Prior to grade four, Casey was illiterate. Reading and writing had always been a huge struggle, and it wasn't until he was in grade five that he felt comfortable. For so long he had to practice his reading and writing skills while thinking he would never get the hang of it. He had to get in the habit of writing as much as possible, just to get himself to grade level, and it was then that he started writing all the time. Whether Casey's writing style may be fragmented, one thing that he is certain of is that writing isn't a burden or a chore but a blessing in his life. With time, Casey found that writing was the best way to express himself when needing to communicate with others. He felt as though it was easier to present all that he was feeling and thinking with the written word. There is always room for growth, and that is exactly what Casey hopes to accomplish with his true passion, writing.

Dedicated to my sister who has been the only constant thing in my life. She deserves our story told, not just for my sake, but for hers. Thanks for always being there for me, even though at times things got really tough to handle.

Special thanks to Matt M. for always believing in me even during the times I wouldn't believe in myself. Thank you for inspiring me on a daily basis to never give up and to always persevere.

Casey Hardman

THIRTEEN YEARS FOSTERED

A Young Man's Struggle for Life

AUSTIN MACAULEY PUBLISHERS™

LONDON · CAMBRIDGE · NEW YORK · SHARJAH

Ordering Information
Quantity sales: Special discounts are available on quantity purchases by corporations, associations, and others. For details, contact the publisher at the address below.

Publisher's Cataloging-in-Publication data
Hardman, Casey
Thirteen Years Fostered

ISBN 9781647502003 (Paperback)
ISBN 9781647501990 (Hardback)
ISBN 9781647502010 (ePub e-book)

Library of Congress Control Number: 2020920334

www.austinmacauley.com/us

First Published (2020)
Austin Macauley Publishers LLC
40 Wall Street, 28th Floor
New York, NY 10005
USA

mail-usa@austinmacauley.com
+1 (646) 5125767

Prologue
The Proposal

What is life, but an adventure down an endless road with many possible turns. Like a road, a person's existence consists of different paths, and the decision that has to be made is done so by either their intuition, peer involvement, or just plain luck. When just starting out, the end result is always unpredictable, and can always differ depending on what path one takes. A person's start is important, and that process involves much guidance from those around them, and shouldn't be taken from whims of judgment.

At times will hear that a first-time mother will automatically know what to do from intuition and or "from within," because something inside of her will truly know what is best. Well, what exactly does that mean? Is it that her intuition is telling her that she would be fine raising a child by herself; that having a low paying job won't matter because somehow she will be able to; that leaving it be to tire itself out will help. That's a load of bull and we both know it. Don't get me wrong, I'm not trying to prove that women can't have "mother's intuition," rather, I'm just stating that that's not always the case. As great as it would be for every woman to experience the tranquility and peace that the mother's intuition has to offer, it's just not realistic. There are quite a lot of women out there who need help and guidance from others because they aren't prepared or ready to bring a child into being. Not only are there women out there who are not ready to take care of a child but also men who aren't. That's where I come in, as both my parents weren't ready for any of the three children they brought into this world.

Over my short and painful life, I have experienced some pretty dark and yet empowering situations. I use the word "empowering" because I find it has that quality of really affecting something. In my life, I had always been overpowered. Overpowered by law, by ways of life, by acts of instinct, by "mother's intuition." I know without a doubt that everything I had been through isn't even comparable to some, where the grim of what they've had to go through is beyond injustice, but still. I feel as though what I have witnessed, can really speak to what could be found behind closed doors. And who knows, perhaps my story could inspire others to speak out, to move on, to find importance in their own lives, or to just be grateful.

In the course of my life, I've had to make some pretty horrific and questionable decisions, and have been faced with many troublesome situations. I just hope that in some way I can touch and open the minds of others to the understanding that there are people out there without a voice, without others to be by their side, all while going through a struggle. My life wasn't given to me to live how I wanted, how my parents had hoped it would turn out. Then again, the choices my parents kept making, made everything difficult, as they were no longer able to make any decision for me.

The actions of my biological parents weren't something I had any control over. The state they were in, was not to be rectified by anyone's actions but themselves. For some time, they didn't even realize what they were doing. The wrong in their behavior. Still, actions have consequences, and their three innocent children were the ones to pay for it. Thirteen years in and out of foster care was the life I had endured because of the actions of my biological parents.

For over a dozen years, I had to deal with situations and witness things most parents would never want for their children. As a parent, it is believed that one would do anything to protect the child in question. Protection from hate, violence, fear, all of the badness in the world. My siblings and I never had that from our parents. For most of our lives, we didn't even have each other. Being moved around in separate homes made life difficult. We had the constant feeling of being alone in the world.

Actions laid against us from infancy, and yet we were the ones poorly viewed from those who didn't understand our situations. Too often outsiders who didn't care to know the truth about why we were in foster care, viewed us as troublesome orphans. Often I had other kids tell me their parents didn't want them hanging around me because of my situation. Little did they know it was not in my control, and yet again, I was the one to suffer. Perhaps if they read my story, they will finally be able to understand foster children aren't always at fault, rather the victim. That's the hope. Hope. Prayer. Faith. Patience. These were the only things I had to hold on to in order to get through my life.

Chapter One

Life's Beginning

Reflection is something that I know too well. As I sit on this chair in the middle of the mall where I work, I'm left reflecting. I'm eighteen years old, and instead of starting an unknown experience and adventure in college or university, I'm stuck working full time in retail. If your reaction just now was *ugh,* I feel the same way. This is definitely not something I saw myself doing at this time of my life. I had so many hopes and dreams, so many things that I wanted to be doing, but when you're broke, you do what you have to do to get by.

As I look into the store to my left, I see my store manager and other coworkers. Looking at them I can't help but think how grateful I am for my job, but am left wondering what could have been if I too was in college where my friends currently are. I'm thinking back to my senior year in high school, which was only a few months ago. Walking through those doors knowing that it was my last year before real life sets in. Thinking at that point what more I could have done leading up to that point, and on and on…

Reflecting on all those small moments that if had been slightly changed, or different, could things have been different and better for me now? The answer is definitely yes. And yet, I'm not a time wizard so can't go back and redo them. I wish I could, but I can't. And so, here I sit. Once again, I find myself writing my inner thoughts, my ramblings, for probably no one to read. And since you can't see me at this point, I just did an eye roll. Something that people in my life could say is my signature move. At least this time it was directed at me.

Often I have heard and had people tell me that our "failures" or things we wish to change from our past is to be used to help shape our future. We take those "mistakes" and make sure to do things differently next time. As much as I would love to live by that, and believe me throughout my life I really wanted to, but at that moment, in the heat of things, it's easier said than done.

Since graduating high school, I have been so down on myself because I threw away an amazing chance at a possible rewarding future. That was very vague, but only because I don't know what could have been, or how things would have turned out. Again, I'm not a wizard, so I can't know. I like to believe it could have been, so in my mind, it was definitely a chance to start fresh with amazing possibilities. I realize perhaps thinking *what could have been* in such a positive outlook might not help, but, oh well. I figure by thinking good things, maybe it will help me make better decisions when faced with more opportunities. In this instance, I just couldn't afford college.

Not only could I not afford tuition, but I also couldn't even afford the applications. Could I have asked for help with paying for the applications, of course. There were resources at my school for that, but when you already feel like a charity case, after four years of being at the same school, it gets less easy to ask for help. I did however ask those I lived with for the money to apply, but was denied because "we couldn't afford it." Story of my life I guess. I couldn't go on my senior class trip, couldn't get a graduation ring, could only get the smallest photo packages each year. Don't think that I'm some spoiled little brat who complains he couldn't get a graduation ring, because I'm not. Those things were just a few of the things I couldn't get because I had no money. Every year there were things like class trips, festivals of some sort, and unless I somehow came up with my own money, it would be a no. Considering throughout my life there had been things over and over I would have to pass up because of the lack of money, my final year of high school was so important. To be honest, it surprised me that I managed to get that far, so I definitely wanted relish in all the perks. Of course, however, I couldn't.

I got my first job at the end of the summer before grade nine. Every year Ottawa had an exhibition fair. I love fairs and rollercoasters, so figured it would be the perfect place for me. The money at the end of the two weeks was actually pretty great, so I definitely couldn't complain. With money being so tight, I used most of that money to buy school supplies, clothes, a really bad hair dye job, and Buffy merchandise. It wasn't until a couple of years later that I realized I would desperately need that fair job each summer in order to pay for my own school belongings.

So much of my life has been a chunk of time that to this day I still can't believe actually happened. When I was younger, I used to keep written recollections on things that went on in my life, so that one day I could look back and wonder, *How could I be the person I am today after having gone through that? Also, how could I use that experience to better myself in the future?* Going through all my past written memories, and all the little notes I've kept to remind myself of things that mattered, what didn't, what caused some kind of grief…made me realize what a shame it is that I didn't write more. Trying to piece together everything I've gone through, the people I met, things I did, things done to me, has not been easy.

Growing up, I'd often wonder how my life would turn out. The question of where I'd be living and with whom is something that I could never be certain of. After my thirteen years in and out of foster care, it seemed only a dream that I would one day be living with my biological family. A dream that often or not felt like a nightmare because of how far out it seemed. Too many times had I been told to be patient, to try harder, that as long as I worked at improving myself, being reunited with my mother could be a possibility. A dream that felt so distant to a young boy, making things seem less real than a reality.

For most of my childhood, I had no idea who my parents were, and the reasons behind everything that they did. The thing that troubled me most of all, was the fact that I knew nothing about them. The only details I did know, was what I was told by my caseworkers and the plan of care packages they made for me. I remembered small details from living with them for short periods of time as a young child, and brief descriptions of their appearance, but nothing fundamentally in-depth. Both my parents have been described to me as *emotionally unstable.* I've been told from my workers, family, and have seen enough to believe it's true, that my father was a woman abuser, and my mother was an alcoholic.

My father was accused of beating on my brother, mother, and myself, and while being so young and not being my brother, I can only recall abuse done on my mother's part and myself. It wasn't until a short while ago that a family member had mentioned my father shoving me against a bookcase at the age of three or four, but that wasn't the abuse I had remembered. Obviously, each family has different ways to pass punishment onto their children, but I do know that my father would hit, and believed he was allowed to do so. From what I can remember, as well as what I have read, there was no accused physical abuse against my older sister. There were, however, allegations of sexual abuse not only against our father but also one or more of his brothers and his friends. Although being so young when that came to light, even to this day I can remember the brief investigation held. Constant conversations with workers, psychologists, but since there were no allegations towards me; I don't know what went on with that. The memory that stuck in my mind from all that, is sitting in the back seat of our worker's car, just my sister and I, and I was asking her if it was true, if our father really had done that. All I remember was my sister crying, saying nothing, and wouldn't even look at me. We must have been around six years old at that point.

My mother wasn't a hitter like our father but definitely had a larger temper. I remember once she smacked me on the ass with a ladle because I wouldn't fall asleep. She was in love with my father and was past the stage to just leave him even though he would hit her constantly. She would be left with black eyes, swollen cheeks, fat and bloody lips, and still, she stayed. She knew what he did was wrong in all sorts of ways, but it didn't seem to matter. She said she loved all three of her children more than life itself, and always wanted what was best for us regardless of what was going on. And what was best for us at the time she thought was to have us stay there with her. If there was a chance for all of us to be a family, she would take it. Going through the abuse brought on by my father, my mother turned to the bottle. She had hoped the booze would drown away her sorrows, and show her that she is making a good decision to stay with him. She became an alcoholic, which only made things worse not only for her but for the children she thought she was protecting while staying with an abuser.

It didn't take long for my brother, sister, and I to be brought to our first foster home. It was just a temporary stay, however. I was two at the time, and way too young to be living in the type of home that I was. The stay was for the Children's Aid to look into the living environment to determine whether or not it was ideal for us to be living with our biological parents.

My father was, and for the most part, still is illiterate. He has never finished high school, nor has my mother. My father was never able to keep a job long, and as far as I can remember, he always had back problems due to a motor vehicle accident from years ago. While reading the plan of cares, which were reports made by my caseworkers to indicate times and events of my past, present and future relations, and updates for my life, I've read how my father had stress issues, anxiety attacks, and depression issues. In complete honesty, I believe he embellished quite a bit on all of that. In order for the caseworkers to get the information needed about our family history, they had to interview our parents, and it seemed as though for the most part, that he was the only one who was interviewed. Whether it was a strategic move on his part, so that he could spin things in his favor or not, I read it while rolling my eyes. What I do know to be true, is that he had a tendency to get mad, yell, and hit very easily.

When you're a small child, it's hard to hold onto memories, but there are those that just stick with you regardless if you want to remember or not. Remembering my father beat my mother, yelling a lot, being mean to my brother because he was conceived from another man prior to meeting my father, are the memories I had no choice but to remember. Growing up, these were the memories that I was left with, and therefore didn't care much at all for him, nor did I want anything to do with him. Having a father who had no problem with beating women, well only my mother, that I know of, didn't give me much of a man to look up to. Instead, it just created a dark side of myself, in myself, only to come out when I would be fuelled with rage.

Having witnessed how he would beat her because he wouldn't agree with what she would say or do, I grew up with the impression that hitting women was okay. That there was nothing wrong with it, other than the obvious knowledge that violence shouldn't be the first resort of action. The abuse didn't just say violence against women was okay. No. It made it seem as though violence against anyone was okay, so long as it was deserving. Watching the altercations between my parents was haunting. Listening to them curse at each other, throw things at each other, beat each other, it was traumatizing.

Before the age of twelve, bullies were a large part of my life. Depending on where I was living at the time, they bullied me for different things. Being the type of person who bottled everything, having a darker side did not pay me any justice. Whenever a bully would start to pick on me, whether it was for my feminine demeanor, living in foster care, not knowing who my biological family was, living with strangers, I would try everything to ignore them at first. Regardless of who the person is, child, teenager, adult, there is only so much they can ignore before coming to blows. Feeling as though most people didn't care enough to do anything since all they would do is tell me to ignore and walk away, it made me feel like it was up to me and me alone to do something about it.

With everything my father had done, it caused me to be distant to the male figures in my life. I tended to have more female friends, would be closer to the foster mothers, I ended up having more respect for females around me. Yet, the majority of bullies in my life were females. I had male bullies as well, but for some reason, the female bullies were crueler to me. Not just things they would say and do, but how they made me feel, and how they would draw in others to join in with them. I found when a male bully would pick on me, he tended to do it solo. Not with my female bullies. I think because they were female made it harder for me. While being young, I had a soft spot for my mother, even though she was just as to blame for everything wrong in my life as my father was. Which was why I tended to gravitate towards females. So when I had a female bully, it hurt even more.

Doing my best to ignore became a challenge. Like I said before, I would bottle everything up. I was like a sponge when it came to being picked on. I would absorb as much as I could until finally it couldn't be held any longer. When it got to be too much for me to ignore and walk away, the person responsible didn't see it coming. Sometimes, people who didn't deserve it also became affected by it. The darker side to me that was created in the hate surrounding my life, mostly because of the abuse from my father, was the part of me I never wanted to come through. It was the part of me that I was most ashamed of, and the part that no one liked.

Thankfully the worst of it didn't surface too often. It almost sounds like a personality disorder, but I assure you it's not. Not truly knowing it was unhealthy for me, it became my way to tackle the challenges and rough times. It was also used to help deal with my bullies when no one else would. It was my bodyguard if you will. One that thankfully one day later in life I would no longer need. When it did surface, however, I myself was even frightened.

Of the many female bullies I had, only three were absolute nightmares. Each one was so different in what they would bully me about. Each one of them knew my weak spots, and where to hurt me. It wasn't until after the third one, which ended the worst, that it really sunk in what I had done. That hitting a girl is NEVER okay, regardless how much she hurts you. Thankfully the third was the last time ever, and it really changed my perspective on how to deal with bullies.

The first girl I hit was when I was nine years old. Now at this point, I was adopted, and everyone I knew, knew that. At first, we were close friends. I think briefly we may have even dated. As much as nine-year-olds would date. She had two close girlfriends who would always be with her. After we "broke up," we weren't really friends anymore. I remember every time I would see her on the playground, she would call me "fefe" "Cassie" and other taunting names. For a while I ignored it. I mostly just thought it was because a boy who lived across the street from me would call me the same things, so just assumed it was his doing.

It became a daily occurrence. On the bus, I would have the boy calling me names, and then at school, her. After a few months of this going on, after telling the teachers who did nothing, I just couldn't take it anymore. I bottled everything up that they had said, but I was at max capacity. The boy received my wrath first. One day on the bus, he and his friends were picking on me, calling me a faggot, fefe, pushing me while trying to get on the bus, while sitting in my seat, and instead of crying like I normally would, I snapped. I turned around and bit him hard! It made him bleed. I was a biter.

Not long after that incident, the girl was still deciding to pick on me and still feeling fuelled, it was just too much for me. The thing that got me though, was that instead of calling me names, she decided to point out how I was adopted. Saying that my own family didn't even want me which was why I'm now living with a new family, who will one day not want me either. That was a subject that hurt me more than anything. I already had issues with being adopted, and having someone tell me I'm not loved nor wanted, was too much. After a bunch more comments from her, I told her to "shut the fuck up and leave me alone" but it didn't work. I ended up grabbing her by the throat. After a few seconds, I let her go and ran away crying.

I got suspended from school. I couldn't begin to imagine what my adoptive parents thought, but I too didn't think highly of myself from what I did. They wanted me to go to her house and apologize for what I had done. I remember when I was on my way to her house, and even before that, I was so sad because I couldn't believe what I had done. At one point, she was a friend of mine. I knew that she had bullied me, but that didn't even matter anymore. The rage I had felt was so strong, and I couldn't even control it. While talking with her and begging for forgiveness, she too had apologized for the things she had said. I didn't feel as though I had deserved her apology but definitely appreciated it.

The second and third time was when I was 11, just before the legal age of getting charged. Both of these times were when I was living at the same residence, and both happened on the bus. The first time happened on our way to school, while the second happened on the way home. I hated that bus ride so much. Nothing good ever came from it. It seemed as though that year and a half taking *that* bus was cursed for me. If it wasn't one person bullying me, it was a different one. And if for some reason I wasn't bullied on the bus, the asshole at my school picked up the slack. Thankfully the school bully wasn't so bad. That damn bus ride though.

With regard to the bus, I had three main bullies. The first was a boy I apparently used to be friends with years earlier, whom I actually didn't remember. Thankfully his presence on the bus was not often due to the fact that he would normally take a different bus. On occasion, my bus would also take the kids on his bus due to whatever reasons. The road I lived on was quite long, so it was made up of two busses. One for the front half of the road, and my bus which was for the back half of the road. To this day I don't know why he seemed so upset with me, causing him to lash out at me. Every time we would take the same bus, he would make it his mission to make my trip to school or home a living hell. Nothing major ever really happened with him thankfully. Just a lot of hoping to not see him. When I didn't see him though, there seemed to be someone else willing to pick up the slack.

Every day for almost a year, there was this one girl who kept harassing me about being in foster care, saying all sorts of cruel things. It seemed like from the moment I moved there, she decided to not like me. Literally the moment. I remember my first day moving to that foster home for the second time

15

(the first was before my adoption), I was so happy to see some old friends again, and when she saw me, she had such a disgusted look on her face as if to be like "Yeah, so what."

The bullying started out small at first. Every time my friends and I would hang out, go swimming, whatever it was, she would make snippet comments to me. The comments would grow larger, more frequent, and more hurtful. It got to the point where I would never want to take the bus, because not only would she say and yell things at me, she occasionally would throw things at me. She would also get other people to say things at me. Never in my life had I cried so much because of a bully. I begged my school to do something, but they didn't. My bus driver never seemed to care, so that wasn't a help. And the days when that boy would take our bus too, those were some of the worst days ever.

One day, after nearly a year of her torment, I bottled up as much as I could. She got under my skin so much that I punched her in the side of the head. As much as I knew how wrong it was, I once again couldn't control myself. I couldn't handle any more of her verbal abuse, and I didn't know what else to do. It was one of those knee-jerk reactions. I felt really bad about it, and after being suspended, I did apologize. I remember having a conversation with her mother about it, and she didn't even know about the teasing. She understood why I did what I did, but told me to tell her next time it happened so that she could speak with her so that I don't get myself in any more trouble. That conversation actually meant a great deal to me. It was one of the most sincere conversations from someone, making me feel as though someone was actually listening. Since then, that girl never teased me again, and we were able to make amends.

The last time was on the way back from school. While dealing with the other bullies, most of the time, she was my friend, but occasionally wasn't. I never understood why one day we would be friends, and the next, we wouldn't. Kids will be kids I guess. In any case, shortly after I hit the last girl, this one seemed to want to take her place. I was already dealing with everything that had happened the last time I hit a girl, and while knowing what subjects are sensitive, she felt the need to continue the teasing. Not only was she saying how no one loves me, and that I'll never be a part of a family, but also mentioned my sister. That became too much for me, and I lashed out.

The day it happened, I was wearing a belt. And for those who know me now, know that I hate belts. This is why. I got so upset, that before being dropped off at my home, I took off my belt and hit her on the back with it. Twice. I remember that day so vividly, and hauntingly. In all the times I have been so enraged because of bullies, never as much as that time. I don't know

16

what it was, but because of that, something awoke in me. It was as if the cloud over my judgment was gone because I had never felt more sorrow and disgust for what I had done. In that moment, I had become the one person I never wanted to become. My father.

If there was any way I could go back to these times, I would definitely do things differently. I never truly wanted to hurt them. I just wanted the pain from the bullying to go away. Looking back at those times, I feel like such a coward for what I did and will always have to live with my actions, but it was then that I was able to come to grasp that what I did could NEVER happen again. I learned from that third occurrence, that violence regardless of who it's being done to is not right. Did it stop me from being violent to guys? No, but never again did I hit a girl, and have not since. From that day onward, I vowed that no matter what a girl says or does to me, I would never allow myself to feel that angry. I hated my father so much because of the violence he did to my mother, siblings, and I. The last thing I wanted was to walk in his shadow. That darkness buried inside me had to go away. Although, once I got rid of it, I seemed to have replaced it with a different dark side.

My father isn't the only one with abusive tendencies and a dark temper. My mother is also. Much like my father, my mother has severe heart problems. To date, my mother has been taking a lot of medication to help her heart and has already been through two surgeries. The last time my mother went into surgery for her heart, she was denied completion because the doctor said she was too overweight and would not be able to operate. Suffering from anxiety attacks, breathing complications, medicating herself, my mother was unable to work. She apparently used to work with children in a daycare. From what she has told me. She believed she always had her children's best interest at heart and did what she could. As time went on, it became problematic.

When my mother started drinking, all I know is that in order to dull the misery and pain inflicted by my father, she lost any desire and hope for her family. No matter how much she loved us, it was clear that she was passed the point of caring about saving herself. From an outside perspective, it would appear that the love she had for an abusive man was greater than the love she had for her children. For some reason, the abuse weighed on her so much, she became dependent on him, and no matter what he had done, she couldn't stay away.

I remember hearing my mother yelling and swearing at my father a lot. I know, and knew when I was younger that everyone's parents would fight here and there, but the vulgar language that I would hear was clearly not something that all parents should say to each other. If it wasn't bitch, it was fuck. Shit. Damn. Goof. The list goes on. I was probably the only kindergarten student who knew so many swear words, in French too. Thanks for the great parenting. I guess I never realized that you actually did teach me French. Not the French one parent aims to teach their child though. Kids on the playground would always get me to teach them how to properly say cursive French sayings, and it made me feel cool.

Looking back to when things first occurred between my parents, it's too difficult to say what the catalyst was that set them both off, and put them down the path that became their dismal marriage. It's one of the most frustrating things I think that goes through my mind. Therefore, whether it's a drinking problem, constant verbal and physical abuse, and adultery, came after having three children, neither of my parents were in any way ready to have and be able to take care of children. I don't even think they were right for each other.

My mother and father were wed early July 1987, only months after giving birth to my half-brother. Being the first and only child at the time meant a great deal to my mother. Although his father was a one-night stand, my mother wanted to keep him. My father understood that he wasn't his child, and at the time appeared to not be bothered by it. He loved my mother and after a short period of months being together, they took vows to cherish their life together no matter what. Well, that was a slap in the face, wasn't it?

My father made a promise to raise and love my mother's firstborn as though he was his own, for anything important to her, was therefore important to him. Even his family at the time took to my brother. There were no current grandchildren at the time, so although not from their blood, they seemed thrilled to be step-grandparents. Everyone appeared happy as can be. If only it had lasted. Two and a half years after the birth of my brother, out came my sister, the middle child. She and I are the only ones with the same father.

Born on March 8th, 1989, my sister weighed just over five pounds. Although being the smallest of the three children my mother gave birth to, she was the most difficult to deliver and was supposed to be a twin. Of course, since I only have one brother and one sister, the twin did not take, and she was the only supposed human baby that came out of my mother. Which at times have been misleading, if you catch my drift? Just teasing sis, you know I love you. Just a few, or more precisely, a couple of months after having my sister, my mother got pregnant for the third time. Noticing that no weight was being lost, and actually more being gained, my mother consulted her doctor and found out that she was with child once again. And might I add "third time's the charm!" Yes, I am referring to myself as charming and good looking, intelligent... *enters daydream*

Casey Daniel Hardman. Born February 23rd, 1990. I weighed eight pounds and eleven and a half ounces. Damn, I was a chubby baby! After giving birth to me, my mother had some minor complications and became quite ill and had to stay in the hospital for a short period of time while her sister took care of me. To this day I still don't understand why my father hadn't taken me, but whatever, that's not the current issue. Before leaving the hospital, I was circumcised and declared a healthy newborn. Being such a little porker, and looking like a month old only after a couple of days, I ended up sleeping in a drawer when I stayed with my aunt until my mother came out of the hospital. I fit perfectly, and my aunt not having the proper bedding to care for me, felt that a drawer was a substantial means for compensating for a crib. Hearing about it didn't really bother me since I have no recollection of that point in my life. It's one of those things that make you grateful for not having a memory of it, although seeing pictures of it makes you giggle.

Often I would have fond memories of my time spent with my aunt. At times, those memories would be a bit strange, however. One thing I remember from being really young was how whenever I would be at her place, I would nibble on the cat's dry kibble. Why? I don't know, but I assume at the time it tasted good to me. I think when you're younger, no one ever really knows why you do the things you do, but it's a way to teach a child what is right, and enables room for development and gives experience.

Growing up, people often reminded me that with each foster home I stayed at, each school I attended, people I met, that everything I had to deal with, was an experience. It was up to me to take that experience and learn how I could benefit from it and become a stronger, more knowledgeable individual. To take each experience while breaking them down to help better my life. To be honest, they were exactly right! I wouldn't be the person I am today if it weren't for each of those experiences. If I had the choice, I would prefer that I wouldn't have had to go through what I did. Sure I look at it as the glass being half full, but who's to say that I wouldn't be the same or better if I would have stayed in a normal functioning family.

It's impossible to tell what my life would have been like if I didn't have to go through foster care, and I know I sure as hell would be interested as to who I would have been…but that's the beauty of life, isn't it? In each person's life, there are many choices and decisions that have to be made, and with each, there are different turnouts. Like, what would have become of my life if I had stayed adopted, stayed in foster care, or not even been put into foster care in the first place. So many obscurities with no real way of knowing. It's that uncertainty that drives me to get to a place in my life where it doesn't matter the, *what if* because things are just so great. That's what I tried to keep in the back of my mind, for thinking so much on this thought; it had plagued my mind and kept me distracted from what really mattered. Since it is difficult to know what exactly my life *would have* been like, instead of concentrating on that, I was always informed that the important thing to focus on was tomorrow. The now and before are in the moment, and there isn't much I can do, except work on fixing the tomorrow to make it better.

With all the wrong judgment calls that I have made, I was constantly reminded by my caseworkers, as-well-as my foster parents that you should never focus on the wrong and ponder what could have been when there is so much room for growth and opportunity to better that situation for the future. If only someone had said these things to my parents.

When I was only two years old, my mother's alcoholism was at its worst. At least, it was the start of her worst. She and my father had been fighting constantly, to the point that the police were being called for domestic disturbances. In retaliation to my father punching her leaving her black and blue, she pulled his hair, and he actually charged HER with assault. Considering the bruises and cuts that she was inflicted with, I am still surprised she would never charge him. While in court, hearing about the charges against my mother, it was dropped from the Judge. According to my mother, the judge laughed at my father and dismissed his case. If the pettiness and violence at that point in time wasn't a clear indication to permanently separate and move on, I don't know what could be.

In early November 1992, my parents had another brief separation due to their arguing and fighting. My mother was still drinking and felt that she couldn't be without my father. During the fight that resulted in their brief separation, aside from my father's volatile attitude and hitting, my mother had thrown a coffee cup at him and threatened him with a knife. Although they were separated for the better, she spent so much time trying to track him down, with no success.

Getting so angry and upset that no one would tell her where he was, she took it out on her children. The end result was that all three of her children would be removed by the police and placed in their first emergency foster home. Feeling as though she couldn't live without her husband, regardless of the fact that he had recently beaten her and not for the first time, she tried to drown her sorrows in alcohol. That didn't work considering she didn't just have one glass of wine to unwind and relax. Like always, it was more than she should have drunk. The things that must have been going through her mind is something I never want to know. NEVER! I don't care that people say you should never say never, because, something like this would be too much for me to handle. No matter how many years have gone by.

I am unsure how long she was thinking about what was about to happen. I am unsure what sort of things she was planning to do. There are so many things I don't know. All I know, all I am certain of, is that her grief was so strong that she didn't care about her children. The only person she could think of or cared about was the so-called man she married. She was charged from the North Bay City Police Department with threatening the lives of her children and herself.

Not getting the answers my mother had wanted regarding the whereabouts of my father, she thought it best to threaten to kill each of my siblings and myself, in a particular order, finishing with herself. Thankfully not following through and being arrested, my siblings and I were taken away. The start of a life that none of us wanted. None of us could have hoped for. And a life that would bring about more torment and baggage than anyone could have thought possible. Our struggle was just beginning.

Chapter Two

Brief Stay

Knowledge of the events that had occurred on that November 10, 1992 night, couldn't have saved me. No matter if I had known then what was about to happen, and even everything that had happened prior, knowing that couldn't have had any effect. I was only two and a half years old. I could barely walk, barely talk, and barely able to dress myself. That's the thing about knowing things.

Knowledge is powerful, and yet, can't always solve your problems, no matter how much you wish it could. At that time in my life, I didn't have the insight into the problems between my parents in their marriage. I barely want to know now, so I sure as heck wouldn't want two-year-old Casey knowing that kind of crap. No child at any age should have to witness and deal with their parents' misdeeds on a regular basis. I do wish I knew enough back then to offer advice to not save their marriage, but my childhood. If only at two years old I could have had proper dialect and speech, enough to tell those two to smarten up and just divorce already. Or send us far away from either of them and their families.

The older I got from such an early age, the more I could see how much my parents weren't right for each other. The thought of divorce did not frighten me. Not one bit. I did not cry and hoped they would stay together forever. I knew better than that. So often through my "childhood," I did wish they could have realized sooner the action of divorce was something that should have happened sooner. Then that just made my mind wander into so many thoughts of *what could have been* and *where would I be now.* No thank you! I remember those headaches, and they never ended well for me, or anyone around me.

All I know is that no matter how many times they fought, took it out on us, and even briefly separated, it wasn't enough to make them realize the path they were headed down. They didn't have the knowledge that the three of us were in harm's way and on our way into a stranger's home in the middle of the night.

My mother was charged with assault against my father on November 8, 1992. The charge was dismissed, and aside from the pettiness of their fighting, it became laughable. In defense of being hit by my father, my mother retaliated by throwing a coffee cup at him and pulled his hair. Apparently, it only took three days afterward, for her to realize she wasn't going to be able to cope on her own. On November 11, 1992, the day after we were admitted into the agency, the police arrested her for threatening to kill my siblings and I, and then herself. This was all because no one would tell her where her abusive husband was hiding out.

Not remembering anything from that night, is what I call a blessing. My older half-brother, who was three years older, I'm sure has some sort of memory of the incident, but it was never discussed. I have no way of knowing, and I'm okay with that. If he was able to push it out of his memory, then I think that's a win for him. My sister and I were too young, and I know for a fact, neither of us ever had any recollection of that night. Of course, it wasn't the first incident of bad parenting towards the three of us. In June 1992, the agency was called due to the fact that our parents were uttering strong and foul language towards us. And from what I've heard, that wasn't even the first time we were subject to that.

The thing I can't wrap my brain around, though, is not the fact that our mother was so desperate for our father that she threatened and wanted to kill us, even after everything he put her through. It's the fact that we never knew about this. Like, NEVER! It wasn't until November 2018 after finally getting my case files, that I read about the real reason for first being admitted into foster care. All my life I had been told that my parents fought, argued, hit us, and that our home was unsafe for us to live in, and so the agency was called and took us away. That was the reason I was given in which I lived my life knowing.

I remember reading my plan of care packages and talking with my social workers throughout my life and never had there been any indication as to the real reason behind being taken away from my family home. After speaking with my mother and father trying to get information to help me deal with my life, I even asked both of them to tell me everything that had happened. Each of them had told me that they weren't managing well together, so had a brief separation, but it wasn't enough to work on their issues, and things got out of hand which lead to more and more fighting. And then we were taken away. Well, I now know that was bullshit.

I'm currently staring at my case files that I had requested many years ago, and it states, "Your birth parents were separated at that time and your birth mother was not managing well on her own." I think not managing well was a scapegoat, as a child needs real answers. In my opinion, maybe not so early on, but as time went on, it was definitely something I needed. Choices are made from persons' surroundings, and what they know. It would help a child make better choices to know the truth. In situations like being in foster care, knowing exactly what my mother did could have made so many things better for me. I would have had all of the facts and could have made my decision making completely different. I went on so long thinking that she was just troubled and needed help, and perhaps being together again could change that. Had I known all the information from the start, it would have opened my eyes and allowed me to not go through life clinging onto the hope of living with her again. In respect, I would have known that I needed to live my life for me, and not her, as I could very well be better without her.

It's easy to say that my life could have been different. It's merely something that I hope more than anything, because I can't be completely sure. Knowing that things would have been different is for sure though. The more a person has knowledge in relation to situations and events, allows for more different possible outcomes. Without knowing this specific information, let's say gave me so so options for going through life. Had I known all along, the options would not have just been so so, but also so, so, and so. The information we are given is incredibly important to a person, especially in these situations. While being so young, we rely on the written word that they provide for us. It is so that we may go through everything that had happened while our minds are still developing and trying to remember things.

They say facts never lie. They say facts tell how a story unfolds in complete truth. They say you can't trust your memory at certain times because that isn't necessarily a true fact. First off, who the hell are *they* anyway? Are *they* in my mind, in my memory? For a lot of things growing up, I had to rely on my memory for things because I didn't always have the facts, and I knew it. The thing I did know though was that my memory never failed me. Traumatic events for me triggered something with my brain, allowing me to not forget most things. There are so many things I wish I could forget, but in a way, being able to remember has allowed me to deal with everything, in my own way.

From when I was five years old and onwards, it's like a video on TV, where I can fast forward and rewind, as much as I want giving me the opportunity to replay events and situations over and over. It wasn't until I was in high school when I got my first moment of pure serenity, where I was able to go through my life in pieces over and over to help my inner self-deal with the moments, giving clarity and peace. Before high school, I never knew how to deal with reliving the moments in my head, and not feeling as though I had a safe space, it caused a lot of friction in my life. It gave me a lot of pain, and I never knew how to process it, which caused my moods to turn on others.

If the written word is to be considered FACT, then my case files have a lot of contradicting facts. Not only that, but I think my birth mother is someone completely different than the woman I knew. I have seen her name spelled three different ways, and none of those are the correct way of spelling. Considering my case file is quite large, since it goes from 1992 until 2005, I would be foolish to not expect inconsistencies. The thing I find strange, though, is that along with the case worker's name on each written file, there is a date. There are multiple written pages for specific times, and there are so many inconsistencies in the information.

One file says the three of us were taken into foster care for the first time on November 10, 1992. Another file says that from November until December 1992 the three of us stayed at a transition house, which is a safe house for families. Another file says that the three of us stayed in a foster home from November 1992, until April 1993. Another file stated that we only stayed at the foster home from November 1992, until January 1993. I guess when you have so many contradicting *facts*, it's about trying to piece together the middle ground. Also, using what *you* know and remember goes a long way. For instance, I remember being at that foster home from late 1992, as I was just starting to walk, until early spring 1993. I remember growing up having photos from that time period, which also helped as they were time-stamped.

While having to deal with so many different people in the course of my life, all who had their own opinions, their own way of seeing how things unfold through their eyes, the only thing I could trust was what I knew. What I remembered. Needing some information to fill in some of the blanks, I relied on these case files. A lot. I read them over and over growing up because I desired knowing the truth. At least what I was led to believe was the truth. Knowing now though, in my adult life, it gives a piece of clarity. In a way it makes me laugh because of how little I truly knew back then.

When I was residing at my first home in 1992, they indicated that although I seemed like a bright, alert toddler, I had a lot of difficulty settling in at night to go to sleep. I'm actually not surprised by this because I have always had difficulty falling asleep. I have always been a night owl. The thing that surprised me the most though was that the file states that not being able to fall asleep was because I appeared to have missed my birth father. Imagine me holding my hands up to my face, eyes wide open, and mouth making a large O. I've never been a fan of my birth father, and I've never preferred him over my birth mother, so this is definitely news to me. I do remember loving my blanket though. That I know I missed. If I didn't have my special blanket, I missed my soother.

According to my mother, trying to get me off my soother was one of the biggest challenges she ever had with me. I even remember always wanting it, until I was almost five. I always had one hidden somewhere in case mine was taken away to try and wean me off of it. There was a time, that the store, they would go to, run out of the blue soothers, and so they had to start buying pink ones. To me, the color never mattered. It was the feeling. The feeling when I had the soother in my mouth was exactly that. Soothing. With all the fighting I could hear and see, when I had my soother, I felt a sense of relaxation. It dimmed the tension a little, and so, I never wanted to part ways with it. Of course, I had to which sucked.

If there was one thing that anyone could agree on, it would be that I was a pretty good eater. I mean, at times picky, but nonetheless, I enjoyed eating. I still do! I was a chunky baby, and after looking at photos of myself, I wouldn't say I was a chunky toddler, but at least had a pretty good appetite. During the brief few months stay at my first foster home, they indicated although a big eater, if I was told no, there was hell to pay. I would get angry with a reaction of throwing things, yelling, and even biting. I guess I must have really liked my food!

One thing I know from dealing with so many people trying to "raise" me while trying to discipline a child, it's tricky. When you're trying to teach them the difference between wrong and right, yes and no, how do you know the proper and best way to do that? From my personal experience, the toddler stage is the most important stage to teach. Saying yes and no, please, and thank you. Getting them to say more and more words. There are so many things to teach a child, and it's not easy knowing when and how to do so. It's a learning curve. When you're on your third child however, you'd almost think you'd be an expert by that point.

For my siblings and I, though, we weren't just told *no, don't do that*. We also weren't just told, *don't forget to say please and thank you*. I can remember even as young as two and three that if we did something we weren't supposed to, our mother especially would yell at us while grabbing onto our arms saying *I said don't fucking do that. Now listen to me next time or you'll get a smack*. It was the same thing she said over and over. Even as we got older. We didn't always get a warning for next time though. Depending on what we did, she would just grab us and smack us on the butt. Too many times I can remember being hit on the butt with a ladle. My sister, the comedian that she was, was the only one brave enough to say after getting hit, *Ha Ha That didn't hurt*. While walking away though I can remember seeing her eyes watering because it did hurt, but she didn't want them to know.

If we were grabbing something on a table or shelf that we weren't supposed to, another thing I can remember either my mother or father doing was throwing something to the other side of the room to get us to go away. For instance, if they were trying to watch something on TV, but we were in their way, they would find something nearby to throw on the other side of the room while saying, *I'm trying to watch TV, go over there and play and leave me alone.* Usually what followed that was *Fuck Sakes.* Or *For Fuck Sakes.*

My mother has always had a shorter fused temper than my father, so she was more prone to swearing. I remember her swearing a lot! When she swore though, it was usually in a yelling tone. I honestly wouldn't be surprised if any of our first words were a curse word. We heard it so often, so of course, we repeated it. We didn't know that we couldn't say it, or that we shouldn't. We all heard it so often, so just assumed that it was acceptable language.

I remember when one of us repeated a curse word in front of either of our parents, there would be a high pitched *HEY*, followed by *what the fuck did you just say? NO! You don't say that!* If it was our father who caught us swearing, he would usually just ask us if we wanted him to get our mother to deal with us. Mostly because he never appeared to want to deal with us, and knew that she would have no trouble disciplining us. If she caught us, she would grab us under the chin, pulling down on it to open up our mouth and ask if we want the soap or hot sauce. At times she wouldn't ask us that because she was already in a mood, so while holding onto our jaw, she would walk over to the kitchen or bathroom, grab the soap, and put it in our mouths. My sister was the only one who didn't cry in front of them. She would say *Thank You.* Or *Mmmm, I like that.*

Hearing the word no for any of us, was never something easy or good. That word was always followed by something bad when we were living at home, even when I was only two years and younger. While living at our first foster home, we didn't react well when they said no, because that is what we were used to. We lived with people who yelled, threw things, swore, when saying no, and so that's how we learned to react when it was said. For myself, I wasn't brave or strong-willed like my sister. I wasn't older with a better comprehension of things like my brother, and so I had to find my own way of dealing with all of that. And so, I became a biter.

I have always had strong teeth, and so my way of putting all that frustration and anger into a way of dealing with it was through biting. If someone was yelling at me, or telling me no, it was time to bite. The way to cope with the bad things happening around me made me feel a need for coming up ahead of it and biting in response made me feel like I was. You want to scream at me, hit me, take away my toys, fine. You're going to get bit, and in my eyes, they deserved it. Of course, I would then get yelled at even more for biting, and then usually I would follow up with crying.

Emotions had always been my downfall. Trying to figure out how to feel wasn't something that came easy to me, and because of that, it was as if my body was telling me to feel everything at once. Which created chaos inside me, and then I would usually just feel overwhelming sadness and then cry. Living in a home that had mostly frustration, anger, violent tendencies, all the bad type of ways of feeling, made it difficult for me knowing how to react to things. Being raised in one specific style showed me that that was how things were supposed to be. It didn't give way for calmness, laughter, warm and fuzzies. That's not to say there weren't ever happy moments or memories, because there were. Just not as many.

I remember one day, my siblings and I were in our basement, or at least someone's basement while our parents were upstairs. We were laughing and running around. We were playing a game where we had to jump couch to couch, chair to chair. It was one of the earliest memories I had where I was actually somewhat happy. With my luck, it didn't last long. As much fun as we were having, being only two, clumsy as heck, I tried to jump further than my tiny little legs would allow. I fell and slightly broke my foot. What I know and remember is having that cast on it. It made me smile, and made me feel special because it seemed cool, and none of my older siblings had it.

While living in our first foster home, smiling was something I tried to do more. I was definitely encouraged to. Although at times being told no, and expecting yelling and whatnot, that didn't usually come, it became somewhat strange to react because they were so different from our parents. We went so long having things being done a specific way, but then one day boom, different parenting skills. Better parenting skills. Smiling at that time became a nervous reaction to things. When I wasn't sure if I was allowed or supposed to do something, and unsure if I was about to get into trouble, I would just smile.

People oftentimes assume when they see someone smiling, it's because they're happy. That can be true, but a lot of the time, they smile to hide the pain and sorrow that's being held within. Or they're trying to hide something else. My entire life, current, all the way back to when I was two years old, this was my reaction to things. It didn't mean I was a happy child. Reading my case files, reading how they would see me smile, and then just directly associate that with being *a happy child, nothing to report*. Sorry, but please pay attention.

My first foster home was necessary for my siblings and I as we were unsafe living at home with our mother, father off somewhere else. The foster home was a drastic change from what we were used to. They had two young children of their own, around the same age as my brother. That was nice for him, as it gave him the opportunity to have others to play with while being of similar age. Especially since my sister and I were more often than not leaving him out because of how close we were in age. Our toys and mentalities were so different, so it was better that he had others to be around.

Although being incredibly necessary, I also feel as though living somewhere different hindered my development. There were too many things different for me, and because of that, the nervous smiling started. I remember being asked from that point onward *why are you not smiling? You should smile more. Are you happy?* I already have a nervous smile, which means I smile when I'm not sure how to feel, and now you want me to smile for your own amusement? The only good thing to come out of that was the fact that it helped me be photogenic and made me work on keeping my teeth as clean as they could be.

More so when I was a bit older, with being told to smile more and more, made it my new reaction to everything. Someone could get hit by a car right in front of me, and there I would be, smiling. I didn't want to wait for someone to say something to me, so before they had a chance, there's that smile! I'm sure most people would prefer to look at a smiling child instead of a grouchy and crying child, but please give that child a reason to do so. I mean, after all the times I witnessed my father hitting my mother, her retaliating, you think I had a lot of reasons to smile? It got to the point where I would actually work on it in front of the mirror.

The older I got, the more sad I became. More and more things started happening all around me, and when people saw that on me, they would tell me to find the happiness and find a reason to smile. Yes, just thinking back to all the times I heard that made me roll my eyes. I couldn't do that in front of the adults, however, because when I did, I would be told I have an attitude, and that next time they see me, they want to see me smiling! Enough with the fucking smiling! Smiling became something for a while I actually hated. Of course, I had to give them what they wanted, and so as soon as I would see someone coming up to me, or if I was in eye contact with an adult, my smile would appear. I could be fuming red, and all of a sudden, all cheers. They'd never know right?

29

While living at my first foster home, aside from the initial caseworker indicating that I appeared to be unaffected by the events that had taken place because I looked happy, my speech was a bit of a problem. I know that was true because for quite a long time I had issues with my speech. I didn't properly talk for quite some time. Probably due to the fact that both my parents were too busy fighting and swearing around us, that I wasn't being taught the basics with speech. At the age of two, mumbles and gibberish was all I was able to muster.

For the longest time, I was unable to pronounce my C's. Instead, I would replace C with R. It was kind of humorous. As so I'm told. Although it might seem to be considered adorable, it was a definite sign that some teaching and training was in order. At that time, however, it wasn't something being done. A slight stutter began to creep its way into my speech. Being considered shy, and mostly afraid to speak, definitely speak out, I did everything I could not to. This hindered my ability to pronounce and make out words, which in turn created a slight stutter. Being stuck on words coming out of my mouth was something that happened too often.

The brief relief of living at home came too quickly. While realizing the struggles that each of my siblings and I clearly had, whether ignored or not, going to live back home should have been something that didn't happen. In early spring 1993, my parents were apparently still briefly separated, and my mother was living with one of her sisters in Ottawa.

Originally from Owen Sound Ontario, my mother's family lived all over. The only family we were accustomed to was her one sister in Ottawa. The rest of the family were basically distant memories that were to be considered rare commodities. Although, not that *rare* in my opinion. We just never really saw or spoke to them. We weren't close. My father's family integrated themselves in our lives a lot more than my mothers, unfortunately.

Looking back at everything, I would bet so much that my father in his brief absence, was in fact staying at his parents, or one of his brothers. And knowing how that family operates, they did everything they could to not let my mother know. Of course, that is just speculation, from things I already know about them, but hey, nothing wrong with guessing.

With a few months having past, and my mother living away from my father residing with her sister in Ottawa, it appeared good enough to allow the Children's Aid Society of North Bay to transfer us back home. While stating that she was in therapy to deal with the issues revolving around her husband, it was enough to impress them, allowing us to return. There appeared to be all these positive blessings and promises surrounding her, which now made her the mother she was supposed to be.

While relocating to Ottawa with our mother, my siblings and I's case files in North Bay closed in April 1993. It is stated that the Ottawa Children's Aid Society would now be visiting us to keep an eye open to make sure things were safe. While still being technically the same agency, it is a different location of foster care, so the North Bay office has no recollection or files on whether or not we were even readmitted after our 1993 departure. To them, what happened afterward, in a different city was none of their concern.

If there were times of happiness I remember from early childhood, it was while being at my aunt's house. She herself had children, four of them. I remember spending a lot of time at her place, with her family, and the memories I have were always so pleasant. Oddly enough, neither of my parents were in those memories. That was probably a sign I should have picked up on, but didn't.

I had never been a fan of my father's family. Well, that's not entirely true. There was one brother and wife of said brother, who I knew I loved and cared for deeply, but aside from them, for some reason, I just couldn't stand his family. Knowing that truly makes me grateful that when being released from CAS, we ended up on my mother's side. The plus to that situation was that her siblings had their own children, while my fathers did not.

My mother's family wasn't perfect at all, but they most definitely weren't as bad as my father's. My aunt and their other siblings weren't as bad as my mother. I swear, my two parents were the worst in each of their already troubled families. Oh, how lucky my siblings and I were. While thinking back to everything, my mother's family wasn't all that bad. With so many things transpiring over the years, I've come to realize that I was misled on so many things, which was made to falter my way of thinking of them. Still, they weren't the greatest, but not as bad as I was led to believe.

To this day, 2019, I am led to believe that my mother had two sisters. That I'm sure about. What I am unsure about is whether or not she has one or two brothers. For some reason, I want to say two, but either way, I don't know or remember if I have ever even met one or two of them. The thing that caused the most friction with my mother and her family, which was what I believe to be the thing that distanced us from them, was my father.

Whether you look at him as a catalyst for trouble, or plain evil in nature, the root for a lot of the bad in my life, is because of that so-called man. My biological father. Not only him but his family. Them as a whole is what I look to as hell on earth. Excluding the one uncle and aunt. (Don't worry, I got you)

My father would always try to weasel his way back because, in retrospect, he has nowhere else to go really. His family sure, but why would anyone want to stay there if they don't have to. It's no surprise that his brief disappearance from my mother and us wouldn't last. When things got really bad, he had to vacate. That's what he did. Now that we were back with her, a chance for some normalcy in the midst, why would he want that for us?

There is always hope in the world. No matter where you are in life. No matter what you have done in the past, and no matter what you are capable of. There is hope! Speaking of hope doesn't always mean positivity and sunshine though. Sorry to rain on your parade. Hope has so many meanings and so many interpretations. In my case, the thought of hope often or not meant getting squashed and trampled over. And over. While I was growing up, hope usually meant an empty promise. It often meant lies, fighting, and never happy endings. For too long, in the beginning of my existence, I referred to *hope* as something to fear. It took years to change my look at what *hope* meant.

For now, however, hope meant that my father was to return because he and my mother were finally ready to give each other another chance at starting over. The two of them had felt that their issues and fighting were that of the past. That the two of them were able to come together and take care of the three children they had made together. It was my father who had felt as though he was able to come back into our lives. My mother still desperate for appreciation and acceptance welcomed him with open arms. After years of abuse, it became something of not being able to live without a man for her. She couldn't and didn't want to be single to properly work on her issues. Regardless of the fact that while staying with her sister, things were actually going really well.

My mother's mind had become so dependent on her husband, which was actually how his family viewed women. They all believed that a woman's place was to take care of the children, stay in the kitchen, while the man comes and goes as he pleased, for he is providing for said family. Well, my father just disproved you because he could barely keep a job long enough to get a paycheque. The things that go through that family's mind, is something I never want to know. Not only would it give me a headache, but I would just be rolling my eyes so much, they might actually fall out.

While living at my aunt's with my mother, my siblings and I were all so happy. These are memories I actually remember. I can truly remember feeling happy. Smiling for real reasons. We were living life with purpose and meaning. Of course, with my luck, that happiness was short-lived. It would appear that so long as I was with either of my parents, luck was not on my side, and only bad things were to follow. Why the others couldn't have seen this, and actually tried to put a stop to it is something I'll never know. What

I do know, is that my mother didn't have the desire, care, or strength to keep moving forward without him. She welcomed him back into our lives just to please herself and her broken heart. She didn't know that some of the worst things imaginable to a child's life and memory, were about to unfold.

Chapter Three

What Went Wrong

There is always more than one side to every story. People's views and opinions tend to differ slightly when discussing a specific event, time, or place. Since everyone has their own mind, their own choice of words and phrasing, it will always be different than others while discussing said event. I can remember constantly asking the same questions to both my biological parents about a specific incident from when I was younger and most times when they do remember themselves, things change from both sides.

At times people will remember what they want, or at least in their mind, will see things how they want to. Believe me, that is not easy when trying to piece things together. For instance, I had asked both of my parents how much my mother would drink back in the day, and because their memories and minds are so different, there were two very different answers. Their opinions and memory are even different from my own. While asking both my mother and father certain questions, I would also have to keep in mind that neither of them has perfect memories, especially since they both have learning disabilities. Having issues of the mind is not helpful, but I would be able to have enough information to put together a good idea of some of the events that took place so many years ago.

The mind is such a tricky thing to comprehend and fully understand, and personally, trying to think about that myself gives me a headache. I know I have a pretty great memory and can piece together quite a lot, while others may not be able to. With my memory being what it was, it was no surprise that I found myself doing a lot of theatre performing growing up. Some people are able to remember names, or faces, while someone else who might even have a better memory, wouldn't be able to. So, the difference in what some people can remember, and what they can't, can actually be fascinating to think about.

While a part of me never wanted to forget specific events, people especially, I started doing mini exercises in order to help myself remember more. Hiding a certain toy somewhere, and later having to remember where it was. I did this often, usually would wait a day. With how busy things got, it actually worked for the most part, because I wouldn't be so focused on trying to remember. I also started trying to remember the smaller details on things. When walking around, I would look at people and basically scan them completely to try to place certain things about them in my mental notes. For instance, freckles, eye color, hair, big or small ears. I figured by doing this, it'll help keep my mind off of the struggles going on around me.

While doing everything I can to build on my own memory, I never would have considered the possibility that I would have to use that to keep my parents and family's memory alive in my mind later in life. The separation regardless of the fact that my parents should not have had custody of my siblings and me, as difficult as that was, my memory definitely came in handy. While at times it was a blessing to be able to remember them as they were, the older I got, the harder it became. So much time was passing by, and more and more troubling situations arose, and the memory of them wasn't what I wanted. The memory of them felt tainted by years of betrayal, and it hurt too much to think about.

It's funny. When you feel a certain way about someone, the memories and thoughts of that person, or persons, is viewed in a specific way. Have you ever noticed that when your feelings change for them, that the memories you hold on to, also change? Not only do your memories feel different, but when going from happy feelings to angry or disappointed feelings, you start to remember things that bring up those feelings. For so long regardless of the fact that my parents weren't just hurting each other, but those around them, the feelings I had towards them were just love, devotion, and the eagerness to be with them. The more I witnessed and saw first-hand, the less I felt. And, the more I remembered regarding that disappointment.

My parents are no strangers to feeling different about things and times from their past. Even current feelings tended to make their memory different. When I would question my mother about things from early on, before us, when she first met my father, I would have to wait until she was in a good mood. That was not easy by the way. A lot of patience and waiting was necessary. I had tried to ask her questions about when they first met, how they first met, and man the responses were filled with such rage, and a lot of curse words. I would have to stop, leave the room slowly, no sudden movements, and then proceed at a later time. I think that's a universal thing though. I'm sure of it. I am definitely someone who's memory is hindered by how my current feeling is.

While there is so much NOW that I know, that I never knew before, there are so many things that make sense while questioning both of my parents. I remember asking time and time again, and there were so many questions I wanted answers for. So many things I needed answers for. Not even just for my sake, but my sister's as well, I believed it could help them in some way to realize what went wrong.

On so many occasions while trying to get the answers, something seemed off with both of my parents. I could never place my finger on it, but their answers seemed distant. As if they were reaching for something that wasn't there. My father has so many learning struggles, that I had always just assumed it was because he was much slower than normal. There wasn't much I had expected from him, but I still wanted and needed his views and opinions on everything. I still needed him to tell me things, so that it came directly from him, for the first time, instead of hearing things from others, and what was written in my plan of care packages. My mother wasn't the brightest of the bunch either, but I knew when she focused she could be. And so, it was always such a struggle to get them to just answer the questions.

My mother was who I decided to question more, only because I knew she had slightly more education and a better dictation than my father. Plus, I had less to ask my father than my mother, so it worked out well. Even though my father gave me many headaches trying to listen to him talk about things. My mother's responses quite often when on a serious topic, seemed as though her brain was trying to search for a way to make things more sympathetic towards her. I often wondered if what she was saying was the truth and whether certain aspects of her story were exactly as they happened. Something just seemed off, but like I said, my parents weren't very bright, and I just assumed it was because of that. Now, I know it's because they were concealing the real truth about a lot of things. Probably due to the fact they didn't want us to know what they had done to us, and how they treated us. Whether it was shame, or the fear of losing us forever, it was something neither of them wanted to share.

My father was apparently a serial dater. Before my parents were a couple, my mother was very close to her sisters. The one I know most was especially close to her, and they were always together. My aunt's friend was the one who had originally met my father while attending a bingo hall. I guess they hit it off, and then they started dating. According to my mother, she got bored of him and dumped him. A wise choice if I may say so. It wasn't long after that, that my father started dating my aunt. I assume she didn't care too much for her friend's opinion about him and felt the desire to see for herself. They began dating, and that too didn't last long. Another indication that should have been looked at more closely on my mother's part. Two people that are close to her have now briefly dated and dumped the same guy. A sign to turn around and run in the opposite direction.

Some things are easily recognizable to the naked eye, while other things require you to experience it for yourself. While having been around my father, seeing how her sister and friend felt and were treated, my mother still felt something for him. Personally, I think it was stupidity, but what do I know. Probably the only three women he knew at the time, and he had to make his way through them all. It wasn't long after my aunt left him, that my mother began dating him. She reports that he was attractive, kind to everyone, polite, a little reserved and quiet, but nonetheless, was someone she wanted to get close with.

At that time he was living in Peterborough Ontario and worked in a factory. Hearing that surprised me since it came as a shock that he actually had a job. It didn't take him long once dating my mother that he began his manipulating behavior. He weaseled his way into a person's mind so carefully, in a way that you wouldn't notice at first, but the end result is to only benefit himself. While knowing how close my mother was with her sister, now that he's dated both, he didn't like nor wanted to share her. Personally, I think it stemmed from his own history with his parents, being neglected while suffering from *mommy issues*.

Not all at once, but slowly, he began to influence my mother by making her perceive her sister as someone she shouldn't be so close with. He would begin to drop hints and suggestions that my aunt was someone who had too much influence on her and that she was too controlling. Calling the kettle black if you ask me. On a side note, that saying makes no sense. I mean, it should be calling the kettle hot, shouldn't it? Anyways, it's ironic that he was saying that my aunt was too controlling over my mother. Without realizing it for herself, just by saying that, he was doing that very thing to her. He was trying to get into my mother's head, making her want to distance herself from her own sister, clouding her judgment.

The main purpose for trying to separate not only my mother from her sister but her entire family. His wish was to move to North Bay, where HIS family was residing. The strange thing about this was that at the time they met, my mother had just recently given birth to my brother. She had a one-night stand with some guy, and in January 1987, she gave birth to him. It wasn't until around March 1987 that she began dating my father. My aunt was not only around so much to be a sister, but rather, to be an aunt, and help my mother who was a single parent. My aunt was already a mother, so knew she would be able to offer advice, assistance, and because she wanted to be there for her.

Tension began to grow the longer my parents were dating, with my father tainting my mother's views of her sister. The two of them would start fighting more and more, and it didn't take long for my mother to turn her back on her sister, which became the start to living her life for my father. She took his side, and ended up packing up, and moving her newborn son to North Bay where my father wanted them to be. They moved in with his parents and were wed only after four months of dating. Another smack to the head if you ask me.

It's astonishing that she wasn't able to see that it wasn't her sister who was controlling her, but rather he was the one. He was inserting himself into her life at every angle, pushing everyone else in her life, out. This was making it so that all she was left with, was him. Doing this made it so that she would live her life for him, and only him, not caring about the fact that she had a child, who was not his. It was an incredibly selfish thing to do on his part. In a way, it wasn't just his fault, because his family was also to be blamed, as that is something they tend to do often.

After speaking with my mother and a few unnamed others, I was able to get some interesting back story in regards to my father's family. His parents especially weren't as they seemed. They had five children, all sons, including my father. He wasn't the youngest, and he wasn't the brightest. At one point my father's parents had a daughter, but she died while still in infancy. Apparently, she was born with many complications, and from what I was told, yes speculation because it was apparently a super delicate topic so it was to never be brought up. As so I was told. She was also born with some form of a mental disability. Not too sure which kind, however. I'm also fairly certain, she was either the youngest, or she would have been around the same age as my father. Either way, my father would have been fairly young when she passed.

While growing up, my father wasn't like his brothers. With having so many learning disabilities, he became a bit of a recluse and would prefer to stay inside the house with his mother. While his father and brothers would be outside working in the yard or doing "manly" things, he would prefer to stay indoors and in the kitchen. He would help his mother out with the household chores, and she would teach him basic cooking skills. Of course, because of the type of guy my grandfather was, he didn't believe men should stay inside. Yes, eyes have been rolled.

My grandfather had that primitive way of thinking, that a woman's place was in the kitchen, while the man was the one who went out and worked. He believed that men didn't have any need to be the house cleaners, cooks, or even looked after the children if they chose not to. To him, his wife was the one in charge of all of that, and from people who knew them, it showed. His basic way of thinking was that his wife was basically his property to do as he wishes. This was a trait that over time he would teach to each of his sons. At least, he definitely tried to.

It's funny because out of his five sons, the one who appeared to have learned the most from his father and acted such a way was my father. The one who probably spent the least amount of time with the man. He was a momma's boy, and although felt better about staying inside doing household things, became the biggest, saddest, excuse of a man. According to sources, my grandparents also fought often, and there were rumors and allegations that my grandfather would beat up my grandmother. Of course, they drank a lot, which never helps those kinds of situations. My grandmother would on occasion have bruises on her face, under the eye, but there would always be an excuse.

Aside from his views on a man's place, and a woman's place in a relationship, my grandfather was very homophobic. Another trait that was passed onto his children. In my opinion, this family was Class A lowlifes. Surprisingly, my mother's family did not share these views. Definitely not to that extent.

My mother's parents had three daughters, who were considered to be strong-willed, and outspoken women. Wouldn't have dreamed to raise them thinking a kitchen was the only place for a woman. My mother and her one sister especially were very carefree in spirit. They all believed that they could do whatever they chose to, which was exactly how they should think and believe. Having such different beliefs and opinions were the main reasons for all of the clashing between my parents.

Even though my brother was not my father's biological child, at the time of starting out with my mother, he began to raise him as if he were. He actually seemed excited to be a father figure, and that went a long way with my mother for she no longer had to be a single parent. Once moving to North Bay to live with his parents, things seemed even better at first for them. No one in the family had children of their own at that time, and so my brother in a way was the only grandchild. The fact that he was a boy, went a long way with everyone because it was another child to groom to their beliefs. My mother was not privy to how the family operated, but it didn't take long for her to realize just what their thoughts were.

After a few short months, the love they had seemed so strong that they could overcome anything that tried to stop them. They got married almost right away, and in my father's eye, the thing that could stop them was my mother's family. Still trying to place a wedge between them, at this point my mother for the most part saw them through his eyes. She was barely speaking with them, and her relationship with her one sister became quite distant, and they started arguing a lot. All my aunt wanted to do was be sisters again, and tried to make my mother see what my father was doing, but to my mother, she just kept hearing what my father would say to her. That she was just trying to tell her what to do while trying to control her every move.

When it came time for their wedding, they had to invite my mother's whole family of course. According to my mother, on her wedding day, she fought so much with her sister that she was pushed down the stairs. Looking at their wedding photos, I never would have known because I didn't see any marks, bruises, nothing. That's good at least. Knowing what I know now though IF my aunt did push my mother down the stairs, there has to be more to the story. All I was told was that they fought about my father, which lead to the stairs. Without being there, and since it's difficult to believe everything she says because of how much she leaves out of a story, it's impossible to know exactly what happened. For all I know, which of course is speculation, but it could have been my father who had done that. All I know is that her telling me this story when she did, was a way for her to change my opinion about my aunt, which didn't work.

At times, hearing certain stories is not enough for a person to believe or change the said belief. From everything I knew about my aunt, and her relationship with my mother, the only thing I could believe was what I witnessed. Growing up, I have so many memories of her and her children, and basically, all of them were positive. I remember at times she and my mother wouldn't get along, but it had nothing to do with myself nor my siblings. Everything that went on between them, was exactly that, between the two of them. Being in a relationship, however, with a man who worked so hard to build wedges between people, it partially rubbed off, and when benefiting herself, tried to build that wedge with her children and her sister.

I am unsure if it was something that had always been a trait with her, or if it was a manifestation from being with my father, but my mother was the type who at times could only see certain things her way. When she was in a frame of mind that her sister was the enemy, we had to agree with her and showed that she was right. It took us forever to realize that this had to be done because if we tried to show that we weren't in agreement with her on a specific subject, she would rip into us. At the end of it, we would be *dead to her*. That was actually something she would say. Later in life, after hearing it so much, it became a family saying.

After their wedding, they continued to live with my father's parents, and at this point because of what happened with the stairs, it was an easy way to convince my mother to cut ties with her family, pretty much altogether. He convinced her that she had a new family with him and that they would be much happier now. Although my brother was a nice addition to the family, he wasn't blood-related, and therefore my father's family kept insisting that he had his own.

Arguing had already been a key factor in their short relationship and marriage, as my mother was not appreciative of my father's views on a woman's duties. He wasn't able to hold a steady job and was constantly being let go after a very short period of time. If my father was hungry, he would expect my mother to make him something to eat, and if it wasn't him insisting she make him something, *his* father would. Situations like that happened quite often, and my mother was not the type of woman who was going to be okay with that. While trying to convince her that her job was to take care of him while he was the one who would work, they would argue because she would bring up the fact that he can't even hold down a job.

On days when my mother would be extremely exhausted with my brother who was colic, she would try to get my father to help out, as he had made a promise to be there for her, and her child. For the most part, while asking and wanting my father's help, my grandfather would step in the middle and pull my father away to help with something else. When my grandfather would see my father was needed to help with a child who was not his, he would find something for him to do, so my mother would have to fend for herself. When my mother would speak out, she would usually be told that mothering a child was a woman's job and that she had to deal with it on her own. It was her job, not my father's. Of course, my father would be present for that, and for the most part wouldn't say anything, which would just become another argument.

No job, no house, no comfortable bed which would lead to terrible nights of sleep, which in turn made for two very uncomfortable and cranky parents. Arguing became the norm at this point, and although my father would on occasion play with my brother, that seemed short-lived. His family was getting very persistent on him to make his own flesh and blood child. My parents had tried and tried, with no results. This was probably the universes way of saying they needed to slow down and fuck off. While agreeing to try and have a child together, it seemed to slightly calm down all of their arguing because, in turn, my father's family was getting exactly what they wanted.

I think the gods were watching and laughing at my parents and their situation. Sure my mother was giving my father's family what they so badly wanted, a blood relative, but it wasn't exactly what they were hoping for. My mother had told me that for a while they tried and tried to conceive another child with no success, and then after a year and a half or so, she found out she was pregnant. While so excited for the good news, my father and his family being in a family that is predominantly male would have a change in scenery since my mother had a daughter growing inside of her.

The birth of my sister in March 1989 brought so much happiness to my mother, for she was thrilled to have a little girl. My father and his family although hoping for a boy to have been born since it was something they were used to, and could groom to their misogynistic beliefs, actually seemed happy themselves. The probability that the reason for all of their excitement was due to the fact that my sister was the firstborn grandchild, and therefore was a huge deal to them. Excitement at first, shortly turned into frustration, neglect, and disappointment for my brother, however.

Speaking to the nature of things, the arrival of a new baby meant that a lot of attention was required for said baby. My sister was no different. Being born at around five pounds, my sister was such a tiny little thing, and being a newborn, needed a lot of attention from my mother. This was the attention that my brother wouldn't be getting now that he's no longer the only child. Thank goodness for my father and his entire family being around so that they could help out and make sure that he's not feeling neglected and cared for. At least, that's what one would assume, but because they are who they are, that didn't happen.

It didn't take long after my sister being born that my father and his family decided they no longer needed him, nor needed their attention. While my mother was trying to be a mother to a newborn, hoping that their attention could be used to care for my brother, they just wanted to do everything for the new baby. While starting to get upset and angry, for she felt as though my brother was just as much their grandchild and my sister, that created a lot of tension between them all. My father was under the impression that he already did his job at helping out with my brother, who wasn't his, and now that he has his own child, that's all that mattered.

When my father's family would only play and give attention to my sister, while my brother would be right there next to her, getting nothing from them, my mother would speak out. More like yell out. I don't actually blame her since it's unfair to have left him out of things. My parents were married, and my father chose to be a father to another child, and just because he now has his own, he can't just go back on that promise. My brother was too young to understand what was going on, and everyone had no problem paying attention before my sister, but now that she's here that's a reasonable excuse to just neglect him. Ugh!

Time and time again, my mother would explain to the family that she has two children. Not just one, but two which means they have two grandchildren. When my father's parents and brothers would constantly pick my sister up, play with her, my mother would repeat and say how they can't just leave my brother out. There are TWO children. My father would respond in front of everyone by telling her to *shut your mouth* and that she can't speak to his parents like that. He would tell her that they can do whatever they wanted because they're in their house. Her opinion didn't seem to matter, and my father would never take my mother's side by explaining the need to pay attention to both children.

The first two months of my sister being born was when my mother had begun to notice a huge difference in my father. They had argued quite a lot before, but now things were seeming different, with a lot more aggression. Not only was he neglecting my brother, but also my mother. Whenever he would take his family's side on things, speaking out against her, as if he was their little trained puppy dog, she would retreat to the basement to be alone and cry. It was getting so bad that my mother found herself in a situation that she didn't want to be in, and knew that something had to change. She decided that she and the kids needed a break and had to leave.

My mother and my two older siblings moved to Coldwell for what was the first separation between my parents. My father ended up getting his own temporary apartment so that he could go back and forth to visit. My mother needed some time away to collect her thoughts, and to get her two children out of a situation that was becoming chaotic and hectic while living at my father's parents' house. She needed a familiar feeling, something that could allow her to breathe and find some peace, and so she visited with one of her best friends.

Her best friend back during that time would later become my aunt. Sadly, the poor woman had to be introduced to my father's family, and being so close to my mother, it was inevitable. The only good aspect of becoming my aunt was that years later she married the only decent brother of my father. The only one I liked. The only one who seemed normal, regardless of the fact that he had a speech impediment. I'm still a little unsure exactly when my parents introduced her to my uncle, as my notes don't actually indicate such details. I do know that she becoming part of the family was a huge blessing, as it offered some peace in a family that was draining all the good out of my mother.

My parents' first separation only lasted around a month or so. According to my mother, my father at the time seemed determined to try and change in order to make things better. He appeared *a changed man* which was what my mother had hoped for, and so that led to them getting back together. They were still married after all, and the separation had only ever been temporary to give each some peace of mind while getting them away from my father's family. Probably one of the best decisions my mother ever made. At least now she has her best friend to be around to help out when needed. As well as her being around, the separation also allowed my mother to slowly get back into contact with her family. Something that appeared to have been very important to my mother.

After my parents were back together, shortly afterward, while trying to make things work with my father, my mother was noticing how she seemed to be putting on weight. She realized that after having two children, and while dealing with all the ongoing stress, that it was probably usual for some weight to be adding on. She had never exactly been a small woman. And after two children, not being super active, she already was a bigger woman. The weight just seemed to be adding on, however, and it was becoming yet another problem between my parents. While becoming upset that she wasn't able to lose any weight since being pregnant with my sister, and having my father not look at her as he once did, my mother consulted her doctor. She was inquiring what could be causing her to not lose weight, and what he had to tell her, actually made her break down in tears.

ME! Finally, I was brought into existence. Finally, and sadly considering the first reactions of my parents. Neither of my parents were working at the time, mostly because my father was lazy, and refused to go out and find a job. Also, my mother was practically a single mother trying to raise two children, and having everything that had already happened, was causing her a lot of depression and anxiety issues. She at the time wanted to go out to work but wanted to make sure her children were looked after. She didn't exactly trust my father to do it by himself. They couldn't afford daycare, and so money was now the number one issue between them while finding out about the newest pregnancy.

Since giving birth to my sister, my parents had begun their fighting, separated, moved cities, gotten back together, and have now found out that my mother was eight weeks pregnant with me. This was all within about four maybe five months after my sister being born. If you're thinking what I'm thinking right now, that *is there a chance that my father might not actually be my father because of the timeline*? I know right? That is definitely hopeful thinking and wishing on my part. The main reason why I believe that could be a possibility is because I remember how in the past my mother had cheated on my father. According to my mother, she said that she doesn't believe I couldn't be his, but for my own personal feelings, I am still hopeful because of the type of man he is.

Neither of my parents were ready nor wanted another child at this time. They had no money, things were becoming quite hectic between them, and they were just unsure how they would be able to handle three children. They had limited time to figure things out because I would soon arrive. There are only 11 months between my sister and I. It seemed like every day taking care of my older siblings, who for the most part were still in diapers, was a daily reminder that a third was arriving soon and that things were going to get a lot more difficult to handle. This feeling caused a lot of arguing between them, as the stress seemed to get to them. They weren't living in the now, dealing with the kids they currently had, instead were too busy thinking about how bad things were going to be later after I would be born.

By the time I was born, tensions seemed to be at an all-time high between my parents. From giving birth to me, my mother had some minor complications and had to remain in the hospital for a little bit. Unable to go home with me, and my father having to take care of my siblings on his own, he didn't feel as though he could also handle me, and so my aunt, my mother's sister, ended up taking me. Thankfully at the time of my birth, we were all living in Ottawa, and so it was easy for my aunt to take me in while my mother healed.

Once my mother was well enough to be released from the hospital, I then joined her from staying with my aunt. Aside from my aunt stepping in often to help out, my mother's best friend also wanted to help. From time to time, when my parents would want a break from having three young children to tend to, her friend would take one or two of us. This gave less for my parents to worry about at a single time, as they found three children were becoming too much to handle all at once. My mother was feeling a little happier though after having me because she was finally able to start losing a bit of the weight she had put on.

While feeling excited that she was losing some weight, and having some help taking care of us, once in a while she would go out for a ladies' night. Thinking that ladies night meant a break, relieving some of the stress and tension, but in reality, it only brought on more. Usually, when my mother would have a ladies' night out, it meant that my father had to stay home with the three children on his own. Since the only help they would get was from my aunt and my mother's best friend, they were ladies, and therefore would be out with my mother unable to help my father. Up until this point, he wasn't exactly fluent in parenting on his own and had been used to my mother being the one to take care of us while he sits back and plays with us when *he* felt like it.

Things appeared quite different for my father after I was born, as it was only then that he had to start parenting, on his own. This was new territory for him, as in the past he always had my mother, but now it was up to him to know what to do and had to do it. He didn't have his family to fall back on, but in retrospect, he was beginning to realize that parenting wasn't even something he wanted to do. While my mother was beginning to feel somewhat happy because she was able to go out and drink with people after she was parenting us, my father was left contemplating alone at home. He was beginning to think that he shouldn't have to be changing diapers, running after the kids, because of the beliefs his parents had raised him in. He had always believed because of them that it was the wife's duty to do everything he was now doing. He was now regretting so much, now believing that being a parent is too much work, and that is not something he even wants.

My mother had the intention of just periodically going out to get a break, however, it was becoming something constant. Being stressed out from her three children, and a husband that didn't want to go out and find a job, while appearing to not even wanting to take care of us, she felt as though she needed more and more nights to unwind. Her going out so often to drink was causing my father to freak and often yell. He wasn't sure how to process everything that was going on around him, which was leading to things building up inside him. He would argue with my mother, telling her that she can't go out anymore, trying to get her to stay home with us. Of course, she felt as though she could, and so would yell back at him telling him to get over it because she was going out if she wanted to.

With feeling incredibly pissed off at my mother for going out so much, but unable to take it out on her while telling her how he feels, he would take it out on us. He was beginning to feel as though he wasn't getting any attention, and that wasn't something he liked. He had it in his mind that if she felt she could just go out and not parent, then he could stay home and not parent there. In a way, to him it felt like payback. It was his childish way of saying… HAHA, in your face.

With our ages ranging from newborn to almost four years old, we of course were all in the stages of needing parental guidance so we could know the difference between right and wrong. We needed someone to watch over us and help us. My father became not wanting to do such. If we were doing something we weren't supposed to or something he didn't want us to do, like crying, he would scream at us to shut up. He became quite temperamental towards us. At times he would refuse to even put us to bed so that when my mother would return from being out, she could put us to bed. A few times he had even broken some of our toys if it meant we were distracting him from watching television. And yes, while feeling so enraged from having to take care of us, he at times would even hit us so we would listen. *You want to cry, well I'll give you something to cry about.*

Although the issues arising between my parents had been ongoing since practically day one, it was still something that neither of them wanted to pay attention to. There had been so many indications over the few years of being together, and yet instead of taking a step back to really focus on them and try to find the right solution on how to deal with it, they chose to ignore and hope for the best. It's never easy to break down issues one might have, and try to find a way to fix the problem. Both of my parents had been so dismissive not only with each other but about the problems within their marriage.

It's possible it was because the problems seemed too complicated to disclose with one another, and they were too afraid of what would happen while dealing with it. It might even be because they were so oblivious to the underlining issue that they were just not good for each other. There are so many explanations and theories as to why they hadn't worked things out, and why they kept choosing to do the wrong thing at every turn. All I know from my memory, and from everything I have learned over the years, is that these two individuals were just not meant to be together.

The sad fact in all of this is that my siblings and I were the ones affected the most because of all of their issues. We were the ones being caught in the middle. Having everything get even worse once I was born, they were just blind to what they were doing to each other and us. My father's temper and violent behavior became more frequent in his daily routine, while my mother's drinking and partying was becoming part of hers. The three of us at the end of the day were the ones to suffer the most.

With not accepting what my parents were doing to each other and to us, for the beginning two years of my life, things between them were only escalating. As time was going on, my father's outbursts of rage and violence had become such the norm, that it almost didn't seem out of place when he would scream or hit us, and even when he would beat out his frustrations on my mother. While trying to go out as often as she could to let off steam and drink, it became something that she would just rather do at home. The alcohol became such a crutch for her, that it turned into something she depended on. Quite a few times they thought brief separations were what they needed to help fix their marriage and issues. The real reasons for them, were for the fact that they were becoming too tired from being together and from being parents, that they wanted to get away from it all. This continued until the first time the Children's Aid Society had been called on my parents in fear of the safety of my siblings and me.

Chapter Four

Quick Passings

For the most part, I think it's safe to assume that we all have an idea as to how we hope our life will turn out. We go through the day to day experiences with the mindset of being able to pull through anything that comes our way. After all, obstacles in our life are the things that generally help make us stronger, by testing us in so many ways. When something doesn't go our way, it's about being able to become determined to not allow that to control how we live tomorrow. It's easier said than done I know, but at times learning from this type of mistake, can be exactly what is needed to be able to not make it again in the future.

Although I was someone who didn't always learn from my mistakes, as it took a very long time, my parents also didn't ever seem to learn from theirs. They appeared to have gone through life making mistake after mistake. Instead of learning from them, so that they could change the outcome the next time, it's as though they completely forgot about the consequences of their previous mistakes. The mindset they had was that of a goldfish, as each time it was as if they were acting on a clean slate. To each other, it felt that the clean slate was necessary in order for them to start over in their marriage. The neglected fact was that their children were the ones currently suffering from their avoided actions.

It is the hopeful thinking that something as traumatic as losing your children to the foster system would be enough to wake you up if you truly wanted them in your life. It is the hope that it's enough to make you realize the decisions you are making might not actually be the right ones. It is also hopeful wishing that that would be enough to make a person want to truly do better, in all aspects of life.

Once my siblings and I were in our first foster home, my father had been informed about my mother's actions. After the two of them consistently fighting and feeling as though running away was a solution, he had been struck with some sort of realization of what had happened. I'm unsure if he returned because he didn't want to lose us, as he never in my life truly seemed as though being a father was something he wanted to do, rather had to do. From what I can remember from that time, his return was something he did in order to get back with my mother.

At that time, not being in the right frame of mind, and knowing what she did was beyond inexcusable, my mother wanted her children home. She also really wanted my father back. After appearing in court, there were certain things that needed to happen in order for us to return, and that included counseling. Since the problems in the home didn't just include my mother, my father also had to participate. While his strides to change for the better weren't as ambitious as my mother's, it took longer for him to come around.

While still being separated, the main thing on my father's mind was to get his wife back. Not so much his children, but her. He knew that in order for him to get her back, he had to do as she asked, which was to help get us back. According to my files, it appeared as though my mother was making some improvement, and following through with the counseling. Apparently, it only took less than six full months of self- improvement after threatening to kill her three children, all because her husband was taking a temper tantrum, for us to return.

After speaking with some relatives about the situation, it was believed that the initial involvement with CAS seemed too complicated and too much to deal with for my father. His lengthy separation was partial to the fact that he didn't want to deal with it. That was one of the reasons for his return AFTER we moved back in with our mother and aunt. The hard work appeared to have been over, and so it was finally time for him to come back home. Having it be so long that my mother was without her husband, she had no quarrels for him returning.

Being so young, my siblings and I were all so confused as to what was going on. Being taken away in the middle of the night was a big *what is happening right now*. Witnessing our parents fight, scream, and then living with strangers was just a lot to understand when we weren't developed for that kind of understanding. We were at the age where we weren't able to have life goals for ourselves. The only things the three of us cared about were to just play, sleep, eat, and watch cartoons. We were infants after all.

In our first foster home, things especially seemed strange as we couldn't see our parents even though we would always ask for them. We had brief supervised phone calls to basically say hi and bye. We had a few supervised visits over the course of our first stay, which was such a tease as we could see our parents, but couldn't go home with them. It was just a confusing time for all of us.

When not being able to sleep at night, we were considered *troublesome* because we wouldn't fall asleep right away. Having difficulty eating for someone else who isn't used to our specific habits, made them refer to us as being *fussy*. We became *temperamental* when told <u>no </u>to as well.

Strange that while being so upset about our situation, we wouldn't be able to fall asleep, or even eat for someone else. It's almost as if something seems missing from our lives, and yet gives reason for labeling us a certain way, which is how others will then on also see us as.

Even though neither of our parents in my opinion were actually ready to have us home, as there were still so many issues between them that hadn't been fixed, I think that our return was necessary for our development. We needed to be in a familiar environment. I agree that the environment we were in wasn't safe, however, I feel as though it was needed. At the end of the day, we kids just wanted to be with *mommy* and *daddy*. We didn't care about the problems going on, as we didn't and couldn't comprehend them. Nonetheless, we returned home and were able to have hope for a normal coexisting family once again.

Memory is a funny and tricky thing to understand. While being so young, it can at times be difficult to hold onto those memories, no matter how good your memory can be. I can remember a lot about being in my first foster home, even before that sitting on the staircase with my siblings watching our parents yell and hit one another. Looking back into my mind's files of early childhood, I seem to have far more bad memories than I do good. Regardless of the fact that there might actually be so many great memories in there, the bad ones just take hold.

Living back with our mother at her sister's place in Ottawa, created some great memories. Those are memories that will forever make me realize she wasn't as bad as we were told, for she went out of her way to make things seem easier for us. The sad thing is, once our father returned into our lives, it's as though my mind knew to stop cataloging as it was probably not going to be what I want to remember.

From the ages of three to five, there are some things I can remember on my own, but most things seem to be a blank screen. From what I've read, and from what others have told me, that time was very transitional. My family moved into our own place out of my aunts, even though the fighting hadn't fully stopped. Children's Aid would occasionally check-in to see how things were going, making sure that they were continuing to work on their issues making our home a safe environment for us. The three of us were continuing to grow, to develop.

My soother faze was in full effect at this time, as that is something I'll never forget. I watched my first horror movie, Chucky, thanks to my father. My toes and knuckles were first cracked, thanks once again to my father. My obsession with the color purple began, as well as my fascination with long hair. It's strange to think and try to remember about those two years, as it seems I have more memories from before that. Maybe it's because, at that time, my parents weren't great, but not AS bad as they had been, and so it wasn't scaring on my mind. It was their *honeymoon* faze I guess.

Once I hit the age of five, it was as if the last two better years were too good. It's almost as if my parents didn't like that things were going too well. Then again, the two of them were just going back on old habits. They acted as though the clean slate they had created was even bigger, and so there was so much room for more bullshit. The memories I had from five on, as bad as they are, they weren't even just from them being them, but all around us. It's as if the universe was reminding us that our lives just suck, and are magnets for trouble.

We were living in a low-income housing area in Ottawa because once again, my father was choosing to not work, as he "didn't feel like it." My mother periodically would work at a daycare center, according to what she told me. We definitely needed the money, and so she would try to find something to do in order to help bring some in. The daycare is actually something I can remember being a part of. One day the daycare went out to McDonald's for lunch, and from what I remember, it was the second time I went there that day and ate too much. By the time I got home, I felt so sick that I couldn't stop throwing up. The daycare had to put me on the lawn, in the shade, curled up in a ball trying to feel better. That was not a fun day, and it wasn't until a long time afterward that I would eat McDonald's again.

As sick as I felt that day on the lawn, which was in the *project* where I lived, the worst part of it was that knowing how I felt, my mother had no sympathy for me. I can remember her telling me that's what I get for eating so much. Regardless of the fact that she was responsible for feeding me one of the two McD meals that day. Her youngest, at five years old couldn't stop throwing up, shaking on the ground in the shade from food sweats, didn't seem to matter as she left me there and went back home. Thankfully one of the ladies at the daycare stayed with me, rubbing my back telling me that I would be okay. As much as I was crying because I just wanted the pain to go away, it felt so nice to actually have someone there with me. A bad memory turned into a good one but wasn't because of my mother.

That project we lived in seemed to be a beacon for traumatic events. There were so many other children who lived there, and all day, every day you would

51

see kids running around playing everywhere. On one side of the project, close to where we would actually meet for daycare, there was a small staircase. There must have only been about five or so steps, and on either side, there were railings to hold onto.

I remember being at the bottom of the steps one day when there were a few slightly older kids playing. There was this one girl who thought she was so cool, so tough, and so funny, and thought that she could walk on the railing. She for some reason thought it was such a great idea, and believe me, it was not. Of course, her shoe slipped, and with one leg on either side of the railing, she fell onto it really hard! Like, REALLY hard. After her lady parts were smacked on the railing she fell off to the side, and things were so bad that she had to get rushed to the hospital. That sight is something that no matter how much I try, I will never be able to get that image out of my head.

Across the street, or should I say almost highway because of how busy it would get, there was a large field. Not really a park, but there was a quite large area that was just grass. A lot of people at the time would go there to run around, throw a Frisbee, play catch, you know, family-type things. On occasion, my parents, siblings, and I would also go over there, mostly because the three of us wanted to. For the record, I have only three memories of ever going there to play. And of the three memories, I can still remember my father's facial expressions of not wanting to be there. I remember how he would huff and puff about having to bring us there.

The last time we went there, it was early evening, still somewhat light out. Especially since we were all still up. We were playing in the field, throwing something. The thing we were throwing is something I can't remember, but I do remember a few teenagers, or at least older kids, playing in the field as well. They weren't super close to us, but they were playing with a ball. Throwing and kicking the ball back and forth to each other. The ball ended up going onto the busy street to the side of where we were. There was this girl in that group who ran after it. She starts running after the ball, and instead of looking both ways before crossing, she ends up getting smacked by a vehicle.

We all saw the whole thing, and let me say it was not favorable. The only good thing that came out of it, was the fact that our parents seemed to have a genuine concern for what we kids had just seen. That, once again, is a memory I had longed to forget! I so badly wanted it out of my mind. The incident as a whole, the blood, the screams, none of that was something I needed to remember. It was something that I would never forget. And if nothing else, it was the moment I learned about the importance of looking both ways before even thinking about crossing a street.

Looking both ways before crossing any street became somewhat of an automatic occurrence with my siblings and me. Even while playing in the project, going from one side to the other, from that incident onwards we would be so afraid to be hit by a car, that we were always looking. Once I started to learn how to ride a bike, with training wheels, watching where I was going was all I could think about. I remember when it came time for me to learn without the training wheels, my father would yell at me to just go, while my mother would tell him to leave me alone and that if I'm not ready, I'm not ready. The biggest fear at that time I had wasn't so much for falling and hurting myself, but my father wanted me to ride my bike down the street in our project, but there was a corner ahead of me, and I couldn't help but fear that a car will run me over.

I have seen other parents try to teach their children to ride a bike by holding the seat while the child pedals, and then slowly the parent would release their hand. This allows the child to feel safe, knowing their parent is there to help them, to not let them go until they are ready. One night, my father and siblings were going to go for a little evening family bike ride, but I still wasn't ready to ride without my training wheels. While my mother is yelling at him to not leave without me, and to help me, he felt it would help to grab my seat while I'm about to pedal, and then just push the bike to go. Yeah, I fell. I cried. I did not learn how to ride a bike that day. I didn't get to join everyone else for the bike ride because my father was too impatient to teach me.

It took a little while for me to learn how to balance myself on my bike while trying to pedal. I was determined to learn because I didn't want to be left behind again. A little bit each day I would practice, and since my sister already knew how to, watching her actually helped. She kept encouraging me to ride, and I wanted so badly to join her and our friends on the little bike ride around the area.

Most of the time, the three of us had to spend the majority of the days outside and around the house. At the time we never really questioned it, and frankly, it was nice. Our parents would be at home usually finding something to fight about, and so being outside was something we enjoyed. When the sun rose, it became something to look forward to because we hated having to listen to them. Once I learned how to ride my bike, I never wanted to leave it. I so badly wished I could have just ridden away from all the screaming coming from our house. Believe me, you could hear them from almost anywhere in the project.

While living in that project, I can account for at least four different times when our father would just take off for a little while. Usually when I would be at the house, and our father wasn't there, and it wasn't because of his freak-outs and taking off, it was because he was off having *daddy/daughter* time, and would be somewhere with my sister. At times I hated it because she was the only one who got special time with our father, but because I was never really close to him, I didn't mind. I would just take that time to spend it with my mother. Since usually she seemed sad, I felt it was better because then I could try and make her smile.

On the times that our father would just leave randomly, we would look around and he would just be gone. I remember when one of us would ask our mother where he was because we all knew he didn't work, she would respond with "I don't fucking know, and I don't fucking care. He just took off because he doesn't love us." I can remember at first when we would hear that, it was quite a shock because we didn't understand that she was just really upset from their earlier fight, and in her mind, she didn't know how to communicate that to us.

The more and more when he would just leave, it became a habit for us. We started not even asking our mother where he was, and when we wouldn't see him, we would look at each other and simply say that "he's fucking gone because he doesn't love us." I can remember giggling with each other because it became somewhat amusing, but a couple of times our mother would hear us say that, and she did not find it funny. Depending just how pissed off or upset she would be from whatever kind of fight they had, we would either get turned upside down on her knee and spanked, or it was the bar of soap shoved in our mouths.

My sister was the most careful of the three of us. She learned how to repeat what we would hear from our parents more under her breath so our mother wouldn't hear, where I was not as careful. Our brother being older, was usually off at school or with his friends, wasn't so much there for all of it. Although my sister would get the knee and soap often, my mother seemed as if she wanted to switch things up with me, because quite a few times I can remember getting the ladle. If she wasn't close to the kitchen we would just get her hand whenever she would have to smack us, but the ladle appeared to be her favorite on all three of us. Sadly, I wasn't as careful as my sister, so I would get it a lot more.

Looking back on everything from being with our parents, while the three of us were each abused in some way, each of us had such different forms of abuse. My brother's abuse being the oldest and not blood-related to my father received more neglect than any of us. My sister's abuse came primarily from our father, while mine came from our mother and that fucking ladle. We each suffered differently over the years being with them, some similar while most times in our own way of punishment. Regardless of how many times we were all hit, the biggest and most striking form of abuse in my eyes was all the verbal abuse suffered.

Day to day living in our home never seemed to include normal dialogue between people. It appeared that the only way to get your point across, and the only way to show who was the boss, was by yelling everything. Anything from us picking up our clothes, to picking up our toys, brushing our teeth, even eating everything on our plates. It felt as though the only way our parents knew how to get their point across to us, was to yell at us to do what they wanted. Whenever the two of them needed to get the others' attention, once again they would yell. That would usually start a fight, and there we would be, watching it all. We of course were never allowed to yell, or swear, even though that's all they actually taught us.

When attending daycare and then school, being around so much swearing and yelling, when things wouldn't go our way, we acted in the only way we knew. When our teacher or even the bus driver would tell us no or seemed as though they had a problem with us, we would tell them to fuck off or call them a bitch. As bad as it was, it just felt right to us, because that's how we would see our parents communicate with one another, and regardless of people saying we shouldn't say those things, we just did. It became a form of instinct for us. With being asked why we had said those things, we would respond with *because that's what you say*. We would then be told that we are to do as they say not as they do! I always hated that double standard saying.

It always felt as though no matter what our parents deemed appropriate, no matter what it was we had to be in agreement, or suffer the consequences. When I was five, my mother for some reason thought that getting my ear pierced was something I needed. Against my father's wishes, as he felt it would make me "queer" to get it done, she still went ahead and I had no say in it.

I remember every minute of not only the experience of having my ear pierced but the events leading up to it and after. I can remember my parents discussing it. My mother told my father that she wanted to bring me to get it done, and he responded with "I'm not making my son a queer. Only fags get their ears pierced." My mother did not like that he said that, and insisted that they would get *the proper ear pierced*, and not the queer ear. Apparently, there is an ear that represents a queer individual while the other is for *normal straight men.* She stated to him that I was her son, and in the end could do as she wants with me. That included bringing me to get my ear pierced.

I really don't understand the things that go through their minds. While listening to what they were both saying, and being only five, I had no idea what queer and fag meant, but I did know that it wasn't something good in their eyes. Hearing their reactions to those two words, it freaked me out, and I didn't want to be those things. I didn't want to get my ear pierced. I didn't want them to not like me and refer to me as those two words since they clearly didn't approve of whatever they meant. I begged them to not get my ear pierced. The entire way to the place, I asked over and over, and still, my mother seemed determined to go through with it.

The entire way back home I don't think there was a time I wasn't crying. I kept reaching for my ear trying to take it out, while my mother would insist I stop and to not touch it. "I don't care if you don't like it. I paid for it, and you're going to wear it whether you like it or not." Well, I didn't listen, nor did I want to, because once we got back to the project, just a few doors down from where we lived, I took it out. There was a small area of grass, near where that girl fell on the railings, and I dropped the earring. For a brief second, I felt relief. I remember a slightly smug smile crept on my face, as it was my way of saying *fuck you* to my mother without actually saying it. I figured, by the time we would get inside and have her notice it, all I would have to say is that it must have fallen out. Oh well, nothing we can do now.

Just a few steps away from where I dropped the earring, my mother turned around to look at me. Probably some creepy mother's intuition that I had done something. I remember her face looked slightly confused why all of a sudden I had a smile while not crying to remove my earring, and she noticed it was gone. She grabbed me by each shoulder screaming in my face, "What the fuck did you just do?" I was so startled and knew that I had to answer quickly, but the words wouldn't come out of my mouth. With her hands still on either side of me, she was moving me side to side, almost as if she was looking at both ears trying to see if she could see it. She kept asking me what I had done with it, and finally, I told her I took it out.

She made me stay outside alone in the grass looking for it until I found it because she did not pay to have my ear pierced just for me to take it out and lose it. Even though I knew I dropped it in the grass just a few steps back, that tiny gold stud earring was difficult to find. My eyes were heavy with tears, as I was so close to being free from it. If I hated the idea of getting it before, having been screamed at in the middle of the project, and spending almost two hours looking for it definitely made me hate it. The two hours were mostly me looking, but my eyes were so cloudy from crying that seeing was a little difficult. Plus, a few times I stopped to pout sitting on the grass, refusing to look. Then I would think about what would happen if I didn't find it, and no thank you!

Considering how absent my father was when it came to parenting, he sure did have a lot of opinions on how he felt we should be raised. For me, he was always concerned and worried that I would turn out gay. He often would express his fears to my mother, with me being able to hear. Even his family would chime in on it saying that I would turn out gay and that he needed to be careful not to encourage my queer behavior. Getting my ear pierced was the first-time hearing this from him. Around the same time, I developed an obsession with the color purple for some reason. I don't know why, but I just loved that color.

I remember asking my mother if I would be allowed to paint my room purple. Oddly enough, she didn't seem to mind and said I could. That made me so happy! When she told my father, once again it was another thing for him to complain about, saying to stop encouraging me to be gay. He went on and on saying the same things as last time, but in the end, my mother and I got our way and my room was painted purple. When it was finished, I remember sitting on my bed looking at the walls, with a great big smile on my face. My happiness wasn't good enough for my father though as I could hear him telling my mother that he hopes she's happy that they are making a fag out of me. Once again those words I don't know the meaning for were creeping their way into my ears, and just like that, I hated my new purple walls.

Whenever my favorite aunt, who was at this point dating my father's brother, would visit me, she would let me brush her hair. She had incredibly long hair, and it always fascinated me. So many times I remember sitting on the floor or the couch, her in front of me, and I would just be brushing her hair. The calmness I felt when brushing her hair felt so nice. Usually, my parents would be somewhere else in the house arguing about something, and so while brushing my aunt's hair, gave me a break from all of it. Although I was able to do a French braid as young as five, that was just another thing to piss off my father.

While spending so much time just trying to be a child, enjoying things that made me happy, everything I liked and did just seemed to piss of my father. His only son, who has an ear-piercing, likes purple, playing with hair, even playing with dolls with his sister, just seemed like too much for him to handle. He never seemed to want to be around me, and he definitely never took the time to play with me. Whenever he would have to be home to watch us, I would do everything I could to be elsewhere, because I wouldn't want to be around him. According to our father, as I can remember him saying

57

in a disgusted tone, that the reason our mother would have him watch us is because she was off *screwing some guy*. Yeah, thanks for sharing that information with your five-year-old.

One day a little before moving from our home in Ottawa, we were all in the house. When I went upstairs to use the washroom, I found my mother laying on the floor in front of the toilet, with blood all over the floor. It looked like something out of one of the Chucky movies my father made me watch. I had no idea what happened, or what was going on. I just saw my mother laying on the floor with blood everywhere. I screamed like I had never screamed before. Everyone came running up, and our father told us all to go away. The sight had sadly already done its damage to all three of us. She was rushed to the hospital, and it wasn't until later that we learned she had a miscarriage.

While my mother was being rushed to the hospital, her parents were informed of what had happened, and from everything I can remember, them arriving to watch the three of us was the first and only time meeting them. Let's just say we did not like them. We liked our mother's sister, but the short period of time that our mother was in the hospital, being watched by our grandparents was not enjoyable. We were all freaked out, and from what we had seen, it looked like she was murdered, and we just wanted answers. We kept asking if she was okay and if we would be able to go see her. Over and over they would tell us that we couldn't see her. They never told us what happened, and they wouldn't let us go to the hospital to visit. I remember being told that if they had to stay at our place to watch us, not being able to see our mother, then we couldn't see her either.

Our parents sat down with us once our mother was back home to explain that mommy had another baby growing in her tummy, but it died. It seemed so weird to all three of us, as I can't remember having ever known she was even pregnant. With her infidelities, she later in life told me that that child she miscarried was in fact supposed to have been my fathers. Having heard that, I couldn't help but think wow, good for you that you lucked out since that miscarriage was his. As if it was supposed to hold some sort of goodwill to me, and it offered nothing. I knew she had cheated on my father, even during that time, but knowing who the father was supposed to be had no meaning to me.

When I was around six years old, sometime towards the beginning of 1996, we made the move back to North Bay. The move actually seemed pretty sudden, but it was suspected that it was due to the fact that our father wanted to be back close to his family. Not one of my siblings nor I really liked them, so it definitely wasn't for our benefit. We were children though, and so we had no say and had to follow where our parents took us.

The actual drive seemed to have taken forever, and we didn't get to our new house until really late at night. It was pitch-black out, and after spending hours driving, all three of us were restless. We were excited to be moving into a new home and were running around all over the place. Our first night in a different city, a new house should have been a fresh start for everyone, and yet, nothing had changed. Our first night seemed like any other day in our home, and it definitely spoke to how the rest of our time living there would be.

I'm a little uncertain as to whom it was, probably because it was my fault, but our door happened to get locked. When I say locked, I mean, it wasn't at first but then someone somehow managed to lock it on us, leaving us stranded outside in the chilly night that it was. I will never forget how quickly things changed that night. We were all exhausted from the move, but we children went from being super excited and laughing while running around, to being completely still while being screamed at. I think people back in Ottawa could hear our mother yelling from what one of us did, locking all of us outside.

Thankfully our new landlord lived across the street, probably heard my mother, and used their key to let us all in. The house seemed smaller than our last one, and this one wasn't even in a project. I remember thinking how cool and nice it was though. Although, the older I got, while driving past it I couldn't help but think how much of a dump it actually was. That's the difference between being a young child and an adult. Everything seems different and almost better when you're a child.

The house only had two bedrooms, one bathroom, and an extra area for a dining room. The kitchen was actually decent sized, so we had our kitchen table set up in there, and used the dining room as an extra bedroom. Of course, there wasn't a wall or a door that separated that room from the rest of the house, and so a sheet was put up for privacy. From what I can remember, it was an orange/yellow sheet. The color of it was so striking and didn't match a single thing in our home, and yet, that was the sheet used to act as a wall. It didn't even cover the entire area, and just looked really bad.

I shared a room with my brother directly across from the homemade bedroom used for my sister. We had bunk beds in our room, and I hated every minute of it. After spending years being yelled at to clean my room, I developed a habit of needing to keep things as clean as possible. Since he was older and seemed not as bothered by needing everything spotless, we clashed. He was slightly messy, and I was just always afraid of being blamed for our room not being clean, and so I would always clean up his messes. This led to me accidentally throwing out his bubble gum comics that he collected, but to me, I just saw garbage. I didn't want the ladle or to be yelled at, and so I threw them out. Of course, he was angry, told our mother, and I got the ladle anyways.

Living at the new house never seemed like a happy place. Our parents more than ever seemed to be fighting all the time. My siblings and I seemed to be clashing more and more. Mostly it was my brother and I. Everyone just seemed to be too close to one another. Probably due to the fact that the house was much smaller, and so there wasn't so much room to be running around, or having our own space. Our parents also just seemed to stop caring about things and started to go through every day with a chip on their shoulder. Our bathroom door seemed never to be closed because, in case of an emergency, the door had to remain open.

There never felt to be any privacy for anyone. It seemed as though our parents were the only ones who were allowed to get it. I wasn't allowed to close my bedroom door, and the bathroom door wasn't allowed to be closed if we kids were in it. Our parents usually kept their bedroom door opened, but at times they would close it. For instance, one time it was the middle of the day and I needed something and so I opened their door to ask, and I saw them going at it on the bed. It was so vile and definitely freaked me out. Of course, I was told to *shut the fucking* door. And I did, and would never open their door again! One of the few other times of privacy was when our father was punishing our sister for something she did. Although she only had a sheet up blocking us from seeing what was going on, we could definitely hear her crying. My brother and I were just told to mind our own business unless we too wanted to be in trouble.

Even though they were still married to one another, moving to North Bay seemed to divide my parents. While spending so much time apart, we kids were also spending time with one of them separately. My brother and I spent most of our time with our mother because we were favorable towards her, while my father preferred to spend time with my sister. My brother was at school full time, and when I didn't have to be in attendance, I would usually spend my time going to the laundry-mat with my mother. My father would be off somewhere with my sister, and would usually be visiting with one of his brothers. I remember always being grateful that I didn't have to go as I didn't like any of them, but also felt bad that my sister would have to be stuck doing that.

My mother had a close friend that actually lived pretty close to our house. I'm uncertain whether she knew him from years past when we used to live there, or if they had only met after moving back there. Nonetheless, while our father would be off doing his own thing, she would at times go and visit with him. A lot of the time she would bring either one of us or all of us with her. My sister was his favorite out of the three of us, and so she spent the most time at his apartment. The guy seemed nice enough. Nicer than our father, and also seemed to have an obsession with cows as his whole place was covered in them. We didn't realize it at the time, but our mother was actually having an affair with him. Shocking! Later in life, I was informed by her that she ended up getting pregnant from him, but lost the baby. Thankfully she didn't lose it like the last one, so we didn't have to be scared once again.

While tensions seemed to be growing out of control, the three of us were beginning to get really tired of it. None of us felt safe, and none of us wanted to stay there another day. While we usually would play on the side of the house, and on top of the roof of our neighbor's shed, we began planning our escape. We spent a few days talking about the best possible way to leave, and when the best time would be. We also had to plan the perfect escape plan knowing when they would be sleeping, when they would be awake. We had to be extra careful because they would tend to sleep with their door open. Our brother being the smartest, was in charge. He actually thought of everything, including where to step so as to not make noise, and how to close the door without any noise. Everything seemed to be perfectly planned out.

One morning, incredibly early before our parents woke up, the three of us got dressed, and after having to listen to them fight the night prior, we just had to leave. One by one we exited through the back door. So far everything was going as planned. So much time was spent on how we would escape, that we completely forgot to plan what to do once we actually left. After fleeing from our property, we quickly ran off down a few different streets. We didn't want it to be easy for our parents to see us, and so we would go street to street. We ended up at one of our brother's friends' house for some reason, and then his friend joined us on our adventure. He wasn't running away from his place but was just going to keep us company. While the two of them were up ahead because they were faster, my sister and I were falling behind.

Completely out of nowhere, our father showed up and started chasing after us. Grabbed my sister's and I's arms, holding really tight. My brother stopped where he was and my father yelled after him. The four of us began to make our way home, and then when my father wasn't looking, my brother took off again. My father was unable to chase after him because he was holding onto my sister and I, swore, and just proceeded to bring us home. We were dropped off at home where our mother was waiting, and then my father ran back out to look for my brother.

At first, our mother was furious, screaming at us, gave us a few good smacks, and then sent us to our room. The day went by and we were both in each of our rooms just crying. We were so hopeful that we were going to be able to leave our crazy home, and yet we were right back. We spent the entire day in our rooms, until later that evening when our father came back with our brother, who was hiding out at the beach. After the kind of day we all had, us kids realized that we were never going to be able to get away on our own, and so we never tried to run away again.

Our mother never really left us like our father had. Usually, after a really big fight, it would be him who would take off for a couple or a few days. After one of the last big fights, I remember our parents having, my mother was the one who was just gone. None of us ever really found out as to why she was even gone, and our father definitely never told us. One day we all got home from school, and when we asked where she was he wouldn't tell us. He would just complain about how she was screwing some guy and needed a break from all of us. I don't know if I had ever seen him so pissed off towards her. She was only gone for about a week, and at that time, every day he wouldn't allow us to talk about her. We weren't allowed to mention her, and he tore up all of her photos, and even the drawings on the fridge we had made for her. We all knew their fights got bad, but we just couldn't believe we couldn't even have our drawings made for her on the fridge. Those were OUR pictures, but he just wanted every reminder of her gone from our house.

Just by walking into our house during that time, you could feel all of the hostility. Things got so bad towards the end that something happened between my brother and my father. My sister was unaware of exactly what had taken place, but all of a sudden we could hear our brother yelling. We ran to the kitchen which was where the two of them were, and they were yelling back and forth, and then all of a sudden, our brother grabbed a knife. He went to go after my father but got pushed back. My father kept antagonizing him, taunting him by saying to "come stab me."

My brother would again go towards him, and then again get pushed back with my father saying "I thought you were going to stab me, come on do it already."

My sister and I were so freaked out, and we had no idea what was happening. While my brother and father were still going at it, I went into the drawers and removed all of the knives. I put them in a large bowl and ran out of the kitchen. Thankfully the whole situation seemed to cool down before anything really bad happened to one of them. In my whole six years of life at that point, that was the first time I had seen my brother so angry. I just knew it had to be for some good reason, even though it may not have been

62

handled the right way. To this day, I still don't know exactly what it was all about.

Having our mother back home was something we all wanted and needed. I especially needed her back because in her own way she allowed me to enjoy the things I liked, without her calling me names. After hearing all the names my father called me while living in Ottawa, moving to North Bay definitely didn't stop the names coming to me. The names actually were repeated more, especially with his family. I was at the point where I decided for myself that when I grew up I was going to be a hairdresser. After watching cartoons with my sister, I started to get into a couple shows she liked, like *Sailor Moon* and *My Little Pony*. Although, I think I might have enjoyed them more than her.

Watching what my father considered to be *girl* television shows, didn't matter to me. I never saw it as a *girl* show, I just saw it as something I enjoyed watching. I also liked *boy* shows such as Mutant Ninja Turtles, Spiderman, and other cartoon shows. I just really liked the other ones better. I never heard the end of it from him though. Always insisting to my mother that they needed to stop letting me watch them. His family would even start insinuating that I was queer, and my *fefe* qualities needed to be stopped. Having her around always helped, as I knew as long as she was there, no matter what my father would say, she would chirp him back.

As much as our mother yelled and hit us, being with just our father was always worse. As bad as she might have seemed, having her around was a sort of mediator that we wanted. After her week-long hiatus details still unknown, things appeared as if nothing ever happened. They never talked about it. They didn't seem to fight about it, and I know all three of us were just so confused. We were starting to know better though and didn't ask either of them. Things seemed slightly better around the house, and so we just went with it. When needing to deal with stressful situations at home, each of us kids had ways to somewhat manage.

After moving to North Bay, there was a school that was walking distance from our house, but in order for us to attend, we had to be baptized. Neither of our parents practiced any type of religion, although my files state that our father grew up Catholic. We had no knowledge about what religion even was. Never attended Church, not even on the holidays. I think the closest my parents were to religion, was when they got married. Unless Satan himself blessed them that day. We had no idea the difference between a Catholic school and a public school, and especially didn't know what being baptized meant.

Looking back on everything, getting baptized in July of 1996, was one of the best things to happen to me when I was younger. I remember afterward, I would attend Sunday mass when I was able to and allowed to. Neither of my parents would join me, and from what I can remember, neither of my siblings did either. I can remember going with a neighbor and friend and I was so grateful for them bringing me along. Those Sundays spent at the church, as new of an experience as it was, I just remember how much joy I felt being in there. With all the craziness going on at home, being in a place where no one yelled, but rather, everyone there seemed to be smiling and were happy. It made me for a brief moment forget about everything crappy that had already happened in my life, and I just wanted to stay there forever.

Growing up I didn't always participate in Sunday mass. I wasn't always allowed to go when I lived at home, and most of my foster parents over my life weren't religious. Most of the schools I attended however were Catholic-based, and so it gave me the opportunity to occasionally practice a faith that had a lot of interest to me. I have never been super religious, but it definitely gave me a chance to believe in something. It allowed me an opportunity to question things that we happening around me, especially regarding things I didn't understand. I then began to start praying to a higher power. I knew I couldn't always ask my parents, and most often never felt as though I could ask my caseworkers or foster parents, and so having someone to talk to in prayer meant a great deal to me.

Although most of the time spent living back home brought us a lot of turmoil and pain, there were brief moments of family happiness. The only problem when living in such a hostile environment was that no matter if we had a good day, we were still fearful. We knew the good would never last, as history had told us that. We would go day to day hoping that today was going to be one of those good days, and when it happened, we would fear what would happen if someone spoke out of turn.

As time would go on, our father became more violent, and our mother became more complacent with his behaviors. I can remember on quite a few occasions her being struck down, being left with bruises and scrapes on the face. Her rage also fuelled more and continued to drink to dull the pain that was our father. Although neither of them was treating the other properly, my mother still felt as though she didn't deserve what was being done to her, and so kept with her infidelity. It no longer became secret as my father always seemed to know. When he would know, and scream at her about it, we would all hear it and then, therefore, know that mommy was screwing someone else.

After years of being together, and after years of doing absolutely nothing to find a way to help deal with the issues that seemed to constantly plague them, my parents still felt being together was the answer. For some reason, they just couldn't see no matter what had happened, that they needed to get help. They needed to wake up. They needed to stop just believing that things would get better on their own. If they actually wanted something to change, they had to be the ones who did the change. The three of us were there witnessing too many problems between the two of them, and it was starting to affect how we acted and behaved.

Tempers started taking over how we would react to things that didn't go our way. Our foul language started to become something that seemed like proper dialogue. I became too tired while being at school, and wouldn't always go, which caused me to be illiterate. I don't think I ever had my parents read me a bedtime story, and I don't ever remember working on school work at home. Education was just something that wasn't viewed as important, and that resulted in me not being able to read or write.

Things started to spiral out of control in all aspects of our home. We barely had the money for food and were always going to the food bank. Fighting was an everyday occurrence, even us kids were beginning to take after our parents with respect to their moods and behaviors. While living in such a home where good days would be almost obsolete, it seemed to spark something within our mother. It was as if for a moment, she had a realization of what was happening, and knew something needed to be done. Thankfully she had that moment, and thankfully she acted on it. She contacted the Children's Aid Society and asked for help. She requested that the three of us be removed, as things were becoming too much to handle, and that it was no longer safe for us to remain in the home.

Chapter Five

Real Consequences

It seems as though with every move made in the course of my life, I would be less and less fazed by it. With fear creeping its way into my day to day life, being around violence was another thing that would start to seem normal. While being in the center of so many issues in my parents' lives, my childhood development was being hindered too much. As it would seem, I was becoming a consequence of my parents' actions. As much as I hated everything that was happening around me, I was starting to expect it while my mind was slowly shutting down.

It took my mother too long to finally come to terms with how bad our home life was to make the call to Children's Aid Society to have us removed. As good of a decision as it was that at least she finally made the call, it was too late. We were once again picked up from our home, to be placed back in the system, where we probably should never have even left. After reading my files, there was such a huge difference in our demeanor from the last time we were in care. When speaking with the worker who had picked us up, the foul language used to describe the type of things we had witnessed seemed to have surprised and appalled them.

We went into detail about the indiscretions of our mother and her "friend" using words that a six, seven, and nine-year-old should not have even known. We had also talked about the punishments we would get, and how our bums would get really red. It was made clear that our return was something that was definitely needed. The only problem was that the three of us had been so tainted by what we went through, and trying to come back from that to have a normal rest of childhood, would be difficult. The process that we would have to go through to seek help on the problems we were then faced with was going to be a long one.

For the first two nights, the three of us were placed in a temporary placement home. From what I remember, for the most part, it was nice. Relaxing and peaceful, especially since it was out of the city. I remember arguing a lot with my brother, so much that he and I barely spoke those two days. As nice as that placement was, I was happy to leave since we were told that we would be returning to our previous foster home from 1992-1993.

As strange as it might seem, I don't remember our worker picking us up to bring us to our new foster home. For some reason, I can remember the three of us taking a bus to North Bay, where we were then picked up. Whether it happened or not, I remember so much about the temporary home and what it looked like, even their dog that would bark, and the mud around their house. So much of that place I remember, and in that memory, I can just remember the three of us having to take a bus by ourselves. It seems weird that we would, and yet that's the memory I have.

All three of us remembered living at the original foster home even though we were all so young. When we were told that we would be returning, we were all filled with such joy. My brother was probably most excited since they had two sons around his age, and then finally he wouldn't be bothered by my sister and I. The foster family also seemed overjoyed to see us and have us return to their home. They had no other foster children, so it seemed to be a great fit.

Not only were the three of us getting a chance to start over in a new and safer home, since it was the beginning of September 1996, that meant the start of a new school year. We weren't able to return to our previous school since it was on the opposite end of the city, and so we were all transferred to a different one. We didn't really mind because at that point everything seemed like an exciting and new adventure.

While starting back out in foster care, we were all just happy to be away from all the fighting. We did miss our parents, but we also knew we couldn't stay in the middle of it all. We had various discussions with people regarding the importance of being removed, and for the most part, understood. At least, we tried to understand the best we could for being our ages. Our worker, other caseworkers, and even the foster parents would ask us about everything that was happening. They wanted to hear in our words the things being done around us and to us.

The comments that seemed constant in my files stated that the three of us presented good manners. Of all of the terrible things that we fell prey to, at least we came out of it with good manners. Of course, credit was given to our mother for teaching us said manners. Truth be told the only reason we had good manners was because if we wouldn't use them, we would get yelled at or even hit, and so we learned quite fast! Fearing how we would be treated if we wouldn't present ourselves in a respected tone and demeanor was something that followed us for years to come. As simple as saying please and thank you is, the way our parents taught us to learn them wasn't to be pleasant while showing our appreciation. We learned to say those things because we were in fear of being in trouble, and hurt.

One of the last fights before being removed from our home was terrifying to us. As much as I can remember about it, it was something we all shared with our worker. While our parents were screaming at each other, throwing punches, one of our tables got flipped over. Not our eating table or anything, I believe it was just a smaller table used to hold things. With things getting so hectic and scary, the three of us being terrified went to hide under our kitchen table. We were left crying, holding each other, and were just hoping things would settle and stop. The reasons why our parents would fight became something that just didn't matter. All the excuses were bullshit, and they were always the same. At the end of the day, we just knew they fought, and we knew that in some way they were both to be blamed.

We spoke often with our worker about the fighting. It seemed as though every so often we would go to the Children's Aid Society's office to meet and discuss. Sometimes they would speak to the three of us together, while other times separately. Every time we would go to the office, I can remember the little playroom we would be placed in. It was a very small room, that had books and toys in it. On the back wall, there was a two-way mirror where someone would be to watch us while in the room. It always creeped me out, because I hated the feeling of being watched. Nonetheless, it was nice to be able to play with the toys.

Once we were back living at the foster home, in the beginning, it seemed as though we would often meet our worker at the office. While trying to figure out exactly what was going on in our home life was something that needed a lot of blanks to be filled in. Our parents would speak with various workers, and in their notes, they indicated it felt as though our parents weren't always being honest, since leaving out details and having their stories change often. After speaking with us, and hearing what we had to say in full detail, the same details over and over, it seemed as though that wasn't enough.

One of the most difficult times having to discuss with our caseworkers was a time that I could never forget. This was a day that is permanently burned into my memory, and no matter how many times replaying I do, it still haunts me because I can't believe I had to deal with it along with my siblings. You hear stories about some things young children especially have to deal with from either their parents or even relatives, and it just makes you completely ill thinking that some people can be so disturbed. You almost like to believe it's fabricated because of how horrendous it is, and the last thing you want to know is that a child had to go through it. It's bad enough that teenagers and even adults have to deal with such things as rape, molestation, but a child?!

One of the worst days of my life was that day in the office. Not necessarily for my sake, but my siblings, sister especially. Individually and altogether, we were asked several questions and were even asked to draw pictures with labels on them. Not sure if someone had made a call to the Children's Aid Society about possibly something happening, but an inquiry was being held in regards to sexual child abuse allegations.

Since having requested my files back in 2009, I have known about these questions and diagrams about the sexual abuse allegations and was really hoping to see them in what I received. Apparently, those were the only things that did not appear. I have gone over and over all the files which are quite a lot of documents, and there isn't even a mention of it. You would think that something so traumatic even just discussing such matters with a child, would be something worth mentioning. Not even counseling or speaking with a professional had been done about it, and definitely no mention about that in my files. When requesting my files, I had even said I wanted those specific, and yet still nothing.

After receiving my files, I called back to ask why I wasn't given them, and apparently, I'm not allowed to have them because of the nature of them, especially since it was to do with our parents. With having to do primarily with my birth parents, I was told I couldn't get them for privacy concerns. My sister having to deal with quite a lot of issues from what had happened requested some of her files, and those reports were basically all she got. It made no sense as to why I wasn't allowed after waiting nine years, and yet she could, being told different things. Thankfully, that day is one of those memories that is permanently etched in my mind, and after speaking with my sister regarding what she received, I can easily say that my memory has not failed me.

I remember the diagrams we were shown, and on them were people. We had been asked if anyone had ever touched us and then had to show where. We also were asked if we knew about areas where no one was allowed to touch us, and to then show where those places were. We were asked if we knew about *private parts*, what specifically that meant, and if we had seen them on our parents or other adults. We were asked if anyone had touched us in our *private parts*. We were asked if there were any games involving our private parts. We were asked if we knew about any of our other siblings being touched in those areas, or if they were shown private areas on someone else.

We had been asked so many questions over and over. After a short period of time, the questions all seemed to sound alike. Although I wasn't fully aware of everything that was currently happening, I knew enough that something most likely did. From what I knew at that time, I wasn't actually aware of something that had happened to myself. I had no memory of being molested, and I was thankful. I did begin to fear for my other siblings though. Although I had memories of seeing more than I should have of my parents in the bedroom or bathroom because they never wanted to close a door, to my knowledge nothing had been done to me. Of course, I would have loved to have seen my files about those situations and meetings, but that's just me complaining again about not getting them.

I remember how much time my father and sister spent together while no one else was allowed to join because it was special daddy/daughter time, and that began to worry me. I knew how much my brother didn't get along with my father, and how close he was to my mother, and that also began to worry me. I was only six years old, and yet it was then I was able to fully understand the meaning of sexual abuse, and it made me fearful. Only six years old, and I was being interrogated by a bunch of people about possible things our parents were involved with.

After we were getting ready to leave the CAS office, my sister and I were sitting in the back seat of someone's car. As panicked as I felt because I didn't remember being badly touched by anyone, it left me questioning so much. After looking at my silent sister who was sitting next to me, I could see just how stunned she looked. Regardless of what was happening, the two of us were always filled with so much energy and were rarely quiet for a long period of time. I just had to look at her once to realize what had happened. Her eyes were beginning to water, lips quivering, while blankly staring straight ahead. She was slightly shaking, and I lightly touched her on her shoulder asking what was wrong.

My sister and I had always been inseparable, and seeing her so shook up freaked me out. Usually in troubling situations, the other would be the only one who could be a calming solution. We were always there for each other, and I just had to make sure she was okay. I kept asking if she was okay, what was wrong, what I can do. After a few minutes of her being silent listening to my questions, I almost began to start crying. I knew something was wrong, and yet she wasn't saying anything. Before I had a chance to cry, she just burst out in tears.

She didn't have to say anything to me. She didn't say a single word in that moment of nonstop crying, and yet I knew enough. With everything that was discussed with us from the workers, my questions were at that moment answered. I felt so much pain for my sister that I hugged her and told her that she would be okay. It was at that exact moment that I made a promise to always be there for her. No matter what was to happen in our lives, I would do everything I could to be her voice, her shoulder to cry on, and her smile. Seeing her in so much pain gave me a sort of strength that was only developed to help her.

In that car ride, we never spoke about what had happened, and what she told our workers, and I knew not to push her into talking when she wasn't ready. Only a few times shortly later had we discussed it. Her comments on the matter had been fragmented, as her mind had been so traumatized, and so her speech was in pieces. She had mentioned something about a camera, someone watching, being touched in her private parts, and having to touch others. She also briefly mentioned something about seeing our brother on top of our mother. Hearing everything scared me. Our brother had never talked about it, and after seeing how my sister was, I never wanted to discuss it.

Over a short period of time, we chose not to talk to each other about it, as we just wanted to move forwards. Little by little, my sister appeared to try and forget everything. It seemed like it was working because she seemed to be getting back to her normal self. Having to deal with situations like that is unimaginable because you never know what kind of effect it will have on someone. While doing everything she can to forget, pushing it out of her mind, she created a block. This block did allow her to somewhat forget about it, however, it created something in her mind unknowingly making her more aggressive in nature. As the years went on, this aggression grew inside her, and completely took over in place of being able to deal with the abuse.

I knew not to speak with my sister about what had happened, and because of that, I had it in my mind that our father was officially the enemy. I knew our parents were deeply troubled and had created such a chaotic home environment for us, but knowing what he did to my big sister was just too much. From that car ride onwards, I promised myself to never forget what he did and what he was capable of. I didn't have enough information about what happened with our brother, and not wanting to ask, I wasn't as upset with our mother. I just didn't know enough, and in time I began to put it out of my mind.

It seemed with everything the three of us had shared with our caseworkers, and although my sister was not wanting to talk about it, nothing had been done. According to the police reports and my sister's files, no charges were ever placed against our parents, and nothing further investigated because a seven-year-old didn't want to testify. Seems like something as severe as what had been discussed, especially since my sister's story had never changed or had been altered, should have been processed. So, just because a seven-year is too fearful about testifying you're going to choose not to proceed with charges or further investigation? Seems rather lazy in my opinion.

While dealing with the aftermath of being returned to foster care, and even the crazy home life prior, education seemed non-existent. I already couldn't read or write, and at this point, even my speech had become problematic. With having to be careful about speaking at home when our parents were fighting, and not being allowed to speak out of turn, I developed a slight speech impediment. I believe it was more due to the fact of being anxious about everything going on, and unsure if I was even allowed to speak. I just had a difficult time trying to find my words. Even when I was two and three, it took me a long time to learn how to speak, as being taught anything wasn't something being done in our home.

Once starting over at our foster home, I attended speech therapy at school. The strange thing is that when switching schools because of where we were now living, I was transferred to a French emersion school. Our father's family is of French-Canadian descent; however, we were never actually taught any French. So, being in a school where I could barely understand a word that was being said, didn't help with my current speech issues. I can still remember being in that classroom on the main floor of the building, right by the doors to the playground. Every day when I would go into the classroom, and our lessons would begin, we would be asked to answer questions in French, and it seemed like an impossible task. At this point I needed to worry about learning my first language, English, so having yet another language to worry about just felt way too overwhelming.

The only enjoyment I seemed to have in that time period of my education, were the bus rides to and from school. There was this older girl who I sat next to, or near most days. Being so young and impressionable, I believed everything she told me. It was probably due to the fact that I found her to be pretty, and just listening to her gave me googly eyes. I loved everything about the *Power Rangers* when I was six years old. The idea of a group of kids having powers to fight the evils of the world spoke to me on a personal level, and it made me wish I could be one. I would talk about them constantly, and so the pretty bus girl knew this. I am unsure if she was teasing me, or just trying to connect with me, but she told me she was one. I actually believed her.

That's the thing about being young and so hopeful minded. You hear something said by someone, and your first instinct is to believe them. You typically listen, because, for the most part, you are learning and hearing things for the first time. You believe everything because you strongly think that those saying things are meant to be telling the truth as they are your teachers, even if they aren't actual teachers. I was so excited when she told me, and for a little while, it gave us something to bond over. She even said that if I was ever in trouble, she would be there to save the day. Knowing now that it was a lie, at that time, it was a lie I needed to hear. Times were becoming too much to deal with, and the people around me seemed to be disappointing me in every turn. Even though she wasn't actually a Power Ranger, our bus ride conversations gave me a sense of power to get through the day. Of course, it was a power that was short-lived.

My brother didn't like the idea of this older girl telling me lies, and so he felt the need to set things straight. He spoke with our foster parents about it, and they all told me that it wasn't true. They said that I needed to stay away from her because it was all nonsense and to not believe everything I hear. They may not have known it, but the conversation I had with them made me feel so stupid. They kept pointing out how dumb it was to believe such things, and so it made me feel as though I was dumb. For the first time in such a long time, I actually felt happy, excited, and safe. Looking back I don't understand the need they had to take that away from me. Yes, it was silly, but someone saw how sad I was and wanted to do something. She might not have been a Power Ranger, but she was a hero to me, and always will be as she gave me something no one else had.

It was a long time after learning the truth that my friend lied to help me, that I tried to make another one. Being so excited at first and then having that happiness torn down, made me question what will happen the next time I make a friend. I just didn't want to have to feel bad again. I did have my siblings, even though my brother wasn't helping to make me want to hang out with him. I purposely chose not to, to maybe teach him a lesson. My sister and I were the only friends we needed. I knew our brother wouldn't try to not allow us to hang out with each other since he couldn't. We were family, so there wasn't anything anyone could do to separate us.

When you're a small child, everything seems much bigger than how they actually are; People seem like they're ten feet tall. Trees touch the sky. Sand piles appear to be dunes, and streams look like rapids. From what I can remember about our foster home, we weren't exactly allowed to go over to friend's houses. We were to remain at our place and find things to do around the house. We had to spend most of our time outside because we weren't allowed inside during the day. Thankfully, there was a lot to explore.

Across the street, there was a small forest that came between the road and a river. Behind our foster parent's house, there was another small forest that came before what I remember to be sandhills. There was much to explore, and having to stay outside most of our days made that quite easy. Of course, being young, and at times bored, we would get into mischief. We at times would venture into our neighbors' yard, and throw things in their pool. We would pull things off the clothesline. And at times would sneak inside the house when we didn't want to be outside. As much as we loved being outside because it was all so different from what we were used to, we just felt as though there was still so much we were missing.

There was so much our parents never taught us. The three of us each had difficulties in different areas of schooling. I had slight speech troubles. We never learned about personal boundaries. The small fundamentals about life were something that we never knew. I to this day am still surprised we were potty trained. For all I know, we learned on our own. From what I can recall, when we had to go, we just went because our parents didn't want to be bothered by it. I can remember when trying to ask for help, our mother would yell at us saying how we are old enough to know how to go. We didn't need help and to figure it out on our own.

Unsure if it was brought on by the frustrations in our home life, or the lack of attention from our parents, but my brother became a bed wetter. It wasn't a constant thing, but it was something that needed to be brought to the adults' attention that was a cry for help. Clearly, something was going on, and he needed help. Nothing had been done to try to fix it, however, as he was just labeled a bed wetter. When moving to our foster home, they were made aware of his situation but still nothing, and he continued to wet the bed. If that was an indication that we weren't being taught anything at home, then plugging the toilet because I didn't know how much toilet paper to use should have been.

A memory that will forever be imprinted on me is the first time I plugged a toilet. I was six years old, and once trying to settle into our foster home, I was trying to do things on my own. It felt as though we basically were on our own, and so I was trying to do everything by myself. I tried to go to the bathroom, and not knowing the "proper" amount of toilet paper to clean myself, it plugged. At this time we were already causing mischief from having to stay outside so much and getting bored, and so when small things happened, it was becoming a lot to deal with. Plugging the toilet seems like it wouldn't be a big deal, but it was. It was just another disruption to our foster parents, and so I was in trouble. I was six years old and was supposed to know already that I shouldn't use it so much. I didn't though. I at that time wasn't aware that you couldn't just use as much as you wanted because it wouldn't go down. I needed to feel clean, and so I just kept using and using.

I remember getting yelled at and once again feeling like a disappointment because I couldn't even go to the bathroom on my own. I tried to explain that I didn't know how much I was supposed to use and was told to stop lying. That day, I not only became someone who needed supervision when it came to toilet paper, but also a liar. For the rest of our time being there, I had to be given a certain amount of toilet paper anytime I needed it. I apparently wasn't allowed free range on toilet paper because I was just going to plug it again. Slowly from that point onwards, I began to fear having to go to the bathroom.

On one of my mischief days with my sister, we were in the basement looking around as it was basically just filled with junk. It was kind of exciting for us because there was so much stuff. The laundry room was also down there, and on one of the laundry piles, there was a pair of dirty woman's underwear. There was a streak on it, and while laughing, I said to my sister that it's probably because she's only allowed a few squares of toilet paper. It may have been a cruel joke, but to us it was super funny. Well, it would seem as though we weren't being as careful as we had thought, and we weren't as quiet as we had wanted to be. Our foster mother heard my comment, and us laughing and was not impressed. I tried to spin it knowing that I was about to get into a lot of trouble, but she knew I wasn't being truthful. Just another example to prove I was a liar.

In 1996 when we were placed back into our foster home, we were only there for a few months. In those few months, it seemed like all we did was get ourselves into trouble. Having so many things neglected in our development from being with our biological parents, it didn't seem to matter. The thing the three of us needed the most was patience. There were so many things we didn't know, that we needed help with, things to be taught. We needed those around us to patiently teach us, show us, in a manner that wasn't fearful. We were just so used to being yelled at, being told we already know, that things weren't sinking in. Our workers at that time in person, and even in their notes, only mention our struggles and the characteristics of our bad behaviors. They don't and didn't mention anything about how they were going to help correct it.

If our foster parents indicate we lie, we from then on become a liar. We are a liar because we aren't believed, not because in that instinct we weren't telling the truth. We are misbehaving when we plug toilets because we are "reckless" and are "acting out," not because we weren't actually taught how much paper to use. We run around and sneak into people's yards because we "don't know how to act responsibly," not because we were bored from feeling neglected and from being forced to stay outside. When one thing is said from our foster parents, and then repeated to our worker, it's a done deal. There is no coming back from it, as wherever we end up, it will follow us.

Each household has its own rules and guidelines. That isn't new information, even to my younger self. I knew even back then my foster home was going to be different than my home life. The only thing at the time I didn't know were the rules. I didn't at the time know we would have to occupy our time by ourselves trying to find things to do outside. During the nighttime, we were meant to be sleeping and had to stay in our rooms. If waking up during the middle of the night we had to use the bathroom, we would be told to get back into our room. We had to go back to bed because we already went before going to sleep and shouldn't need to again. That became another thing that we were labeled with. Sneaking out of our rooms in the middle of the night, even though we had to pee.

We got yelled at quite a few times for having to use the bathroom in the middle of the night, that it made my sister fearful when she would wake up having to go. One time she woke up and instead of going to the bathroom worrying that she would get into trouble again, she went pee in a toy antique stroller. To us, we didn't realize that it was an antique, or even what that meant. We just saw it was a stroller for her dolls in our shared bedroom. Yes, the three of us all shared a bedroom. When she woke up, she really had to pee, and so she went in the stroller. She went back to bed, and the next morning completely forgot about it. We continued on with our day until the three of us were all summoned up to our room.

We were all asked to line up while both of our foster parents started yelling at us. Clearly, they were all very upset as they found urine in the stroller and didn't understand why any of us would do such a terrible thing. Hearing them yell at each of us just made me think as though we were back living with our parents while having to listen to them yell. Instead of actually talking to us and asking us why, or even who had done it, they chose not to. My brother and I knew we hadn't done it and right away said we didn't. Our sister was quiet, standing beside us beginning to cry because at that moment knew she was in trouble. She realized at that moment that she had forgotten to clean the stroller. I remember looking over at her, and how scared she was.

This became the last straw for our foster parents. In the moment of grabbing my sister by the arm to bring her in front of the stroller to show her what she had done, they made it clear to each of us that this kind of behavior will no longer be acceptable. They told us that they would be contacting our worker to have our sister removed from the home and that maybe having some separation from each other will do us some good.

Things started to feel like the beginning of the end. It was now only my brother and I left at our foster home. Already he and I weren't close and rarely spent time together. He was always off with the foster parents' two sons, and they would never allow me to tag along. Losing my sister, my only friend, made me feel so alone. I tried to go on the same walks in the woods, along the river, but they always felt empty. I would usually have to stop, find somewhere to sit and cry. I never felt as though I was allowed to cry because I was told boys need to be strong, and crying was for girls. Thankfully, I was now alone most of the time, and so I could cry without any comments from anyone.

About a month or so after my sister left, my brother and I were told we would be able to move back in with our parents. My first response was filled with excitement because I thought that meant my sister would also be moving back. We were told that she is having much trouble dealing with her anger and misbehaviors to go back home, so at this time would have to remain in a foster home. And just like that, my face went from smiling to frowning. I was excited to be leaving my foster home, but all I could think about was if our parents were going to be okay for us to be living back home. There were so many issues, and it almost seemed too soon once again for us to return.

We were assured that both of our parents had been given help to deal with their issues, and so we would be safe to return. We were told something by an adult, and so we assumed it was the truth. We were a little skeptical but did have hope since we didn't want to be in a foster home again.

We moved back into the house we were previously living in. A part of us had hoped our parents would have moved, but they didn't. Everything seemed the exact same. Once again, my brother and I were sharing a room, and once again our bickering continued to grow. He didn't want to spend time with me, nor I with him. A few times he had mentioned that he wished our previous foster parents' sons were his brothers because he didn't want me as a brother. I would tell him that I wish he had stayed in a foster home instead of our sister. Our distaste for one another only grew as our parents' hatred for each other grew.

It seemed almost instantly that things resorted back to how it was only a few months earlier. We were told things would be different, that they would be better, but they weren't. Our parents were fighting about the same things they did before, and nothing had seemed to be different. The only thing that was actually different this time around, was that this was when I started to lose my belief in things.

One thing I have always heard parents discussing, was when to tell their child that Santa isn't real. The same with the Tooth Fairy, Easter Bunny, etc. It was Christmas 1996 that I lost that belief. It's weird, but all the previous Christmas' that I've had prior barely stand out. I can remember glimpses of them, but nothing full. Christmas 1996 was the first year I can remember everything about it. The Halloween that we had just a couple months earlier, was also one of the only two I can remember. For the longest time, I was beginning to believe that while in my home life, celebrating holidays wasn't something our parents wanted to do. I mean, what six years old only has memories of two Halloweens and one Christmas?

By the time Christmas came around, it had only been about a month and a half that my brother and I were back living with our parents. On Christmas Eve, I can remember our mother telling us to stay in our room and go to sleep because if we don't Santa won't be leaving any presents for us. I was so excited not only for the presents, but we were told that our sister would be allowed to come visit us on Christmas Day. So, it was a very exciting and important sleep. Of course, my mind was busy racing that I couldn't sleep. I stayed up laying in my bed for so long, that I had to pee. I quietly snuck out of my bed to use the washroom. Slowly I opened the bedroom door and could hear that my parents were both in their bedroom, and so I quickly made a dash for the bathroom.

I left the light off as there was a nightlight in the bathroom, and so I could see enough. I didn't fully shut the door, but enough so that you couldn't see inside. When I was finished, I didn't flush because I didn't want to make any noise. I was about to wash my hands when I could hear my mother asking if my father had grabbed everything, and he said that there were still a few in the bedroom. I peeped through the crack of the door and saw him putting the presents under the tree. I swung the door opened and asked what he was doing. I said that I thought Santa was supposed to be bringing our presents. He then stopped what he was doing and looked at my mother. She started walking towards me while saying "What the fuck are you doing out of bed? You were supposed to be sleeping, and should not still be up."

I can remember them saying to me, that since I already saw them bringing out the presents, that the surprise is already ruined. Santa is not real, and its actually mommy and daddy who get the presents. And just like that everything I believed in was shattered. Going to bed seemed easy after that because I was less excited to wake up. Now all I could be excited about was to see my sister and share with her what I had learned. My brother thought it was the perfect time to also tell me that all of the other holidays were also make-believe. What a shitty Christmas this was turning out to be.

What we didn't know at the time, and something I didn't even know until I received my files, was that a couple of weeks after returning to live with our parents, CAS received a letter from someone stating that our father knocked out our mother in one of their fights. The funny thing is, I can remember seeing her bruised, but no one had explained to me as to why. It was reported so that they wouldn't have CAS take us away again, that she was attacked behind a Tim Hortons. The stories that were shared with the caseworkers changed a few times between the two of them, but because there was no actual proof of what happened, we remained living with them.

It was two days before Christmas that after seeing her doctor, that my mother was diagnosed to have an antisocial personality with no conscience, remorse, or guilt. Also, they were able to determine from tests that she had a low IQ. To be honest, I could have told you that. This information was also not shared with my siblings and I, even though it does sound like something we should have had some knowledge about.

From mid-November 1996 until late January 1997, no matter how many times we were told that things would be better, the short time we lived back at home proved otherwise. Our parents' fighting didn't seem to even take a pause, and tensions in our house just seemed to keep growing. The hate that was developing between the two rubbed off on my brother and I. My father began to show that he didn't even care for the two of us.

The teasing that my father showed towards me for certain shows or for the fact that purple was my favorite color, only escalated. I loved playing with long hair as at that time I wanted to become a hairdresser when I grew up. I then started wanting to play with barbies, but my father wasn't going to have any of it. His distaste for such became much more in the open and would insinuate I was a girl and not a boy. He kept insisting to me that I would become queer, and that he should have called me Cassie instead. So much of what he would say made no sense to me. I still didn't understand or really even know what queer meant. I knew I wasn't a girl. At that time, I didn't have attractions to the same sex. I just loved playing with long hair, and the "girlier" shows tended to be more colorful which made me feel happier.

My mother in those couple of months was too busy getting black eyes, sleeping with their friend down the street, to even notice or say something to my father. Later I would be told that her disconnect from us was due to having yet another miscarriage from the friend she was sleeping with. I was feeling so lost, confused, and very much alone. Fighting with my brother seemed like the only way I could get out my frustrations. Our bickering wasn't entirely focused on the other but was a result of not being able to do anything from our parents.

One day, fighting with my brother got so bad that he grabbed a fireplace poker, and swung it at my head. Thankfully he missed, but my father saw it. The only time in my life where my father actually seemed genuinely concerned for my well-being, although did not react well. He grabbed my brother by the throat and screamed at him. In all of my parents fighting, the threat of calling Children's Aid to have us taken away was something my father used often with my mother. It was this however that not only made her threaten my father with but actually did.

The thing that wasn't made aware to any of us that January 1997, was that there is only so much that can happen before drastic changes are made from other people. Where people outside the home have to take a stand, and demand changes to be made. To make those changes themselves. My parents had spent years thinking they knew best, and that one way or another they would be able to work things out. As time had proven otherwise, there was nothing left for them to try with. They had been given more than enough chances to get better, to give a safe home to three children. It was then that the three of us would never again be returning *home* for a chance to be a family.

Chapter Six

Kill the Chipmunk

With history repeating itself more and more, being taken from our home to be driven to a foster home was becoming the norm. When my brother and I were being driven away, we didn't even question it. We once again were fully aware that things were quite hectic at home, and so it came as a relief to be leaving. The thing that seemed to matter the most was the question of where we would be going to this time.

To no surprise, for the third time now we were heading to our original foster home. I was not pleased, while my brother seemed excited. I always felt a disconnection from that home because anytime one small thing would happen, they would hold it against you. My brother felt so much joy because it was as if he was one of their own. He was the perfect age as he was in the same age group as their children. The two of us already weren't getting along at all, fighting constantly, and now that he has his better "brothers" where will I fit in?

After a couple of months being away from the foster home, didn't seem to matter what-so-ever, and it appeared as though we just picked up right where we left off. While hoping for a reset button to start fresh, I was immediately shown otherwise. On my first day back, I was reintroduced to my four-square toilet paper rule. I was also spoken with about no fighting with my brother or their two sons. I was not allowed to venture into other people's yards, and not to go wandering by the stream in the woods. The way I felt was as if I wasn't allowed to do anything, because all I was told were things I couldn't do. Nothing was said about things I could do, as their expectations were low on how I was going to behave. It didn't give me much of a great start, as it just made me feel as though I could only disappoint. Just like that, my brother went on his own leaving me completely alone. Yay for day one of the rest of my life.

I can remember feeling so many different emotions, and it seemed to all come on at once. This was the first time I have felt truly alone, and I hated it. At the moment, all I could think about was the fact that I needed to use the washroom, but because of the stupid rule, I was too afraid to go. I held out as long as I could until I just couldn't hold it in any longer.

While realizing that my sister needed to be on her own to work out her issues, it became a question whether I too would benefit from my own foster home. The fighting between my brother and I hadn't stopped, and so after about five days, I too would be moved. The short time while living at my original foster home seemed much longer than it was. While it seemed like all I did was upset everyone around me, I began to feel quite depressed from feeling so left out. The toilet paper rule was making me feel very unclean and was told that I couldn't be trusted with more, and so I was never given more.

I had done what was told of me when I had a concern, talk about it. I did that, and yet nothing was being done. I didn't like having to walk around all day, as I wasn't allowed to bathe every day. I was left feeling dirty because I wasn't allowed to clean myself properly. With that, I felt as though maybe they needed to be taught a lesson of some kind. To my six-year-old mind, I figured that since I wasn't being heard, that I needed to find a way to show them. For less than a week of living there, I began to smear one of the walls in my bedroom with what couldn't be cleaned from their rule. Yes, it was completely disgusting, and it's embarrassing for me even to this day. I just didn't know what else to do to make them realize what I had been trying to tell them.

It wasn't until about a week after being moved that the foster parents finally realized what I had done. While living at my new foster home just down the street, they received a phone call about the smearing, and I had to return to clean it up. I tried to explain to my caseworker at the time as to why I had done it, but I wasn't being heard. The foster parents basically called me a liar, and so then I became a smearing child to "get attention." Another label. I just couldn't believe that it took them so long to realize what I had done. Then again, while there I never felt as though they paid close attention to me, so I guess it wasn't that surprising.

Moving away from my brother wasn't that big of a deal to me. I was more upset about the fact that I couldn't live with my sister, and that it had been so long since I had even seen her. I kept asking my worker when I would be able to see her, and all I would ever be told, was that she was working on things so "now wasn't a good time." I never found it to be a stretch that a child who is separated from their siblings would want to be reunited. Every time I would ask, and I would be told no, it broke a piece of my heart.

Since the few times being sent to a foster home, it had been the same one, moving to a new one actually kind of excited me. I thought it could be really good to have a fresh start regardless if it was just down the road from where I already was. What I didn't realize at the time, was that there had to have been some sort of dimensional portal because I wasn't just moving down the road, rather I was moving to the center of hell.

In all of my years in foster care, and all of the families I lived with, the next several months were not only going to be the most painful for me, but the time that really fucked me up. Already my development had been hindered because of my home environment, and there were so many things that were confusing to me. There were so many people telling me all sorts of things, and it had become so difficult to determine the proper way to act, speak, dress, just live every day. All of the conflicting messages from all the people currently in my life were only going to be added with the next batch of craziness.

After being dropped off by my worker with my new foster parents who appeared like the great grandparents of someone, it started. My worker barely had time to leave, and I was told they had already spoken with my previous foster parents who filled them in on me. I was told that I would NOT be plugging their toilet and so the toilet paper rule was back in session. I was also told that the living room was for them to have their TV time at the end of the day, and not for me to watch television. I was not allowed to venture into any of their neighbors' yards, and when in their yard I had to not go near their truck. My room was in the basement, and the only other room down there was basically their junk and storage space. I was told nothing in there is mine, and so no stealing, and no getting any ideas. They from time to time foster other children on weekends, and so there would be a second child sharing the bedroom with me. There was zero tolerance for fighting, and I was told to get along with whomever should stay down there with me. They notified me that they visit with their son and daughter-in-law often, and when they should visit the house, I was to be elsewhere to give them privacy. When we would go to their place, I may go into their basement and watch TV or play outside.

It took less than a few hours for myself to realize these people were set out to ruin my life. I just knew that however long I was going to have to live with them, that I was going to be miserable. People my whole life have told me to think positively and to smile because things may not be as they seem and could be an exceptional experience for me. There was no amount of positivity that could make these people pleasant, and make my stay go well. Believe me, I tried.

When you walk into the home, if you go straight, there is a staircase that leads downstairs which has two rooms. My large bedroom which had two beds in it. The other room was a quite large storage and junk room. So much junk down there, it seemed impossible to walk around. Instead of walking downstairs, if you turned left, there were a few stairs that lead to the main floor. Looking straight ahead, to the left is the kitchen and dining area. At the back of the house was the living room, which did not look like many people would be able to sit and enjoy each other's company. It was almost as if they intended to never have anyone else join the two of them in there. To the right side of the small house, there is one bathroom, and then their bedroom. Pretty standard, and small of a house. I almost preferred my biological parents' shitty house that I lived in before my reentry into foster care.

After many conversations with my worker since I had found myself getting into some trouble at school, being told to try and stay positive was something I figured I would really need to work on. I mean, this was the first official time I would be living solo, and if I wanted to see my sister, or maybe even move back home, I needed to show them I could be good. What I didn't realize at this time, was that according to my files, my worker found me to be emotionally disconnected. It stated that I don't smile and seem flat. Apparently, I tried to be the center of attention at any chance I would get and was very needy.

With being teased from girls at school, I was told from not only my caseworkers but teachers, that it's probably because they liked me. When they would tease me, I would then think, "Oh they like me, fine I'll chase them pretending to kiss them." I never did actually kiss them because I knew I was being lied to about them liking me. They were teasing me because they were bullies. I of course got into a lot of trouble, and with that was labeled *the six-year-old who was making unwanted advances at girls*. That was just another thing that stuck with me in my files.

The past year at this point in my life had been such a sandstorm because so much had happened, and I didn't know what to do or how to react. In my personal life, it didn't seem like anyone was listening to anything I had to say, and at school, it was no different. It didn't even seem like anyone knew what was going on at home, and I found them to not be bothered to even care. I had so many people telling me to smile, but there was literally no reason to smile. I felt like no one was listening to me, and so of course I acted out. I was being teased for being "fem" at school, mostly by girl peers, but no one would say anything or do anything to adjust the problem for me. I would react by swearing at the teacher and had even thrown chairs or objects. Had that not worked, I would resort to biting. It was something that just became a reaction while knowing how strong my teeth were.

It felt as though every person in my life had a better understanding as to the person I was, rather than me. Everyone wanted me to be a different person, in their eyes, and when you're six years old, all you want to do is be a kid, which I could not. It toyed with my mind, and the only thing I knew or understood was anger since it was the one thing that had been constant in my current life. Considering how the first few hours went at my new foster home, I knew the anger that was residing inside wasn't going to get me anywhere, despite how easily they were making me feel it.

With moving just down the street, thankfully I didn't have to move schools once again. I was stuck spending most of my time alone, and outside. It kind of sucked though, because when I would be outside, I would go across the street to play in the woods. The woods which I had made myself familiar with while living in my previous home. While I would be out there by myself, at times I could hear my brother and his foster parents' sons. I had fairly good hearing, but it was also because I wasn't that far from him. Listening to them talk, laugh, seeming to be having a great time made me sad. At times, there was this one clearing in the woods with a wood stump, and I would just sit there trying to listen to them while crying because I had to be alone.

I had been told that my sister was struggling a lot with her anger and other problems, while I seemed to be suffering from similar issues. My brother was the only one of us who seemed better than ever. He was in the same home and had in some way his own little family going on. As much as I didn't care to not be with him, it bothered me that I couldn't have that. I wanted to no longer be alone while being left crying instead of laughing and being happy with siblings. I just missed having someone I could run around with. When you have to play outside as much as I had to, it wasn't so much fun when it was just yourself.

During the days or late afternoons after school, I usually had to find something to do outside. This was becoming a usual boring daily habit, and yet never got easier. When it was time to come inside for dinner, there was a routine I had to follow. First, I had to change into my pajamas, and then go to the washroom to thoroughly wash my hands. Once I was finished, I had to sit down at the table. My first week living at this home opened my eyes to so many eating rituals I had not been made aware of. At times, which usually depended on my foster mother's mood, I had to show either her or her husband my hands so they could inspect them. I wouldn't be allowed to sit at the table if they were dirty. My hands were not allowed on the table, and not only that but neither could my elbows. Not so bad considering even I had been told elbows on the table was considered to be rude.

Once sitting at the table, my hands were to be placed on my lap. I learned this after getting my hands swatted to be removed. I was told that while waiting, and while I eat, my elbows had to remain below the table. Anytime my elbows would be above the table, my foster mother would hit my arm so I would know to remove them. She wouldn't hit like my parents would, but to a six-year-old, it definitely didn't feel nice.

While everyone sits at the table waiting to be served food, it was a quiet time. Without even being said anything, I would generally do everything I could to not look at my foster father. A part of me was too scared, not knowing if he would like it, or if I was even allowed. He was the first to be served, and then my foster mother would be served next. I would be served last. No matter who would be at the table, even when the company would be over, I was always served last. That meant I got what was left, and not that it really mattered, but I always got the "smaller" piece of whatever was being served.

Whenever living in someone else's home, there is a period where you have to get used to the new house rules and ways of life. There should be a grace period especially for a child, as they have yet to not only learn the rules but at times make mistakes. It is the thought that they are not used to living such ways, and so there should be some time where you allow them the chance to mess up, but then quickly learn. I had figured I would be given such a grace period, but my new foster parents acted as if I should have already known these insane rules. The worst rules they had were to do with being at the table for dinner.

While we were eating, we were not allowed to eat with both hands, unless we needed to cut something, and then a second hand was allowed to be used for the knife. Once again, I learned this by getting my hand smacked and told that it's rude to use two hands to eat. We didn't need both hands unless the knife was needed to cut something. I'm right-handed, and so most of the time my left hand had to be placed on my lap. It was actually a custom that seemed difficult to me. Eating with only one hand made me feel strange. I often found myself wanting to use my second hand, at least having it up by my plate. Placing it on my lap while I ate just felt weird. A few times I even pretended to need my knife just so I could have both hands up. I soon got told I didn't need my knife and to put it down. I remember so badly thinking to myself without saying anything, why put a knife at my place setting if you know I don't need it?

Another thing I had to learn the hard way, while eating and cutting food, as soon as you were finished with the knife, it had to be placed on the side of the plate. Had you placed your knife and or fork on the plate, it meant that you were all finished with your meal. Without being told anything about this, I made the mistake a couple of times of placing my knife and or fork on my plate while I was busy chewing, and so that made my foster mother assume that I was all finished. Regardless if she herself was still eating, she would quickly get up to grab my plate and bring it into the kitchen. I remember the first time this happened, I didn't know what I had done. I remember asking what I did, and why she took my plate away. She preceded to tell me that I gave her the signal that I was all finished with my meal, and so she took my plate away. I would respond by telling her that I was chewing and placed my fork and knife down to wait till my next bite. She then told me that in their house the knife and fork go on the side of the plate. If someone puts them on the plate that meant they were finished eating.

I most definitely wasn't finished eating my food. I tried to tell her that, but it didn't matter. My plate remained in the kitchen until she and her husband were all done eating, and then it was thrown out. I did not get it back to finish, and that was to "learn my lesson." The lesson was not being allowed to finish. I remember the first time it happened I was only about half finished my plate. While my plate remained in the kitchen, I had to sit at the table and watch them eat their meal, and could only leave the table once they were finished. It felt so cruel that they would eat right in front of me, my food about ten feet away, and yet I couldn't finish it because I didn't know where my fork and knife were destined to be placed.

I can remember my dinners not exactly being the greatest, and yet my lunches were worse. The entire time I was living at this hellish foster home, I would be sent to school with a sandwich and a juice box. I hated my lunches, and always found myself still hungry. When it came time for lunch every day, I would see all the other kids with snacks, and amazing looking lunches. I would have a flimsy sandwich and a drink, that's it. We had snack time, but I would never be able to eat anything because I wasn't given a snack. Sometimes I would get so hungry that during recess I would sneak inside and take someone else's snack from their lunch pail. It didn't take long for people to realize that someone was taking people's food, but I always denied it was me because I didn't want to get into trouble. I tried to be sneaky like how I was at my last school when my sister and I would sneak inside to do the same thing.

One day close to the end of the school year, I got so hungry because my dinner had been taken away the night before, and with people realizing the snack thief was still at large, I decided to try to steal money from my teacher's purse so I could get something from the vending machine. I got caught and got into a lot of trouble. The funny thing was, I think my teacher was the less mad person who knew what I had done. My worker and especially foster parents were furious, and then I became known as a thief. I tried to explain to them, but according to my foster parents, I was given enough food and that there was no reason for needing anymore.

It was at this point, towards the beginning of February 1997, and a little before my seventh birthday weekend. This one week, leading up to the weekend, my foster parents seemed very happy. It was strange because I was not at all used to those emotions from them, other than what I could hear at night when it was time for me to go to my room. I was told that their favorite foster child was coming for a relief visit. It was as if this child was made of gold, considering how he lit some dimmed light in their eyes.

The closer the weekend got, the more I kept hearing them speak about him. I had barely been living there, and yet already I seemed to have caused much grief for them. They kept telling me how I better be on my best behavior. I was informed that he and I would be sharing a room and that I was to not get him into trouble, as I tend to get myself in trouble. I remember thinking how that seemed insane since I didn't even have time at that point to get myself into any trouble. Nonetheless, I was beginning to realize that I would never be able to win with these people, and so I agreed. I made sure they knew I would behave around this golden child.

Things about people tend to stick in one's memory. Some people can never remember specific traits or features regarding people, and this relief foster child was no different to me. He was a couple of years older than me, and yet he was slightly shorter than myself. I will never forget the cringe-worthy laugh he had, and how when he would smile, it was as if it stole life from the room. That wasn't a compliment by the way. It felt very much like a joker type of smile. His eyes closed shut with his smile, and it was kind of creepy. He wore glasses and let's just say it didn't take long for me to not like him. Frankly, I couldn't imagine how many people would like him. He was definitely the type of kid that was a suck-up while trying to prove he was better than anyone else.

I was beginning to accept while growing accustom to being alone. It hurt a little less each day, but I knew it was never going to be fully okay. Rather, I knew I wasn't going to be okay, but I knew there wasn't anything I could do. The first time this kid came to stay at my foster home, I just wanted to continue being alone, especially if they were already convinced I would be a bad influence on him. I tried everything I could to distance myself from him, just so I wouldn't be put in a situation that could bring me even further down. Before his arrival, I had begun to start digging and building a snow tunnel and hideaway in one corner of the property. I put it on pause and did everything

I could to stay away from it while he was there because I wanted it to be my secret little hideaway. It worked for a little while.

After a couple of times of him coming to visit, it was starting to get more difficult to hide from him while getting away to my finished tunnel and fort in the snow. He ended up finding me one day, but I refused to let him in. I explained that the whole purpose of me being in there was to get away from him and that he was not allowed in it. I refused him entry a few times because I was tired of not only seeing him but having him trying to get me in trouble for his misdeeds. He had blamed me for things he did that should have gotten him in trouble, but my foster parents adored him, and almost seemed relieved when he placed blame on me.

The first weekend I met him, my foster parents, right in front of him, explained to me that I was having difficulty in school, that people were "apparently" picking on me and so I would start fights. They also said that I had a toilet paper rule because I plug toilets and smear feces on the walls, so to make sure I don't try to sneak more than four squares. I could feel myself boiling on the inside because he didn't need to know any of that. My foster parents seemed the need to share with him ALL of my past issues, including my biological parents fighting which lead to me going into foster care. They insisted that he watch out for me, and to not allow me to get him into trouble, and to let them know if he saw anything.

One night while I was asleep, he got up to use the washroom and then came down in a panic waking me up. My eyes barely open, I could feel him shaking me to wake up, while quietly saying my name. I remember that night because it was the night I realized just how much of an asshole he really was. It was that night I said to myself I could never trust him nor like him. He, in a panic, begged me to help him. He apparently couldn't make it to the bathroom, and some of his poop landed on the floor in the bathroom. I held my hand up against my face, wanting to laugh out because of the irony, and yet I didn't. For some reason, he felt the need to ask me to help clean it up. Apparently, the smell was making him gag, so he couldn't. I told him boldly NO! I was not going to help him because I had enough to deal with and didn't need any more trouble.

Apparently, even nine-year-olds can be straight-up pricks. With me saying no, that I wasn't going to help him, that he should deal with his own messes and problems, didn't fly with this kid. I knew he didn't want to get in trouble, and yet he felt the need to blackmail me. He told me that if I didn't help him, he would wake up the foster parents and tell them that it was me who did it. The instant he said that I couldn't believe it. I became blank, because I knew if he would do that, just how much trouble I would get into. I could just hear them now. See the anger from them, and that was not something I wanted. So, of course, I quickly got up to go clean it. To be honest, there was barely anything to clean as it looked like a rabbit went to the bathroom. I couldn't believe he couldn't clean it, but at least it was done, and thankfully I was safe. This time anyways.

When I denied access to my snow fort thing, he got so angry with me. He went straight inside to tell them I had built a fort in the snow, and that I wouldn't let him in. The foster father came outside furious. Not only was he furious because I wouldn't let this little devil in my fort, but because he thought my fort wasn't safe. He screamed at me to come out, and at that moment all I could hear were my parents and how they used to yell just the same. If you want me to get out of the fort, especially because it was unsafe, just *say* it, nicely. There isn't a need to scream at a seven-year-old. After hearing him yell, I felt uneasy, and not safe. So, I said no I wasn't going to get out. I told him I wanted to stay in there by myself. He didn't appreciate the backtalk. I had a couple of tunnels leading to one big center hole where I would sit. He saw one of my tunnels and filled it in with a shovel.

He told me that if I wouldn't come out on my own, he would make me come out. My fort was being filled in with snow, and it was coming in quickly. I responded to him by saying, "Fine, fine. I'm coming out, just stop ruining my fort." Before completely getting out of the one tunnel left, he reached in and pulled me out by my arm. He was yelling so much, I could barely understand anything he was saying. He made a point that my fort was unsafe, and yet he was the one filling it in with snow while I was inside. Didn't seem to make much sense to me, but then again, I was just a child, so what did I know. Walking inside after my fort was demolished, I saw that demon child, and he was just staring at me smirking. I wanted to punch his face in so badly, but I was sent to my room, yet again, where I was to remain until they wanted to call me out.

The only good thing about this kid staying for a weekend, was that we were allowed to watch a bit of TV. If he wasn't staying with us, I wasn't allowed to watch TV, unless we were visiting their son's place. When he was there though, I didn't have a say as to what we would watch. Only he was allowed to choose something to watch. It drove me nuts, but a part of me was just happy to be allowed some TV time. I just couldn't believe how I never had a choice for what seemed like anything.

My 7th birthday will forever be my second worst birthday ever! After begging my foster parents and worker to allow my sister to come visit me, I was denied. It seemed I was always being denied that one request. They said that she was unable to make it, but that they would have my brother come to my foster parents to celebrate with me. I was actually not so thrilled about that. He didn't seem to want anything to do with me, as he was so happy down the street with his new family and their two sons. I remember telling them that I didn't want him there, but they told me that it was too late because it was already scheduled. They said that it would be good for me to have him there. I didn't think so, and I was right.

Just before the weekend, I was informed that the devil's son was going to be staying once again for relief at my foster parents. From what I can remember, this would have been the second time since I had moved there, and the time before my snow fort incident. Since the blackmailing weekend of meeting him, I really didn't want him there. I mean, this was supposed to be my birthday, and I was already being forced to have my brother, his foster parents, and their two kids stay for a "birthday party." Now, I'm being forced to have another person who I don't like, and definitely don't want there, but there was nothing I could do about it.

The day before my party, I saw my foster mother in the kitchen baking a cake. It was going to be my birthday cake, and I asked her what kind she was making. She proceeded to tell me that it was a chocolate cake because it was her golden child's favorite. She was making a cake to make sure that he would like it. I couldn't believe it. I remember being so stunned because she knew I didn't really like chocolate cake. It was good, but not my favorite, and she knew it. I asked why she's making his favorite when it's my birthday. She replied with if I don't like it or want it, I just don't have to eat any. I couldn't believe her. I can remember nearly calling her a bitch, because I was so angry at her. I can recall biting my lip to stop myself, and then I left.

Before my brother and his foster family arrived, I and the asshole were stuck having to play outside. In the backyard, there was a massive snow hill created from what was plowed from the driveway. It thankfully wasn't super close to my fort, so no one that day saw it.

We began playing on the hill, sliding down. We had these plastic body sheet things that we would use to go down the hill. For some reason, the word has slipped my mind, but I'm sure you know what I'm talking about. We went down so many times because there wasn't really anything else to do. Apparently, my slippery sheet thing was better than the demon child's, and so he demanded I switch with him. I laughed and said no. We were standing at the top of the hill, and he pushed me when I said no. I didn't fall down the part we would slide on, rather, it was off the edge that had no slide. I tried to catch myself because I knew it was going to hurt if I would fall straight down. I barely caught my footing, but it still wasn't enough to refrain from falling. Thankfully my fall wasn't as bad as it could have been but still landed pretty hard. I smacked my face on the ground, and my nose began to bleed a lot.

We both ran inside, blood falling pretty hard from my nose. He actually seemed pretty freaked out, and actually admitted right away to "accidentally" pushing me off the edge of the hill. My foster mother barely seemed affected by blood pouring out of my nose. She pulled my hand down from trying to stop the blood coming out. She looked at me and said that I'm fine. I'll be fine, and that I just need to go wash away the blood. Bitch!

I shoved Kleenex up my nose to stop the bleeding, and my whole face hurt. It felt so numb, and even my eyes hurt. My nose was swollen, and under my eyes were slightly bruised from the impact. After washing the blood, we had to return outside to continue playing. I was not happy, but I couldn't say anything. By this point, my brother and the rest were making their way over.

There were now five of us kids playing outside on the snow hill while the adults were nice and warm inside. I just wanted this day to be over, as it didn't even feel like my birthday. This day should have been about me, but in every way, it didn't feel like it. My brother was over to visit me and spend my birthday with me, and yet he seemed more interested in spending time with the demon child. I think the demon child partially knew it would upset me to take away my brother's attention, and so he did. I would see them talking, laughing, and wouldn't include me. I wondered why I was even there, or why anyone else was. Once again, I was left alone, and I knew had my sister been there, I wouldn't have been alone. I would have been laughing and actually enjoying my birthday.

I made my way to the top of the hill for my turn to slide down, and for some reason, my brother felt it would be funny to watch me fall down the same edge I had fallen down earlier. For the second time I fell down, and once again my nose started gushing blood. I will never forget how much that hurt. I cried so loud and hard. I was also so mad because the others were actually laughing from watching me fall down. It was as if they wanted to see me fall and to see how much I would bleed from the nose. After making our way inside, I actually got into trouble. My foster mother said that I was trying to seek attention and that it wasn't going to work. I needed to relax as it wasn't that big of a deal. At this point, I thought I could have had my arm sliced off, and somehow, I would have been blamed.

The rest of the day, I was not happy. I didn't want to smile, and I definitely didn't want to play with anyone. I had two bloody noses, a bruised face, my feelings hurt, and not a single person seemed to care. I just wanted everyone to leave, especially my brother at this point. He and I began to argue, but of course, I was the one overreacting. I was sent to my room, and everyone left. I didn't eat any cake, mostly because I didn't even want any since it wasn't even made for me. I kind of welcomed being sent to my room, because at least I could finally be alone. As crappy as this birthday was, it was only the second-worst birthday I have ever had.

Demon Child is the best way I know how to define this kid. Since he too was in foster care, I realize he also has a story. I'm sure that there were so many things going on in his life, that may actually be the reason for his behavior and actions. The thing is, I felt victimized by him. Instead of trying to place blame on me, making me feel left out, he should have tried to include me. He should have tried to in a way, be on my side since I too was a foster child. Times were already tough enough for each of us, and yet he went out of his way to make my time even more difficult. That was the one thing I hated the most about him. I was being bullied by enough people, the last person that should have been bullying, was another foster child.

Another time when he visited, I was again sleeping, when my foster mother had made her way into our room. She very loudly woke me up screaming at me. I had no idea what was going on. My bed was against the wall that leads to the door to leave the room. The other bed was on the other side of the room. Apparently, there was a wet spot near the end of my bed on the floor, which was on the path to leave the room. While walking in the room she stepped in the spot and started accusing me of peeing on the floor. NEVER had I had any issues with peeing my bed. My brother was the one who wet the bed, but not me. In my lifetime I think I may have peed the bed maybe max three times, but that was mostly because of fear, too much water, and nightmares.

I just couldn't believe I was once again being automatically blamed for something I didn't do. Since day one this woman has had it out for me because of what she heard and was told by other people before even trying, or making an effort with me herself. I immediately told her that it wasn't me. I don't wet the bed I said, and I definitely don't pee on the floor. I had pretty good bladder control and would be able to hold it in quite a long time, so would have had no problems making it to the bathroom. I told her it had to be the demon child who I could see laughing, or maybe even her cat. All I knew was that it wasn't me. She told me to stop lying because they couldn't have done it as they know better. I said, "Whatever" and she did not like that. I was stuck cleaning it up and then spending the rest of the day downstairs by myself.

For several months, I remained in the hellish foster home, if I wasn't off somewhere, usually in the woods by myself, I would be stuck downstairs in my room. I had some toys, but looking back, I didn't have a lot. Not at this point anyways. Being stuck in my room wasn't that great because there wasn't much I could do. I had fairly good hearing, and so while being stuck downstairs, I would sneak to the stairs and sit at the bottom listening to everyone upstairs. With having my bedtime being quite early, and the fact that it took me forever to fall asleep, I would at times do this then too. In some weird way, it made me feel like I was a part of whatever was going on without me. I often sat wondering what it would be like to be able to be up there with them, laughing too with whatever they found funny.

One evening while I was supposed to be downstairs in my room, my foster parent's son was over visiting, but I wasn't allowed to be up there. I was so tired of being in my room, so I sat on the stairs, this time near the top. I just wanted to listen to what was going on. I thought I had heard someone making their way over to the stairs, and so I quickly got up to try and sneak back to my room. I tripped over my feet and fell down the stairs. I landed on my back, and it actually really hurt. The thump of me falling was loud and so everyone upstairs heard. They came over to see what had happened, and instead of asking if I was okay, they asked why I was at the stairs listening to them when I was told to stay in my room. I made an excuse knowing I would be in a lot of trouble for listening, saying that I needed to use the bathroom.

I tried to make my way back to my room, but my back was really sore. I had just been called a liar because they didn't believe my story about needing the bathroom, and they told me to stop faking my back hurting. I most definitely wasn't because it felt as if the wind had been taken out of me, and it was a little painful to breathe. They apparently told my worker that I pushed myself down the stairs to get attention while they had company over. That was the last time I sat by the stairs to listen. I was a clumsy child, and I didn't want to feel that kind of a pain in my back again. The lesson was learned, although I tried to tell my worker that I didn't push myself down the stairs. He didn't seem to believe me, but at that point, I was becoming used to it.

My worker's job no matter where I was living was to make sure that I was safe and doing well in my foster home. While knowing my home life brought much trouble and traumatic events, my foster homes needed to be the opposite. When speaking with myself about how I was doing, he would usually make up his mind after speaking with my foster parents. Looking back, I did like him, and I still do, but the fact is that he never seemed to take my word for how *I was doing* in my foster home. We got along great whenever we saw each other, and I was genuinely happy every time I saw him. Reading his notes, however, has made me aware that any time I would say something it would be disputed by my foster parents as he would immediately ask their opinion on everything I had said. He would read to them the notes I would tell him, giving them the chance to correct it, by making themselves seem in the right, while me in the wrong. A lot of the time, they would even leave things out that they couldn't spin around to make themselves the good guys.

When you're a child in the foster system, one of the most important things needed is the feeling of not only being believed, but having people on your side. It is extremely important to have someone who is truly there for you, who dedicates their time to make sure that you are well looked after. Mind, body, and soul. The caseworker I feel is supposed to be that person. Even more so than the foster parent. The caseworker tends to stay with the child longer, and so it's their job to ensure that they are being listened to, and taken care of. Although my worker was kind and made me happy to see him, I didn't feel as though he was there for me, instead showed he was there for the foster parents. So many times I remember telling him about things that these foster parents had done, but he could never just take my word for it, and that made it difficult for me to want to tell him anything.

Making a good impression to my caseworker seemed to be the number one priority for my current foster parents. Every time he would make a visit, there they were full of smiles, house fully cleaned, fresh baked goods, and they especially made it clear to me that I had to be clean and on my best behavior. I am unsure if it was asked by my worker or someone else at the CAS office, but occasionally they would whip out the camera to take photos. It wasn't often that this would happen, but when they did, I was told to pose for them. I don't just mean to look at the camera, say cheese, and then smile big.

During Easter, while I was staying in hell, I woke up hoping for lots of chocolate, maybe an Easter egg hunt, just something fun and special. I slowly walked upstairs to the living room with the demon child who was once again staying with us, and he had just woken me up with too much excitement. I wanted to slap him because I just wanted more sleep. When I got to the living room, there were things placed on two spots in the room. The chair had a few things on it; chocolate bunnies, eggs, a couple of other chocolate pieces. On the other side of the room, there was another spot that had a bunch of Easter chocolate and goodies. The few things on the chair were for me, while the demon child got at least three times the amount I got. I looked at both of the spots, and was like, *Why does he get so much more than I do?*

I should have learned by this point that anything I have to say should just not be said. I should have just shut up, leave things alone, and have hope that one day I would move away. My foster mother did not like my question. Just before I asked why I was given much less Easter goodies, she was standing between us, a little back from the furniture. She was clinching a camera while looking at the demon child with a huge smile as if to wait to see his reaction to all of the things she had gotten for him. When I asked why he got so much more, she turned to me, face fell flat, and you could almost tell she was going to burst out in anger. She responded that *if I didn't want anything, I could just give it to him. I should be happy I got anything considering how much trouble I cause them.*

Of course, I wanted something for Easter, I was just surprised I barely got anything. As crappy as my home life was, one thing that had always been made sure of, was that each child got equal amounts. Not speaking about attention or whatever, but when it came to holiday presents, each of my siblings and I got the same amount of things. To make it fair, so no one would feel left out. I guess they did do something nice after all.

I was left staring at the couple of things in front of me on the chair thinking how shitty this stuff is. I'm already not a big chocolate fan, and this kid next to me is getting toys, a camera, a bunch of stuff, and the best thing I got was a lousy chocolate bunny. Literally, that's it. I was told to smile and sit by my stuff for a photo. I didn't want to, mostly because I just wanted to go back to sleep. I sat down on the floor, held my hand up to my hear, and then she took my photo. She asked me what I was doing, and I told her I was listening for the Easter bunny. I don't think she understood what I meant, but I remember thinking it was funny and clever because clearly, he couldn't have come by as I barely had anything.

The demon child was sitting next to me going through all of his stuff. I remained sitting on the ground because I wasn't allowed to sit on the chair, with the few things behind me. Every time he would pick something up to look at it, he would look at me and smile ear to ear. Clearly, he was trying to rub in my face that he got so much stuff, and it just pissed me off. I was just sitting on the ground, and it wasn't as if I got a toy to play with, so there wasn't anything for me to do with the few things I was given. My foster mother asked if I liked my stuff, and I said no. This little asshole was pissing me off with all of his stares and smiles, that I just didn't care. I remember with much surprise and anger, she said, "What did you just say?" I told her I was told not to lie. I don't like what I got because I don't think it is fair that I got practically nothing, and yet someone who only comes for the weekend got everything he did.

Easter 1997 taught me to be grateful for whatever and however much I get. Although I may have only got one bunny, and a couple of other chocolates, I still got something. I should have looked at it like that back then, but I was just really hoping to be treated like an equal child in the home I was living in. When I said that I wasn't happy with what I got because I didn't think it was fair that the other kid got so much more, my stuff became his, and I was sent to my room. At that time, being sent to my room for being "ungrateful" actually came as a blessing. It was one of the few times I was actually happy to be going to my room. I wasn't even mad at the fact that my one chocolate bunny was going to Satan's spawn.

Like Easter, there were a couple of other times that my foster parents searched for a time to take a photo to show just how amazing my time there was. Sorry, but if you look closely at each photo, I swear you can see me screaming to be helped, in my eyes. It had just always amazed me at how important appearances were to them. At the same time, they knew that the workers would believe anything that had to say because they were the adult, I was the child, and they had been fostering for a long time.

The last memory I have of the demon child, and of course, it was another one where he somehow managed to get me into trouble, came one night when he and I were sitting at the table. I am unsure how the topic came up, but it was sex. I remember him asking if I knew what it was, or how people did it, and I said that I did know. I don't know why, and I don't remember everything about the discussion, but I do remember grabbing a pen from the table and putting it between my legs while making the up and down movements to show him that I knew what sex was. To my seven-year-old mind, that's what sex was. Our foster mother was in the kitchen doing dishes, and I think he waited for the perfect time to get me to show him what it was, where she would see what I was doing, and I of course got yelled at. I was told that I was disturbed and that that behavior was unacceptable and to go to my room. She spoke with my caseworker, who also told me how inappropriate it was. At that point, I was so used to getting into trouble, that I just didn't even bother to explain. I knew the demon child could do no wrong, so didn't even bother to give them an explanation. Looking to the future, I just made sure not to ever do anything like that again.

My siblings and I all have our birthdays at the beginning of the year. My brother in January, mine in February, and my sister's in March. With all of our birthdays so close together, and with our supervised hour-long visits with our biological parents becoming more and more spaced apart, it was decided to have one birthday visit for all three of us. At the beginning of our visit, our parents gave each of us our birthday present. My brother and sister each got some kind of toy(s), while I got a card with 20 dollars in it. After looking at each of my siblings who could be seen smiling and playing with their birthday gift, I was there standing with a 20-dollar bill.

At this point in my life, family visits were something that didn't come around often, and with that, I knew something was going on. It had been so long since I had seen my sister, and it was almost just as long since I had seen my mother and father. I didn't have a lot of possessions at this point in my life, so anytime I could have something that I could hold, look at, even hug, while knowing it came from my parents, meant a great deal to me. I wanted what my siblings had, something to hold to look back on with the memory that my parents gave it to me. What I didn't realize, is that this was going to be my last birthday celebration with them.

I was upset to not have gotten a toy that I could play with like my siblings. I admittedly took a bit of a fit as I wanted a toy instead of money. I didn't want to have to explain to everyone that it was because I wanted something that I could have which could remind me of my parents since our supervised visits were less and less frequent. I handed back the twenty and asked if they could use that to get me a toy. My father took it and left to go buy me something. I honestly didn't mean at that very moment, but I did at some point want them to buy me something. I just knew that in the time I couldn't see them, I would want to have something that I could hold, smile in the thought of them, and probably cry.

It took nearly the entire hour visit for my father to return with a present for me. I actually felt bad, and I'm pretty sure my siblings were upset with me because he was gone for the whole visit. In some ways, I didn't mind too much because I didn't like the man, and it gave us a chance to spend time with our mother. When my father did return though, he actually came back with one of the best toys I ever had. Like, in my entire life. I don't know if it was because of my age, and everything going on around me, but the toy he came back with just seemed like the best thing I had ever seen.

When I lived with my biological parents, I had some toys. I didn't have a lot, but I did have enough to keep me busy when there was fighting going on. We didn't really have any money, so unless it was a holiday like Christmas, we would usually get one toy every so often when our parents were able to get a bit of money somehow. My father didn't like the fact that I loved playing with barbies because of the hair, and so would always try to get me to play with toy trucks or something. When he came back with my present on our shared last birthday, he brought with him the biggest toy car I had ever seen. It was maybe about a foot long but was super cool. It was a black sports car that turned into a police car. It made noises and everything. I wasn't fond of toy cars much, but this was definitely something that brought much excitement to my eyes.

When I returned to my foster home with my new amazing birthday present, every time I thought of it, I had a huge smile on my face. When you first walk into my room, there was a dresser along the left wall that could be seen from my bed, and that's where I put my new toy. I wanted to be able to put it up so you could see it from every spot of the room. It was up on display, and aside from smiling so much, it did exactly what I had hoped it would do. I barely had any good memories of my parents, but now that has changed. I would be able to look upon my toy and think how wonderful they were for getting me the best present I had ever received. When I would have to stay in my room because the company would be over, or when I would get into trouble, at least now I had a rad toy to play with.

By the time early March 1997 came around, there weren't many things that made me truly smile or be grateful for. I would try to smile as I was always asked to because I would be constantly told that by showing I'm happy, happy things will happen to me. The thing about that, is does it really work if the happiness is forced? I never thought so, but was tired of hearing the same things over and over from my worker and foster parents. One day, my foster parents brought me over to their son's house to visit. I wasn't allowed to be with them and had to entertain myself. I was actually tired of watching movies in the basement, and so I went outside to play with a friend from school.

I wasn't allowed to be over at anyone else's home, and so I never told my foster parents where I was. We played outside for a bit, but then she told me about this new show that was airing for the first time. I'm fairly certain it was its premiere night, but nonetheless, it was the very first episode. I didn't get to watch TV much, so when it came to new shows I had no idea what was what. I was just glad to be hanging out with a friend, so was like sure, let's watch it. Of course, I had to be back by a certain time so made sure to watch the clock.

To this very day, in 2019, that show I watched for the very first time, on its premiere night still remains my all-time favorite show. A show about a teenage girl who fights vampires with her friends while saving the world on a weekly basis. Buffy The Vampire Slayer. I'm uncertain exactly what about the show at the time sparked something in me, but I remember watching that show completely intrigued. I just didn't want that episode to end. That first episode ended with the captions *To Be Continued*. I immediately rushed out of my friend's house to run back to my foster parents' son's house. I didn't want to be later than I probably was going to be. The last thing I needed was to be in trouble again.

During my entire run back, I couldn't stop thinking about the show I just watched. Even though I was doing everything I could to not be late and get into trouble, I was smiling the whole way back. I thought how cool it was, and I wished so badly that she could come and save me from all the horrors in my life. Sure, I knew vampires and demons weren't real, so she couldn't save me from those. She was just so kickass awesome, and I felt as though I needed definite saving. I just couldn't wait for the next time I would be able to watch the show. It was the first time in such a really long time where I found something that actually made me excited. Every time I thought about the show, I smiled and wondered what would happen next. I didn't get to watch it every week, but the couple times I was able to, it just filled me with so much warmth and happiness. And the thing I loved most about it, was that it wasn't forced happiness.

After a couple of times going to my friend's place to watch my new favorite show, my foster mother found out that I wasn't just playing outside, and that was the end of me being able to leave while we were at her son's house. I got into so much trouble, and when we were at *home* I would have to stay downstairs to think about what I had done. Before I got my amazing toy car from my birthday, I had nothing to do. Sitting on my bed got tiresome after like five minutes, and so I would make my way into the storage room beside my bedroom. I wasn't exactly able to go into it, but I was seven and had no toys.

I would quietly walk around the room looking at everything. There were bins with papers and floppy disks in them. There was so much junk everywhere. While walking around the room, I couldn't help but think of my new favorite show, coming up with my own next episodes. I wasn't allowed to watch them anymore, but I wasn't ready for the show to end in my mind. Every time I would look at a bin, I tried so hard to put everything back where I found it. I had never seen floppy disks before, so had no idea what they were at the time. There was this one bin that was just filled with them, and they were all lined up in rows. I would pick one up and then put it back. I spent a few days when having to stay in my room, making my way around that room looking at everything.

It seemed as though nothing I did could make my foster parents happy. Every time we would eat dinner, at times with habit, I would want to eat with two hands when I didn't need to. I would then get yelled at because I should know the rules. It's not that I don't know the rules, it's that I just hate having to keep one arm and hand on my lap while eating. I'm not royalty, they're not royalty, so why do we even need to eat with such poise. It seemed even with looks, I would get into trouble, and so I just wanted to do something that could be perceived as helping. I wanted to do a nice gesture to get into their good books.

After I got my amazing car toy, but while having to stay downstairs in my room, I wanted to do something that I thought would be helping. Instead of just playing with my toy like I should have, I went into the storage room. In one corner of the room, there was a huge fish tank. My foster parents had a bunch of fish in it, and often I had seen my foster mother feed them from something beside the tank. I thought to myself how nice it would be to go and feed her fish for her, so she wouldn't have to. I thought that would be a good thing I could do. Well, I was a "fucking idiot."

When I was seven years old, I was illiterate and was for some reason at a French school, which wasn't helping. When I got to the fish tank, there were a few bottles beside the tank, but I couldn't read any of them. I had no idea which one was the food for the fish. I remember staring at them wondering which to use, and so I used all of them. I didn't pour a ton of each into the tank, but what I thought was enough to feed them just to be safe. After I fed the fish, I actually felt good. I remember smiling to myself thinking that finally, I did something my foster mother could be happy about. I thought maybe now that I did a good deed that maybe I could be able to leave my room.

The next day when my foster mother went downstairs to go feed the fish, I was sleeping and was woken up to yelling and screaming. I jumped out of my bed and ran into the next room where she was. She was in front of the tank freaking out. I looked at the tank and had seen that all of the fish were dead. She heard me behind her and turned to me swearing at me, asking what I had done. In that very instant I knew I was about to be in more trouble than I had ever been. Trying not to cry, I told her that I was trying to do something nice by feeding her fish for her. I showed her what I used, and she called me fucking idiot as it wasn't food but poison for fish. My files say it was liquid paper, but back then I was never told what it was. I began to cry and was saying how sorry I was, but I was just trying to help and do something nice. She slapped me, told me I was fucking stupid, and to go to my room and get comfortable because it would be a very long time until I was going to leave it.

I spent the entire day in my room crying. My face was sore, and I didn't know what to do. Her son came rushing over, and like her, he too was screaming and swearing, mostly at me. When he first came over, he called me to the stairs, so I rushed over to see what he wanted. I stood at the bottom of the stairs, and all he wanted me for was to yell at me. I was already crying, so getting screamed at more from someone else didn't help me to stop. I was told to stop crying and to listen very carefully. He didn't have anything to say that I needed to hear but just kept yelling at me. That day felt so much as if I was back home with my parents, except the entirety of the yelling was directed at me. I just wanted the day to be over.

The next couple of days were beyond stressful. I was only allowed to show my face when I needed the bathroom or to eat dinner. Even then it seemed as though neither of my foster parents wanted to see me. They barely spoke to me, and I surely wasn't going to try and talk to them. One night when I was sleeping, I was woken up to my foster mother screaming at me to wake up. I was laying in my bed, and when I heard the yelling I sat up. That night will forever be one of the worst moments of my life because of how much pain it brought me. Every bit of that night still haunts my memories and will be something I could never forget.

My foster mother was still furious about the fish being killed, and after spending a couple of days not speaking to me, even after I had apologized so many times. She turned the light on and demanded I wake up. Once I was sitting in my bed freaking out on the inside because I wondered what I could have possibly had done now to make her even more upset. She said while yelling at me, "Is it not enough that you killed my fish, but you also had to go through all of my papers as well?" At first, I had no idea what she was talking about until I remembered that I actually did, but thought I had put everything back in their original place. I told her that I was sorry, but I was bored sitting in my room, but tried to put everything back where I found it. Apparently, her floppy disks were out of order, and some of her papers were also out of order. To be honest, it didn't even seem as though anything in that room was in some sort of order.

No matter what I would have said to her that night was going to make a difference. She was furious about her fish still, which I can understand. She went on about how all I do is piss her off, getting into things I shouldn't. She told me that all I ever do is touch and break things that aren't mine, and that it was time I learned a lesson. At the time, what I didn't know, was that the toy car I got for my birthday, was actually going to be the second to last thing I would ever get from my biological parents. It was going to be the last toy I would ever receive from them.

My foster mother's face was red from all of her yelling. As she said it was time I learned a lesson, she turned to her left which was where my toy car was on the dresser. She picked it up, and right in front of me, she smashed it on the ground. Before walking out smiling, she said, "Now you know how it feels to lose something you love." She knew very well how much that toy meant to me, not only because it was basically the only toy I had, but because it came from my biological parents. I busted out crying while repeating no.

I may have found myself getting into a lot of trouble, but never had I intentionally done something to cause harm. I didn't kill her fish because I wanted to. I didn't mess up her papers in spite of her. I had done things with thinking of good intentions, I just didn't know enough at the time, and it just didn't work out. What happened to her fish was terrible, and I did feel bad, I did apologize, but I didn't think what she did was right at all. In the moment of her swinging her arms down with my toy car locked in her hands, I felt my heart stopped. That toy car was more than just a toy. It was more than just my only toy. It represented a kind of peace and happiness from when I would think of my biological parents. That toy gave me a sense of assurance that with all of the terrible things going on, something good could come out of it. Of course, it would have to be ripped away right in front of me.

I barely slept that night. I just couldn't stop crying, and my chest was hurting. I spent the majority of the night trying to put my broken toy back together. There were so many pieces, and it didn't seem like I was going to be able to salvage it. I ended up keeping the broken toy that could no longer change form, or even make noise. I even kept the small pieces that I couldn't figure out where they went. Although the toy was broken, it meant more to me than just a toy, and so for that reason alone, I couldn't just throw it out.

In early spring 1997, as soon as the nicer weather came out, it seemed as though I graduated from the basement to once again having to remain outside. I actually welcomed it so much considering the basement was a dark and dank place, and I was beginning to hate it with much passion. There was this one spot on the side of the house that I wasn't allowed to go to, but I was never told why. I was just told that it was off-limits. I didn't so much mind as I had my favorite spot across the road in the woods. It was my reflection and crying log spot. Reading my file, it stated that my foster parents spoke about how there were many children in the neighborhood I was able to play with, and yet the only other children were from my brother's foster home down the street, where I never went. I spent all my time there alone, and usually across the street listening to them.

Every so often I would hear a loud bang coming from the side of the house that I was not allowed to go to. I never knew exactly what it was. Since I wasn't allowed to play there, I would at times play in the front of the house on the grass. There were many chipmunks and squirrels that would be running around all over the place. I would make a sort of game out of it by chasing them trying to catch one. There was this one chipmunk that I would see almost every day, and I would be able to differentiate it because of its red stripe on its tail. It was actually pretty friendly, and would often come close to me. There would be nuts and such on the ground as if my foster parents were trying to feed them, and so I would use them to feed my new friend.

I spent a lot of time sitting on the lawn, watching my chipmunk friend run around and eat the nuts I would place close to me. I would have lots of conversations with it. I had no one else to talk with, and so I found enjoyment talking to something that couldn't yell at me, and something that couldn't make me feel like shit on a daily basis. My foster mother would see me sitting on the grass talking with what looked to be no one, and had a few times mentioned how weird I was for doing that. I explained that I made friends with a chipmunk, and I would sit there to feed it. I remember the strange look she would give me, followed by calling me weird again, and then would mutter to herself.

I wasn't allowed to go visit with my friend from school to continue watching my new favorite show when we would go to my foster parents' sons' home. I no longer had the coolest toy ever to play with as it's broken and hidden in my room. I wasn't allowed to visit with my sister, and I was barely allowed to visit with my parents. I was beginning to have less and fewer things and events in my life to bring myself joy. The chipmunk I would see and speak with was the only friend it seemed I had, and it was becoming the only thing that would make me smile. One day before having to play outside, I heard the loud bang once again coming from the side of the house. When I was told I could go outside since the loud noise had stopped, I went to where I would normally sit to speak with my friend.

I made my way to the lawn, and before I sat down, I saw something strange on the grass. My chipmunk friend with the red stripe was laying on the grass with blood pouring out of it. As it turned out, the loud noise that I would hear was my foster father's gun. They would put food down on the grass to draw in the squirrels and chipmunks so he could shoot and kill them. When I saw my chipmunk laying there dead, it made me so upset and I couldn't help but cry. It was the only good thing in my current life and was my only friend. I know it was just a chipmunk, but it just meant a lot to me at that time. I looked up after I held my dead friend in my hands, and all I could see was my foster mother staring at me with a slight smirk on her face. As soon as it was established that I had seen her watching me, so turned and walked out of view sight.

Emotions had never been something I was good at figuring out. I never really knew what I should be feeling, or how to react to certain things or people. I was always told so many different things, and how I should be feeling. In certain moments like getting my toy car smashed or seeing my dead chipmunk friend, it was a natural reaction of sadness, loneliness, and grief. Emotions like those were what seemed to fuel my mind during 1997, as those were the only feelings that would naturally come around. I rarely had natural reactions of happiness, and that was becoming a problem because being seven years old, I should be able to know how to find things to be happy about.

I took my chipmunk friend in my hands and rushed across the street to my spot. It was a little away from the tree line, and so no one could see me. I sat on my log with my eyes filling with tears, and I placed my friend on the log in front of me. I sat there for a good hour crying, and just staring at it. I didn't know what to do. I had seen enough horror in my life, but I never knew what I should do about a dead animal. I knew enough about dead things, and how it would begin to rot and smell. Thinking that my friend wasn't going to be running around me, allowing me to feed it anymore just made me even sadder. It was going to soon begin to smell and rot and I didn't want that happening. There was this hole in the log, and so I placed it in there. It remained there for two days, and during those two days, I would make my way over there to continue to cry and talk to a now-dead animal. I wasn't ready to leave it though.

When I was leaving the house to go over across the street to speak with my dead friend, I noticed on the driveway a small piece of metal. It had a sharp edge to it, and at that moment, I had an idea. I remember hearing about how some people would have a lucky rabbit's foot. I remembered how they would have it on a string and would carry it around everywhere they went to bring them luck. I knew that my chipmunk friend didn't exactly have a foot like a rabbit, and so I couldn't carry around a lucky chipmunk foot. I did however think it would be a great idea to have a piece of my friend with me, to maybe watch over me, and bring me luck which was something I desperately needed. I went across the street and while crying, I cut its tail off. The one thing that allowed me to know it was my friend and not a different chipmunk was because of its tail.

Very carefully so my foster parents wouldn't know what I was doing or had done, I cleaned the chipmunk's tail. I didn't want it to smell or anything, so I did everything I could to make sure it was clean and smelt good because of the soap. Every time I felt sad or alone, I would go into the small cigar box that it was kept in, so I could look at it and rub it. It made me feel close to it and allowed me to believe there could be good things to come my way every time I would rub it.

Spring 1997 brought many unanswered questions for me. I had no idea what was going on with my biological parents. No one was explaining anything to me, just that their issues weren't going away, and seemed to be getting worse. Our visits were becoming something that should have brought happiness to myself and my siblings, but with how spaced apart they were, just made us confused. It sucked being stuck in a tiny room with people watching us through a glass window for an hour. There didn't seem to be much time for anything. I didn't know it then, but the reason for me starting up with therapy sessions was to help me deal with the later decision of no longer having them in my life. The sessions were to pinpoint all of the circumstances leading up to my current state, and how it had affected me.

Once a month starting in April 1997, I would go and speak about all kinds of issues surrounding my life. I tried to explain all of the issues in my foster home, but nothing ever seemed to be done about it. I had always felt closer to my mother, and with not having many visits, it brought much sadness to my life. In my sessions, I would be told I could speak about whatever I wanted, and we could play games or even dress up if I chose to. At times I would dress in woman's clothes in my sessions because in some strange way it made me feel close to my mother who appeared to be disappearing from my eyes. I would try to find clothes that I thought she would wear and then it was as if she was right there with me. I didn't do it often, only because in the back of my head I could hear my father and his family calling me names, which always made me feel very sad and low. My sessions became a time that I could get away from everything going on, and I could just be free to be me. Although it took some time, it did give me the chance to let go of things and gave me the feeling of doing whatever I wanted.

I had already celebrated Easter at my hellish foster home, but a late Easter visit with my biological parents came at a much needed time. Like my birthday visit, it was some time afterward, that actually brought some happiness. My siblings and I didn't just get chocolate and candy, but also a birthstone gift set. It was the coolest thing I had seen. Before moving to my current foster home, I had taken out my earring. In the birthstone gift set, there was an amethyst earring stud. I hated having an earring, but when I looked it, something changed. The last gift I got from my parents was destroyed, and so this became my most precious gift.

The last gift I would receive from my biological parents would have been that Easter 1997 amethyst gift set. Purple was my favorite color and so it just seemed perfect in every way. Just one look at it and I would have a smile ear to ear. Finally, I was able to smile for real instead of the fake smiling that everyone around me was telling me to have.

One day shortly after receiving my Easter amethyst gift set, my foster parents were driving me to school. I was sitting in the back, and I had yet to put my earring in since getting it. I wanted to bring the gift set to school because it brought me pride that my parents had gotten me something so beautiful. While I was sitting in the back, in the eyesight of my foster mother, I put my earring in as the hole hadn't closed over. I sat there for a few amazing moments with a smile on my face. Before that moment I hadn't shown my foster parents my gift because I was too afraid since the last time she destroyed my present.

I was staring out the window with a huge smile on my face, and my amethyst earring in my ear. My foster mother turned around and looked at me. She said in a disgusted voice, "What the hell is that in your ear?" I turned to her still smiling and told her it was an Easter gift from my parents. She then turned to her husband who was driving and let out a bit of a chuckle. He blurts out asking if I'm a fefe. The word that I had heard my father call me, so I knew at that moment this car ride was not going to be fun. My smile disappeared instantly. I told them, *no*, but they didn't agree. My foster mother told me that "only faggots wear earrings" and to hand it over because no faggots are allowed to live in their house.

There was no way I was going to hand over the only gift I had left from my parents. When I refused to take out the earring, my foster mother leans back and pulls out my earring. The backing was in, so it really hurt when she pulled it out. The gift set I had only had the one stud, so I didn't have another I could put in to replace it. She looks at it, looked at her husband, and said that *it's even purple*. I told her that it's amethyst and to give it back to me. I was trying to not cry because of how much my ear was hurting, but I was just focused on trying to get my present back. At that point, I was passed feeling sad and was now feeling anger. My foster father speaks up and says that "purple is a girl's color." The two of them begin to laugh. My foster mother turns to me and said "So you're a faggot who likes a girl's color?" At that moment I started to yell at her to give me back my earring and that I was not a faggot. She didn't appreciate my yelling and so she opened her window and threw it outside while we were driving.

Before I got to school, I told myself that no matter what, I was never going to forget what had happened and that I could never forgive them for doing and saying what they had. As upset as I was for what they were calling me, the fact that they threw away that earring hurt me more. In a couple of months, I would learn that that earring would be the last gift I would ever receive from my biological parents. I didn't know it then, but it still really hurt. For my short and brutal seven years of life, purple was my favorite color. I didn't know why, and even though my father made little jokes about it along with his family, I tried not to let it bother me. Hearing what my foster parents said in that car ride though, made me really start to wonder if it should be my favorite color. In that moment, I changed it to red. I was tired of being called names, and so I made sure to later tell them that my new favorite color was red. As if to be like, *there, are you happy now?*

One day after watching my earring being tossed out the window, I had some hope that it remained in the truck. One day when it was parked in the driveway, I tried to look for it but had no luck. It was really gone. I was so sad and mad at the same time. My foster parents had some random papers on the floor of their truck, and so I figured I would return the favor. They wanted to throw my earring out the window, and so I threw out a few of the papers on the ground of the truck. I didn't know what they were, and I didn't care. In a way, they shouldn't have either, since they clearly treated the papers like trash. Apparently, the papers meant something because they became angry and told my worker what I had done while leaving out what they did. Like always though, they chose not to tell him. I tried to though, but no-one ever believed me.

In June 1997, my school was having an end of the school year water day. There would be snacks, tons of water games, and a full day of staying outside having fun. The only problem with hearing about this day of fun was the fact that I didn't have a bathing suit. I spoke with my foster mother about how I would need swimming shorts so I could play the water games, as it was asked by the teacher to pack a bathing suit. I told her that I didn't have one, and would like one as I was excited to participate in all the fun at school before the summer hits. She seemed fine with that and then went out the next day to get me one.

When I came home from school, I was so excited to see my new swimming shorts. She told me to go look on my bed. I ran downstairs to my room and looked at my bed. What I saw wasn't what I had asked for. It looked like a pair of tiny underwear. It was not only a speedo but one that was a little too small for me. In that moment I knew she had done it on purpose because she knew I wanted swimming *shorts*, and she knew my size. I told her that I didn't want a speedo and that it was too small for me. She told me too bad, and that if I wanted to participate in the water day, I would have to wear them. She said that she already spent money on them and that she wasn't going to go back out to spend more money on something that I didn't need. I needed to be grateful for what I got.

What a bitch. I didn't say it to her, but I definitely thought it. I knew what a speedo was, and I knew that no one was going to wear one. I went to school for the water day, and I had to bring it with me. My foster mother went with me to school that day, and wouldn't leave until I put it on. I looked around

108

and didn't see a single other boy wearing one. I begged her to get me shorts and to not make me wear it, but she refused. I put it on and felt an overwhelming embarrassment taking over. That was the first moment in my life I had felt self-conscience.

The second I stepped out to where everyone else was so I could also play, I was being pointed and laughed at. I wasn't a tiny skinny kid, although I wasn't large either. I was a middle awkward stage of the two. I had some chub, and being in a speedo that was too small for me, it emphasized everything that much more. I tried to go to a different area where there weren't many kids, but the entire time I would walk, more and more kids would point and laugh at me. No one was wearing a speedo, which was what I had told my foster mother, but she disagreed. Well, I was right. I finally found a spot to the far end of the water area where no one was. It was near a tree that was full of shade. I did everything I could to hide from everyone.

The only thing that saved me from a full day of embarrassment, was my teacher who had seen me hiding out. I spent much time crying to her about everything. I told her everything and she gave me a big hug and told me that I would be okay. I was able to put my clothes back on and just didn't participate in the water fun. At that point, I didn't even care anymore.

It seemed like my school's water day inspired my foster parents to have one of their own. I'm uncertain if the water day in their back yard was a way to make me even more embarrassed or to just really piss me off. One way or another, I knew it was to make me upset. They invited my brother's foster parents and their kids, their sons' family, and a relief foster child was also there. Once again, I was told I had to wear the speedo they bought me. I had just spent a horrible day being laughed at because of it, so there was no way I was putting it on again when I knew no other kid would be wearing it. Plus, it didn't fit. I think even her cat would have been too big for it.

The water day they decided to have also meant that they would be having BBQ food and a bunch of snacks. Since I didn't want to wear the small speedo, I was told that I had to stay in my room and listen to everyone else having fun. With where my room was located, and it's window, I was in perfect earshot of their little water party. After a couple of hours go by I was getting pissed off that I wasn't allowed to join in on the fun just because I didn't want to wear that stupid speedo. All I could think about was how hungry I was getting. I decided that I was tired of staying in my room, and if I wanted some food I would have to put it on.

I yelled for my foster mother's attention. She came inside and I told her that I would wear the speedo if I could come out and get some food. She told me that it was too late and that I had already decided I didn't want to join them. Apparently, the only window of opportunity to join in the fun was at the beginning, and so now I had to stay down there for the rest of the day. I was not happy and started crying and yelling saying how that wasn't fair. Mostly, I was just so hungry as I hadn't eaten anything all day, which I think made me quite cranky. She told me that I could get food when I calm down, and when she would have some time to bring me some.

About another hour or so later, my foster mother came back downstairs while I was sitting on my bed, eyes still wet from crying earlier. Once she had left, my little outburst stopped because I knew it had to if I wanted to eat something. I just didn't stop crying. On a paper plate, she handed me a cold, and plain burger. She told me that's what was left, and if I'm still hungry I can eat that. I so badly wanted to throw it at her face, but I was too hungry. After she left I quickly ate it, and then remained sitting on my bed. The longer I sat, the more angry I felt. All I could hear was laughing and cheering outside, and it just didn't seem fair. With much anger, I grabbed that stupid speedo which had caused much chaos and tore it up.

Once I finished destroying the speedo, to myself I actually smiled. It felt so good, and as if it was a big *fuck you* to my foster mother. After the water day had ended, it didn't take long for her to figure out that I had ruined the speedo she had bought me, but she almost didn't seem to care.

Shortly after my foster parents' water day, I was informed that I would be moving. Thank the heavens, my prayers had been answered. I knew rubbing my chipmunk's tail would come into good use. As it turned out, my foster parents were retiring, and so I needed a new home to live. At that moment I didn't care where I would be moving to, just as long as I didn't have to see these people again. I had dealt with enough crap living with my biological parents, and yet, it almost seemed as though I had to deal with more in this foster home. Since day one, I was labeled, and there was nothing I could do to change that. I was finally being given a chance to have things changed. Finally, I could have a fresh start, and I didn't want to mess that up. I was going to take this fresh start, this new foster home, and do everything I could to make it better.

Chapter Seven

Lakeview Round One

No matter the circumstances, moving anywhere is never an easy thing to do. There is always so much involved, and when you're a child, you're left with so many questions and worries. Every time I was to be moved somewhere in the foster system, my mind would spin as it was filled with questions that I wanted answers to. For myself, the questions I found I had were different when I would be moved without asking my worker, then when I requested said move. In the case of my move from the hell house at the end of June 1997, the excitement I felt to move was powerful, but still, I didn't know what to expect.

I never imagined my move from my brother's foster home to the hell house that things would only get worse for me in the home, and so there were a lot of concerns about this move. The only thing I had to go on, was hope that the worse was behind me, and I had to find the inner strength within myself to get me through whatever was about to unfold.

In early Spring 1997, I had begun therapy to help deal with the trauma I had witnessed while living with my biological parents. My monthly sessions started out with hesitation because I hadn't had therapy previously, and so I didn't understand what it meant. I had enough people trying to talk with me in my life, and it made no sense why I would have yet another person. What I hadn't known at this time of therapy, regardless of any cause for worry within myself for my home life, was that the talk of adoption had been in the works.

The Children's Aid had been speaking with both of my biological parents regarding the safety concerns of our home life. There was much discussion about whether or not the three of us would ever be able to return, and more importantly if we even should. There had been countless times where both of my parents had the opportunity to grow for the better, and change their violent and intoxicating behaviors. The choice of not dealing with any of their problems only made things worse for everyone involved. After realizing that the Children's Aid Society had been right, and the thought of what would be best for all three children was for us to be adopted into new homes where we could have a chance at normalcy, my parents agreed to give us up.

After speaking with my biological parents on the subject, I was told that it was my mother who had been the first to agree to put us up for adoption. Our father seemed hesitant and did not want us to have a chance at a better home life. Whatever his motives and thoughts were on the matter, didn't last because on June 4th, 1997 all three of us had become Crown Wardship so we could be placed on the adoption list.

Prior to the final decision for us three children being put up for adoption, there had been no discussion with us to prepare us for what was to come. In my therapy sessions, I can remember little hints from specific questions being asked, but at the time, didn't think anything of it. Once the decision for adoption was decided, my therapy sessions changed drastically. Then again, how do you tell a seven-year-old that he will no longer have his mother and father in his life, but will have to start looking for a new family, all while not expecting him to act out?

It wasn't until after the move to my new foster home, that things began to change for me and my siblings. With every foster home I stayed at, it always started with a drive, that always seemed to take forever. While staying at the hell house, I had gone to a couple of relief foster homes. It was to only last a weekend, which gave the foster parents a break, but there was always the knowledge of returning, and so the drive never seemed to matter. Actually, moving for a new placement in a home, made everything change.

I've made the drive from North Bay where I was living to my new foster home as an adult, and it was probably a twenty to thirty-minute drive. As a child, with so many questions and concerns swirling around my brain, the drive had seemed like hours of sitting in a car. I was stuck staring out the window wondering what this new home was going to be like. I had hopes when moving to my last home, and things just seemed to get as bad as they could. Everything that had been said and done seemed to transfer over, and I wasn't allowed to start anew. From my experiences, the thing that a lot of foster parents weren't aware of, was the fact that each child just wants a chance to start fresh.

Regardless of any faults a person may have, there is usually always the possibility of making up for those mistakes. When moving to somewhere new, the hope that any issues or problems you had would almost be erased, allowing the new foster parents make their own conclusions from having you stay with them. The hell house never allowed me to start over and show them the kid I wanted them to see. They had their minds made up that I was to only bring trouble, and so they couldn't see anything else. In this drive to my new home, all I was left with, was having faith that things could and would get better for me.

My social worker turned off the highway onto a dirt road. There appeared to be many turns down this dirt road, as well, it didn't seem to want to end. I remember looking out both sides of the car to see the houses that we were passing. In the background to my left behind the houses, I spotted water. Typically in the car rides with my worker, he would be speaking to me, but I usually blanked especially when looking at the scenery. I started to become excited because of the water I had seen. I had so much hope that I would be living on the side that was attached to a lake.

Before living at the Lakeview foster home, never had I lived on the water. I didn't even live that close to it before. Aside from the small cheap pool my siblings and I had in our backyard while living in Ottawa, I hadn't even swum before. I feel as though the fact that I'm a Pisces, is the reason why I had always been drawn to water, even though I never had the opportunity to be in it. The instant I saw that lake, I made it my mission to make sure that this foster home was going to work out.

We pulled into a driveway that was on the side of the lake! An instant smile filled my face. The driveway we turned in on, had a house on the left side, and if you continue about fifty feet, there is a second house on the right side. Past that house is a U shape of the land with water filling the middle. The middle part with water was used to store boats for going out on the water.

After driving in and parking, my worker brought me inside the first house which was on the left. I remember seeing in the background a few other kids. For so long I had been alone, with no other kids near me, and not only do I get to live on a lake, but I get to live somewhere that had lots of other children. I felt like I hit the jackpot and just couldn't wait to get settled in my new home. The joy and excitement I felt just driving up to the house, was met with even more joy once I met my new foster parents. They were an older French couple, who just exuded kindness.

After only maybe an hour or two of meeting my new foster mother, I had noticed she smiled more at that time, then my previous one did while my whole stay there. Up until this point in my life, I had gone from a terrifying home life to a couple of scary foster homes and only hoped that one day I would be placed somewhere completely different. Thankfully, for what was to come into my life this upcoming year, this Lakeview home was by far the best place I could have lived at.

Even though my new foster parents were made aware of all of the issues surrounding my life up until this point, it didn't seem to have an effect on how I would live with them. They knew I had some troubles at my previous foster homes, as well as my biological home, but they chose to see how things would be for themselves. Exactly what I had hoped for, as well as how it should always be. I did have a lot of issues, especially when it came to my behavior, after all, all I knew was aggression and anger. This new foster home felt like a great place to be able to work on that. I have found that the best way to work on things like the anger and aggression I had, was to have a home environment that was opposite. This allowed myself to be able to see that not everything in life has to be filled with such badness. This helped me to see that there is kindness out in the world and that I deserved a little of it.

This move to my new foster home came at the perfect time. It was the beginning of summer, which meant, I was able to get settled in the new environment, meet the new kids in my area, before a new school year. I was allowed to let go of the troubles previously I had experienced, to finally just be a kid for a bit. Little did I know at the time, but some of the relationships I would make that summer, with those kids who lived near me would go on to last a lifetime. Some of the relationships to this current day in my life as I sit writing my life story, I am still friends with. It's times like that, that really make an impact on someone's life.

One of the best things about my new foster parents were the fact that they didn't care about my previous foster parents' rules. I was finally able to be rid of the toilet paper rule, although at this point I had started having bathroom issues. I had been so worried for so long about needing to have to go, that I would try not to. I would hold it in as long as I could because there was always the fear of going, using more than a few squares of toilet paper, and then plugging the toilet. Even though it had only been one time, I was made to feel bad about it. I just couldn't help but feel as though it would be better if I just didn't go at all. I eventually would go when I couldn't hold it in any longer, but still, the stomach pain I would have, became too much, and the feeling of not knowing if I would get into trouble was always there. As time would go on, things would get better, but a small fraction of that pain remains inside of me. Probably one of the reasons I could never use a public restroom.

In the hell house, I was only allowed to take a bath when the foster parents allowed me to. I was never allowed to be in the bath without them being present, even though I would ask for privacy. I hated that because it felt strange that I needed one of them to be there while I was naked, in the bath with barely half a tub filled with water. I had thought I was old enough, but I was told that I couldn't be trusted to be in the bath by myself. Moving to my new foster home, not only was I allowed total privacy when taking a bath, but I was allowed a full bath of water. As small of a thing as that may seem, it felt like a big deal to me. I was even given permission to close the door so that no one could see me naked in the bath.

I had gone so long of my life without privacy, that it became an everyday occurrence where I would never expect it. I would obviously have wanted it but was always told in my homes that there wasn't a need for it. While moving from a biological home where lines had been crossed regarding sexual abuse allegations, it was a strange concept that even in my first couple of foster homes I couldn't even take a bath with a door closed. I had been told about how my private parts are exactly that; They are meant to be private and not seen or touched by anyone else, and yet, while in the care of my first couple foster homes, they were not kept private.

Had I been younger, like when I was first in the system at two years old, I would understand the need for someone to assist in my bathing. When I am six and seven years old, after all of the allegations against both of my biological parents, I would assume the need and desire for privacy would be even greater. I am no expert, however, it makes sense to me that saying one thing, and then doing another would only confuse a child while they are trying to grow. I was trying to figure out what needed to happen, and how things were meant to be since my care workers were saying to keep myself private, and yet my hellish foster parents were doing the opposite.

Being in a home where I now felt as though I had privacy meant a great deal to me. I knew the difference between a bath and a shower, and how being a younger child meant that it wasn't time for me to shower quite yet. My new foster parents after a little while, allowed me to have my first shower. They wanted to wait to make sure that I was big enough to stand and clean myself off. Plus, I also enjoyed my baths because I could play in the tub with some toys and bubbles. It was a small enjoyment, but still something I was not used to.

I often wondered if the new things I was being allowed to do were things that I could have always done. At the current foster home I was seven years old, and yet I had been used to so many other habits and routines. So much was changing, and in a way, it felt amazing but still confused me so much. I had wondered why I couldn't have lived this way before. If all of these new things were deemed acceptable, why couldn't I have been allowed them before? I was starting to realize that there was so much being kept from me, but no one was explaining anything to me.

I had always known that in my home life with my parents, there were a lot of things that were troubling. I had heard on many occasions that things that had happened shouldn't have happened. All three of us had been explained that we were stuck in an environment that was not suitable for children. I remember being told to trust the adults in my life now as they are all there to help and fix the mistakes done to us. I was left feeling unsure about things because it didn't always feel like we were actually being helped. Our parents were being kept from us. The three of us were separated, unable to have constant visitation, and we weren't really being listened to when discussing current foster home issues. Thankfully, my therapy sessions gave me yet another opportunity to discuss these concerns I had.

A part of myself still to this day feels as though the only reason the therapy sessions began, was because the care workers, or social workers, had known adoption was the next step for us. Everyone involved needed to make sure while covering their asses that these adoptions into separate homes would work out. There were so many problems and issues arising in all of us, and in order for an adoption to work out, we the children needed to show that we could handle it.

During the summer of 1997, everything seemed to blur by. Finally, after so long I was given a chance to be around other children. Finally, I was living in a home where I felt as though people actually wanted me around. I was finally experiencing new and simple things life had to offer, and yet there was more uncertainty than ever. My siblings and I were briefly explained that things had become too much for our parents to handle, and so it was decided that each of us would need to find a new permanent home to be raised in. It was decided that it was unsafe for any of us to return and that this was in our best interest. We needed an environment where we could finally be children as we were, and start to live a good life. Sounds great in theory.

From the end of June 1997 until March 1998, I would remain at the Lakeview foster home. In the nine months of living at this foster home, all I was left with were happy memories from the foster parents. For the first time in my life, I was living in a home that felt surrounded by love, compassion, and care. Everything they made me feel was what I had wanted to feel previously, but didn't think I would be able to. Although the foster parents had shown me all of the good things life could offer a child, there was still so much darkness surrounding my life.

I had been told along with my siblings that we would no longer be able to have our parents in our lives. As much as this was a good thing from an outside viewer, to us children it seemed unfair and wrong. We didn't, and couldn't have known exactly just how bad things were. Our minds couldn't have been able to comprehend just how wrong some of the things that occurred in our home were. At the end of it, we just wanted our parents and to be a family. Hearing the news out of nowhere struck much confusion because we didn't know what that meant. At this point, I was still illiterate, and so having to understand the logistics of having a court order saying I was no longer allowed to have any contact with my biological family seemed way too complicated.

Each of my siblings and I had endured much pain and abuse which was carried out in different ways. My sister had spoken about the sexual abuse from our father and others against her, while she had seen our brother sitting naked on top of our mother. She had even mentioned something about there being a camera in the room at times. Each of us had spoken on numerous occasions about being smacked and hit by both of our parents. There was a constant volume of screaming between both our parents, while also being directed at us. There were so many terrifying issues and concerns being brought up, but nothing ever seemed to come of them. We would share with those telling us to tell them, and yet nothing happened. Never any charges or investigations were drawn up.

It would seem as though after hearing about all of the concerns being shared with our caseworkers that we were never believed. We were always being told about the horrendous acts in our home life, but then why was nothing ever being done about it. Taking us away from our home doesn't make the problems go away. Keeping us from seeing or speaking with our parents doesn't mean we weren't abused. Putting the three of us up for adoption isn't a solution to make all of the allegations and conversations just go away. It became something that only added to the confusion we already had. We were always being told about how unsafe our home life was, and how our parents weren't equipped for parenting us, but then why not actually do something to punish them for what they had done. It seemed like everything that occurred prior, just vanished. Their slates were scrubbed clean, and the only solution in place, was put us in a room with another stranger to speak about our concerns and problems, and hope adoption would make everything better.

I had always been closer to my mother. Even at seven years old I hated my father, and I knew that would never change. Hearing that I would no longer have her in my life troubled me. With all of the growing problems I had, that she had, a lot of the time I felt as though she was on my side. She stuck up for me against my father when he would tease me, call me names, or would argue certain criteria for being male. It was the one good thing that always stuck with me, and it was something that I held on to. Having her stick up for me regardless of everything she had done and been a part of, made me want to have her in my life. Hearing she would no longer be my mother troubled me and made me miss her before she was even gone. At times, in my therapy sessions, I would play dress-up, which allowed me to feel connected with her. When she was no longer in my life, dressing up wasn't about being gay, or wanting to wear women's clothing. It was about somehow feeling as though my mother was a part of me.

During some of the supervised visits I would have with my siblings, my sister and I would play dolls as we had in the past. I would hold and cradle a doll as if it were a baby, pretending that I would always care for it. I would pretend that I would never leave it, and would always love it. It seemed as though this appeared troubling to our worker. In my files, it was written how unsettling it was because I shouldn't have been doing that. It had been indicated that I showed behavior that only brought up more questions that would be passed on to my therapist to go over. One might assume that losing both parents and then being put on the adoption list, might stir up mixed feelings about wanting to be looked after while wondering if the child was even loved.

When my sister and I would play dolls, especially after no longer being allowed to have any contact with our parents, holding the doll represented how I wished I could have been cared for. I was able to pretend for the moment that I was the parent showing how the child in my arms should have been cared for. I had always just wished I could have been shown affection from my biological parents that didn't come with screams and abuse. I wanted to convey that message as silly as it sounds to the doll I would play with. I know I was developing issues based on the fact that my parents and family would no longer be in my life. I was struggling internally with so many questions that remained unanswered, and I needed a way to cope and sort through them in my own way.

After witnessing me playing with the doll, rocking it in my arms, my worker informed me that I was not allowed to anymore. He felt I shouldn't have been doing it, and that it was a sign of disturbing behavior. Hearing what was said from my worker only made me feel really crappy because it actually made me feel slightly better. I wasn't hurting anyone. I wasn't trying to upset anyone. I just needed something to allow myself to process everything that was currently going on in my life. It just brought up memories and feelings when my father would see me playing with dolls and the names that would be called to me. In a way, it just made me retreat even further down in myself because I didn't know what to do.

Without even realizing it, it seemed as though when I was seven years old, I brought much cause of alarm to my worker. If playing with a doll was bad, then my first kiss with a girl must have been really bad. At my new foster home, there were so many children in the neighborhood, of all ages. I became close especially with my direct neighbors that I shared a driveway with. There were two boys and one girl. All similar in age, and similar to my age. The girl was the same age as me, and she became someone I would play with daily. She had been living there longer than myself and introduced me to other children on the street. Those kids became my friends, and those friendships became something I would appreciate for years to come. My direct neighbor friend even introduced me to other kids, friends of hers from the tiny town where I would be attending school in the fall.

One night my neighbor friend had invited another girl from the town for a sleepover. The three of us camped outside in a tent, on our property. We had watched some movies, and after seeing the older kids and adults kiss, we all thought we would try it. It wasn't anything serious, as it was only meant to be out of fun. We were all seven, so we were just curious. It was only kissing after all, and all three of us wanted to. Each of them was on either side of me, and to kiss one of them, I had to prop my upper torso slightly on top of them so our lips could touch. Well, what we didn't know was that we were being watched from my foster brother. He went and told our foster mother that he had seen me laying on top of the two girls and we were all kissing. That message got passed on to my social worker, and I got in trouble from everyone.

The incident was passed on to my friend's parents, who seemed to understand better than anyone that none of us meant any harm from what happened. We were all just curious, as it was something we had all seen the other kids do. No one was being forced into the kiss, and we had all wanted it. My worker seemed to be more upset than anyone and called it *disturbing behavior, brought on from witnessing and being exposed to sexual acts in my home life.* Yes, while living with my biological parents I had been prey to troubling things, but that's not what this was. Considering my first kiss was with a girl, and how everyone seemed concerned I would turn out gay, I'm surprised they weren't all happy. Nonetheless, the incident was addressed, and we all moved on from it.

Summer at my new foster home aside from my first kiss ending in getting into trouble, actually brought a lot of needed fond memories. I had gone so long with only being able to remember trouble, and bad times wherever I lived. This home gave me a chance to create new memories that could actually make me smile. My foster parents loved being outside, and had a pretty close relationship with each other, even if they all didn't live directly close. The fact that we lived on a lake, definitely helped when there would be times of family get-togethers.

My foster parents had, I want to say four children, but it could very well be three. It probably is three, and I'm counting one of them twice. One of the foster parent's children, had children of their own who occasionally would come over for visits. It seemed like the number one fun thing we could all do together, would be to take the boat out on the lake for the day. We would all climb into my foster parents' boat and go out on the water to a small island where we could play and swim. At times, we would even fish off of the boat. Just being on a boat was new territory to me, and so it seemed like the best possible experience I could have had.

I practically lived in the water the entire summer of 1997. When I wasn't swimming or going out on the boat, my foster parents here or there would go fruit picking. They had a few locations picked out for the best collection of blueberries especially. I was brought along on some of those day trips which was actually a lot of fun. I had never gone out in nature to pick wild fruit. It was away from the city, with no people around, and was very calming. A couple of times I was even allowed to bring friends to join in. Picking blueberries as longing as it may seem today, back then, it was as if time had stood still, and I was allowed to just enjoy being a kid who had too much energy while eating more than I should have. It was one of my favorite memories that I was able to create with my foster parents. A true smile created in a moment of the simple act of picking fruit from a small bush.

September came too quickly. I was having so much fun for the first time ever, being able to put out of my mind all of the troubles that seemed to plague my life. I felt like an actual kid for the first time in my life. It seemed as though Fall came faster than I had hoped, and that the name wasn't just for the season, but a description for my life to come. Having only one therapy session a month didn't seem enough to help me try to deal with my issues or concerns. During the summer I had been told that my parents couldn't work things out, and so I would be put up for adoption at some point. It seemed like I had just been told this, and now that September came around, that time was present.

Without even realizing it, and partially not being able to comprehend it, September 1997 was when my "Goodbye Visit" with my biological parents had taken place. I remember barely even being able to remember being told that come September, I would have to say goodbye to my parents in order to be put up for adoption. The whole process was basically a wash on my mind as I didn't really understand what that meant. My siblings and I were notified that we would have an hour or so supervised visit in a larger room at the Children's Aid Society office. In this brief time, we would be allowed to play, have a few snacks, talk with our parents, but that it would be the last time we could. We were told to make the visit count and to make sure to say "goodbye" because we wouldn't have another opportunity to do so.

I remember when I was seven years old being told that I would have to say goodbye to my biological family since it was a must in order to look for a new family. I remember wondering if that had also meant saying goodbye to my siblings. What about my relatives? I remember not knowing any of this and having it explained, that by the court's order, the only biological family I was allowed to continue contact with was my sister and brother. I wasn't very close with my relatives, and I actually didn't care for my father's entire family, so not being allowed to see or speak to them didn't seem to matter. I did wonder why I wasn't even allowed to say goodbye, but it was a thought that quickly left my mind. The most important concern I was faced with was what it meant regarding my siblings. If I wasn't allowed my parents, I just needed to make sure I could still have my sister in my life.

There could never be enough preparation, especially for a child to say a final goodbye to their parents. Regardless of how bad things got, were, they were still the only parents I knew. My mother and father are the definition of bad parents, and yet, I was just a child unsure how I could possibly say goodbye. I was struck with the fear of what would happen to me. I didn't exactly have a stellar track record with being placed in homes, and the current foster home I was living at seemed like a one in a million. How on earth was I going to be able to find another home that could be equally as great? As sad as it may seem, the fears and concerns I had for saying goodbye were more to do with the days to come after and not the actual goodbye.

I was a child who was taken away from his home starting at the age of two. There were circumstances that called for this, and I have always been aware of the importance of me being removed, but that doesn't make it easier. The memory of a stranger coming to my home each time to remove my siblings and I isn't something out of a movie where first there were visits from a saint asking everyone questions about our home life. It wasn't something that had been planned. Being taken out of the only home we had known came suddenly and there was no choice. There were reasons that called for us to be removed, but what I have found most people in my life have not realized, is that the memory of it happening is something that scars. As a child, there was no possible way to prepare myself, nor comprehend the situation, and so all I was left with was a terrifying feeling.

Up until I was seven when I had my goodbye visit, I knew the reasons for being taken away into the foster system were because of the unsafe environment I was born into. I knew that when things were getting really bad at home, it meant that I wasn't able to live there. When violence and vulgar language are used on a daily basis, it called questions for the appropriate parenting. When all of these things were occurring, it was embedded in my mind that I would no longer be allowed to live there. All of this created a fear in my mind that at any point I could be taken away without a moment's pause, and I would have no choice. This was something I was unaware of at the time, therefore I couldn't properly deal with it because I didn't know. In my monthly therapy sessions, it wasn't something I could speak about because there were already other situations to talk about. This fear of being removed from my home at any time because of bad behavior was something that would build as time would go on.

Before the fall of 1997, each of the hour-long supervised visits with my parents came and went in the blink of an eye. The visits never seemed long enough, and when there are three children, trying to get our parents' attention was not easy. Between the three of us, we had to try and find ways to spend time with them getting their attention, which always leads to us trying to be the center of attention. This is something that my worker found I did most. It was written in my files that during our visits I would fight for attention, and to that, I say so what. I mean, I was a young child who barely got to see his parents, and in one hour, evenly splitting the time between two parents for each child doesn't give a lot of time. Each of us wanted to play and spend time with each of our parents. The sad aspect of these visits though, was that we never knew there would come a time where there would be a last one.

When I was told about my goodbye visit, I wanted to do everything I could to make it memorable. I even wore a button-down long sleeve shirt. It was the only one I had, and it was given to me by my parents, so I felt as though in a way it would let them know I will always have a way to remember them. I could do something as simple as putting on a shirt while knowing it came from them. The last two things I was given from them had been destroyed by my previous foster home, and so I didn't have a lot of possessions to remember them by. My smashed toy car remained in my room at my new foster home, with a plastic baggie that had the broken pieces in. I would try to fix it and turn it on so I could play with it, but it was just too broken to do so. Still, it came from them, and I needed to keep it.

During my visit, I remember being stuck in my head about so many things. A part of myself knew of the terrible things I had been born into, and yet still I didn't want to say goodbye. I remember thinking about all of the ways I could remember them once the visit would come to an end, but I didn't know how I could. I hated having my earring, and yet I would have worn it in their memory, but it was tossed away. My car was broken and didn't work. I barely had any toys, and none of them came from my parents. I just couldn't believe that the shirt I was wearing was one of the few things I would have from them. What kind of seven-year-old can't even go through his things to find something given to him from his birth parents. It brought me a lot of pain and sadness that day.

The Children's Aid office had these small stuff hand-knitted doll things that they would hand out to families. A nice gesture, but cheaply made, and kind of creepy looking. I remember getting one or two of these in the past when I had a visit with my biological parents, but always knew it was given to them from the social workers to give to us. During our goodbye visit, the three of us were given another one of these. Gosh, they were creepy! Still, it created a bookmark for that day. It created a memory I could look back to and remember the last day I had with both of my parents.

One good thing that came from the goodbye visit was that a lot of photos were taken. The social workers wanted to take lots of photos so that each of us would be able to get a copy and look back to remember. These photos would be the last photos each of us would have of our parents, and for the rest of our lives when wanting to look back would have to go back to that day. For myself, I used the photos to try and remember the fun and happy moments in that short visit, but I couldn't help but feel sad. As nice as it may have seemed to be able to look back at our last memory together being a happy one, it was also a reminder that it was the LAST memory. For the time to come, I would have to go through life knowing that I could never make another memory.

Before the visit was even over, my mind was done. I just couldn't deal with everything. I remember having a small freakout towards the end because I knew I didn't want to say goodbye. I couldn't understand how these adults were expecting all of us to be able to do something like that. How does a person come to find the strength to be able to say goodbye to their own flesh and blood, knowing they will never have an opportunity to speak or see them again. The thing the adults didn't realize at the time, was there was no amount of preparation that could enable any of us to do this with ease. It was going to be something that no moral person could do. My parents were terrible, and yet, still they surprisingly had feelings. They too didn't want to say goodbye.

The end of the goodbye visit came way too quickly. When we were all told that it was the end of the visit, no one was ready. No one wanted it to end. No one was prepared to say the words. Everyone was filled with tears, and all we could do was hug each other and just hope that we would be okay. Our mother seemed more affectionate and sad that she had to say goodbye to us. I could barely understand any words spoken, but I remember being hugged tightly and told that she loved me. Tears falling from her face onto my head, her arms wrapped around me, through sobs she told me to be a good boy and never forget how much she loves me. It was a moment I could have never imagined nor be prepared for. Seeing them walked out of the room with a worker, the three of us were left alone with other workers crying and yelling for them to come back. No matter how many times we said goodbye and that we loved them, it wasn't enough.

The pain that filled me at that moment was overwhelming. My entire body ached, and I felt as though I just lost a piece of myself. Seeing the door close behind my parents made everything around me go dark, and it was then that I retreated in myself. It was the exact moment of no longer being able to see my birth parents that I lost the will for any feelings. Being taken away from our home was one thing, but when it feels like all of a sudden I was no longer able to have them in my life, how could I continue to live. What was my purpose now that I'm left alone? Without realizing and especially without knowing what it meant, I became deeply depressed. I had no idea what to expect in the days to come, and I just couldn't imagine life without them.

Chapter Eight

Adoption

The beginning of second grade at a new school gave me an opportunity to distance myself from the misfortunes that were happening in my life. Distraction was something that I needed because the thought of my goodbye visit with my birth parents seemed to be the one thing on my mind that I wanted to go away. I wasn't the brightest child when it came to education, but I did feel much joy from attending school. Up until my September 1997 enrolment, I became a bit of an introvert since the feeling of being alone in my home life was the only thing I knew. Making friends hadn't been easy because, in a way, I wasn't allowed to. I wasn't allowed to go and play with friends after school, and with the occasional teasing, I just found it easier to remain on my own.

Living on the lake where there were kids everywhere, and I was actually encouraged to make friends and play with them, slowly, I was trying to change my ways. Starting out at school seemed easier because I already knew a few kids, and so it gave me the self-confidence I never had. Needing something to distract myself from the knowledge that I won't have a family anymore fuelled my desire to make friends so I wouldn't be completely alone. I was tired of having to go through life with no one, and feeling as though I had lost my sister since I rarely got to see her, made something missing in my life. My second grade came at a much-needed time. I still had literacy issues though, since that was one thing not being changed or worked on yet.

Prior to starting grade two, I had some problems with my previous schools. Whether I was getting into mischief during recess or lunch hours, biting my teacher, screaming and swearing, throwing chairs, there were a lot of unresolved issues going on all around me, and I didn't know how to deal with them. Looking back to the time I lived at the lake and attended half of grade two in Sturgeon Falls Ontario, it seemed as though I didn't have as many behavioral issues. Granted, my foster home was a better fit for me, and the foster parents actually showed that they cared for me and wanted me in their home, which went a long way in allowing me to feel belonged. Although there were a lot of better things going on around me in my foster home, the fact of losing my biological family felt worse than anything I had to face and deal with, but instead of acting out even more so right away, it just numbed me completely.

The goodbye visit with my birth parents struck me in waves. Some days were better than others, and on the not so good days, it became difficult to not lash out. Surprisingly, I found that I didn't get into as much trouble as I had previously, but still had some bad behaved days. For the most part, I had a lot of friends at school, and teasing wasn't something as bad as it had been before, so that relieved a lot of stress. Whenever I had felt abandoned and sad from my goodbye visit, it did make me have little freak outs though. It was never anything that someone couldn't handle but was still enough to make my social worker cause for panic.

As a child, over time I developed a sense of needing to be left alone because that's how I felt. I had so many people telling me how to act, what to do, and it was confusing and bothered me. I wasn't one to show my feelings all of the time, and all I knew was to scream out my frustrations. Being on the school bus or even in the classroom, when something bothered me, I didn't want to talk about it. I didn't want to acknowledge it, and I just wanted silence so the moment of frustration would pass on its own. When someone wouldn't allow that to happen, I would burst out with yelling, screaming, or even foul language. I had been trying to work on my biting, punching, and kicking, so that wasn't the biggest of issues. My temper was the thing that seemed to spark concern in the adults in my life.

In my therapy sessions post goodbye visit, with my temper becoming the number one concern, trying to learn ways to deal with it was what was being worked on. For me, during that time the hardest part of dealing with my temper was the fact that it would just sneak up on me, and most times I wasn't in control. The sessions with the therapist turned into a way so that I could learn how to be in control. There were so many issues going on in my life and it was becoming problematic. There felt to be no way I could possibly have enough time to work on everything. It was always just one thing being worked on, and so the other issues were being avoided.

When my sessions began back in April 1997, they were only once a month to deal with the pressures from my biological home life. When I had my goodbye visit, the sessions became something that would occur every two weeks. When my behavior became something to worry about, in order to prepare me for adoption, they became weekly.

When speaking about the bullying I had faced in the past, and odd times in my current foster home, mostly from the older foster sibling residing with me, the only advice I was given was to *ignore, tell someone, walk away, and tell the individual, "So?"* Over and over I would be told the same thing from not only my therapist but social worker as well. Funny, because there I am telling someone, which was one of the things I was told to do, and yet, I was still being told to tell someone. It became a cycle that just never went anywhere. At school, I didn't really have many bullies. Only the odd times I would be teased because of my high-pitched voice, my girlish name, as well as my quiet and kept demeanor. At times, I would even be called a queer because of how I would act, and that was a word to stick much hate.

Prior to the second grade, it seemed as though the bulk of the teasing I had been faced with was actually from adults. It was mostly my father and his family. My attitude and behavior seemed *girlish*, and was always told to act more boyish, and that I should make more friends who were boys. The reason why I preferred to make friends who were female, was because of the fact that I missed my sister, and from how close we were but was kept apart, I figured in a way it was like having her back in my life. I did make some really great friends who were boys in my class though. Those friendships actually came as a great surprise and were different from other friendships in my life.

Whenever I would speak to someone about the teasing, asking for help, letting the adult know of the struggles I was faced with, it never seemed as though something would be done about it. It almost seemed as though my social worker as well as my therapist would only respond with the steps I needed to make to deal with frustrations so that they wouldn't have to personally deal with them. I was always told to tell my teacher and principal, but still, that never seemed to help either. At my school, I found that there were only two teachers who actually seemed to want to help, and they weren't even my direct main teachers.

From what I know, for the most part, my school was made aware of my situation and most of the issues going on in my life. Considering the fact that I had quite a few problems in my previous schools, they needed to be made aware just in case something happens, and they would have no idea why I was acting the way I was. Having some knowledge about my situation, and that I was dealing with some bullying which only added flames to the fire, the eighth-grade teacher, and another teacher (whom I can't quite recall what she taught, even though I want to say some form of resource or Ojibway classes. Sorry!), did everything they could to make me feel better. I remember many conversations where I would be told that if ever I was having a bad day or when something would happen, to go to them and talk about it. I remember even a few times, the eighth-grade teacher would let me sit in the back of her class, which allowed me to feel better because I knew there was someone close by who seemed to actually care about me. It was a feeling that I had hoped for and needed. I especially needed them after my goodbye visit, because the waves of frustrations always came without notice.

Up until my departure in March 1998, for my adoption, my behavior at school started out rough. I was trying to deal with the loss of my birth parents, but slowly once the process had begun to look for an adoptive family, things began to improve. I had been emotionally disconnected because the loss of my family came as a shock, and I didn't know what my future entailed. There was always the fear of more rejection, being moved around, and the separation from my sister. My school was trying their hardest to help me in finding ways to come together and be there for me. Special treatment if you want to call it something. It was actually something that enabled me to finally feel a sense of compassion from people around me. I had it in my mind that people were working against me since things just seemed to keep getting worse for me.

When losing one's family, it becomes difficult to attach yourself to things and people. Becoming disconnected from so many things because of the thought of not being wanted, desired, or needed, even loved, takes over your entire being. As much as I had tried to be okay with the idea that I had to move on from my biological family and join a new family, it was a concept that appeared to be unreachable at times. Some kids at school had heard that I was in foster care, as well as they had heard that I had a "goodbye visit" with my birth parents. Being that they were seven-year-olds, it wasn't something they could have much knowledge about, and so questions had been asked. I remember at times being asked why I don't live with my parents, why can't I see them, why do I live with strangers. It was in my second grade where teasing for being in foster care had first occurred. I had been teased for being queer, or having a girl's name, and now about my tragic home life.

Going through my second grade was not an easy task. Little by little, I was losing a part of myself because there were so many questions I had that no one would answer because I was told I was too young to understand. Of course, I was too young to have to deal with those sorts of issues, but it was too late. I was already in the middle of it all and was having to deal with them, and so I just wanted to know. Not having things fully explained, I wasn't able to properly deal with the loss of my birth parents. It felt like everything was being taken away from me as if parts of myself were being stripped away, and there was nothing I could do. There was so much I didn't know, and I thought everything that was happening was because of something I did, or something about me that was making people leave me.

For a while, it was difficult to find something, anything, to make myself happy. I didn't feel like I had any reasons to smile. Of course, the people around me had noticed that I wasn't smiling much or that I seemed happy. In my files, it states that my worker and therapist found me to be very much disconnected and that I appear emotionless as I don't smile much. During that time I was often told to smile. "Smile, Casey." "Why aren't you smiling, Casey?" "You need to smile more." I hated hearing that. I had already had to deal with people telling me to smile, even though I had no reason to. At this point in time, I definitely didn't feel like I had any reason to smile. One of the things I hated the most, was having people telling me to smile because they didn't want to see the pain I was feeling. Never mind them trying to give me reasons to put a smile on my face, they just found it easier to tell me to do it.

In one of my empty feeling days at school, there were a couple of kids asking me more questions about my situation. Kids being kids while knowing even less than I did at that time, didn't know how much the questions affected me. When I was asked why I don't have my parents in my life, not being able to answer, they proceeded to assume that it had to have been something I did. They asked if something was wrong with me. They asked me if I had done something to make them not love me, and so sent me away. What was harmless questions at first, turned into an attack, insinuating that something was seriously wrong with me. Already there had been a couple of friends at my school who had been told by their parents to stay away from me because I was a foster child. Being a foster child, there had to be bad reasons why I was there and therefore didn't want me hanging around their child in case I would affect them in some way.

While waiting for my bus one day after school, I ran into the bathroom to get away from the taunting kids, and I was crying. I was so sad because of the things they were saying to me. I didn't think there was something wrong with me, at least I had hoped not, but what if there was. I stood in front of the mirror, still crying, and just staring at myself. All I could think about was everything being asked, and while staring at myself, I was asking myself the same things. I was thinking about everything that had happened before, from living in Ottawa, watching my parents fight, to watching them fight after moving to North Bay. I was just thinking about everything that had happened and was wondering if it was because of me. Was I really that horrible of a child, to bring so much pain? Was there something about myself that doesn't allow anyone to love me? Am I so troubled that I can't be capable of any good?

After a few minutes of staring at myself, tears running down my face, it became too difficult to look at myself. I wanted the pain and fear to stop flooding my mind, and the sight of myself to go away. I smashed my head against the mirror a couple of times until I couldn't see my own reflection. Thankfully, no damage had been done to my face, but I was faced with the problem of damaging school property. Right away I feared what would happen when someone would see it. Once I was being asked if I had broken the mirror, I did everything I could to deny it because I didn't want to get into any more trouble. With no marks on my face at the time, they couldn't exactly prove that I had. Thankfully, the situation had gone away, and nothing had been done, although the adults were under the impression that I did do it.

Once I had my goodbye visit with my birth parents, it seemed as though the CAS wanted to waste no time in trying to find me a new home. Even though I was having more frequent therapy sessions, that in a lot of ways seemed to do nothing for me, it felt rushed to me. I had just had an incredibly difficult event to process in my life, and I needed the proper time to grieve my loss. There was an adoption conference in October in Toronto, and my social worker and others wanted to get myself and my siblings on the list to present us to potential families.

The process to get us prepared for adoption entailed ten "Lifebook Sessions" where we were to look over everything in our lives up until the current time. The sessions with our workers were videotaped, although I had never seen any of them. These videos would allow our adoptive parents to watch them to get an idea as to the children we were, and where we came from. It was hoped to help determine whether it was a good fit or not. Photos had been collected from various foster parents, as well as our birth parents in order for our *Lifebook* to be created. If we were to have found a home, our Lifebook was to allow us to look back and not forget about where we had come from.

At the beginning of these sessions, a few photos were taken of myself sitting at the table getting ready to begin the sessions. I was asked to smile because potential families would see these pictures of me, and I should look as happy as possible. When I was seven, I had messed up teeth. I'm not even joking. I had some teeth that were missing, as well as gaps between some, and I had what I called *Bamby spots*. The Bamby spots were actually white circles on my teeth but always reminded me of the white spots found on baby deer, hence, Bamby spots. At times I had been embarrassed of my teeth, but still, I smiled. I'm just glad that over time, they seemed to correct themselves without any work needing to be done.

Prior to beginning my Lifebook sessions, my worker had my biological mother provide some photos from when my siblings and I were living at home. Some photos of our relatives were also given. At the beginning of the Lifebook, which was basically a photo album, my mother had written some descriptions as to who certain people were in case I would one day forget. My father was illiterate, so he wasn't able to write anything. Since I couldn't read very well, as I still hadn't had any extra help with reading and writing, I had to sit with my worker in my sessions to read over everything my mother had written.

Aside from writing descriptions, she had written each of us a personal letter, that was an additional goodbye.

I was already feeling quite numb since having my goodbye visit, and there was nothing that could have prepared me for the session where I was introduced to my mother's goodbye letter. It was just a one-page handwritten letter, and yet it was the most difficult thing I have ever read in my entire life. The first time my worker had told me about the letter, he said that we would read it together, especially since I needed help to read. What should have taken five minutes to read to a normal person, this letter took about three sessions for me to finish.

For so long emotions were something that was difficult for me to not only show, but also figuring out which to feel. Being closed off, I felt as though I may not be capable of ever feeling anything again until I started reading that letter from my mother. The moment I started reading it, I couldn't help but start crying. It brought up so much I had tried to put behind me and made me remember everything. It was incredibly overwhelming, and I couldn't finish reading the letter in one sitting because it made me so sad that I couldn't stop crying. My worker and I had to spend almost three sessions to read through the whole thing because all of it at once was too much for me. That letter remained in my Lifebook, as well it traveled with me everywhere I went afterward for years to come. It became something I held onto whenever I thought of and missed my mother. That letter became something that allowed me to feel a connection to my biological family.

When I received my files from the Children's Aid Society, for privacy concerns, a lot of names had been removed to protect people's identity and privacy. It's funny, because I had never forgotten the people's names, and so was always able to fill in the blanks from all of the redactions. They even removed the names of certain pets of homes I lived at. The redactions made weren't always the greatest though, because there were many they had forgotten in some places, where in other areas, they had been removed. Printed copies were made of absolutely everything from my life while in the foster system. Everything from my Lifebook, photos, letters, report cards, plan of care, incident reports, even medical reports. The only thing that was never recorded nor copied were my own personal thoughts and reports on certain events. Whoever was in charge of the redactions, even felt the need to remove my own nickname given from my birth mother in my letter.

131

Casey   (My Boo Boo) – Redacted nickname

Casey my man I know you won't understand this but in time I hope with your strength & wisdom (knowing more) you can look in this book and have some good memories. If you choose not too that's o.k. too. It's you're wants & needs right now that have to be meet and that's why mommy & daddy want these new things for you. Why? I know it's hard right now to believe but it's because our love for you is so strong we (mom & Dad) want more in life for you than you are now getting. You're a special little boy with the brains & know how to do whatever you want. Casey don't blame yourself because you weren't bad, it was nothing you did. It's not your fault. It's mom & dad who fought and need help. But don't worry we're getting help and trying hard so we can be like we were in the picture we gave you. So please Boo (not redacted nickname) *remember that it's not your fault or anything you done. You weren't bad. Your dad and I feel you deserve more of a whole family life, a part of a family with no fighting. If your angry, hateful, or just plain mad please <u>talk</u> it out don't act out. You're life is too presious (good) to have a life like that. Be strong and when you feel the need to see dad or me look at the picture it might help.*

Boo (not redacted nickname) *remember all the good things we done & the good times we had not the bad. Remember Boo* (not redacted nickname) *it<u>'s not</u> your fault and keep on smiling. We love you very much and hope that smile of your's will never go away. You're always in our hearts and in our minds so be proud of yourself*

You're a good boy.   Love Always's & Forever
XXOO   Mommy, Daddy

The photo that had been mentioned a few times in my letter, referred to one of them on their wedding day, where they were smiling. This letter, as short as it may have been, felt like the longest thing I had ever read. It struck every emotion that had been buried deep inside of myself since having to say goodbye. The letter played with every sense I had about feeling like the reason for them leaving me in the world alone. As sad as it was to read the letter, in some ways it brought some peace of mind to me at different times. It didn't change every way I felt, because at the end of the day they still weren't in my life, and so those feelings couldn't just go away. It did help ease some of the pain, but when having to listen to other kids pick on me for my situation, it removed everything I had read from this letter. Being told that there had to be something wrong with me, that I couldn't be loved, made what my mother had written just vanish from my mind. As much as I would try to keep her words in my thoughts, the more I would hear the teasing, the less I would believe the letter.

The last few months of 1997 were stressful and difficult to get through. There seemed to be so much going on, and I was left feeling as though I was never going to find happiness again. My Lifebook sessions seemed difficult to sit through, as it just brought up too many emotions, and made me think about so many terrible memories I had. My mother in my letter spoke about me needing to remember the good times, but those were taken over from the bad ones. I had more bad memories than good, so that was difficult. So many times I didn't want to continue with my sessions because at seven years old, it just felt like something I shouldn't have to do. I was barely able to speak with or even see my siblings, and so that was another thing that only brought pain into my life. Still, everyone was telling me to smile.

When trying to find something that brought any bit of happiness into my life, I found that quite often I would sit on my bed, alone, holding my chipmunk's tail. I would close my eyes, and think how I just wanted something good to happen. I needed something good to happen. Without realizing it at the time, I was praying for something good to come into my life. I was tired of being sad and upset, and I needed something to distract me. One of the things I liked the most about my Lakeview foster home, was that I was actually allowed to watch television.

One night I was trying to find something to watch, and I stumbled across the show I had seen towards the beginning of the year. The show about a young girl saving the world from vampires. For a brief time, I had actually forgotten about the show, and so as soon as I had seen it, my eyes went wide open and I literally jumped with excitement. Some people may not understand, but sometimes when things feel so down and low in life, at times even the smallest things can change everything for the better.

It was late fall, snow was practically falling to the ground, and now that I had found my favorite television show, it felt as though all of my problems had gone away. A simple thing like a television show was the one and only thing at that time to make me forget about all of my troubles in life and gave me a reason to smile. It wasn't a forced smile but was something that came naturally. As silly as it may sound, starting to watch that show again, helped in so many other ways. Having felt as though so many things in my life were being taken away from me, leaving me in the dark, all alone, it gave me something to actually look forward to. When would the next episode be on? It reminded me that there are joys in life. They may not come as soon as you would want, but they are out there if you are patient. In some ways, that show saved my life. Finally feeling like I had something to look forward to, it helped me to try and find things to look forward to at school, and even in my sessions.

I was not the only child living at my foster home, and so things had to be shared. I was the youngest in the home, and because of my "girlish" characteristics, I was teased heavily from one of the other males in my home. Aside from the teasing, I would often be left out of things. Being someone who had been used to having siblings, I missed that bond. When we would all go swimming in the lake, I would often be left behind because I was that young annoying kid who would want to tag along. In the evenings or even in the morning, I wouldn't have a say what got watched on the shared television because it was always what the other kid wanted. Sometimes I didn't mind, so long as I could watch my show. My foster mother had seen and heard the teasing and would do what she could to get him to stop, but it wasn't always successful.

On the nights when my show would be on, but the kids shared TV that was located upstairs was occupied, she felt bad for me. She had seen how happy that show had made me, and considering the latest stresses in my life, knew it was something I would look forward to. My foster mother wanted to do something nice for me, and at times had even let me watch my show on the main television that she would normally use. When she had done that, it felt like the best kind of gesture someone could make, and always made me feel so good.

The kindness that I would receive from my foster mother always came at the perfect times. Seeing how I was smiling less and less, she could feel the pain I was in, and actually tried to do little things to get me excited about something. She and her husband would go hunting each year, and us foster children living in her home would typically go away for the few days to a relief foster family. Going hunting wasn't exactly a safe thing to do with children, and so we would never go. I didn't mind that as it was never anything I had any sort of knowledge about. I was curious though as it was a new concept to me. I wasn't allowed to go hunting, but one day they did take me to one of their hunting locations to show me the tree fort thing that they would sit in to watch out for deer. They even showed me the salt licks that were used to draw in the animals. That day we didn't end up seeing any deer, or other hunters, but it was a great day for walking in the woods, exploring nature.

On the way back to my foster parents' truck to drive back home, I tripped over some branches, and a small tree bark fragment went into my eye. I remember screaming in pain because of how much it hurt. In a panic, my foster parents rushed to my side while having no idea what happened. They had asked what happened, and if I was okay. I told them that I had something in my eye, and it really hurt. I could barely open my eye, but I did long enough for my foster mother to help get the piece of bark out. The entire drive home, my eye remained incredibly sore. Once we returned, we washed out my eye as it had become red, and eye drops were placed in my eye. It was the first time I had ever received drops, and it was a weird feeling. They put a patch on my eye, and I had to wear it for a couple of days to make sure that my eye wouldn't get infected or anything else in it. I didn't go hunting, and yet, I had my first hunting accident. As much as I can remember the pain from my eye, the joy from walking around out in the woods with my foster parents was a greater feeling. The first part of that memory that I think about.

Before the end of my stay on the lake, I had gone and stayed on a few occasions for relief at a different foster home. There was one relief in particular that has always stood out for me, for a couple of different reasons. The very small town that I attended school at, Sturgeon Falls Ontario, was primarily a French and Ojibway town. Growing up, I wasn't introduced much to the diversity in the community. It's a shame really, but for some reason in the small towns that I had lived in aside from Ottawa, there wasn't much diversity. Even at the school, I was attending in grade two, from the people I can remember, there had only been one black student. The only form of multi-culture I had experienced was that of French and Ojibway. Thankfully, one of my relief foster homes changed that.

In the thirteen years in and out of the foster system, there was only one black family that I stayed with. To be honest, they were the only family I had even seen who weren't Caucasian. Being seven years old, I hadn't been aware of the racism or of the derogatory hate that was out in the world. Thankfully, when I made my way to the foster home, I hadn't even noticed their color until years later because, it never mattered. For so long, looking back on my stay with them, all I can remember was how kind and nice they all were. They had children of their own, which gave me another opportunity to play with others. The small town that we were in does have some known racism, and I am so grateful that it didn't have an effect on me. As ridiculous as it may sound, staying with the relief family was something I look back on as something that was needed in my life.

While growing, I was developing in so many ways, and one of those ways was how I saw other people. I needed to be shown that the color of our skin doesn't matter. What matters is how we treat others in our community. Being that the community especially in the 90s was privy to racism and homophobia, I needed to be taught that those views are wrong, and it's not fair to judge someone based on something that shouldn't matter. Staying with this family was actually something that was necessary because it allowed me to for the first-time experience diversity. The kindness I was shown from the family allowed me to see past the racist hate in the world, giving me the chance to make my own conclusions that a person's skin color has no effect on who they are.

While staying at the relief foster home, the other thing that stood out for me, was the fact that it came after my goodbye visit. The only bad thing that came from my stay, was how suddenly I was struck with sadness. I remember the couple of nights how I could barely fall asleep. For some reason, I was left thinking of my parents, and even my siblings. I couldn't stop thinking about how basically I was left alone without a family of my own, and it hit me hard. I couldn't help the feeling and ended up crying all night long. The pain and sadness I was feeling was overwhelming and wouldn't allow me to stop long enough to fall asleep. That's one of the struggles of dealing with forms of grief, as it hits you when you least expect it.

During the few months meeting at the Children's Aid offices to work on my Lifebook, preparing for adoption, the time seemed to drag on. The decision was made for myself and my siblings to be placed in separate homes, and I had often wondered how their sessions were going. I wasn't allowed to know because the sessions were theirs, so it was none of my business. My sessions were taking a toll on me, because I had wondered so much if they were ever going to end, concluding with a placement.

It felt as though my sessions would never end, and after hearing that my file was presented at a conference, I couldn't help wonder what the potential families had thought about me. I was left feeling abandoned and unwanted since my goodbye visit, and it was something I couldn't help feeling. Regardless of what my mother had written in her letter, it was something that was on my mind. I would go day to day wondering and hoping that the perfect family would see my picture, read my file, and out of all of the children, would pick me. I had hoped so much that I would be chosen over others for what felt like the first time in my life.

A part of myself had even hoped that a miracle would happen, where a family would want me and my siblings. That was until I went to an event for my brother. While still at the same foster home since we were brought back into care, he started attending Cadets. I think it was Cadets anyways. Either way, he was part of some community enrolment thing. He was getting a badge or something at a ceremony. Clearly, since how fuzzy the details for what it was all about, and what he was a part of, shows how much I paid attention. All I remember was being invited to go see him, and since I couldn't see my sister, I was going to take what I could get.

I got to his foster home to see him, but he had already left. When I got to his ceremony to congratulate him on whatever it was he did, he didn't seem to have the desire to see me. We practically shared no words with one another, and it left a sore note on my mind. I was actually really upset. We had lost our family, and the tiny bit of family we still had, didn't seem to matter to him. In that moment, I changed my miracle hope of all three of us finding one adoptive family together, to just my sister and I. He invited me to his event, and yet he had no desire to even see or speak to me. It was a feeling that just added to the many terrible ones I already had.

The end of 1997, couldn't have come soon enough. December brought a lot of potential to my life, which teased me for the positive things that the new year would bring my way. I had been informed that there was a family who seemed interested in adopting me. The news came as a relief, and yet surprising. I had been spending a lot of nights holding my chipmunks tail wishing for exactly that news. No matter how much I tried to stay positive about potentially finding a home, the fact that I was getting older, only brought worry. I had been told that the older you are, generally speaking, the more difficult it can be to find an adoptive home.

Hearing the news that there was actually a family out in the world that wanted to adopt me made me really hopeful that things could finally be going my way. From what I can remember, I was the first out of the three children to find an adoptive family. The fact that I was the youngest made me realize what my workers had said to me was true; The younger you are, the better chance of finding a home. That's how it made me feel in any case. As happy as I was to have found a potential home, I was left sad for my siblings. I had no idea how long it would be for either of them to find a home, but I was really hoping that they would soon after me.

Of all of my childhood Christmas holidays, the one that has always stood out for me was that from 1997. All of the Christmas' I had experienced previously had a lot of sadness involved with them. None of them had only brought joy to me, as all I can remember from them was the fighting between my birth parents, my father's family, and then the one in 1996 where my sister had been absent for most of it. So much had changed in my life, and my time living on the lake was finally bringing some happiness into my life.

Christmas with my foster parents was a memory that could never be forgotten. I can remember waking up on Christmas morning running out to the living room where the tree was, seeing all of the presents. There were actually lots of presents for me. I had received some presents while living with my birth parents, but it was never a lot because of their financial struggles. This year was different as there were tons. One of my favorite presents were these three stuffed raccoons. It was like a little family, and I just loved them. I think I loved that present the most because it resembled everything I had wanted for myself. I can't quite remember why or if I had an obsession with the raccoons prior to Christmas morning, but I surely did afterward.

A few days before Christmas morning, I had a three-hour visit with both of my siblings. Arranged from our workers, we had spent some time opening presents from each other, followed by food and ice-skating. Christmas 1996 was the last Holiday spent with our parents, and Christmas 1997 was the last Christmas the three of us would spend with one another. We didn't know it at the time, even though we all knew there was a possibility of finding separate adoptive families. There was still so much about the adoption process that none of us knew about. Mostly, whether that meant we would no longer how contact with each other.

The afternoon of our Christmas party was a beautiful distraction. We were all left in smiles and laughter. Unaware that this would be one of the last interactions all three of us would have together, we just lived in the moment. We ate pizza, had cake, and we were even allowed to drink some pop. I hadn't exactly been ice skating before, so going to the hockey arena brought a new experience to my life. I wasn't the greatest, but still, it was a lot of fun. It was such a fun day, and no one wanted it to end. It was one of the best memories I had with my siblings and was definitely the best Christmas Holiday we had spent together.

Once the new year came, everything changed for me. Between January and March 1998, proceedings had begun for me to transition from foster care into an adoptive home. I had still been struggling with internal issues surrounding my goodbye visit but was doing my best to put those feelings aside. Hearing that I would be able to meet my adoptive family came as a Godsend. For so long, all I wanted was to be part of a family, and my birth family didn't allow for that to happen. Finally, I had that chance.

Before the move to my new adoptive family's home in March of 1998, I would meet with them a few times. The meet and greets were to introduce everyone involved so that we could find a connection. We needed to get to know each other before I permanently moved in with them. Each time that I met with them, the feeling that I was always left in, was awe. They had two daughters who were older than me. The youngest who was five years older than me was the first I had met. Each of our get-togethers went amazing. I couldn't believe how much I liked them. I had been hoping and wishing so much to be placed in a perfect and loving home. I wanted so badly for a family to come into my life that actually seemed to want me the same amount that I wanted them. Every time I met with this family, that was the only feeling I was left with. Everything they said and had done showed me just how invested they were, dedicated to giving me the perfect home and family.

With proceedings beginning for my adoption, I was unable to spend my brother's birthday in January with him. I wasn't able to spend my eighth birthday in February with either of them also. In March of 1998, just before my departure to my new adoptive home, our social workers and adoption workers planned one last shared birthday celebration. My sister's birthday was in March, so it definitely worked out in her favor. The sad thing was, this birthday celebration was more than just for our birthdays. It was in fact going to be the second to last time all three of us would ever spend time together.

Having known that I was about to embark on a new adventure into adoption, the workers needed there to be an opportunity for me to say goodbye. It became a goodbye, without saying goodbye while wishing me luck into my adoptive home. At the time, I knew that this birthday celebration had some hidden meaning, but I was doing everything I could to not let it bother me. I wanted this day with my siblings, that might have been the last, to go really well. I wanted another day like Christmas, where we had fun, laughed, created memories to carry on to wherever we would end up. I wanted this day to be as special as it felt to me.

Looking back on everything, the closer I got to being adopted, certain, and yet small things about me changed. For one, my appearance changed. It could have something to do with the fact that my teeth were finally starting to correct themselves. Mostly, I think it was because of how happier I was becoming from the knowledge that I was being given a chance at a normal family dynamic. I was beginning to dress differently too. I wanted to take pride in my appearance to represent the better feeling I was starting to feel. For the birthday party, I even wore a dress shirt and tie. Dressing up made me feel like I was wearing how I felt on the outside. It was something I hadn't felt prior in my life, and it was something I had hoped would continue.

I met my siblings at the Children's Aid offices to begin our birthday party. I can remember the surprise on both of my siblings' faces when they saw how dressed up I was. They laughed, and then I laughed because of how different it was to all of us. We had cake, took photos together, and even shared blowing out the candles. After opening some presents, we made our way over to *Airzone Play Centre*. It was a place in North Bay that did a lot of planned events like birthday parties for kids. There were slides, tunnels to crawl through, ball pits, and even bouncing castles.

As amazing as the birthday party was for everyone, it didn't leave the same feeling as the Christmas party did. We all knew I was taking off for my adoption, and none of us knew what that meant for the three of us being siblings. When it was time to leave, we were all sad, and I can remember crying a lot because I knew I had to say goodbye. I was tired of having to say goodbye to people that I didn't want to say that to. Why must I continue saying that dreadful word? I was incredibly grateful for what I had thought to be one last memory with my siblings, finding an adoptive family, but was inevitably sad for leaving them behind.

For my eighth birthday in February 1998, I couldn't spend it with my biological siblings. Instead, I was given an opportunity to visit my new adoptive family at their home for my first overnight stay. It was one of the best solo birthday's I had in my entire life. The overnight visit represented so much at that time, and it gave me the chance to see where I would be moving to and hoping to live for the rest of my life. When I got to the home, I was presented with a huge surprise.

As a *WELCOME HOME*, they invited kids in the neighborhood and from the school, I would be attending once I make the move, for a birthday party. The house was decorated, and there were so many people there to celebrate *me*. Up until that moment, I never had someone go above and beyond like that for me. I had never felt that special, and as though I could matter that much to someone, especially enough for them to do something like that for me. They had shown me some of the most beautiful and best possible love in that moment, and I hadn't even moved in yet. When I walked into their house and saw my surprise, they had shown me how it wasn't just their house. It was now my home too, and it was then that I knew I loved them. I might be moving in their home, but they had just moved into my heart. Something so simple, and yet it had such a huge impact on me. It was the first time I was able to experience something like that, and it showed me the kind of love and care that can be out there, and what I was missing from my birth family.

My birthday party was so much fun. I was a little taken back from everything I was feeling and was a tad overwhelmed from all the people, but in a good way. It was so new to me, and I was just overjoyed. I had one of the best days and met some incredible people. One of the games that were played was hide and seek. Everything up until that last game was going perfect! Being at the home was my first time, and so I wasn't used to anything. I didn't know anything about farm-life, which was what I was being adopted into, and I hadn't been introduced to the process of drying out certain vegetables. For instance, I didn't know anything about peppers.

During the last game of hide and seek played, I was in the basement trying to find a hiding spot. In one part of the basement, there was a sheet laid down on the floor with peppers on it. At the time, I didn't know what they were, so I didn't know that they were hot peppers and that I shouldn't touch them. I especially didn't know that I shouldn't touch my face after touching the peppers without washing my hands. I was curious as to what they were, so I bent down to pick a couple of them up so I could get a better look at them. Shrugged when I didn't know, and so put them back down. I proceeded to look for a hiding spot, when my eyes became itchy. I rubbed them with the hand I used to pick the peppers up. After a few moments, I began to feel a burning sensation in my eyes.

My eyes started watering, and yet burning at the same time. I had to shut my eyes because it felt as though it helped, but I didn't think anything was going to help. I screamed so loud, as I was in so much pain. I began crying and still shouting. My eyes wouldn't stop burning, and I didn't think they were ever going to. They actually felt as though they were melting while being on fire. As much fun as I had up until that moment, it was time for my party to come to an end. My adoptive parents rushed to me when I was screaming and crying. They helped to clean out my eyes, and the *pepper story* as scary as it was when it happened, became something to look back on as a somewhat funny story.

My first home visit with my adoptive family finished on such a happy note. It left me wanting more, and excited to be moving in permanently. After my shared birthday party with my siblings, exactly that happened.

Leaving my Lakeview foster home wasn't easy. I had grown attached to the foster parents, as they had done so much to try and make things better for me. They came into my life during a really traumatic time, after a terrible previous foster home. I appreciated everything they had done for me and knew I would miss them terribly. I was just so appreciative of the time I spent with them and was excited to be starting the new chapter of my life. As an adoptive child.

There are many forms of goodbye. There are so many instances that require such a word or phrase. There are so many meanings behind each time it can be used. For me, I have always hated the word. Whenever it was used in my life, it represented something being taken away, in the thought that I would never have it once again make an appearance. Typically, the word goodbye meant that certain people would be leaving my life. Here and there, the phrase was used to represent an aspect of my life, and how it needed to be said to help better myself. That comes later though.

I had already said goodbye to everyone at my school, my siblings. It was now time to say goodbye to my workers and my foster parents. If there was one thing I had learned from this past year while I lived on the lake, was that goodbyes shouldn't happen so often at once to a person. Every time it is said, it gets harder and harder. It makes the mind more and more sad. At least for me, it did. This was supposed to be a happy goodbye. This was supposed to be a goodbye that meant better things to come, leaving everything that held me back in my past. I was to look to the future, and hope for better things to come. First, I had to finish saying this dreadful word over and over.

I had always thought I deserved to be happy. I had hoped that amid all of the pain I had currently been faced with, that something would change giving me a chance at a normal life. I was tired of moving around, living with strangers, having to deal with sad briefings about my home situation. I had lost so much by the time I was eight, and I wasn't sure what else I might lose. There were so many things surrounding my life that seemed uncertain, and all I could do was have hope and wishes that things would just settle down. Everything seemed to be happening so fast, and I was being caught up in it.

Finally, I was being gifted with the ideal family situation from my lingering adoption. It came at a time where I was beginning to lose hope that I could finally have what I had always wanted and hoped for. My adoption gave me a sense of salvation to all of the horrors that plagued my life. The only thing was to move on from everything in my past and make something of my future. The only real question now though, was if I would be able to do that. Had I truly dealt with everything I had witnessed as a child in my biological home? Was I properly dealing with those traumas so that they wouldn't sneak up on me, causing only more pain and suffering? Would I be able to move on from my siblings, positioning myself within a new family? Was I too old to be adopted where all of the memories are too great to just simply ignore, forget, or move past?

With everything involved in this adoption process moving so quickly directly after my goodbye visit, was I given enough time to determine if I was even ready? Yes, I wanted to be a part of a family, especially this family, but was I <u>ready</u>? That was a question I hadn't known at the time and was something I would soon learn. There was nothing I wanted more than a happy ending for myself, my life. Was this adoption my happy ending, or the start to only more and worse problems shaping the rest of my life. I'll soon find out.

Chapter Nine

Theatre Happy

In life, there is so much time, and yet in so many ways, not enough. We go through our days creating memories, building relationships, and experiencing new things. We are molded into the people we become from those experiences and the influences in our everyday lives. There are things that can never be forgotten in our lives that hold a special place in our hearts, while other things we can only hope to forget. It is the hope that a child, born into a world of hate, violence, and ignorance, is somehow able to overcome everything to live a peaceful, meaningful, and better life. The struggles that the child must overcome should not be something that they do on their own, as they will need help and guidance from those in their life.

Like so many children who are raised in the foster system, the feeling of being alone in the world is overwhelming and unbearable. It is something that cannot be ignored and is a feeling that we cannot help but feel. We should be entitled to feel as we do, without question or judgment. Just because one adult says something, or suggests how we should feel, doesn't make it so. Foster children should be allowed to voice their own opinions on such matters without being stopped and told otherwise. Our feelings deserve to be valid because they are valid. The social workers or even foster parents aren't the ones who had to deal with the struggles and turmoil that lead to the initial foster system intake. The foster child's voice needs validation in the eyes of the adults that chose to be there to help and assist them in their recovery for a life.

In my years of experience living within the foster system, one thing I have learned was that feelings cannot be helped. At times when things seemed to be going really well for me, little things would creep up on me, and old feelings or triggers from situations or events would make an appearance. The feelings I once had even if they have no barring on the current situation, would take over making it really difficult to live in the moment. The feelings from these triggers were a sign that things hadn't been properly and fully worked out. As a young child, trying to determine and figure that out isn't an easy task. At times, it isn't even as easy as simply asking for help. There is a lot of uncertainty, and it becomes a question of what is really bothering me, and is there someone in my life that I can trust enough to share anything with. People would come and go, and building that bond where you know you won't ever be judged isn't something that comes around often.

While living the beginning years in heartache, there was much for me to work out. There were so many situations and triggers from the violence that I had witnessed in my biological home life. In my first couple of foster homes, things didn't seem to go well for me either, which only added to create blocks in my mind. These homes instead of helping me to work on the issues already in my life, just made more of a mess, that would have to one day be worked out as well. I started to have to look for ways to try and deal with things on my own because it felt as though I didn't have anyone that truly felt on my side.

The year leading up to my adoption was a long and troubling year, as so much seemed to happen at once. I was finally beginning therapy to start helping with all of the troubles, but that didn't always feel like much was being done. There were too many issues to work on, and not enough time. Trying to live in the moment, finally having something to be excited about, hearing about a family that wanted me to become a part of their family and home, gave me a brief break. The news of my adoption came as a relief that there was a possibility for normalcy in my life. The thing I didn't know at the time and was something I wish I could have known was that I needed more time to work on my past struggles. I needed to know what the triggers were so that they wouldn't confuse me and cause only more pain. I needed to be able to recognize what hidden troubles were lurking beneath the surface of my mind so that I could understand how to deal with them in a healthy way.

Becoming an adopted child isn't as simple as just finding a family and moving in right away. There are many steps involved in order to determine if it is even a good fit for both sides. I had a couple of months to begin communication and visitation with my adoptive family to see how everyone got along. Once the initial move took place, we were officially on a six-month probation period. Within these six months, it allows the family to see how the progress of integration goes, in case it turns out that it isn't a good match. Generally speaking, adopting a baby instead of a child or even teenager, tends to be easier, because the baby won't have the memories or knowledge of what happened in their biological home life.

I had heard from so many people that the older you are, the more difficult it is for finding a home. In so many ways I know this to be true from my own experience. As excited and happy as a child can be to finally find a family that wants you, letting go of whatever past you had, isn't always so easy. It's the memories that can stop you in your tracks, without warning. The smallest of things can trigger even memories that had been buried, causing you to lash out when you don't want to, or mean to. There can be things that play on your insecurities, making everything difficult to find the happiness you have longed for.

Knowing what I know now, I wish so many things could have gone different from my adoption. For one, I wish that I had more time prior to my move. Everything about the adopted family was perfect in my eyes and everything I could have hoped for. The problem wasn't with them, but were my own issues and troubles that made it an impossible feeling to have it succeed. I was on such a high of excitement in my move from foster care to my adopted family that my past had been temporarily stunned and paralyzed. I had honestly felt better than I ever did in my life, and had hoped while assuming everything would work out. My adoption only lasted two years, and in that time, it was never finalized.

The first year while living with my new family, had its bumps, but it was the second year where everything went to hell. Things kept piling up, and I was becoming the child and person I had hoped I wouldn't. In so many ways, the traits of my parents that caused my move into the foster system became a part of myself. All of the bad aspects of my biological parents that I was trying to get away from, seemed to be creeping their way into my way of living. Without realizing it, I was creating the worst version of themselves in me. There had been too many memories of living with them that stayed in my mind, and too many concerns regarding them that hadn't been talked about or worked out prior to my adoptive move.

Looking back on all of the troubles I was faced with within my adoption, I asked myself if they could have just been fixed by speaking up. The answer is no. Thinking back to those two years, had I even been made aware of the exact issues I was dealing with, and then proceeded to notify my family, it wouldn't have made the problems simply go away. The real problems I was facing were internal and needed time to be worked out. It was time that I didn't have. It was time that I wasn't given.

Before I moved in with my adoptive family, there were certain traits that I developed in a result of dealing with the abuses and problems while living with my birth parents. There were things that also arose while living in my first couple of foster homes that seemed to take over aspects of my life becoming a way to deal. Never having a proper upbringing and receiving the extra help with my education, I became illiterate. For so long I often feared speaking because I didn't want to get into trouble for what I would say, and therefore developed a slight speech impediment. It was more of a nervous tick that made me stumble on most of my words and therefore would repeat them.

Often times while living with my birth parents, and while living in my first couple of foster homes, I had to remain quiet. I often felt as though I needed to walk quietly while not making noise, because I didn't want to get into trouble, and so I started tiptoeing my way around. Without even realizing it, something I find I still do to this current year of 2019, I will walk on my tippy toes. It became habit regardless if I didn't have to walk softly.

My first two foster homes made a ridiculous toilet paper rule, which made me feel bad for needing to use the washroom. Although my last foster home didn't use this rule, still, I had the fear of needing to go because what if I use too much and plug the toilet. Would I then be made a fool once again, resulting in doubting myself in doing simple everyday things that everyone does? This feeling made me do everything I could to not go when I needed to and ended up causing a lot of stomach pain, and uncomfortable feeling.

Being so young while first dealing with violence, I had no way to defend myself when dealing with forms of abuse. I became a biter which became a way for myself to show I wasn't going to allow to be taken down. It was the only way I felt as though I could defend myself in times of trouble.

When I would try to speak up in my past, I was made to feel as though my opinions or side of the story wasn't valid, and therefore was a lie. I began to start keeping things to myself. I felt as though I was never believed, and so why bother trying to convey how I felt or what had happened if no one would listen. I started bottling up everything, doing everything I could to keep it inside of me.

Often I felt as though I was alone in the world, with no one to trust because people in my life kept going away or being taken away from me. This hindered my desire to attach to people, building relationships. Feeling as though there wasn't anyone in my life who would be a constant bond, made me want to hold onto the close friendship I had with my sister. Having her being taken away from me, kept at a distance only made the fight to keep her in my life that much stronger. It became something that I felt I needed in order to deal with the troubles within our home life, and the thought that a "sister" was something that could never be replaced lasting for life.

When moving in with my adoptive family, for a moment, all of the issues and traits that I had developed were on pause. Difficult to explain, but the feeling I had every time I was near my adoptive family made these issues disappear in a way. Not fully gone, but hard to find within me. I was fuelled by the love and devotion that these people exuded in their actions and even speech. There was a sense of calmness about them, that allowed me to feel at ease, which was something I had never experienced before. The second I walked in during my birthday visit, I felt a love that had been void in my life until that point. I had hoped those feelings would remain, taking over all of the issues buried inside of me, but as great and needed the feelings were, they weren't a solution.

My adopted parents were fully aware of all the issues and problems I had. To them, none of my problems mattered, because they still wanted me in their lives. They felt as though my issues could be worked out, and so right away began to try. Knowing that there was going to be a process, and a lot of time required to get through everything, still they remained hopeful. It's difficult to know exactly where to start when there are so many issues in a person's life. Looking back, no matter how they started to tackle these things, wouldn't have mattered. As hopeful as we all were, there were just too many to go through. Like I said, there needed to be more time prior to my move, to deal with the trauma of my birth parents.

From the start of my adoption, I was told that until I felt comfortable, I didn't have to call them *mom and dad*. They made sure to let me know that the adoption wasn't something designed to replace my previous life, but rather a chance to start fresh. Having them in my life wasn't something to take over and therefore I had to forget my birth parents and siblings. They wanted to make sure that I knew they understood it was going to be a process and were willing to wait while doing what they could to ensure I felt like a part of the family. They told me before my move, and ever since day one of living with them that I was in fact part of the family.

A part of myself since meeting them felt an instant connection allowing me to feel like I belonged with them. Although I was told from day one I could wait to call them mom and dad, I didn't want to. I did end up waiting a little bit of time, but I still didn't want to. They felt like "Mom" and "Dad."

To me growing up, the term *mother* and *father* didn't represent a parent's title. The two terms to me meant a formal way to describe who they are. When dealing with strict people, you may hear that someone will refer to them as *Sir* or *Madam* because of the fear involved with addressing them. My parents brought much fear to my life, and although wanting to be called "Mom" and "Dad," they always felt like mother and father. My birth parents never made me feel safe and loved enough to want to title them with endearment, for it felt as though they didn't deserve it. When I think of the words Mom and Dad, I think of two people who are a representation of unconditional love and devotion to the child in question. My adoptive parents were such people.

During my birthday visit, I was able to introduce myself and meet a few other children who I would be attending school with. These kids lived in the area I was in, which helped because it gave me an opportunity to make friends near me. I suffered from a fear of being teased, and at first would appear as shy and kept to myself. Before separating from my siblings, having my sister close to me helped with those feelings because at least there was one person I could rely on for support and help. Being adopted into a new home life, I wasn't prepared for the need of separating them from my birth family. Slowly I had to learn how different things would be now, but there were still things and behaviors that I clung to.

Although I had met some kids that I would be going to school with, still, my first day filled me with nervousness. Starting at a new school had never been easy for me because there were too many things that brought panic to my mind. Bullying had become my main concern, as this new school meant possible bullies I had never met before. I couldn't possibly have known how much teasing would fall upon me, if any. If I was going to be bullied, would it be an everyday occurrence? There were just too many unknowns.

On my first day of school, I could feel all of the glares directed at me since I was the "New Kid." I was feeling slightly overwhelmed by it all and didn't know what to do, or who to talk to. Had I been going to school with my sister, I wouldn't need to have worried because she would have been at my side, and just by talking to me would have calmed my nerves. Since my new adoptive sister was also attending the same school as me, I thought I would look for her. I had hoped that once I found her, I would be able to talk with her, perhaps stay close by until my nerves settled a bit, and then would get some confidence to go on my own.

Once I spotted her with her friends, I quickly made my way over to her. In the moment, I wasn't thinking that there was a larger age difference between us, five years, and so hanging out with the new little adoptive brother probably wasn't an ideal thought. She never told me to go away. She never told me to leave her alone. She never spoke to me in a distasteful manner. She suggested that I try and make new friends by speaking to some of the kids from my party, who were also my age. She assured me that I would be okay, but to give it a chance because once I talk to them, I will have lots of fun with my new friends.

My new sister never did or never said anything wrong or against me in that brief conversation. In my mind, I was just so nervous and scared and wanted something or someone to be near me that I knew so I could feel safe and secure. I should have tried to explain more to her, but I didn't, and off I went. I can remember looking all around at all of the other kids. When I realized that I didn't know anyone, and couldn't spot anyone from my party, it drew panic. I trembled in fear and worry because I didn't know what I was going to do. Already when I don't know anyone, I tend to remain shy and quiet, and that's exactly what I was doing.

In the moment of hearing what she had said to me, with my fragile and emotional mind, it made me feel as though she didn't want me to be around her. It wasn't the case at all, but because of my insecurities, it felt as though she was almost embarrassed to have me there while being with her friends. Once I knew I was out of eyesight from her, I continued to make my way to an area where I could be alone. There was this one corner of the playground where no one was. I stayed there until it was time to go inside. I got caught up with feeling distant and uneasy about my new school, as well as the assumed avoidance from my adoptive sister, that I couldn't help but cry to myself.

People say that within the first few meetings with new people, minds are made up of how you view them for time to come. Actually, I think they say it's within the first five minutes. To come up with a conclusion of what you think of them in your eyes. I've never found five minutes to be long enough, and so I prefer to use a longer timetable. The first few instances of meeting my new adoptive sister, she seemed incredibly kind, excited to finally be a big sister since she was the youngest of two. She made me feel a sense of ease on my mind because I felt as though we would be able to create a wonderful sibling bond. The moment I had with her on the playground on my first day of school, unknowingly and unfairly soured my view of her slightly.

My new adoptive parents had two daughters. There was the one I was attending the same school with who was five years older, where the other was even more older. The eldest was still living with us, at my new home, but was engaged and preparing to move out by the time I moved in. It wasn't until my final move into the home where I got to really start trying to connect with her. The difference between the two daughters in my mind was the knowledge of the age difference between myself and the eldest. I knew full well that I would never be able to have as close of a bond with her, as I had with my biological sister. I knew the two of us would never be playing silly games, running around, all the things I had been used to previously. This knowledge never mattered to me, because I was able to recognize that she was in fact older. Having the mindset of already knowing this before having the chance to start getting to know her, helped in so many ways to build the relationship we ended up having.

I was aware that there was still an age gap between myself and the youngest daughter but was so much hoping for a closer bond where I could be a kid playing with his older sister. I had spent so many years fighting for that opportunity with my biological sister, that it was something I missed. My adoptive sister was completely unaware of this at the time, and it was something I didn't know how to explain. I was just used to having a sister that I was able to play with, run around, laugh, and create memories with. In the end, that's all I wanted.

The first few months of living with my new adoptive family was an adjustment period more than anything. As excited as they all were to bring in a new child into their family, especially a boy since they only had two girls, they soon learned that they weren't just bringing in a new child. When you are adopting an older child, you are also adopting all of their flaws, issues, problems, struggles, their entire history of living. In my case, I was still allowed to have some minor contact with my siblings, and so that was another thing that was being brought into the family.

With living in a different part of the province, now outside of London Ontario, my adoption file was transferred over to the Children's Aid Offices in London. I was living with my new family under a probationary period and there still had to be meetings set up with the adoption workers there to ensure that everything is going well. The meetings needed to ensure that each person was still in favor of this adoption. I had already been used to an adoption worker out of North Bay since I had seen and spoke with her and others during my sessions along with my social worker. Way too many different workers if you ask me, as it always confused the heck out of me.

Since my first day of school, I had continued to try and connect and get close with the youngest daughter. When she would be watching TV, or playing on the trampoline outside in the backyard, I would want to tag along. To me, it wasn't about trying to invade anyone's space, especially to the point of annoyance. I was tired of being alone, and missed a sibling bond, and wanted a sister again. Looking back, I realize now that at times I pushed it too much, and would have even annoyed myself. It got to the point that she felt as though I was always around, and became needy for her attention. She felt as though she had no space, a lot of the time said how she just wanted to be left alone, and for me to find my own things to do. This resulted in the start of the tension that only grew between us.

After a while of hearing how annoyed she had become from me wanting to be around, the issue was discussed with the new adoption worker. There was a meeting within the family to discuss it, and boundaries were put in place to give everyone the space they wanted. It was an adjustment that needed to be talked about and dealt with, which it had. Admittedly, while knowing how annoyed my new sister had become of me wanting to be around, it was at that moment I realized just how different everything was. I knew at that moment that I wouldn't be able to have a sister as I once had, and had fought so hard to keep in my life. A part of me knew that I was still going to have two new sisters, but that things were going to be different. I just didn't know how different and worried that once again, I would be left feeling alone. A part of myself blamed her for this, even though I shouldn't have, I did. From that point forward I was almost too afraid to try and do things with her, because I didn't want to upset or bother her, and so at times would show disgust for her instead.

Although at times during the beginning of my adoption, there were mixed feelings from both sides, the youngest daughter did try a lot. As an outside viewer, you could tell she at first felt bad. Although she still wanted space and boundaries, she would do what she could to make it up to me. Just because she didn't want me around every moment of every day, that didn't mean she didn't ever want me around. This was a concept that was difficult for me to understand back then, which was why I acted out towards her a lot. There are so many memories I have with her that brings a smile to my face. More memories of good times than bad. The problem, in the end, was that those bad memories stacked up, and became something she, I, and everyone couldn't just ignore or forget. Still, to this day I choose to remember her from those good memories because focusing on the bad ones only becomes a reminder of how much trouble I created in her life. How much chaos I made for her.

Before my adoption, there was so much in life I hadn't experienced. There were so many things I had never done or even knew about. I hadn't even swum in a lake until this past year. People say you never forget your first kiss, your first love. I say that tends to happen to most of the "firsts" in one's life. In my case, I never forgot any of my firsts. At least the ones that occurred post infancy. During the course of my adoption, I would be flooded with firsts, and every single one of those experiences had shown me all of the wonders this world has to offer. So many of these instances were simple, and yet to me, seemed like the biggest of special events.

I had never seen a trampoline in my eight years of life, until my adoption. I had briefly heard of them, but not enough to really know what the purpose of them was. Once adopted, the youngest daughter actually had shown me how to jump on it. My first time on a trampoline was because of her, and she taught me how to jump on it while staying safe to not get hurt. I remember so many times going out to jump on that thing, and every time we did, it seemed even more fun. She even taught me some fun games to play on it. Crack the egg was always my favorite.

Being a child brought up in foster care, who had many restrictions as well as a home life that negated simple pleasures, every day within my adoption seemed to bring new and fascinating joys. My new parents were privy to everything since having spoken with the workers involved with my adoption, as well as what they read from my files. They understood in many aspects of my life, there were specific troubles I was faced with. With great confusion, I had always wondered why so many things were never tackled while in foster care, but thankfully that would soon be fixed.

One of my greatest struggles at the time was the fact that I couldn't read and write. I can remember once I made the move into my adoptive home, they had quickly realized just how much I struggled with it. One of the first things, almost instantly, was looking into ways of helping me with it. Never in my life prior had I had someone read to me. Not at bedtime, and not for help with my school work. I was quickly shown how simple it was to have someone read to me. My new parents took about fifteen to twenty minutes before going to sleep each night to read me a story.

At first, they would read to me and would ask me here and there to sound out specific words. Over time, the role of reading was switched to me, so that I had the chance to try and read the stories I was enjoying. The simplicity of taking barely any time at all once a day was already making a huge difference. The storybooks they would get to read with me gave me something to look forward to each night because I wanted to know more. Of all the things we read together, *"Curious George"* was my favorite. He was always getting up to no good, which reminded me of myself a bit. The struggles I had with reading and writing couldn't have been fixed with just reading bedtime stories to me, and they knew it. While speaking with my school about getting some extra help for me, they also looked into some private tutoring.

The private tutoring didn't occur right away once I moved in with my adoptive parents. Sometime within my first year, they were able to find a woman in our community who specialized in helping children in academic struggles. I remember going over to her house, and over the course of my adoption, I had learned so much from her. She didn't help me just with my reading and writing, but other areas of school, such as math. I had been left so far behind with my school work because of my pre-adoption home life, and so her lessons always helped. She had even given advice to my new parents on how to help me while at home. With each of our tutoring sessions, I felt as though a slight burden had been lifted because finally, I was beginning to learn something as fundamental as reading.

I had been teased a lot previously for being someone who couldn't read, and who could barely sound simple words out. While living within my adoption, at times throughout my school life, I was still being teased. With beginning to get better, it was slowly going away. I always hated when my teachers would ask one of the students to continue reading for them during a lesson, to get the children reading. I was always so fearful that my name would be called because I knew I would be that student who would be left having to sound out almost every word. On some occasions, my name would be called, and the anxiety I felt from potentially not knowing any words only made things worse. I can remember at times being laughed at from others in the classroom because I struggled so much. It was never a fun feeling, which was why my tutoring sessions were so important to me.

Finally, I was receiving the help I had always needed. By the end of my adoption, I had learned so much, and the progress I had made was something that would carry on for the rest of my life. By the end, I was actually able to read for the most part on my own, unless it was a really big word, but then would think back to my lessons. I would then know ways of sounding out the words so that I could continue with whatever it was I was reading.

There were so many things I needed to learn, in school, in life, but also within myself. My whole life I had to deal with so much trauma, and the issues that came from trauma within myself. I had never truly been able to find ways to deal with it all, and therefore acted out a lot. I needed to learn how to process everything I went through, in healthy ways of dealing. My adoptive parents were instrumental in that. It was everything they began to teach me that carried on to later years of life that would allow me to look back, and think of ways to cope with the inner pain I had. During my adoption, while trying to teach me ways to deal with stress, anger, and emotional baggage, the lessons they had bestowed upon me sadly didn't take full effect until it was too late. It was times of truly hitting rock bottom that I was able to reflect back on things they had taught me. I was able to think back to everything they were trying to teach me, which enabled me to find some inner peace. Unfortunately, it came during a time I no longer had them in my life.

In the beginning few months of my adoption, everything that was happening seemed to be an adjustment for everyone. I hadn't been able to process grief or stress at all, which didn't help with ensuring the finalization of my adoption. Processing situations, and learning the proper ways to deal with these issues was a top priority for my new parents. I can remember how much they tried to come up with new techniques in the hope that I would be able to communicate better, so I wouldn't lash out. One of these ways came from the bonding time I spent with the eldest daughter.

My two new sisters had different fathers. Although not the same father, that never seemed to matter to anyone, because in the end, they were all family. Family to them didn't mean you had to share blood. It was something that you felt within yourself, and the overwhelming and unconditional love shared with one another. The fact that family to all of them meant you didn't need to share the same blood, came as something I would cherish quite a lot. The qualities of what it meant to be a family was something I learned quickly from them because since day one they had already made me feel like part of their family.

I was a little scared at first to call my new parents *mom* and *dad*. It wasn't because they didn't feel like my mother and father. It was because I was afraid of letting go of my previous life, regardless of the fact that I wanted to, and needed to. I was scared that by letting go I would be simply forgetting them, as well as my sister, and what that meant for my future. I was fearful that once I call them mom and dad, it would lead to the insecurity of one day being taken away from them. I had barely known them, barely lived with them, and yet I had already loved them more than anyone in my life. The thought of being taken away from them was a great fear of mine because it was something I never wanted to happen.

Without helping it, one day, not long after moving in with them, the words just came out. I remember the moment perfectly. I was on the staircase, and after saying it, I was left in smiles. They were officially "Mom" and "Dad" and I didn't regret calling them that. It was a simple gesture of what they represented to me. Being able to call them that made me feel as though in some way I was repaying them back for what they were doing for me. They were giving me a chance at a life, which was all I wanted.

There was much promise and hope that my adoption was going to change my life for the better, but there were a lot of things that needed to be worked on. My anger was something that had been somewhat suppressed and would pop it's head out when no one expected it to. The reason was because the hidden anger issues hadn't been worked out, and I hadn't been shown ways to deal and cope with them. My mom and dad were trying to find ways to try and help me deal with my anger, and one of those ways came from a quiet and relaxing technique.

The eldest daughter and I at first didn't spend as much time together as I had with the youngest. It was understandable since she was preparing for her wedding, and was an adult. She was excited to finally have a younger brother and seemed extremely happy to see me every time she did. Knowing how many struggles I was faced with, and wanting to do something to help, while spending time with me, she began to teach me how to knit.

My adoption had only lasted two years, and within that time, I found the relationship I had built with the eldest daughter came with ease. I never had the tension with her that I did with the youngest. It wasn't anyone's fault, although mostly mine, but it came as a relief. A lot of the time I did feel bad that I made things difficult for the youngest daughter, and so when it came to the eldest, I was grateful that our time together always brought calmness to my mind. Needing a lot of help dealing with taking deep breathes so I wouldn't act out, knitting was a way to do that. It gave me a chance to pay close attention to what I was doing while working on my breathing. It was a hobby that the two of us shared together, which always brought some calmness to my life instead of tension and headaches.

Throughout the course of my adoption, when dealing with issues and struggles, I always found spending time with the eldest daughter to be one thing that helped. Spending time with her and her husband, always allowed me to feel safe, and gave me a sense of knowing that there wouldn't be judgment. I was around someone who had enough patience to calmly settle me down. It became time that I appreciated and created a bond that I have always looked back fondly on.

In fairness to the youngest daughter, I could very well have had a similar bond and relationship with her. It was those starting months of my adoption, that my mind had been made up from feeling the disconnect with her. I had hoped for a similar sibling relationship that I had with my sister, that I didn't allow for a difference. It wasn't something in her control, and she did quite often try to do things with me and spend time with me, but it was difficult for me to let go. I had it in my mind that I wanted a specific version of my sister, and because of that I never gave her the chance she deserved.

Every time that I would try to spend time with her, and she would ask me to leave her alone, it hurt. I remember she had a game system and had a few games that she would play on occasion. The console was located in our basement living room and would have her time where she would be down there either by herself or with friends. I had never really had a game console before, and so it intrigued me. I was so curious as it looked like so much fun, especially since how much joy I saw it brought to her. I would often try and sit with her so that we could play together, but she at times didn't seem to want me there. It became something where I didn't even really want to play, but rather just to sit with her while she played. I would insist that I just wanted to watch, but all I wanted to do was to spend time with her.

Each time I would get my feelings hurt because I just wanted to be near her, it added to my distaste for her. That resulted with me later calling her names and making her feel quite down. Feeling such a disconnect with her, I felt quite sad because the one thing I wanted the most was not just a sibling, but a sister. When it felt as though I barely had that with her, a way for me to feel somewhat connected, was to have something of hers. I at times resorted to sneaking into her bedroom when she wasn't around to try and find something that I could take so that I could hold onto it, and therefore would have something I could feel connected with. As weird as it seems, to me back then, it made sense. After noticing that a few things here or there would go missing, it was brought to everyone's attention, and so a lock was put on her door to keep me out. Another conversation about boundaries had needed to be discussed, as it was a violation of privacy.

My mom and dad seemed to always be working overtime when trying to find new ways to help me with the issues and problems in my life. One of the greatest problems I had was finding the balance between knowing the difference between what was right and wrong. Learning to respect other people's privacy was an issue that had been a problem at first, but was being worked out. One way I was helped with understanding the importance of privacy, was having my dad build a treehouse with me.

In the middle of my adoption, my dad decided that a way the two of us could spend time together, while learning the importance of needing privacy, was with the construction of my very first treehouse. To the side of our home, there was a small patch of trees that extended around our property. There was this large tree in the patch, that was in a slight opening. It was the perfect location to build a treehouse. It allowed for some privacy, while still being close enough to check up on me.

In my life, it had always been difficult to get close to, as well as trust, adult men. This was a reaction to my biological father and from all of the trauma, he had caused me. Needing to work on that, since my dad wasn't my father, it became important that I was being shown the difference. My dad really wasn't my father, in every single way. This man was kind, compassionate, driven, and showed how much he cared for the people in his life, which now included me. I was never judged, or teased by him for my "girlish" demeanor, and it was something I hadn't been used to.

The treehouse had never been finished before leaving my adoption. Towards the end, the anger that was inside of me was too great and was too difficult to deal with. I lashed out on everyone, especially my dad. I made things so bad, that we were never able to finish building it because I would refuse to spend the time with him. When things would get bad, it would make me think back to everything I had dealt with previously. Instead of taking it out on my father because I couldn't, I would use my dad as a punching bag so to speak, so that it felt as though I was punishing my father. My dad never deserved the hate I gave him, as he was always trying to show me that he wasn't like my father. In my mind, I didn't want to hear it, and I was too fearful that someday he may show similar characteristics that would bring more pain to my life. The closer I had become to him, the more I began to fear that I would be hurt and left aside while being tormented by his actions. No matter how much he tried to prove how different he was to my biological father, the fear in my mind was too great to be proven otherwise, and I just couldn't find a way to let go of my insecurities and trust issues involving my father.

When building my treehouse didn't seem to help matters, my dad tried to find alternatives in creating memories while spending time together. We lived on a farm of sorts, and so he tried to involve me with a few different things. Each year they would pull vegetables from the large garden they had on one side of the property. They would spend time jarring all sorts of things, that we would sell at farmers' markets or to friends and family. He encouraged me to help him jar some vegetables, and I found the experience to be new and exciting, and so I did. It was actually a great experience. We got to spend some time together, while I was able to sell the jars and make some money to put in the bank account my mom and dad had set up for me. I was learning so much, without it even feeling as though I was being taught life lessons.

While we had a large garden on the property, we also had an area where each year we would raise chickens. There was a chicken coup that attached to an enclosed caged area that also had some geese. I never had any farm animals living with me in any previous home, and so it was once again a new experience. I remember one year I went out to help my dad pick out the chicks that we would get to raise. The whole experience was a lot of fun to me because I found the chicks to be so cute. At the time I didn't understand that we were getting the chicks to raise so we could eventually send them to the factory to become food. I had just seen it as an experience to have farm animals that I could feed, look at, and talk to. It was another way I could spend time with my dad, and was something just the two of us did together.

When we picked up our batch of baby chickens, we brought them home to the prepared coup. We had some geese already in the caged area, and the mother goose was sitting on some eggs she had laid. Not knowing at the time, but geese can be very protective as well as vicious. I was full of excitement for the baby chickens, that I was actually proud of in a way. While my dad was placing them all in the coup getting them settled, I picked up one of the chicks. I walked over to the mother goose who was sitting on her nest. I wanted to introduce her to the new chick, as it seemed like such a happy day. When I held the chick up to the mother goose she turned to the chick, and in a quick gesture, snapped its neck while it was in my hands.

I was devastated, frightened, and now holding a bloody dead baby chicken. I had no idea the mother goose was going to react like that, and I had no idea what to do. I screamed with panic, crying because my happy day turned bloody. Not only was I sad and terrified about the baby chicken being killed in my hands, but I was worried about what would happen to me. In my life, I had been punished for the smallest of things, that were out of my control, as well as things I didn't even do. I was worried that I would get into trouble because I *should have known better*. That was one of the things I loved about my new parents. They understood better. My dad knew it was just a tragic mistake, and that I didn't realize what would happen, because I never had farm animals before. I didn't get into trouble, although I did learn a lesson that day, that the mother goose was just in protection mode since she was sitting on her eggs.

In the course of my life, prior to my adoption, it seemed to the adults around me that I should have known everything. I had always been made to feel as though any mistakes made shouldn't have been made in the first place. They seemed to think and believe that I already knew certain things were right or wrong, therefore there should be no excuse for my actions. I would always get in trouble because of it. The thing that always bothered me the most was the fact that I didn't. I never had people sit me down to calmly go over things to explain whatever the situation was. I was never told in detail what was right, or wrong, or what should have happened instead. I was just told I was "bad" and needed to do better.

One of the things in my adoption that became a great appreciation, was that I finally had people to explain things to me. I finally had people who wouldn't just react, and punish me, but rather try to help me understand what I had done. The only way I could learn so I don't keep making the same mistakes over and over is to be properly explained where I don't feel attacked, judged, or blamed. My mom and dad offered me exactly that. With each mistake I would make, we would sit down to discuss it as a family, to help me from making it again. Of course, I didn't always learn the first time, but it definitely allowed me to realize how things should be handled.

During the times where I would be left in frustrations because some things seemed too great to be dealt with, the anger inside would take over. I would yell and swear, and call people names. It was a way I was able to attack others when feeling attacked myself. I would stomp my feet, slam doors, and tell everyone to get away from me and leave me alone. The thing was, my mom and dad never wanted to leave me alone. They recognized that I was clearly hurting and in pain, which was why I was acting out in the first place, and always felt that leaving me alone wasn't going to help. They would insist my bedroom door remain open so that I knew when I wanted to, after calming down, I could rejoin everyone. For so long in my life, I had been left alone, especially while feeling alone. They always wanted to assure me that I didn't need to be alone anymore because I had them. It was a feeling I never had before, and as great as it felt, it was something that seemed undeserving.

Depending where I had been living in the course of my life, there was typically one of the adults that I attached myself to more. It usually ended up being the mother figure, as men had been a struggle to get close with. My adoption was no exception. Although my dad was the kindest, most helping man that I had met, I still found myself preferring to be close with my mom. When I look back on the time I spent being adopted, there was never just one specific thing or event involving her that showed me how much she wanted to help and be there for me. She had done so much for me, probably more than anyone, and it was every single thing she had done that always made me feel loved.

When I was being read for the first time in my life before bed, most of the time it was from her. It had become something the two of us shared together. Within time, and after advice from my tutor, the two of us started reading at other times as well. I needed a lot of help, and she was always trying to help. Towards the end of my adoption, I was given the Harry Potter books, and in order for me to go to the movies to watch them, I had to read the books first. It was a compromise that gave me something to look forward to, as well as a chance to learn and work on my reading skills. Obviously, the time had been limited, but I did continue to read them on my own once my adoption failed. Every time I think of the books and even movies, it became a reminder of the time I would spend reading with my mom and has always made me smile.

One of my favorite things to do with my mom, was actually when we would be driving somewhere. Something that was simple, and yet brought so much joy to my mind. Whenever we had things to do, or places to go, driving with her had become a way to spend more time together. We would have music going, at times would sing along, and just being next to her felt like the best of times.

I remember this one time, that still makes me laugh, was when we were running late for one of her salon appointments. Often I would go with her while she was getting her hair done, and this one time, she was slightly speeding so we would make it. We got pulled over by the police, and when the officer made it to the window, I could feel the frustration my mom was feeling. I ended up bursting out, "Now we're definitely going to be late for your hair appointment." In the moment of running late, and then being pulled over, it came as a slight comic relief that made her smile and laugh. Something so small as that, and yet has always been a memory I love.

During one of the Halloweens, I had spent with my adoptive parents, my mom had driven me all around to collect candy. There was this one memory that I'll never forget, and as somewhat scary as it had been at the time, ended up bringing laughter to us. We had just gone to a few houses to collect candy, and I was standing to the backside of her car. Without thinking, she assumed I was out of the way. I was in a daze as I was looking at all of my candy in my pillowcase. Since my costume was dark, and hard to see in the night, she thought I was out of the way so went to back up a bit. The tire slightly ran over a part of my foot, to which I screamed out. Not sure what had happened, she made her way out to check on me, but thankfully no damage had been done to my foot. I remember how bad she felt, and how worried she was, but it ended up being a funny story to tell.

Being a child with many different issues and insecurities, bonding time with both my mom and dad became something that felt needed. I needed to be able to trust them, and I needed one on one time with both as well as separately. The one on one time was to give me the opportunity for us to talk about things in my childhood, or even in the current days while finding ways to cope with them. They wanted to show me that they were there for me and that our time together was a safe space to be as open as possible with no judgment. I can remember my dad taking me for *Lime Rickies*, nonalcoholic of course, and it became something that we shared together.

While at times as a family we would all to go this one spot in the small town of St. Mary's for ice-cream and then take a walk down the river. It was a memory we would create where we were all enjoying each other's company. Going for walks became something we did a lot. A lot of the time we would take an evening walk down the road as a family, but it was also something I would continue to do with just my mom. It gave us the chance for one on one time to discuss any problems, issues, or even to just talk about our day.

Back to school shopping was a thing I enjoyed doing, especially later in life. Shopping, in general, was always fun because it gave me the chance to look at all the cool toys and clothes. I usually couldn't get anything, but at least looking at the items was enjoyable. When I was adopted, shopping with my mom made that joy even more strong. I loved walking around the mall or stores with her. As to my surprise, at times depending on my behavior, I would even get something during our trips. Our shopping trips had always been filled with so much fun. At times we would get something to eat while we were out, and since I had never been taken to a restaurant prior to my adoption, that was another new thing I was able to experience. Our shopping trips, or our car rides at some times, came after I had been dropped off at her work.

On days that my mom needed to be at work longer than anticipated, I would go to her office and wait while she finished up. I always loved going to her office. There were other people there, and everyone was always so nice. She had a close friend that she worked with, who had a daughter my age, and after a while, became one of my friends. It worked out perfect because my mom could spend grownup time with her friend, while I was able to spend time with my friend. I always valued each friendship I would make because it wasn't something that came easy to me. My mom knew this, and so she always helped me to ensure that I would be able to see my new friend so I could keep building new relationships.

There were so many gestures and things about my adoptive parents that showed me just how much they cared and loved me. The question of whether or not they did, was never the issue. The thing that had always worried me was the insecurity that perhaps one day they wouldn't, and when would that day come. Of all the ways I was shown by them just how much they cared and loved me, my favorite came whenever we were at the gym.

My mom and dad were pretty active people. They always enjoyed being outdoors, taking part in activities, as well as working out. They all had gym memberships, and once I became a part of the family, I too got one. Some of my favorite memories were from going to the gym. There was this one mall in London Ontario, where they had a massive GoodLife in the lower part. Being a small child, it at least seemed like a massive gym. There was a pool, squash quarts, a large daycare center, snack and drink bar, and of course areas for working out.

On the days that I was to stay at the daycare center, as it was also used not just for babies, but children, my mom would drop me off there. Before going to change and get ready for her workout, she would walk me to the center. I always knew just how much she cared about me, because I always knew I would see her before the end of her workout. Typically, she would always make her way back to stop in and see if I was doing okay. She may have worked out for only an hour or so, and yet still always managed to make her way to see me. Knowing that every time she would drop me off before we would leave, I would see her again because she would be expected to make an appearance. It was so small of a gesture and yet felt like such a for sure sign that she cared about me. It was something I always appreciated because I never had someone who cared enough to check in on me that much.

My mom and dad loved playing squash. Tennis too, but I think they preferred squash. A lot of the time, when we would go to the gym, they would play a round of squash with either each other, or others in the gym. I was even taught how to play, and after learning, squash became something everyone could do as a family. We at times would have matches with one another, to see who would win. It was a great exercise and was something that always made everyone smile. I was even given my own squash racket.

We as a family ended up spending a lot of time at that gym. There was always so much to do there, and every one of us always had our own things to do. I was enrolled in swimming lessons since I had only swum a bit from living at the lake. I wasn't the greatest swimmer but did love the water. Before I moved away, I got all the way up to level eight, which became something I had always been proud of. I actually still have all the badges I received, as my lessons became something to always bring fond memories to look back on.

Although loving my swimming lessons, one downfall was the creation of some insecurities.

I had never been a slender, stick-figure boy. I loved food, and although I was never "fat" I did have some extra bit of weight. There had been some other kids when I would go swimming that would poke fun at my chub, and at times would ask why I wasn't wearing my bra. It created some doubt in my appearance, and at times would make me feel too uncomfortable to go swimming. It got to the point where I would have to make my way as fast as possible to be in the water, where no one could see my chub. If I couldn't make my way into the water fast enough, I would wrap my arms around my front until I could go in. During times of feeling the most insecure, especially if we were at a beach or something, I would prefer to wear a t-shirt. I was too afraid to be made fun of and figured if people couldn't see my chub, or "man-boobs" then I would be okay. Considering how active I had become since my adoption, to this day I'm surprised that I didn't get in better shape than I was. My mom and dad understood the pain I felt about my body issues and tried their best to assure me that I had nothing to worry about.

While hoping to become more active, I started to be involved in more than just swimming lessons, as well as squash or working out. For a short period of time, I had been enrolled in Karate lessons. Those were short-lived for me though because, when I would be teased, I found myself getting into more and more fights at school. So, the need to disconnect from things that could help me with fighting had occurred. It sucked because I did enjoy the lessons, although I also knew there was truth in the fear of learning fighting techniques and using them to help defend myself from bullies. The saddest thing about becoming more and more violent in school, due to the growing bullying, was having to remove all "violent" things in my life.

Having my all-time favorite television show, which came during a time that I felt the lowest in my life, brought joy to my life when I thought I had none. Since the show was about a girl who fights vampires, it was found to be one of the things that should be removed from my life for a while. I needed things surrounding me that had no violence in them, to hopefully help with minimizing my violent tendencies. The thought wasn't so much that by watching the show I would learn how to fight, or give me ideas because that show only ever made me happy. It was just about the need for less violence in my life. Sadly, the show had fighting in it, and so it was considered violent to a young child. My mom and dad did know how much I loved that show, but they loved me and wanted to help stabilize my moods.

Something I had never been familiar with since it seemed like something that didn't even really happen, was doing things together as a family. It wasn't until my adoption that I began to learn the value of what it meant to be a family. It was only since living with my mom and dad that I was shown through activities we would do together, the importance of being a family. There were so many things we would always do together, and some of our favorite things to do together were our skiing trips. I had never been skiing before in my life, and so I began to learn. My mom skied while my dad and the youngest daughter snowboarded. I tried snowboarding but found it too difficult, and so I stuck with skiing. I did lessons and eventually found that I was pretty good at it. My lessons really helped, since often during the winter we would all take trips together. We would travel all over the place to ski at different resorts and mountains, and it was always something that was one of the most fun things to do as a family.

Since unable to ski during the summer months, we would substitute that with other activities. For the first time in my life, I was introduced to a few summer activities that we would again, typically do as a family. My mom and dad loved playing golf, and so on occasion, I would join them since I had never been before, and so I became intrigued. I wasn't much of a golfer, but I did enjoy going with them. The one thing I did enjoy doing during the summer, were our camping trips. I loved being outside in the wilderness, and so did they. We would find a campground that usually had hiking trails or bodies of water where we could swim or even fish.

Trying to find activities to keep me busy seemed like a never-ending task. Never had I had someone or people in my life who kept trying to find ways to help me deal with things. Over my two years, they tried to find so many different things. At times, some worked, but as time went on, the issues in my mind were becoming too strong to be overpowered by an activity. Going to the gym and taking evening walks had been a really nice way for distraction, but wasn't enough to help channel all of my problems. In school, I started to get involved in track and field, and cross country running. At some points, the cross-country running did help a little, as it made me focus everything on trying to control my breathing. The best part of it was that when I had meets, my parents would always be there to watch and support me. I wasn't the fastest runner or came in the top ten, but I didn't give up and always finished.

Participating in cross country running opened the door for me to want to try other sports. I had never done any sports before or been a part of any team. It was the hope that being a member of a team would help me work on getting along with others so that I could make more friends which could become another needed distraction. I began hockey and ice-skating lessons. I did that for one season but didn't actually like it. Still to this day, I'm not a fan of hockey. Nothing against the sport as I enjoy watching it, but playing, no thank you. I also tried to play baseball.

Thanks to my mom and dad, I went to my very first baseball game to watch the Blue Jays. It was a trip that brought many amazing memories and has always been one of my favorite things being done with them. I had actually gone to a couple of games with them. Enjoying my time watching the games, it was the thought to try to get me on a team since some of my friends already were. I began to start playing baseball, and I actually loved it. I played a season on the team, and every game I had one or both of my adoptive parents in the stands cheering me on. Seeing them there to support me always lifted my spirits because it showed me that they could be proud of something I did. I had done so many things wrong, that finally, I had a chance to feel pride in something.

The thing about sports though, is that they come and go throughout the year, and interests come and go as well. I loved playing baseball, but the season of playing only lasts so long, and then it becomes the point of needing to find something else. Typically speaking, whenever I am doing something that I really enjoy, things do somewhat seem to go better, because I have the distraction I need. The problem is that it's exactly that; A distraction. My mom and dad during each distraction actually tried to help deal with the issues within myself, but a part of me didn't seem to be ready for such a task. There were just too many things I didn't even know weighing on my mind, that it became impossible to work on things. One of the main things that always weighed on me because of how often it would occur, was the teasing and bullying in my school life.

When living with new people, I had always tried to find separation in comparison from those previously. The feelings I had towards my biological parents filled my head, and I never had the chance to share my thoughts and opinions with them. They caused so much pain and brought so much trauma into my life, and before I knew it, they were taken away from me before I ever had the chance to tell them. Once they were out of my life, it had no longer been about that inner pain I felt, but the sadness that they were no longer around. I suffered from mixed feelings, and I couldn't help it. Still, I had the untreated feelings of needing to make sure they knew how bad they made things for me. While unable to pass those feelings on my mother and father, I would look to those closest to me, and misguidedly let them become the focal point of my suppressed rage.

Looking back to the relationships I had built with any of my foster parents, especially with my adoptive parents, post-goodbye visit, feeling, and fearing abandonment became my worst nightmare. While I had a therapist to discuss specific issues, there wasn't enough time for me to go over everything, and have them worked out. When hearing about the news of my adoption, I had been fuelled by excitement. So much so, that all of my fears and worries went away from my mind for a bit. This allowed me to have a small taste of freedom, but the issues and fears had always been there.

Little by little, and one by one, all of my buried emotions, fears, and trauma that had been thought to be gone, crept their way back. At times when thoughts and memories would pop into my head, especially regarding my sister, it would make me sad, and make me want to spend time with the youngest adoptive sister. If I would be told to go away, or that she didn't want to spend time with me, it would tear me apart inside, remembering all the time I had spent alone.

Feelings would slowly make their way back whenever being triggered by small things because they had never been worked out. At the time, I didn't have the realization of what was happening, so discussing it wasn't easy. When feeling alone and abandoned, I would try to reach out to my sister through my new adoption worker. I used her and thought of her as a way to reach out to my previous life. I only had a few instances of communication with my sister, since her adoption process was unsuccessful, and I needed to focus on my own.

Before the summer of 1999, the issues that had been developing in my adoptive home, and the things that had triggered old feelings and memories came from my school life. Thankfully, I did have friends, my best friend even lived down the road from me. People can have many friends, and yet still feel alone, and it can take just one bully to make all of the difference. Looking back to the two years spent being adopted, there were three main bullies that seemed to make my days at school a living hell.

I lived in the country on a long dirt road. There were many houses, but it was a majority farm country, and so houses were separated from large spaces. Directly across the street from my new home, was the home of my main bully. At first, things seemed fine, as they usually start out that way until the bully is able to establish ways to torment someone. Unsure what the problems were that he had with me, became something that would no longer matter. Within our community, at times there would be BBQs, get together of sorts, where everyone was welcomed to join in for food, drinks, games, and just to enjoy the company of the community.

At first, I would enjoy these types of get-togethers because they were something I had never been able to be a part of wherever I lived. After some time had passed, this neighbor kid would feel the need to call me fefe, fudgepacker, Cassie, girlie, queerboy, just any cruel name he could think of. Anytime he would walk past me, he would whisper the name-calling to me, hoping to get under my skin. I couldn't go anywhere that he was, without him trying to find an opportunity to call me names. A couple of times, he had even gone to the extent of chasing me around calling me names.

One day, there was one of those get-togethers at his house across the street. I chose not to go in fear because I didn't like him. I remained at home but even that didn't save me, because he made his way over to my house with someone. The both of them found the need to taunt me by knocking on my doors and ended up chasing me all over the place, after making their way into our basement. Whether or not the only purpose of chasing me was to call me names, I didn't know what to expect. I didn't know if they were going to hit me, beat me up, and so I was filled with so much fear. That day they did end up hitting me.

My mom and dad were told about what had happened and weren't happy about the situation. Discussions had been made, but the teasing didn't stop. There's only so long you can boil water before it becomes too much and escapes the pot. That's the best way I can describe myself when dealing with bullying. There was only so much of this kid's persistent teasing until I couldn't take it anymore.

I shared the bus to go to school with many kids, and unfortunately that included my bully across the street. After having things thrown at me, name-calling, the house chase, I got to my boiling point. He always found it amusing especially when others were around. Perhaps made him feel good about his own insecurities when teasing someone else. I don't know, but it was uncalled for and definitely unnecessary.

Although I have always hated being teased about my feminine qualities, when people brought my personal life into it, it became something I couldn't deal with. One day on the bus, the teasing had commenced, as usual, this time had brought up the fact that my adoptive parents weren't my real parents. While laughing and in a taunting tone, went on to say how my real parents didn't want me, and how soon my adoptive parents wouldn't either.

I had already been having feelings of worry that my adoption wouldn't work out, because of my abandonment issues, so hearing this didn't help. I just couldn't take anymore, and so the monster that was inside of me came out. When I was younger, I resorted to biting because that was the only way I knew I could for surely defend myself. I knew I wasn't strong enough to punch, and so I bit him. I bit him hard, to the point of breaking skin. I screamed out of anger, vulgarly telling him to shut up and to stop teasing me.

The bus incident was the first incident where the full rage monster that was inside of me, came out. It came as a huge surprise to everyone, especially my mom and dad. Worry came with the surprise, but the only good thing to come of it was that I no longer had further issues with that bully.

When looking back to all of my bullying instances, the freak out always came from two things. The first thing that enacted the rage monster was dependent upon how often, and much teasing would occur. The second and final straw to unleashing the rage monster, usually always came when discussing my adoptive/foster care situation. There had been other instances of violence that didn't include the rage monster. He became a part of an inner version of myself when I felt nothing but rage and all things bad. It represented the worst parts of myself that had been created in the image of the bad things in my life and allowed me a chance to enact my own version of revenge. He didn't come out too often but did make an appearance every so often over the years.

A second bully came when I least expected her to. When I look back on my life, surprisingly there had been more female bullies than males. There had been a huge difference between the two, and although the male bullies tended to be more violent towards me, the females ended up hurting me more because of all of the psychological trauma they brought to my life.

There was this girl who was a year or so older than I was at my school, but somehow we managed to cross each other's paths. During the time of my neighbor's bully, she had been made aware of the torment he caused me, and how hurt I became of him. We had become friends, and for a short period of time even became "boyfriend and girlfriend." The two of us hung out often during recess, and even joined gymnastics together. That was the first experience for me, but I actually loved it! The two of us shared a lot together while we were at school. That all came to an end when we *broke up*, which if I'm not mistaken, came from her.

Once the two of us had broken up, I had hoped and assumed that we would remain friends as we were before. I was mistaken. For some reason, she had it in her mind that I was now the enemy. Along with her two best friends by her side, anytime she had seen me, found the urge to call me names. If having known all of the torment I had been going through with my neighbor wasn't enough, now I have her to worry about?

I can remember her going on about how stupid she must have been because she should have known I was queer. She kept saying how she must have been a lesbian because I was such a girl. This had gone on for a while, which became my second everyday bullying occurrence. The end of her bullying once again when the rage monster couldn't be contained any longer. The teachers at school kept insisted when I spoke about the bullying, that it's probably because she just liked me. I remember shaking my head, telling them that there was no way, and it seemed to be the opposite. Still hearing about it, they did nothing and resulted in me snapping.

One day outside it became too much to ignore while trying to walk away. She kept going on while following me, that my real family couldn't have loved me because they gave me up, and I had to find another family, who will probably do the same. Pretty much the same things I had already been teased about. Even though I had already heard the same things from my neighbor, hearing it once again from someone I once viewed as a friend hurt me even more. It made the pain I felt that much worse.

That day when she began teasing me, taunting me, following me around the schoolyard, I kept asking her to leave me alone, but she wouldn't. Finally, when I couldn't take anymore, I turned to her and put my hands around her neck. I remember screaming at her to "shut the F up" while squeezing her neck. After a few seconds, I realized what I was doing and let go of her. The teachers that were outside came running over to her and helped her up when she fell to the ground clutching her throat.

This girl was my first female bully, the first girl I had put my hands on, and became the first moment I feared turning into my biological father. Once again, since getting hurt from me, the bullying with her came to an end.

The last main bully I had suffered from came at the end of my adoption. Prior to hearing about how my adoption wasn't going to work out and was probably one of the reasons for it coming to an end, came the last time I would be encountered with a bully.

Since the strangulation incident, things had been made clear to me how unacceptable it is to react in such a way. If I would be bullied like that again, I needed to find other ways to deal with it. Over the last several months prior to February 2000, I had been dealing with secret traumas that felt to be destroying me. I was already in constant pain, so when I started grade four in September, having my last bully on occasion finding it necessary to attack me, it bothered more than it should have. His bullying didn't happen every day, but he was more violent in his torment. Pushing me to the ground, throwing punches at me became his method of teasing.

I was already feeling victimized in my personal life, and I didn't want to have someone else add on to that already felt agony. I felt as though I couldn't do anything to protect myself from what had already happened, and so I decided that instead of unleashing the rage monster where I would become violent, I would try something else.

I found a small pocket knife in the basement and decided to put it in my school bag in case I needed to defend myself from getting hurt again. I never had any intentions of using it, especially since it was old and quite dull. When I was out on the ground trying to hide from my bully, he managed to find me. When he wouldn't get away from me after I kept asking, I pulled out the knife.

I held it in my hand and said to him once again, "Get the fuck away from me." At his surprise, not knowing if I would use it, ran away quickly.

In the brief moment after pulling out the knife, I could feel the worst part of myself trying to make an appearance, but thankfully no such luck. My bully ended up telling the teacher that I had a knife, and it was then I was suspended. Although I had known I wouldn't actually use it, no one else could have been aware of that with certainty. The fact that I felt the need to bring a knife to school even if it was to defend myself against a bully made a lot of people scared, and concerned.

In all my years of being bullied and getting into fights, the end result was always the same when it happened before and after my failed adoption. Having heard about the violent behavior I seemed to be continuing to develop and lashing out towards others, it became the thought that I needed to be punished. Every time I resorted to fighting back, it was only then that the adults found the need to step in. Many times prior I had spoken with teachers, bus drivers, foster parents, my social worker, even therapist, and yet I was always given no help. Most of my bullies had been picking on me over long periods of time before I would snap back, but it was only once I snapped that something would be done about it. Not to my bullies though, to me.

I had been suspended from school, kicked off my busses, denied recess privileges, and punished in my home life. I would have some or all of whatever privileges I had in my foster home taken away, because of the fights that I found myself getting into. It was the thought that I needed to be punished and made aware that what I did wasn't right. All anyone could think about was how wrong I was, and punishment was their only thought. I knew I deserved some consequences for my actions because I always did go overboard, but what about all of the times I tried asking for help? Everyone around me when I had gone to them would tell me to just ignore them, walk away, tell a teacher or an adult. You don't think I've tried that already? Do you honestly think I would just resort to hitting back without trying all of those things for months of having to endure the ridicule and bullying? Please!

The approach everyone in my life had taken when it became after the fact of my bullying, only involved punishment for myself. While I was adopted, for the first and only times in my life, they took a different approach. While at times my mom and dad were aware of some of the bullying, I had so many other things going on in my life, and so always going to them with again another problem, wasn't something I wanted to do. Instead, I tried going to the adults at my school.

Once I would be suspended for fighting, bringing the knife to school, my adoptive parents knew in those moments that clearly something was going on.

They didn't just want to simply place blame on me, but rather try to get to the bottom of where it all started. They felt that I needed more than just discipline for what had happened. For each of my main bullies, as well as others at times, they had the thought that I needed to get together with them for a face to face apology. This apology wasn't just to have me saying sorry to them but to discuss the ongoing bullying and fighting between both parties. My mom and dad would speak with the parents of the bully, and then once agreed, we would all sit down to discuss. The hope was that we would be able to talk things out so that in the future we wouldn't have these issues again.

These meetings actually seemed to help I think because it made everyone including the parents aware of what was going on at school, and on the bus. The most difficult one of these apology meetings was the one I had with the girl. I had never felt so much shame, guilt, and remorse for anyone that I had hurt as I did for her. I cried so much prior to seeing her because of how badly I felt. Even during the time that I went to her house to apologize, I cried a lot because I didn't think I would ever be deserving of her forgiveness. Thankfully, she had shown kindness to me and accepted my apology.

The approach taken from my adoptive parents seemed like a better way to deal with the fighting and violence I had been showing since it allowed me to get to whatever underlining issues were going on. It showed me how much they wanted to help, and that they didn't just want to punish me. It gave me the opportunity to see and deal with what I had done so that I could hopefully not make the same mistakes again. Although I found it to be an excellent approach, I was just too deeply troubled, and anytime a new bully would come into my life, I retreated back to square one. The knowledge of how to deal with them just went out the window, and the process had to start over.

Towards the end of my adoption, the last attempt of trying to find some inner peace of mind came from taking art lessons. My mom would usually drive me to and from them, which was always one of my favorite things to do with her. Our car drives were always something to look forward to. My lessons even became something that surprised me, since I never really knew I liked art. I learned a lot from the classes, and they showed me just how artistic I could be when I focused. Once I was no longer adopted, I even tried to keep up with my art because of how much I enjoyed it. I wasn't the greatest artist, but it did allow me to drown out everyone and everything in my life.

Although incredibly enjoyable, my classes came to a halt when my adoption ended because there had been some new trauma that occurred in my life. I was in no way capable of dealing with or talking about the trauma that happened starting in the summer of 1999. There are some things that are easier to talk about and work out than others. No matter how much you may trust and care for someone, that doesn't automatically mean you feel as though you can share absolutely everything. As much as I loved, cared for, and trusted my mom and dad, I was overwhelmed with the feeling of shame and was terrified to share certain things with them. I had always been afraid during my adoption that something would happen, or something would be said that would change how they viewed me, resulting in me being taken away. I was fearful that one day they would realize that they didn't want me in their life, then send me back to foster care, since that had happened with my biological parents. I had never been this happy in my life, and so I was trying to everything I could to prevent that, which meant the need to keep some things to myself. Also, I had never been faced with the type of trauma that started occurring in the summer of 1999, and so I became fully closed off not knowing a single thing about what to do.

Throughout my adoption, when one on one times with my mom or dad didn't seem to help certain situations, there were other ways that had been tried to see if I would open up. I had grown quite fond of the eldest daughter and always enjoyed spending time with her. After her wedding which took place not long after initially moving into my adoption, she moved in with her husband to a farmhouse. Although newly added into the family, I was made welcome with every aspect of her wedding. That was something I always knew I could rely on with her. She always did everything she could to make me feel welcomed, and part of the family. She always tried to take the time to bring a smile to my face, and with her relaxing and calming demeanor, smiling around her became simple. I always loved going over to her new farmhouse because I was able to explore the barn and farm life with her. It was a way I was able to bond with her, building a sibling relationship that meant a great deal to me.

If there was one other person within my new family that came as a great joy to spend time with, it was my new grandma. If things at home or school were getting bad, and one on one times weren't helping, spending time with her eased my mind a lot. I think one of the reasons for taking overnight visits with her at her house, gave my parents the chance for a small break while making sure my new sister was okay with everything going on. Considering how at times I treated her, I believe it was necessary to get small breaks.

Although not blood related, still my grandma seemed eager to have a desire to build a relationship with me. This was a new concept to me because none of my biological relatives seemed to express that kind of interest towards me. I had often been teased by them, and they would often insinuate that I was going to turn out *queer*. Almost as if warning my mother and father. My new grandma never made me feel awkward, or bad about myself. And she certainly never even thought to mistreat me with cruel words. Although at times, I may not have made things easy on her, the time we had spent together was fulfilling. After a while, she had become someone that meant a great deal to me and gave me the sense of relief when needing to escape certain problems within my adoption.

Finding an opportunity to take a step back from certain issues while in my adoption was something that was becoming more needed as time went on. Both my mom and dad had been in a constant search for what could be that one thing to help me deal with the inner struggles from what I had to go through before living with them. There had been on some occasions where the activity seemed to be helping, but they only seemed to put the problems on pause and not actually help to make them go away. Even though activity after activity wasn't helping as much as the hope had been, they did seem to bring joy to my life, which was why my mom and dad never wanted to put an end to them.

There were many constant struggles I was faced with in my life. One that brought probably the most fear and pain to my mind, was that I couldn't be myself. In my biological home life, I had been teased so much from my own family for certain things I had liked, which always made me feel as though I couldn't be myself. At school, I would be poked fun at for my feminine demeanor, which only made me realize that I could never share certain pleasures or joys with those at school. The thing I loved the most about my mom and dad, was that they never judged me. Something that I hadn't experienced from people before, and it came as such a relief. Finally, I had a home life where I could be myself, and share a part of me that I had been under the impression should have been kept quiet.

I had always loved horses. I don't know why, but just looking at a photo of one always put a smile on my face, because of how magnanimous they appeared. They seemed majestic in nature, and I found them to be the most beautiful creatures on earth. At first, I had feared sharing this passion for horses with my adoptive parents because I didn't want to be teased as I had with my biological father. I was able to feel comfortable to share with them, and to my surprise, they embraced it. They had shown me that I shouldn't be ashamed of the things I liked and enjoyed, which opened a door to share so much with them.

My mom and dad had a close friend, who also had a daughter that was close friends with their youngest. This woman had a horse, who I found to be so enchanting. He was a buckskin appaloosa, which was how he received his name. Knowing how passionate I felt about horses, riding lessons had been put in place giving me the chance to experience something I never had before. I began collecting toy horses, and my dad even built me a miniature horse barn to keep them in. Knowing that I was safe from ridicule, enabled me to completely enjoy something I had always been afraid to share.

Over the course of my adoption, I would make my way over to the horse woman's house, where I would spend a lot of time. It took a while before beginning to ride her horse because I needed to be introduced to the family, as well as the horse. Communication and trust had to be developed before I would first saddle up. I couldn't just hop on the horse before not knowing a single thing about riding and about horses. Yes, I had a strong passion for them, but I knew nothing. I didn't know the proper grooming techniques, what they ate, the difference between riding English and western. There was so much I didn't know, and therefore I began learning. This woman knew how excited and eager I was to begin riding her horse but wanted to teach me everything there was to know about a horse first.

We began our lessons by going over all of the parts of a horse. She had created lesson plans, workbooks, and kind of homework of sorts so that I would be able to have the information I needed. As excited as I was to start riding, I came to appreciate her horse so much more because of how much I knew. I learned so much because of her, and with all of the lessons prior to my actual riding lessons, I found it allowed me to create a stronger bond with her horse.

I spent so much time at this woman's house, and my visits became so much more than just riding lessons. This family had been so incredibly kind to me, and in a way became a second home to my adoptive home. On times of stress and issues within my adoption, the little breaks of going to the horse house became something that allowed me to take a step back and breathe. The daughter of this home even became someone I enjoyed spending time with. At times we would go swimming in her pool, or even bond over a shared interest of a girl singing group, Spice Girls. Having people not judge me for certain interests became something that was incredibly needed. The fact that I felt comfortable enough to even share my interest in a girl group, came as a relief. More importantly, it felt really great to share that with someone.

I had always thought I loved animals, although there had been some instances in my life that would make some people think differently. It wasn't until I began spending time with the horse that I truly realized just how much I loved animals, especially horses.

When I was about four years old, my birth parents had a cat in our home. I don't know everything involved in the situation, but I ended up swinging it around by its tail, which caused it to attack me. It scratched me pretty bad, as it left a large scar on my chest. I can remember being scratched by it, but don't know why I would have swung it by its tail. It might have something to do with how at times I had seen my birth parents hitting it, so I thought it was okay.

Before I was adopted, I only had a dog living with me at one foster home. It was my initial foster home, but barely had any contact with it since it was usually left tied up outside. Being adopted, gave me the chance to have not one, but two family dogs. One female and one male, and both were different breeds. The smaller of the two, who was female, was primarily kept inside and was an everyone kind of dog. The golden lab, I believe that was the breed, was primarily the youngest daughter's dog. Not exactly having much experience with dogs or animals, I was unaware of certain "poisons" in food.

I can remember one afternoon, I had a craving for something sweet, and all I could find was chocolate. I wasn't a big chocolate fan but was hungry so figured why not. I poured a lot of the chocolate chips in a bowl and made my way to the living room. The smaller dog followed me in and kept staring at me eating the chocolate chips. She kept looking at me with her adorable eyes as if expecting me to drop some, or to feed her. I started feeding her the chocolate chips out of my hand. When she would finish, she would lick my hand, which kind of tickled, and then made me laugh. She seemed so cute, and I was having fun. I kept feeding her the chocolate chips until I became distracted and then left the living room.

Not long after leaving the living room, was I startled from hearing screams. I came rushing in and had seen that there was throw up all over the place, and the dog was laying on the floor. She almost looked dead. I noticed that the vomit was brown, and some of the chips were still visible. Everyone was freaking out, and then they found out I was the one who had fed the chocolate chips to her. I had no idea that chocolate was a form of poison to dogs, especially small ones. No one had ever told me, and so I had no way of knowing. My mom and dad were very upset respectfully, but it was then that I realized what not to feed a dog. They managed to take the dog to the vet, and thankfully she made a full recovery.

To this day, I still don't understand why I did it, as it was cause for serious alarm. One evening when we were all outside enjoying a bonfire as a family, I was stuck in my thoughts. Kind of in a daze, my mind was being flooded with so many things. Thinking about all of the bullying, the fact that I didn't seem to be bonding with my new sister which made me miss my birth sister. Although happy with my adoption, I found myself wondering what had happened with my birth parents. Where they were and if they had any more kids since abandoning their first three. The more I was being teased for being adopted, the more I found myself thinking about my birth family. It was something that I just couldn't help.

While in my thoughts, I had seen a frog on the ground. I picked it up, held it in my hand, and all I could feel was rage. I was so angry at all of the things popping in my head, that I felt the need to unleash my feelings on something. I wanted someone or something to feel the pain I was feeling. It was becoming overwhelming, leaving me numb, and no one who deserved my anger was around me. Without thinking, I threw the frog on the fire. I remember the moment I did it, I couldn't believe what I had done. I didn't know why I had done it. And it honestly scared me, because I wasn't thinking. It also scared my mom and dad. I was yelled at for what I did and then sent to my room.

It was extremely rare in my adoption that I was yelled at for something. My mom and dad weren't angry people and found reacting to things in such a manner wasn't the right way to get one's point across. I did get in trouble for things I had done, but still, it was rare that I would be yelled at. I remember this one time, I was being babysat from my best friend's sister. I loved having her as a babysitter because we always had so much fun. She would jump on the trampoline with me, which was one of my favorite things to do with people. Randomly, one day when she was watching me, we started prank calling people.

Still to this day I can't help but laugh, even though I know how wrong it was. We ended up calling random numbers, and we pranked this one-man good. We told him that he won a free vacation, and had to make his way to the airport to pick up his flight tickets and information regarding his free vacation. At the time we made the prank, everything seemed to go well, and he seemed to buy the prank. It was later that night that I found out, we had been caught. Apparently, he made his way to the airport, but there was nothing there for him. Not realizing that there were ways to track one's phone number, he called my house back and spoke to my mom and dad. The incident got me into trouble, not to the point of being yelled at though. My babysitter and I had to stop our prank calls though.

Getting into mischief was something that came easy to me. I had always been a curious child. The problem was, that my curious and mischievous ways usually resulted in me getting into trouble. The need for finding something, anything, that would keep me busy, distracting my mind from getting into trouble had been the most difficult thing to do. In the two years of being adopted, I had done more activities, tried more new hobbies, combined in comparison to the rest of my foster care living.

In the spring of 1999, before the end of the third grade, I stumbled into something that became the one thing I had been looking for without realizing it. My third-grade class was putting on a school play, and I was put in the lead role. I had never performed in a play before, and yet my teacher who I had always found to dislike me, put me as the lead. The play was an interpretation of *Jack and the Beanstock*, to which I played *The Giant*.

To my surprise, it wasn't until after the performance that I realized just how much I loved acting. When the play finished, I had so many people coming up to me, congratulating me on a job well done. Some of the people even included other kids who I had thought hated me. Everyone seemed to enjoy watching me perform, and the celebratory cheers I received gave me a sense of accomplishment I never had before. I had so many problems and thought so many people had just viewed me as a child who could do no good. I finally felt a bit of pride in something I had done, and I didn't want that to go away.

When I was performing, I wasn't the foster child or adopted kid anymore. I was able to put myself fully in a character, completely forgetting who I was, and all of the problems I had in my life. It was so freeing, and I found it gave me the chance to show people that I was capable of doing something good.

My adoptive parents seeing how excited I felt with acting, wanted to help me continue in it, as it seemed to work better than anything else they had tried. After searching, they found a theatre summer camp, where kids could sign up. Over the course of I believe three weeks, the kids in the summer program would be put into groups depending on the age brackets, and then put on a final performance. Within the camp, we would also experience singing and dance classes. The camp wasn't an overnight experience, but during the time, there were so many fun exercises that we would be able to participate in.

After being placed in my theatre group, the staff that were involved with directing and casting didn't see me as "role worthy." I didn't mind so much that I wasn't given a role, other than being a tree that got chopped. The whole experience was amazing, and I was just starting out. I was learning about acting techniques, singing, and dancing. The whole theatre camp left an amazing feeling, and I was excited to go back the following year. It gave me a chance to return after having more acting experience, and the hope of getting a role.

The summer of 1999 when I think back to it, is something that has always seemed conflicting. While certain parts of it had been some of the best moments of my life, it was also something that became some of the worst in my life. Once a child is adopted, typically there is a celebratory party. The fact that I had siblings, meant that the party needed to be waited for each of us to be in our new homes. It was a way to bring us all back together, to visit with one another, while congratulating on our steps to be in a new forever home.

Initially, there had been a planned party, however, my sister's adoption fell through almost instantly, and therefore it wasn't the right time. The Children's Aid wanted to wait until she was more stable in a home. My brother hadn't found his adoptive family until I believe a year after I found mine. The second time there had been a planned party, my adoptive family had suffered a great scare, which prolonged the party once again.

My mom was out riding her bike when she had found herself in an accident. She wasn't wearing her helmet, and so there had been a lot of head trauma. She

176

was in the hospital for a while and was pretty banged up. The road for recovery was thought to be a long one since there was much fear that her memory was to be affected. I remember being told to remain calm when I would first see her laying in her hospital bed. Already in my life, I had witnessed some scares, but nothing could have prepared me for this. I remember walking into her room, seeing her, and instantly began freaking out.

Never in my life had I become so attached to people as I had with my adoptive parents. I had often felt as though I was in a constant tare away from the parental figures in my life. The thought of possibly losing one or both of my adoptive parents was my greatest fear. Seeing my mom in that bed made me worry a great deal that I was going to lose her, and if not, what if I was sent away because they wouldn't be able to handle me. The fears I was struck with from her accident affected me more than I realized. All I knew was that I wasn't ready to leave this family. She was going to need time and help to recover, and I didn't want her to do it on her own. I wanted to be there as much as I could, so she knew how much I cared for her.

After the necessary time for my mom to recover from her accident, finally, there had seemed to be a time to plan this adoption party. The more I fought with the youngest daughter, the more I missed my birth siblings. I only had minimal contact with either of them and so I had been looking forward to this celebratory party. Looking back on everything, to this day I wish I never had that party, because of the events that would follow it.

Before my adoptive family and I made our way back to North Bay to visit with my birth siblings, I felt in a lot of ways content within my new family setting. After the first year, I had realized just how happy I had become, and to surprise, realized I would be able to let go of emotional ties. For so long I had kept my chipmunk's tail, so that any time I would feel alone, scared, I would hold it, and pray for better things to come. In times of great sadness where I would be left thinking about my birth parents, I would hold the broken car which I received on my seventh birthday. These two items held so much weight in giving me the strength I thought I needed to be able to move forward. Once I finally felt as though I no longer needed them, because of the security I found with my mom and dad, I threw them out.

It had been a year and a half since I had seen either of my birth siblings. As much as I didn't really like my brother, I was still somewhat excited to see him and meet his adoptive parents. My sister was still in foster care, but hearing that I would still be able to visit with her was what excited me the most. The day we were all able to get together was such a joyous occasion. It was as if all of us had grown so much, and yet, in some ways, nothing had changed.

Smiles and laughter filled the air that day. At the time of our party, which was the beginning of July 1999, I had yet to attend my theatre camp. So excited and proud of it, I talked about it so much to my siblings. All of us were sharing so many things that we were all doing in our separate lives, and I could tell each of us felt some form of pride. After years of heartache, having some good things to talk about and share, seemed to be one of the most important things to discuss.

While at the adoption party, it seemed as though my adoptive parents and my brother's hit it off. After seeing how happy everyone appeared to be, they decided to remain in contact, so that perhaps additional visits could be planned. Although I much would have preferred having had visits planned with my sister, she wasn't in an adoptive home, so it wouldn't have been as easy. The thing that no one saw coming, was how that adoption party should have been the last time we had been together. For all I know, having no further contact with my brother could have possibly saved my adoption.

Before summer's end, my adoptive parents as well as my brother's got in touch with each other to plan the first adoptive get together. After seeing both of my siblings in North Bay for our celebratory party, it did make me miss them. My sister was not in a good place and was experiencing quite a few problems while still being in foster care. Unable to make similar plans with her, I figured I might as well take this opportunity to visit with my brother. The two of us had never been close, so I saw this as a chance to start fresh.

My mom and dad brought me to a part of Toronto where my brother and his new family were living. Whitby to be exact. I had never been there before, so the travel was something to look forward to. At first, everything seemed to be going great! We had all formally met, so we were able to not worry about an initial meet. My brother's new mom and dad, both seemed like really great people, and so I was truly happy for him.

I remember the day when we arrived at my brother's house like it was yesterday. I can remember my brother wanting to bring me around his neighborhood, and then down to the docks where his family had a boat. The entire time we were out walking around, being shown his new life, he wouldn't stop talking. He kept going on and on about his new friends, his new family, all of the things he gets to do and see. He also seemed quite happy to now be an only child, since his adoptive parents had none of their own.

I understand the excitement he must have felt for becoming a part of a new family. The problem was that he took it to the extreme of being so selfish to not even give me the chance to talk. He seemed to have stories after stories to share with me, but still, I remained quiet. I remember thinking how had this been my sister, even if she would talk so much, at least we would be laughing because of how she always put a humorous spin on things. I was most definitely not laughing, and I was becoming bored, and just wanted to go back to my home.

Once the evening came around, all of us decided to spend time in the living room chatting and playing games. The time seemed to go by quite fast, and before we knew it, it was time for bed. I was sharing a room with my brother for our stay, and since he had a large bed, we were supposed to share it. It had been a long day, and I was ready to fall asleep!

Our adoptive parents remained downstairs while my brother and I were supposed to be going to sleep. I brushed my teeth, got on my side of the bed, and was ready to call it a night. Once again, my brother felt as though it was a perfect opportunity to talk, although he should have just gone to sleep. At first, I just thought he was making idle chit chat, but to my shock, it became something I never saw coming, nor had any way to prepare myself for.

While laying in the bed, he turns to me and says that we are no longer brothers. I had no idea what he was talking about. Yes, we are half-brothers, but still to my knowledge, that made us brothers. I told him that we were brothers, and asked why he would even say that. He knew full well how important having a familial bond in my life was, so first hearing that was a small jab. He sits up in the bed and repeated his comment. "No, there are certain things that make people brothers, and we haven't bonded that way, and so we are not brothers."

At this point, I sat up too because I had no idea what he was talking about. He told me that when he lived in his previous foster home, he and one of the sons there had what he referred to as "Brother's Bonding" which made them brothers. Since he and I had never bonded like he had with the other, we were not brothers. At this point, I was wanting to start crying, because he was making me feel like how I always felt with him. I felt as though he didn't care for me, and was just throwing me to the curb yet again. He told me that just because we are not brothers now, that doesn't mean we can't become brothers. He asked me if I wanted to be his brother, and to my oblivious mind to what was going to happen next, I said yes. I told him I wanted to be brothers because I already thought we were.

He grabbed me by the arm, right above my wrists, and put my hand on his crotch. I pulled away instantly and asked him what he was doing. He told me that it's okay. "It's what brothers do. By doing this, it will make us brothers." I told him that I didn't want to do that. I said that's not what brothers do. He replied that he thought I wanted to be his brother. He grabbed my arm again, putting it back on him. I pulled away again and said that I didn't want to do that. There were a lot of things I didn't understand, nor knew about, but this was something I knew wasn't right. I knew that this wasn't normal, and was something that shouldn't be happening. I remember hearing everything that my sister had to go through with our father, and in our CAS meetings, we were told about the importance of keeping our *private parts* to ourselves.

After pulling away for the second time, I insisted that I wasn't going to touch him, and then I turned over to go to sleep. Once I was facing the other way, he grabbed my arm again, only this time tighter, making it difficult for my nine-year-old strength to pull away. Clinching above my wrist, once he put my hand on his crotch, he began to move it around in a rubbing motion. I tried to pull back my arm and asked him to stop because we weren't supposed to be doing that. He insisted that it's okay because afterward, we will be brothers like I wanted. I told I didn't want to be brothers anymore, and that I just wanted to go to sleep. While still holding my arm with one of his hands, he used the other to try and push my head down. I told him to let me go, and if he wouldn't stop I was going to call out to my mom. His hand was removed from my head, but still had a grip on my arm with the other. He said just a few more seconds, and then he let go.

There are so many things I remember as clear as day in the life, and the look on his face after he finally let my arm go, was one of them. He turned me, had a smirk on his face, and said to me; "See, that wasn't so bad. And now, we are officially brothers." He went on to tell me that the only way we could remain brothers was by keeping this between us. He told me that I wasn't allowed to tell anyone, because this was something that could only be shared with brothers. He continued to tell me that there was nothing to worry about, as we were done and could go to sleep. By the end of my visit, I was so sick and tired of hearing the word brother and was grateful for having so many sisters.

He went to use the bathroom, and I was at that point sitting up in the bed, unsure what just happened, and what to do. I remember thinking about everything my sister had to go through, how hurt she was, but how nothing ever happened. She had told so many people about things our father and others had done, and still, nothing came of it. I was thinking to myself what if I say something and the same thing happens to me. What if nothing will happen, and then I'm left having to deal with it all alone. I loved my adoptive family, and I felt safe with them and trusted them. The problem was, that I was so fearful that if I were to mention this, what it could mean for my future.

Once my brother returned from the bathroom, I got up and said that I needed to use it. I walked right inside, locked the door, and started to cry. I didn't want to make noise, so I was trying to be as quiet as I could. Tears were falling down my face, I looked in the mirror, and remember thinking how awful and disgusting I felt. I washed my hands right away because all I could feel was dirty. I splashed water on my face, and then caught my breath so I could stop crying. I dried my hands and face and then started to very slowly unlock and open the door. So many thoughts were filling my head at that point, and still, I was at a standstill as to what I should do.

Once I opened the door, I could hear our adoptive parents, and while looking down the hall from the bathroom, all I wanted to do was yell out to my mom and dad. No words and no sound could leave my mouth, and I felt stunned at that moment. The fear of not knowing what would happen if I tell them was too strong. I already had so many problems in my life, and I didn't want to add another and risk ending my adoption. As much as I wanted to call out to them, I opted not to and wanted to try and put the incident behind me.

For the remainder of our visit, my brother oddly enough seemed better. He wasn't ignoring me as much and actually treated me like a brother. I wish he didn't, because I was just ready to be home, away from him, where I didn't have any brothers. Not knowing what had happened, our respected parents seemed to have enjoyed themselves, and so they insisted on making more plans to get together at a later time.

I knew if I wanted to get over what had happened, I needed to try and put the situation out of mind as if it never happened. I needed to think back to before the visit and stay in that mindset. Seeing how it affected my sister, made me realize it may not be easy, but that it could be done. Up until Christmas 1999, I did exactly that, although at times had some issues.

When being bullied, a few times had my arm grabbed, which made me think back to my brother, and it freaked me out. I felt numb and unable to do anything about what my brother had done, and I didn't want that to happen again. Whenever a bully had grabbed my arm, or called me a queer, it triggered what had happened. Instead of the usual telling them to leave me alone, I resorted to extreme foul language, yelling, and hitting back. I wasn't able to defend myself against my brother, and I wasn't going to let a bully do the same. In a way, yelling and fighting back, was my way to get back at my brother, wishing it was him I was yelling at or hitting.

The added aggression and acting out didn't start escalating until after my Christmas holiday of 1999. I had thought what happened in the summer was behind me, but I was reminded with even more trauma. A Christmas holiday had been planned with both my brother's adoptive parents and mine to take a skiing trip to Mount Tremblant in Quebec. Thankfully, during this vacation, I wasn't sharing a room with my brother, and so I felt some relief. The thing was, any chance that my brother seemed to get when it was just the two us of, he felt the need to try and grab my arm again.

I kept pulling away because I didn't want him to be able to get a tight grip. I tried to stay close to my mom and dad, or at least always have someone else around so I wouldn't be alone with my brother. With having no luck getting a hold on my arm to touch himself again, he began to show hostility towards me. I didn't mind, because there was no way I wanted to have happened what did in the summer. I wasn't ready to say anything at that time, only because I was still worried about the possibility of being taken away from my adoptive family.

The whole Christmas trip had my brother not wanting to be around me, which made our parents wonder why. I remember being told that I needed to get along with him and that this whole trip had been planned so we had a chance to see and spend time together. Wanting to tell them what happened, I was always stopped. I was thinking that the only reason why my brother was avoiding me, was probably because he was fearful that I would say something, while also being pissed off that I kept pulling away at his advances to grab my arm. The situation was causing me to remain in my head, as I couldn't help but have an internal conflict on what I should do. Typically, when I was having internal thoughts bothering me, I lashed out on others around me. This usually gave me the chance to get my revenge of sorts for the issues I had, regardless of the directed person wasn't deserving of it.

During my Christmas holiday, I lashed out at my adoptive sister. My brother had been avoiding me, and I needed to lash out at someone, and she just seemed like an easy target. I remember feeling quite bad about it because she was always the target of unnecessary attitude and feelings hurt by me. She never did anything wrong, but this was the only way I knew how to let out the feelings trapped inside my mind.

The last time my adoptive parents made a get together with my brothers, was during February 2000. The visit was close to Valentine's Day, and I was at the point where I didn't even want to see him. Still, I wasn't ready to talk about the previous couple of visits, and so he and his parents made their way to my house. Thankfully it was a short visit.

Up until my brother and his parents were about to leave my house, there seemed to be no incident. I made sure to do whatever I could to ensure that he was never alone with me. I didn't want to give him another chance to try anything. Thinking that since nothing thankfully happened during Christmas, maybe it made him realize what he had done. I had the hope that he wouldn't try anything again since he didn't until the end of the visit.

In the evening of the last day, my brother and his parents were at my house, I had a Valentine's Day party at one of my school friends' place. Before my brother was about to leave, which was the same time I needed to leave for my party, I went up to my room to get ready. Getting ready for my party, my brother came up to my room. At first, I just thought he was going to talk, and say goodbye. I was sitting on my bed, putting on some socks, and then he sat beside me.

Without even saying anything he once again grabbed my arm and put it on his crotch, and tried to rub it around. Feeling beyond enraged, I took back control of my arm using more strength than I thought I even had. Although his grip was strong, finally I felt as though my strength was greater. I told him that I wasn't doing that again. I told him that wasn't what brothers do, and that I was his brother even if I didn't do it. Trying to keep my arm away from him, I stood up so I could go downstairs. He stood up, and instead of grabbing my arm, he grabbed one side of my head. He leaned in and placed his lips on my neck while holding onto my head. I tried to pull away, told him to stop since it was actually hurting my neck. I pushed him off of me and told him to leave me alone.

My neck was hurting where he grabbed me, and also where his lips were. I didn't know why it was hurting, and so I made my way to the bathroom to take a look. I noticed that there was a mark on my neck. A hickey. And I didn't know what to do. I had heard of them but never had one before. I began to freak out. I tried to wash it away with water, but it wouldn't go away. I went back to my room and told him to look at my neck. I told him to look at what he did. I asked what I was supposed to do. I so badly wanted to start crying, because I thought that because of the mark now my parents are going to know, but I wasn't able or ready to explain what had happened.

It was time for my brother to leave, and so we were called to go downstairs. Freaking out because I still didn't know what I was going to say. I tried to find something to cover it up, but I couldn't. My parents had seen the hickey, and immediately became freaked out. They knew what a hickey was, and I could only imagine what thoughts they had to have had. They kept asking what had happened. Where did it come from? But I became speechless.

I had the chance to finally speak about what had happened, and after seeing how freaked out they were, more than ever, I felt as though I couldn't. I thought I would rather them think what they wanted than to tell them everything. I kept saying I don't know. Tried to say anything to avoid the subject. I just couldn't get any words out and began to cry.

I had my Valentine's Day party, which came as a great welcome because I needed some time to get away from the situation. My brother and his parents left, and I was so glad. I never wanted to see him again. I was told that after my party, there was going to be a discussion because they wanted to know what had happened. My dad picked me up from my party and had tried to talk with me, but the entire time I was hoping nothing would be mentioned. Trying to keep from crying, I just kept saying I don't know.

I have never felt so disgusting and ashamed in my life. I have had some pretty terrible incidents and situations throughout the course of my life, and nothing compares to what I had to deal with from my brother. So badly I had hoped the anger and sadness I felt from what he did to me would go away. So badly I had thought by not talking about it, would make the problems go away. I just wished I never had to see him for those visits. I just wished that the whole situation could be put aside because I didn't know how to deal with it. I so badly wanted to speak with my mom and dad and tell them everything, but the pain and worry I felt was too overwhelming. I didn't know if they would understand, and if they would still love me.

On February 20th, 2000 I was told that my adoption was not going to work out. Over the last two years, there had been problems, situations that caused alarm within my mom and dad, and so they kept requesting to extend the adoption probation. My adoption had never been finalized, and so they were able to extend in the hopes that things would get better. Since the summer of 1999, problems in my life had only escalated even more than before, which made things so much more difficult to deal with. The anger and aggression I was showing became more evident, and lashing out to others became more frequent.

Aside from the usual frustrations of being a foster child with struggles and worries, what happened with my brother only added to them. He caused more pain to me than anything else I had dealt with, and it caused me to act out more violently than ever before. Fighting was becoming the usual way for me to deal with bullying and any means for disagreeable conflicts.

My mom and dad were not able to extend the adoption probation any longer. I don't even know if they would have wanted to. Problems within our home seemed to be getting worse, and they still hadn't known what actually occurred with my brother. I had just been suspended for bringing a pocket knife to school. I was making their youngest daughter feel frightened from my behavior, and I was mistreating her by constantly calling her names. Things just seemed to be not going well, and they were out of options. I know they had wished the adoption could have worked, as I could tell they loved and cared about me. The problem was, they just didn't know what to do anymore, and they needed to think about their daughter, and how this was affecting her.

I remember feeling more sad hearing that I would be returning to foster care than I ever had before. I cried so much, begging them to not send me back. I kept thinking how in a way, I was glad that I didn't tell them what my brother had done, because, without knowing it felt as though they were sending me away. What would have happened had I told them. I asked them when would I be returning to foster care, to which they responded with February 24th.

My tenth birthday was on February 23rd, 2000. A day that should have brought excitement, and happy memories. Instead, I was left feeling nothing but sad. I didn't want the day to end, because I knew first thing in the morning I would be picked up, and taken away. I wanted to try and enjoy my last evening with my adoptive family, but it was difficult. Everyone seemed sad, and emotions were taking over. It was hard to enjoy what was known to be our last day together.

Before the start of my adoption, I never knew things would get worse for me. There were so many issues I had that I didn't realize or were even made aware of until it was too late. I walked into my new life, with my new family head held high. I was so hopeful thinking that I would be able to put my past behind me, but on so many occasions, I realized it wasn't so easy to do. As much as I wanted my adoption to work, and no matter how much I thought I was ready to move on, things got in the way. I thought I tried to make my adoption work, but it was made clear that my mind wasn't healed from what had happened in my life before. I was living in such a happy place, and I had been in a happy mindset when I initially moved, that the problems I had were not visible.

I have often wondered if I had more time to sort through my mind from the issues I had from early childhood if that would have been enough to ensure my adoption's success. There were too many *what-ifs* and *what could have been done differently* in this situation. All that was certain, was that I felt as though I was moving on in my life, in reverse. I was supposed to be moving forward, to better things, and yet I was going back to where I had started. I was going back to foster care and didn't know what that would mean for my life. I had been so hopeful for a better life, a better future, and I had the perfect family. What were the chances that I would be able to find that again?

Having to say goodbye yet again, was something I didn't want to do. I didn't know how I was going to be able to do that with my mom and dad. They had shown me all the great things life has to offer. They had given me a reason to smile. I was just so down on myself for allowing things to get so bad, that it only created even more conflict within myself, that I didn't know if I would ever be able to get over or work through. And now, only time was going to tell.

Chapter Ten

Sky

Forgive me. I haven't finished crying yet. As I try to wipe away the tears streaming down my face, I might as well let them continue to fall, because they aren't ready to end. I try to understand what happened, what is currently happening, and what will happen. Nothing makes sense to me, and it was as if I was left in the thickest fog. I left my foster care life behind me so I could be placed with an adoptive family in the hopes of regaining a life that seemed lost. Two years later, and I'm right back where I started. The only difference is that I am driving in the opposite direction.

Once my adoption came to a messy end, it seemed as though all I knew was how to go into my new life, backward. I had spent so much time in the hope that I would be able to move forward, away from all of my past troubles, but this ruined me. This failed adoption that meant the world to me, left me feeling as though there was no way to be picked back up. I was at my rock bottom, and I couldn't imagine anything getting better for me. In many ways, I was right, because having my adoption failed was only the start to even more problems.

I have never been in denial that situations and things just kept piling up within my adoption which made it too difficult to continue, which was the result of it ending. I was the reason my adoption failed because I was just too damaged with my past. I allowed it to take over and was unaware of how to ask for help, and with most of those situations, was too afraid to. Always having known it was me and only me to be blamed for the best thing in my life to come to an end, made it that much more unbearable. The guilt I was faced with was something I wasn't sure if I could ever get over. Then again, I was beginning to realize that had I been more prepared and had the issues actually dealt with prior to moving, things might have ended differently. Perhaps there would have been a higher chance that I could still be living with my adoptive family instead of moving to my new foster home.

I spent most of my drive back towards North Bay staring out the window. I was covered in shame for allowing myself to be returned to foster care, and couldn't bring myself to look or speak to the woman driving me. I had known her from a couple of years earlier, which only made the situation feel even more real. Not to mention the fact that she didn't even appear to want to talk to me. She seemed as though she was angry at the fact that I could have let things get so bad after all the hard work to find me the perfect home. It wasn't as though I purposefully sabotaged my adoption so I could continue living with uncertainty, and without stability.

During my drive which became an all-day event, I barely felt the desire to talk. I was feeling so disappointed and angry at the situation and just needed time to myself. There were a few moments where on occasion this woman would speak up. Having just dealt with the most difficult goodbye of my life, I was in no way ready to discuss what had happened with my brother. If this woman was going to choose to speak to me, it was the hope that the topic of what happened with my brother was not going to come up. Every time she would begin speaking, my whole body began to tremble, and I was left hoping she would say nothing about my brother. I wasn't ready to talk about him. I wasn't able to come to terms with what happened. I didn't have time to sort things out on my own, so prayed that this woman would say nothing!

I guess when you hope and pray for something so much, it's possible that the universe comes through for you. The problem was, it became something I almost hoped wouldn't happen. The entire drive to my new foster home was a very quiet and awkward drive. Although hoping my brother wasn't a topic of discussion, it turned out that it wasn't. Not just with the drive, but moving forward in life, nothing had ever been discussed. Not one single time had I had someone sit me down, to ask me what happened when I was adopted.

I had really hoped I wouldn't be asked, but I think a small part of myself was waiting to see if someone would show me they cared enough to find out. I think a small part of myself wanted to be asked the difficult questions making me feel comfortable enough to confide in them, which would allow me to start healing. I just wanted anyone to want to help me. Not one single time and not one single person ever bothered to.

Once I was returned to the foster system, I decided I wanted little to no contact with my brother. I needed to find my own ways of dealing and healing and figured the best way would be to find separation. Anytime a social worker would remotely discuss my brother, all that would be said was that "he is still in his adoption, and if I choose, I may continue to contact him. If I would want visitation, it would have to be supervised." I remember hearing so many times that IF I wanted visitation it would be supervised. One might assume to ask why that is, but no, it wasn't asked. One might assume that perhaps the fact that my two-year adoption came to a messy end, I might be full of many unresolved feelings, and might need to discuss them with someone. Someone who talks to people about problems for a living, but that never happened. Not only did I just experience a tremendous loss, but there was also something clearly bothering me about my brother. I just couldn't believe how oblivious everyone was, and didn't even think to ask if I was okay, what happened or make me speak with a therapist once again. I didn't have a choice to speak to one before my adoption, so why would now be different.

Looking back to my first year after my adoption failed, I know with full certainty that I suffered from some forms of depression. The thing I don't understand is how not a single person was able to figure it out. In all fairness, I would say that it was most likely a mild case, as I did have a lot of periods where I was happy as I could be. I believe the only reason why I didn't spend every waking hour crying although I remember wanting to, was because of my new foster parents.

One of the greatest fears I had while being a foster child, was the unknown regarding placement. Typically, you don't get to choose where you live so you never have an idea about who the foster parents are, if there are other foster children there, what kind of house and rules do they have. Before my adoption, I had stayed with several different homes, three full-time homes, with even more relief foster homes. There was only one I actually truly enjoyed and so there was the fear of what kind of new home I would be moving to.

The worker and I began driving down this one road before the end of our long drive, and I remember looking at all of the houses wondering which was my new one. All of the houses actually looked pretty nice, and I was becoming excited. There was the worry that you'll end up in a small, crowded, and unclean house, and so seeing these fairy large homes excited me. I was told that we were just about at the house, and then we pulled up to it, turning clicker came on.

We turned to the right, into the driveway, and I remember looking at the house thinking WOW! It was one of the most beautiful wooden style homes I had ever seen. It looked massive to my eyes, and then the front door opens. Three other kids, who all looked to be teenagers, made their way out of the house. And then what looked like a horse came running out. It was the biggest dog I had ever seen. The first thing that popped its way into my mind, was how I hoped the other kids weren't going to become my new bullies. When you start at a new school, or at a new foster home, there's always the worry of whether or not you will get along with others. I did not have a good track record when it came to new bullies finding their way into my life. I was just really hoping that I would be able to live here without the fear of being teased on a daily basis.

Once I made my way out of the car, the new foster mom made her way out of the house behind the other kids. She had a big smile on her face while she greeted us. She asked the other kids to help bring in my belongings. I couldn't help but think how amazing that was since I for the first time in my life had a lot of belongings. It was going to take me a long time to bring everything in, so the help that was unasked, was very much appreciated.

My worker, my new foster mom, and I, all sat down in the kitchen at the table for the initial introductory meeting. We were introduced to each other, and then we went over why I was being placed in my new foster home. Nothing had been mentioned about my brother, except that there was an *inappropriate touching incident*, and that we were to have supervision if a visit was put in place. The worker also included that there was *no need to go into detail regarding it*. She spoke about how I was placed within my adoption home for the past two years, but then things started to fall apart, and the decision had been made to not finalize it. I was sent back into the foster system, where I had been previously on and off since the age of two due to many issues within my biological home life. The worker went on to describe all of the potential future issues that I had prior to my adoption, which for some reason there had been a need to rehash them. Never mind I had new issues, but the old ones I thought were behind me, now became a part of my life once again.

So many times in my meeting, I kept thinking that there could be no way this woman would even want me in her home. This worker was not painting me in any light and seemed to only want to mention all of my misdeeds, even the ones that happened once, years earlier. The worker spoke about how although the adoption hadn't been finalized, I would be allowed to continue contact with the family, should both parties want to. The fact that I found enjoyment while performing in community theatre, and was something important to me, it was mentioned to my new foster mom. Should I want to continue to look for opportunities to perform, that could be something they would look into for me.

By the end of the meeting, after hearing everything being said to my new foster mom, I couldn't help but wonder if I even liked myself. It made me feel as though all anyone sees in me was trouble, cause for worry, panic from my violent behavior, and wondering if I could ever get better. The thing I didn't know at the time, was that had any other foster parent listened to all of the things being said about me, they probably wouldn't have liked me. Thankfully, my new foster mom wasn't like any other foster parent.

My foster mom was in complete understanding that I came from a troubled past and had just been through even more pain from dealing with my adoption failing. She and her husband had been foster parents for a long time and knew that my past is a part of me, but shouldn't define who I am while living in her home. I have always believed you tell a lot from a person, from the impression given off by their home. My first impression of this new home radiated warm embrace feelings, which became evident with how my foster mom seemed.

Once the worker left my new foster home, it was time to get settled in, but to my surprise, all of my belongings had already been taken up to my room from the other kids. I was not used to that type of kindness and welcoming feeling from a foster home before. First nights are typically the hardest because everything is new. There is so much to get used to, and there's so much you don't know. My first night went a lot better than I could have expected. Any moments I did feel sad because of the fact I was no longer with my adoptive family, I played with my birthday gift.

Over the past year or so, while trying to find a new television show to get into since my favorite had been considered too violent for me, I became obsessed with Pokemon. For my tenth birthday, I was given a new gameboy, and yellow version of the Pokemon game. I also got what you could call a cheat sheet book for the whole game. It showed me maps and clues to get through the game. It actually helped me a lot. The game was the last thing I got from my mom and dad, and so playing it always made me think of them. I knew there were going to be many sad days and nights, and this game helped me a lot.

My whole life I had always been an emotional person. Most times, I couldn't control my emotions, which was why I was always encouraged to try and work on controlling them. I easily cry, because I was always under the impression I was undesirable to those around me. I always felt attacked because it never seemed as though I was being heard when I would try to speak up. Every time a new situation came into my life that felt to be holding me back, or when a placement fell through, I retreated in myself thinking there has to be something wrong with me.

My birth parents gave me up for adoption because they would rather send us away than trying to work out their problems. My adoption failed because of how troubled I had become. These were the thoughts I had regardless if they were true, because in the end I had to look at the bigger picture, and the evidence pointed to these conclusions. I had been bullied so much, and even they had teased me about this. The thoughts were driven so deep in my mind, it was too difficult not to think this way. At the point of moving to my new foster home, I was flooded with the fear that I was damaged goods. I worried that there would never come a time where I would be able to regain some self-worth.

One thing that really helped when I moved to my new foster home, was the fact that I already knew one of the other kids. When I lived in the Hell House, one of the foster kids that would come for the occasional relief stays, was this kid. He wasn't the Demon Child, thank goodness. Having at least one person I already knew, made a huge difference because that meant not every aspect of this new placement was new and uncertain. The other great surprise was the fact that my new foster family attended Church every Sunday.

Prior to being taken away from my birth parents, I attended Church on my own since no one else in my home wanted to. Going to church when I was able to, gave me a safe feeling, which was something I was missing in my life. When I was adopted, they too attended Church. I was baptized Catholic, but my adoptive parents were members of a united church. At the age I was, I didn't understand or know the difference. At the time I just knew it was a church, and everyone was getting together in a church to pray to God. The lessons and teachings seemed the same, and so I never questioned the difference. My new foster parents attended *The Church of Christ*, and that made me excited.

Now that I was no longer adopted, I felt the need more than ever to attend Church. It was when I was ten that I started to get into my faith more. I finally knew the importance of prayer, and since I felt as though I needed much guidance, praying to God seemed something I would do since I had so many questions about where to go from here.

For the most part, the time I spent at my new foster home with the massive dog, was something I always looked back on fondly. Yes, there were issues and problems that crept their way into my life, but overall the experience was one to never forget. The first little while after my adoption, I spent many nights crying myself to sleep. Being someone who was overrun by their emotions, the one constant emotion I had was sadness. The anger and frustration was on a break, and for the first while I blamed myself so much, and the pain I had was replaced by sadness.

To what I can remember, I only had one true nightmare in my childhood. For some reason after all of the horrors I had witnessed as a kid, still, there was only one huge scare that I will always remember. When I was adopted, I had my first movie theatre experience. Prior, I had never been to a movie theatre, and yet I had always wanted to. I went quite a few times and loved every one of those experiences. Not thinking about it at first, I went to go see The Mummy. A movie that to this current day in 2019, is one of my all-time favorites. The movie wasn't exactly terrifying, and yet, for some reason, it made me unable to sleep. My mom and dad had the most difficult time getting me to fall asleep because I couldn't stop crying from the horrible nightmare I had. I was left fearing that I would be eaten from the mummy. Looking back at it now I laugh, but can't understand why it scared me so much.

While living in my new foster home, my nights of sleep always made me think of my adoption and the problems I had. I would wake up upset and scared, because of the fear that my mom and dad didn't even love or care for me. I was plagued with the thought that I could never have that again, and it terrified me even more than the mummy dream. The greatest struggle I was going to be faced with during my time in my new foster home, was trying to figure out where I belonged. There was the unknowing of what will happen to me now that I've returned to the foster system.

I was still a *Crown Wordship without Access* and therefore had no legal rights to my birth family. I had zero desire to continue contact with my brother, and I was told that I would have to wait a long while before it was even considered to restart a relationship with my sister. My adoption had ended, but I was allowed to continue to call, write, and even see them. Still having them in my life was something that meant a lot to me, but still, it confused me because I didn't know what that meant. Was the occasional contact a way to have them say goodbye to me, or were they staying in my life in the hopes that one day we could try again to be a family?

After a few days of living in my new foster home, I was brought to my new school to be enrolled. At the time, I had the last name of my adoptive family. I still don't know if the name change had ever been legalized, but was asked if I wanted to continue using it. I remember the first time I wrote my new last name during my adoption, the feeling I felt was empowering. Looking at it written down on paper, brought a smile to my face, and made me feel like I actually had a place in this world. The name had shown me that there actually was a family in the world who cared so much that they gave me their name. It was the best feeling in the world.

When I was sitting in the office at my new school, I took a few moments. I had no idea if I would ever see my mom and dad again. I had no idea what my future had in store for me. All I knew was that I felt so alone and that I once again had no family. I felt as though if I kept going by my adoptive family's name, it would just leave me miserable. Every time I would have to see it, I would be reminded of the fact that I had everything I ever wanted and was the reason for it no longer being a part of my life. That was something I didn't want to feel. I didn't think I would be able to handle it, and I needed to try and pick myself up. That day was when I started using my birth name once again, and it hit me hard. I felt incredible when my name had changed prior, but this time made me feel the opposite.

When a person suffers a loss, the grief that they feel is something they can't control. To lose someone, they don't have to die in order for it to be considered a loss. The loss is represented by the absence in your life. Prior to my adoption, I had lost many people. I often wondered if I would ever be able to overcome the losses I had. Before having the time needed to handle the losses, I was sent into my adoption. The happiness I felt replaced the grief, but it was only a temporary feeling. The loss had always been there, and it was now that I was back in foster care that those feelings came rushing back.

Once entering into my new foster home, I once again was in an adjustment period. I was told that my foster parents were in the process of designing a new home to where we would all be moving to once it was built. Building a house was something I had never experienced, and so I became excited to go through it with them. Until the spring, when we would move from our home, I went through my days trying to figure out my new place in the world. I needed to find balance post-adoption and needed to find the stability that had been taken away from me.

Having wished to be a part of a family for so long, and then finally finding it with my mom and dad, that desire once again came to me. I wanted so desperately to become a part of a family again but feared getting close to people. Every time I had gotten close, it would be short-lived and I would move somewhere else. My new foster parents surprised me with their kindness and overwhelming love shared with all of the foster children. I honestly felt as though I hit the jackpot with the foster home on the lake, but this one felt like an even bigger jackpot.

My foster parents had six children of their own, who were all grown up and moved out. They had many grandchildren, and so the family was big. Over time, I would be introduced to each of the family members. They were all so different, and yet, the one thing they had in common was the overwhelming love. Every time my foster family would visit with one of the children and their spouse and or children, they would treat us as if we were part of the family. Having been taken away from so many families, feeling alone, it came as something I desperately needed.

Over the time I spent with this foster family, there were three children that were around more often than others. One of the sons and his wife was where we moved to while the new house was being built. Another one of the sons and his wife ended up moving close by which made it easier to visit with them. I don't know why, but the one son's wife had a voice that resonated calmness. I don't know if it was a slight accent that she had, but I can still remember always asking her to say *car*. It's hard to explain and to be honest, I don't know why. For some reason, her voice just had this quality to it that was like being hit with something that relaxed me. I think after a while she became annoyed because I would always ask her to say *car*.

The third child that made more appearances than the remaining three, was one of their daughters. Of all of the six children, I think she was the most outgoing. She had this rock star personality, and every time I would see her, I just knew I would be in smiles and laughter. Each of the six children became a huge part of living with this foster family, and each of them all did what they could to ensure us foster children felt welcomed.

By the end of spring 2000, my adjustment period in my new foster home seemed to go fairly well. It certainly wasn't perfect, as there had been the odd time where I found myself getting into trouble. Thankfully the issues weren't extreme and had been able to get resolved easily. I wasn't being faced with daily doses of bullying at school, which definitely helped. I was having slow contact with my mom and dad, which always gave me something to look forward to. I never found it to be enough, but this was the time to focus on me, and I had to try to resolve the problems currently in my life.

If there was the ideal foster home to be living after having an adoption fail, it was this one. I have always felt as though there couldn't have been a more perfect placement for me to help deal with the losses in my life. I struggled with the desire for belonging and family, and although I felt as though it had been voided once again in my life, my foster parents' family picked up those pieces. It became something to admire, and appreciate. Even during yearly holidays, we, foster children were always made welcomed to stay and participate.

By the time it was Spring when we would move to our foster parents' son's house with his wife, we were one foster kid down. At the start, there had been four of us, but after a couple of days living there, one left due to problems in his life. There was another kid in my foster home who had begun the process of adoption, which was something I was familiar with. As much as I should have been happy for him, it was difficult. Seeing this foster kid go through what I could remember about starting out in my adoption, raised too many memories and feelings.

I was starting to slightly heal from my failed adoption, and having someone else show their excitement for their adoption became overwhelming and undesirable. Of course, I had become jealous, because I missed that feeling, and all I could think about was my mom and dad. I was left wondering if they were still my mom and dad and if one day they would be once again. I was not someone who was in control of their emotions, and so it was difficult to control.

The son and his wife became the one child of my foster parents that were around more than anyone. Truth be told, they were my favorite, even though I found the others to still be favorable. They too had a Great Dane, which meant for a while there were two living with me. Two massive dogs to play outside with, and two massive dogs to make me feel safe. We all lived with the son and daughter in law until the Fall. They were both filled with so much joy and excitement. The son had the spirit of a young man, which helped when we would have days spent on the water. The new house was being built on a lake, and after long days working on the house, we would all enjoy ourselves with being out on the water. We spent so much time that summer swimming, boating, water tubing, and everyone participated.

As excited as I initially was from the idea of helping my new foster family build their house, there was so much I wasn't expecting. Every aspect of this was something I hadn't experienced prior, and so there was a lot I never knew. I never realized just how exhausting some days would be. I never realized just how much work would be needed. At the time of living in my foster home, at times I hated being outside so much. It was later in life that I actually came to appreciate most of all from living there.

There was so much to experience from being outside and having experienced it, I would much rather be outdoors now than staying inside all day watching television. We as a family would watch some television, but for the most part, especially during the days, we would be outside. The outdoors was our TV, and we were to create the program being watched. Okay, that was a lame, but still, there was always so much fun to be had outside.

When I would become tired, any control I may have had on my emotions went away. Being tired has always been my weakness in lashing out, and it seemed as though I could never think before saying or doing something. I would become agitated, and small things would seem like monsters. Then again, I also still had a lot of internal issues needing to be worked out, so having those thoughts also didn't help when I would be tired.

In the summer while trying to help my foster parents the best I could being ten years old, I found myself getting tired often. I was not used to being outside so much, and I especially wasn't used to the things I was experiencing. Tempers flared at times, but during those times were tantrums that they could handle. The odd time I would find myself not getting along with the other foster children, but that never lasted long. Having known that there wasn't going to be *the perfect foster child* who was never going to get into trouble, my foster parents knew I was trying. They understood that I was going to have rough days. It became a matter of trying to show me how I was acting, and what I needed to do to fix the problems I was having and creating. The way about they did it, was something I wished everyone did.

They never resorted to screaming at us when we did something wrong. They would recommend that we take time out to breathe and relax. Usually, there would be somewhere that we, usually me, would go sit. We would stay there until we had calmed down, and then we would speak with them about what had happened. Trying to get us in a settled state of mind always helped us become aware of what had happened so that the issue at hand could be fixed. They never wanted us to feel ignored, and so it was important that while taking time out we knew we could rejoin everyone, but only when things had settled.

The summer of 2000 came with much to be excited for. Finally, after so long of asking and begging for contact with my sister, I would have my first visit. When hearing that I would be allowed to have a visit, I was filled with excitement. For so long I had wished I could get back in touch with her, and after everything I had to deal with my brother, I knew things would be better with her. I never had to worry about crossing boundaries, or feeling ashamed because of being inappropriately touched by her. We were siblings, and she had always made me feel safe. It was something I had missed and was something I needed. I never really wanted contact and visitation with my brother, and what he did made me appreciate my sister even more.

There had been a few times where my sister and I had written to one another, but it was very sporadic in nature. When we saw each other for the first time after so long of no contact, we were both filled with happiness. It made me feel like I had a family once again, which was a feeling I missed most. I remember during our visit, her foster mother had organized a few arts and craft things for us to do. We each made some things that we would give to the other. Pictures, and whatnot. They were actually decorative things that I still have to this day. It marked the start of us reconnecting, and became something that resembled importance in my life. I tend to keep all things that have important meaning from a point in my life, and that day I was able to add to my collection.

If finally being able to see my sister once again wasn't the best news I could have received, being told I would be able to spend time with my mom and dad definitely was. We had been keeping in contact via telephone and letters. Knowing how much I struggled with my literacy, they had the hope that I would continue while living in my foster home. They even gave me incentives so I would continue practicing my writing and reading. In my letters, I would write a certain amount of sentences, and if it was enough, I would get a special treat to congratulate me. Knowing how much I enjoyed art, it would usually be something to do with that.

The planned visit with my mom and dad wasn't as long as I had hoped, which meant I wasn't able to go back to the theatre summer program. The visit actually gave me hope, because I had been feeling in the dark in regards to where we stood at the potential of being a family. Although extremely excited to spend some time with my previously adoptive family, I would soon find out that my visit wasn't what I had in mind.

Although being able to spend some time after months of no visitation with my adoptive family, I was also told about how it had been planned to include my brother and his family. Still, at this point, no one was aware of what had happened, and so it gave me mixed feelings. I had been working very hard to put the incidents behind me so that I could move on, and not have any more blow-ups. I had felt as though, finally, I was making progress, so there was concern about how this visit was going to affect that.

Thinking that the best possible thing I could do would be to pretend as though the previous incidents hadn't happened, I would try to get through this visit. I went into my visit with the thought of showing forgiveness towards my brother. I really wanted to enjoy my time with my adoptive family, and with having him on my visit, I needed things to go over well. Thankfully, we had never been alone together, and there wasn't a time where he tried to grab my arm. We had gone horseback riding, which was something that brought much excitement since I had missed dearly my horse riding lessons. Although nothing bad happened with my brother during the visit, there was some hostility shown towards me from him.

I was actually surprised since he was the one who had caused me such pain and grief. So much I couldn't believe how his adoption continued, while mine had to come to an end. It felt so unfair that since I was the one who had been afflicted with abuse from him, that he was the one who was able to continue within his adoption. Then again, I didn't speak out, because I was still trembling with fear and disgust.

The visit I had with my mom and dad went extremely well. We were able to remember the feeling of being together, and it made us all miss it. The summer visit with them became the start of more contact and visitation in the time to come. Everyone seemed to be filled with hope that we may be able to work on fixing the issues that were in my adoption. It was the hope that perhaps one day it could be something to revisit down the road.

By the time Fall of 2000 came around, I was in a weird place emotionally. Things had picked up in regards to contact with my adoptive family, but things started to slow down with my sister. We had some visits during the summer, but by the time fall came around, she had moved to a group home out of town, which made visiting more difficult. I thought there was progress in reconnecting, but it was stopped all of a sudden. I knew at the time that she was having some problems, but so was I. We were the only family, the only blood family either of us had left. Both of us had felt so disconnected from life, and staying close to each other became extremely important.

197

While trying to understand the separation that was happening with my sister, I was trying to be excited about the fact things were picking up with my adoptive family. My school life was going okay, although the odd time I was experiencing slight bullying. The one kid finally had moved out to be with his adoptive family, which only made me sad and reminded me that I couldn't with mine. We were still living with my foster parents' son and daughter in law, although for a short while longer.

Unable to progress all of the different types of emotions I had been feeling, I never knew how to act. When someone would say something that I didn't understand, or took the wrong way, I felt attacked. I would lash out thinking the worse. Feeling uncertain about so many things, it had become difficult to ascertain situations around me, and I always assumed the worst. It seemed as though people were working against me, even though they weren't, and it affected my moods. I was easily frustrated, and trying to control my moods was still something I hadn't dealt with. I actually felt bad, because here was a family who had done everything they could to show me how much they cared, and yet I still managed to assume they didn't.

I had many miniature blowups while living with my foster family with the Great Dane. I ended up living with them for a little over a year, and within that time, only two major blow-ups come to mind. The first happened in the fall of 2000 before we were able to move into the new house. The second came at the end, which resulted in my departure into another foster home.

The thing I wasn't able to recognize during my stay but became something so clear later, was how with each of my blow-ups, my foster parents still wanted me around. A lot of the time, I didn't make things easy on them, and yet in the end, still tried to make me feel wanted within their home. The tried their hardest to show they weren't giving up on me, which was something I had really hoped for.

Before we moved into our newly built home, I had my first giant blow-up, to which the rage monster made an appearance. I had been stuck in my head, thinking everyone was working against me. I had it stuck in my mind that things in my life were seeming sour and that I was never going to make progress. I was snapping at everyone in the home, and I was unable to listen to what was being said. It was a big problem I had back then. The thing about it was that I had actually begun to really love this family, and I was being overwhelmed with the fear that this home would too come to an end. I would once again since finding a home, and family that I admired so much, would be taken away like my previous ones. It was something I was unable to comprehend and therefore lashed out.

Within my freakout, I was about to storm off when my arm had been grabbed so I wouldn't just walk away. It wasn't grabbed to the extent of harm, but rather when you want to keep someone from taking off. It had actually been the first time my arm had been grabbed since my brother, and with it being in the same spot, I was flooded with having to remember what he did. All of the memories I had been trying to forget came rushing back. If there had been any hope of things settling down, at that moment there was none. My mood escalated, and my demeanor became aggressive.

When the incidents with my brother occurred, I felt incapable of helping myself. I wasn't able to escape his grip, and I felt more fearful than any other time in my life. In the moment with my foster parents, I didn't want to feel trapped again. I wanted to show myself that I wouldn't be held down and that I could find a way to leave the situation. At the moment, all I knew and could feel was the need to leave. I wanted to leave the situation, and a part of myself felt as though I wouldn't be able to continue living there as I wasn't capable of dealing with the trauma of my brother.

I took off from the house and ended up running off towards the new house. I didn't know where I was going, but I knew I just needed to get away. On the way to the new house, I ran into a friend from school. I needed a distraction, and I took advantage of the situation. I made a call to the CAS to ask to be removed because I was manhandled. I definitely overplayed the situation, as I wasn't harmed. I just needed a way to leave the situation behind me. I had the overwhelming feeling of needing to exaggerate things because the freakout came from thinking of my brother. I wasn't ready to share that with anyone, and so I needed a way around it.

I still can't believe to this day the level of compassion my foster family had, because they still wanted me to stay with them. After everything I had done and said, they still seemed to want to foster me. It was something that came as a surprise to me but was something I would forever be grateful for. In that moment it showed me that I really did have people in my life who wanted me around, and that cared for me.

Once the freakout became something of the past, things were able to slowly get better. My mood and behavior seemed to slowly improve, which made things go a lot better for me in my foster home. I was continuing my phone calls with my sister, which always helped. My contact with my adoptive family also continued, and there had been talks of going to spend the Christmas holiday with them.

Finally after so long it seemed, I was once again finding myself to be a part of a theatre experience. My school was putting on a Christmas musical, and I was cast as the lead. It was a combination of Disney stories, and my part was

The Big Bad Wolf. I was actually a little surprised I was cast as the lead because I was not a singer. I did enjoy singing but was definitely not any good. Being cast in the musical brought a great and needed distraction in my life. It gave me an opportunity to find pleasure in doing something that showcased me and my talent. It allowed me to forget all of my problems, and I was focused on wanting to do something people could be proud to watch.

To my surprise, when I had started driving to and from the new house starting in the summer, I recognized a house. Whenever we were driving somewhere, we would always pass this one road, and something about it seemed familiar. After a while, something clicked, and I remembered why that one house seemed familiar. It was the house that my biological father's parents lived in.

Curious about it, and not realizing the court order in place meant I wasn't allowed any contact with any biological relatives, excluding my siblings, I drove my bike to the house. I had minimal memories of them, and since wishing for some familial bonds, I decided to make my way over. It had been years since I saw them, and so had wondered if they would even recognize me. They had a yard sale going on in their front yard, and so it was a perfect opportunity. I began walking around, and sure enough, I recognized a couple of my biological uncles and grandparents. At first, no one recognized me. It took a bit of time, and then finally I said who I was. Oddly enough, they appeared excited to see me. They wanted to take a group photo together, and so I did.

I was still dealing with insecurities of my weight, feeling overweight and ashamed of my man-boobs, and of course, the moment had to be ruined. My paternal grandfather while taking a photo, moved his hand down and squeezed one of my man-boobs. I don't understand why, and it definitely didn't make me feel good. Here I was trying to have a moment, but of course, the fact that I had a bit of extra weight made him feel the need to inappropriately show he also knew.

My father thankfully wasn't there, because I definitely wasn't ready to see him, nor wanted to. I made my way back with my foster sibling who waited for me on the road. I spoke with my foster parents and shared with them that it was in fact my biological grandparents' house. Unsure if it was something I was even allowed to do, they said they had to inform my worker, and that until I hear anything, I was to stay away. I understood where they were coming from because being a crown ward without access had a lot of questions involved.

When I began attending school in the fall, I was approached by a girl a little bit younger than myself. Somehow she recognized me and asked if I remembered her. At the time I did not. She informed me that she was actually one of my cousins, from my biological father's side. It intrigued me, because I had been wanting to feel like I had a family again, and so I embraced it.

When Christmas came around in 2000, the biggest thing on my mind, was the school play. I felt so much joy from rehearsal, and I couldn't wait for people to watch. I hoped so badly that people would think I did a great job, and actually couldn't wait to hear what would be said after the performance. One afternoon, we were in rehearsal, when a photographer and journalist from the North Bay newspaper made their way to my school. I guess they had heard about the musical about to be performed, and so they wanted to capture a photo to write a small blurb.

I had just finished one of my big musical numbers, and then the photographer captured the moment. He took my name and age, and off he went. What no one knew at the time, until after the article had been published, was that I actually wasn't allowed to be photographed nor mentioned by name. With my crown wardship with no access, my foster parents and I were explained that there had to be privacy put in place to protect my identity and where I was living. Had either of my biological parents had seen it, or relatives for that matter, and made their way to my school, it could cause many unwanted troubles. Thankfully, nothing came from the article and became the first time I was in a newspaper for a theatre performance. The original photo and small blurb is one of the most cherished things I have, as I have kept it these past 19 years.

My foster mom was the only one able to make my performance, which was all I needed. After the performance, I had a lot of people coming up to me to congratulate me on a job well done, which lifted my spirits. Hearing all of the kind things said to me, made me feel so good, and accomplished. Since my newly discovered cousin was in the play in a small part, my biological family, minus my father, was in the audience. After the performance, I had seen them all, and they had seen me, and yet not a single one of them came up to me to congratulate me. It was a little unsettling as I thought even though we had to remain apart, they would have at least said great job, but nothing.

My foster mom's praise was really all I needed though. She seemed extremely happy for me and went on to tell me how great I was. Hearing what she had said, gave me a sort of high, but was an amazing feeling. I knew in that moment if I was to do another performance, I wanted her to show up and watch. Knowing I had someone in the audience who would appreciate it, meant a great deal to me.

When you are faced with issues, distractions can be nice, but when the memories return, it can become scary. Leading up to Christmas, I was given a second chance to start fresh within my foster home, and I was trying really hard to show I could do better. When Christmas approached, I had a lot of worries come to mind. I knew I was going to be visiting with my adoptive family, and there was uncertainty about whether the visit would also include my brother. I had really hoped to not see him, but the fear was something on my mind. I was left remembering what had happened the previous Christmas, and although technically nothing happened then, there had been times when he tried. I also had my sister making a surprise visit to my foster home, as the son and daughter in law decided to begin fostering themselves. Everyone knew how much I missed my sister and wanted to show me that I didn't have to be alone during this season.

Christmas within my foster home was actually something I had never experienced before. The entire family made their way over, and so the large house we were in, was jam-packed with people. There was always something fun to do, sledding especially. Everyone seemed to be in great spirits. It was just an overall exciting time to be living in my foster home. While trying to be embraced with the excitement, I still couldn't help but feel worried about how my Christmas visit would go. I had to get through Christmas morning at my foster home first.

To my surprise, when everyone woke up on Christmas morning, the entire main floor living room where the tree was, had been covered with presents. I had never seen so many presents in my life. Of course, there were tons of people at the house, so it made sense. Everyone received a lot of presents, including me. There were three in particular that I received that day, that for a long time after my stay, meant a great deal to me.

One of my foster parents' daughters made me a red winter hat, that resembled something a jokester would wear. It even had little bells on the ends of it. When I saw it, it was the coolest and nicest hat I had ever seen. For years I kept that hat because it came from someone I barely even knew, and yet still she felt the need to get me something.

Since my adoption, I had a lot of days where I found myself feeling sad and alone. I would play the game I got on my tenth birthday anytime I felt down. It always made me feel better. There had been a couple of additional games out there, and so one of the presents I got was another one of those games. I was beyond excited, and couldn't wait to start playing it.

If there was one gift that meant more to me than any other gift I received that year, and possibly any other year, was a blanket. The blanket I got wasn't just any blanket though. This blanket was incredibly soft and had adorable little bears on it. It was the first blanket I got that was just mine. I never really had a special blanket as an infant, and so this felt like my first. Looking at the blanket made me feel like I had something that was just mine, and made me feel like I could snuggle up to it while feeling warm and safe. As simple as it was, being a blanket, it became one of the most prized possessions I ever received. It was actually the item I thought to be my second most favorite of all time. I even kept it until I was twenty years old.

To great appreciation, the Christmas visit with my mom and dad was something spent at their home, that did not include my brother. The whole Christmas holiday seemed to go by way too fast. Before I knew, it was time to go back to my foster home. The good thing was that I had another memory of great times spent with this family I was eagerly trying to hold on to. As much as I felt I needed to stay in contact with my adoptive family, the more I did, the more I felt sad knowing I wasn't living with them. Still, there had been no definitive answer for where this was all going, although we did have hope.

My eleventh birthday is the one birthday that brought a lot of sad memories to me since the year earlier was the last day I spent adopted. While feeling quite upset about my birthday, I would have my spirits lifted when I received one of my presents. To this current time of my life, the one thing that has meant more to me than anything was a cross I received. I still keep it beside my bed, and every day it reminds me to never let go of the faith I have always had for a better tomorrow. My mom and dad got it for me and wrote on the back of it to remind me when I got it. Every time I look at it, I know I will be okay because it represents the devotion I need to have to get through every day.

Over the course of my life, I had to face situations that I honestly wasn't sure if I would be able to make it out alive. I had a lot of scares, and most of the time didn't know how to overcome them. It's the small things in life that remind me to not lose hope, and to have faith that things can get better. It's the little things in my life that seemed to hold the most meaning. For so long, all I had was my faith, and I found myself praying for the strength I didn't feel like I had. I prayed for a better life, and although it seemed to take forever, it eventually in some ways worked out. It was the path I was taking, that was difficult, as it seemed like I was taking the long, and painful way to get to the end.

I remember one day at my foster home, we had another foster kid stay with us during the winter. He was only staying for relief, and that was something I became grateful for. Since he was closer in age to the other foster kid already living with me, the two of them decided to stick together. Feeling like I didn't belong and that I wasn't good enough to hang out with them, I stayed on my own for the most part. Down by the lake, I had built myself an igloo. I was actually really proud of it, and it allowed me the chance to get away. I was able to go inside and leave all of my insecurities and problems outside. I remember sitting in it and feeling a sense of freedom.

One evening, when I was inside the igloo because the relief foster child decided to start bullying me, I needed a way to escape him. Sitting inside, I found myself crying because I hated being teased and called names. Yes, my voice was a bit high, but I couldn't help it. When I was inside, all of a sudden, the kid decided it would be a fun idea to jump on top of the igloo. Not only was he destroying what I had built, but I was trapped inside. He jumped a few times until I was completely buried in the snow. I remember the feeling I had at that moment. I had no way to prepare myself for what he did, and before I knew it, I was trapped. There was no air, and I couldn't move. I tried and I tried, but I was becoming worried as I couldn't breathe.

I remember freaking out and in the moment was hoping and praying that I would be able to make my way out. Not being able to breathe, I couldn't yell out, and I couldn't ask for help. Finally, I was able to make a small hole, and I kept digging until I was free. Finally gasping for air, I kept taking small breathes as it felt as though my chest was tight. I remember shaking from the fear that I wouldn't make it out. I started crying like I never had before, and then ran up to the house. I told my foster mom what happened, and at that point became nearly frozen. She made me a hot chocolate and covered me in a blanket. She was not happy, and not impressed. She spoke with the two other foster kids, and thankfully, I didn't see the relief kid again.

The year 2001 is the year I can remember being the start of receiving the majority of my bullying. I lived in two different foster homes that year, and yet, it seemed like I had a target on my back. While living in my current foster home, the majority of the bullying came from the bus. There was this little blonde bitch that for some reason even though I barely knew her, found the need to torment me. She would throw things at me when I would be sitting in my seat. She would call me names and would try to get others included in her name-calling.

Things had become so bad for me on that bus when I would try to yell back at her, I would get into trouble. When this happened, I was forced to sit at the front of the bus, so the driver could keep an eye on me. Barely anyone ever wanted to talk to me on that bus. One day, another kid was assigned to sit next to me. He was a few years younger than I was, but thankfully never joined in on the teasing. It was something that was nice because finally, I could talk to someone who wasn't going to tease me.

What I didn't realize at first, was that he was the younger brother of my bully. She found out he was assigned to sit next to me, she freaked out. She kept insisting that she didn't want her brother to be sitting next to a faggot. She didn't want my gayness to rub off on her brother. She even tried to blurt out that I tried to touch her brother when everyone could see I didn't, and that she was just being a bitch. Her brother seemed unbothered by sitting next to me, but I was becoming tired of having to deal with his sister. I insisted that he be moved somewhere else so that she could stop with her torment. Once he had been moved somewhere else, the teasing had slowed down thankfully, but every day it was becoming harder and harder to resist lashing out.

I ended up having a minor blowout, but I think to everyone on the bus, seemed like a major one. I couldn't take the name-calling, her throwing things at me, even the ludicrous accusations that even the bus driver knew were false. After having dealt with what I did with my brother, the pain I was left in, there was never a possibility that I could unleash that on someone else, regardless of who they were. I didn't exactly resort to violence, but I did unleash a lot of horrid words towards her. I think she got the message because she seemed to remain quiet afterward. It had become clear to me that all of the bullies only become quiet once you finally show them that you will no longer take their bull crap. It's sad because it shouldn't come to that, but with my experiences, things only got better after my blow-ups.

Until the spring of 2001, things at my foster home seemed to be going fairly well. Aside from the bullying, I was getting on the bus, my home life for the most part was going well. When the weather started to clear up, having the snow melt, we were found outside continuing on the house. Since the fall, there were still some things in the house that needed to be finished. It was a log/wood style home. On the outside of the house, between each wooden board, there was a space for what is called chinking. It's a substance used for visual appeal or something. Honestly, I don't really know its purpose except for the fact that it was being placed between each board.

The closer I got to the summer, the more I had on my mind. There was so much feeling unresolved in my life, and I found myself dazing out quite a lot, deep in thought. One day while being trapped in my thoughts, I was on a scaffolding with my foster mom and her teenage grandson working on the chinking. Already I was in one of my moods, so being stuck in thought didn't help matters. I wasn't paying attention to what I was doing, and it resulted in messing up the chinking.

When my foster mom had seen what I was doing, she had also noticed I didn't seem to be paying attention. I could only imagine I would have seemed to be out of it. To try and snap me out of it, and to stop making a mess of the chinking, she grabbed my arm, above the wrist, and lightly tapped it with the chinking stick. It definitely snapped me out of my daze.

As soon as she had done what she did, I pulled my arm away and yelled for her to not touch me. I became livid and aggressive. Once again, I was flooded with the memory of my brother and since this had been the second time while living with her that my arm had been grabbed, I freaked out. To me, at the time, although it was a harmless grab and tap to tell me to pay attention to what I was doing, it seemed worse. It wasn't even so much what she had done, but the fact that my brother would grab my arm, and I hated that. I felt powerless, and I was done feeling like that.

Being so oblivious to what was happening, all I could think about was that my foster mom grabbed my arm, tapped the top of my hand, and then in order for my mind to process it, it became much worse than that. It made me feel as though she had tugged on my arm so much, almost tearing it off, while smacking my hand with a wooden stick. Once again, I felt as though I needed to leave, and get away. I quickly climbed down the ladder that allowed us to get on the scaffolding and then knocked it down. I didn't want them to have an opportunity to stop me, and so I trapped them up there. I ran inside and made my way to the phone. I paused for a moment, wondering what to do. During that time, all I could feel was terrified. I was so enraged, and it had nothing to do with my foster mom. She didn't know what happened, or what I was feeling from having my arm grabbed at. I had just made a huge ordeal out of nothing, and I didn't think I was going to come back from it.

I called the Children's Aid, told them that I had my arm yanked, and then smacked with a wooden stick. It was something that they couldn't just ignore, and so they made their way over. I was removed from my foster home that night. I remember feeling slight relief because I was running away from a problem that I created in a moment of panic and not knowing how to deal with the trauma no one knew about. It was in that moment of freaking out that it made me realize that I wasn't actually handling things properly, or how I had hoped. I realized that I had just allowed it to ruin another amazing placement, but it seemed too late.

I was left feeling like this was my punishment for not speaking out. It hurt a lot because it felt as though my brother was always winning when he should have been the one dealing with the pain I had. Since it was late, I had to be placed in an emergency relief foster home for the night, until proper placement could be made for me. During that time, I felt much regret for what I had done but didn't think there was any way I could change it, or make up for it. I was left with more concerns as to what was going to happen to me.

Chapter Eleven

Lakeview Round Two

I have heard from people that you never forget your first love. There tends to be a lot of things that people say is too difficult to forget. What we choose to remember becomes a big part of our lives. What we consider to have a lasting effect on the type of people we see in ourselves, becomes the very essence of who we become.

Before requesting to be moved from the foster family with the Great Dane, I was at the Children's Aid office one day. It had been decided that I needed to begin a social skills program to help me in my day to day life. It was not something that became a choice but was something I was told I had to take part in. After one of my sessions, I was in the parking lot when I spotted a familiar face. The Lakeview foster mom was at the office, and to my surprise, I had to say hello.

It had been years since I had seen her. The mere sight of her filled me with all of the fond memories I had while living with her. We had a brief greeting, but then we said goodbye.

When I requested my move from my foster family, I was left thinking of the Lakeview foster mom. I remembered how happy I felt during my stay with her, and how much fun I had with all of the friends I had made. Thinking about that home, and with the knowledge that I had just ruined another great placement, I felt as though I needed some familiarity. I needed to be somewhere that could give me another chance at being happy, and where I could try to work on the issues developing within my mind.

For the only time, while I was a part of the foster system, my request to be moved to the Lakeview home was approved. Hearing that excited me so much. The only sadness I was left with at the time was how I wouldn't be able to see some of my previous friends. During my adoption celebratory visit with my siblings in the summer of 1999, I made my way to say hello to my foster parents at the lake. I felt to be in a great place and wanted to share what I found to be a success with them. When hoping to see my friends who lived in the house right next door, I was informed of a tragedy.

Sometime after I moved away, the family decided to move. Unsure as not all of the information had been passed on, but there were one or two accidents. Within those accidents that involved a drunk driver, all except the girl was killed. The details were gossip in nature since it was only what was given word of mouth. All I was left with, was that only she survived. Hearing that devastated me. The entire family meant a great deal to me when I lived there. I spent most of my time with them, and the news became the first time I would experience a tragic, life-ending loss.

When I was moved to the Lakeview home, although unable to see some old friends, there were still others to be excited for. There was actually quite a lot to be excited for. With my new foster home, I was also given a new social worker, to whom I found to like quite a lot more. In all honesty, the first worker I received once returning to the system, was someone I barely remember, because of her absence in my life. This new worker was a lot more frequent and became someone I would often want to see, and speak with.

While trying to relish in the fact that I was given a fresh start at a place that I was familiar with already, there were still discussions needed about the ongoing issues.

Once I was returned into the foster system, almost right away, people seemed to want to start over by looking for a new adoptive family. Between February and September 2000, I was asked about my desire to be readopted. I wasn't ready, and since I had still been in contact with my previous adoptive parents, I wasn't wanting to think about others. I asked for more time to make a decision. I was given six months to make up my mind whether I wanted to try to find another home. They had it planned out to present me at another conference in April 2001.

Before the end of the given six months, I had been asked a few times if I had given any more thought to finding a new adoptive family. I was trying to enjoy my time with my mom and dad. Although I wasn't living with them, I had still considered them to be a part of my life, and I felt as though I still needed them. I didn't want to start over, and the connection I had with them was stronger than any other familial bond I had. I had asked if it could be possible to try being adopted by them again. The thought I had was that since we were still remaining in each other's lives, it almost made sense we could. This was something that my worker was uncertain of. I was told that the whole idea of readopting me, was to be with a different family.

Moving back to the Lakeview home, left me sad at times because of how I ended my previous foster home. There were still some upsides to look forward to though. Watching television wasn't something that I always did. At the time I would in the evening, but it was the hope to not have us foster children glued in front of the TV. I didn't mind it, and it was actually great because I was able to experience so much from being outside. With my new foster home though, we were able to watch television as we pleased. While still loving the outdoors, I became excited because I knew what that meant.

The only thing I ever wanted to watch, was my favorite television show. I was always talking about it. I would always tell everyone how it came into my life when I felt as though I had nothing else, which finally brought some happiness in my life. It finally gave me a reason to smile. After so long of talking about it, when I wasn't even always able to watch it, it still remained incredibly important to me. Now, I had the opportunity to watch it every time a new episode would air. I had to wait until the fall, but still, I was left feeling excited, which gave me something to look forward to. Knowing how important it was in my life, it even became something that people would use against me as a punishment for bad behavior.

While spending so much time outside at my previous foster home, one of my favorite things to do, was to walk their dog. So often in my life, I felt small and unable to protect myself from bullies and those who seem to want to make my life a living hell. The dog that was in my foster home was massive, nearly bigger than me, so walking him gave me a sense of protection that I didn't have. Every time I would walk him, I felt as though nothing could hurt me. He was by far the best dog I have ever lived with, and despite his size, was incredibly gentle and kind. Having him walk beside allowed me to feel as though I had someone out there protecting me. The safe feeling I had in my previous home majorly from their dog, was going to be something I would miss tremendously.

When I think about what makes a home safe, I am left thinking about the rules put in place, as well as the parents' views on life. Each foster family has their own ways of living. Some families have pets, which offer a sense of friendship and safety, while others try to offer that from their own word of mouth. While the home with the Great Dane and the Lakeview foster parents are quite different, from all of my foster families, both of them tried to offer that safe feeling more so than any others. Aside from having their dog acting as a trusting protector, my previous foster parents offered something I had never heard of before.

Before the time where almost every person including children would possess a cell phone, when playing outside, all we children had to go on was to watch the sunset or a watch. We were told to be back at a certain time, and away we went. Having access to a phone was not as easy as it is in today's society. When out in public, typically people would have to use a payphone in order to make a call to someone. The Great Dane foster parents wanted to make sure each of the foster children that would stay with them, were safe. Having only a payphone to communicate when staying out late, or perhaps while in some form of trouble, meant we always needed loose change with us to make a call. Well, never did we need change.

As soon as I moved in, I was given a special 1-800 phone number that was toll-free. This special number was a direct line to our home, additional to our normal phone number. They wanted to make sure that no matter where we were, we would always be able to contact them without the need for a quarter. The number wasn't just good for a payphone, but any phone. The level of safety I felt just from that became something that meant a great deal whether I would need it or not.

While I had been used to having a dog and a special number for feeling safe, I would now rely on my foster mom's voice. The Lakeview foster mom always tried to talk with each of the foster children, making sure to stay in our lives and listen to our concerns. Standard communication should be usual in any home. You would think at least. She was probably the most made aware foster parent I had ever lived with. My previous couple of placements had been quite aware, but this was next level. It gave a different but appreciative, nurturing sense. It made swimming in the lake and walking around the woods easy because she always seemed to know where anyone was. Most times anyway.

In the meantime, my top priority once I moved was to reconnect with old friends. To everyone's surprise, randomly out of the blue, I just showed up. I was recognized instantly, and for the most part, received a warm welcome. This was something that occurred both on my street, and at school. I went to a different school than most of the kids on my street, so there was always some separation there.

From the first time of seeing everyone, there seemed to be only one girl who didn't appear impressed to see me. I never understood why, but I could still remember the look on her face when she first saw me. It was almost as if she looked me up and down, being like, *oh, okay. So what, he's back.* Trying not to think about it at first, I was trying to be excited to be seeing old friends. I was wanting to rebuild our friendships.

The slight hostility I felt from the one girl, only grew into aggression and intense bullying. Over the course of my stay at the Lakeview home for the second time, her taunting words and actions got worse as time went on. Like most things, it was bottled up because it made me feel so low, and belittled. For so long I never understood what I even did to make her hate me so much. I actually kind of liked her, so the fact that she seemed to have so much hate for me, confused me.

The bullying from her went on for about a year, with moments of nothing when some of my friends would ask her to just stop, and let everyone enjoy their time together. Those moments became really nice but never lasted. After things became too much for me to endure, the rage monster came out in full force, and in a moment's reaction, I lashed out and punched her in the side of the head. I didn't know what more I could have done. It was only getting worse, and I couldn't take any more torment and cruel words.

That incident became something to never forget because of how violent I had become within an instant. It scared me, and others, but in some ways kind of helped things. I had a heartfelt conversation with her mother afterward, which meant a great deal. She understood the pain I was feeling, and although wishing I didn't resort to violence, knew it became unavoidable due to her daughter's on-going constant bullying. The incident even somewhat helped with the girl. There was no more bullying by her, and feeling beyond sorry, I was able to apologize to her. Before moving again, things between us had even begun to actually get better. I was shown a different side to her, which made me like her. I wasn't able to be her friend for most of the time I knew her, but towards the end, I felt like progress had been made, and it was something I appreciated.

Of course, the one girl wasn't the only one who received the worst of my violent tendencies. One of my neighbors while knowing how much I had been hurt from ongoing bullying from multiple people in my life, decided to join in. The sad thing was how we at times were friends. When it benefited her, she felt the need to lash out at someone, chose me as an easy target. The bullying from her didn't last as long, mostly because I was still fuelling from the last big blow-up, and so it was easier to react. I hit her with my belt a couple of times on the back.

There was no reason for reacting that way. I soon learned that and it has been something to live with my whole life. I went years refusing to wear belts because of it. The guilt and shame I had to live with, was my punishment. Regardless of how I was left feeling because of her bullying, I still shouldn't have done what I did. Even to this current day, I hate wearing belts and am reminded of the incident every time I see one.

If dealing with bullying in my home life wasn't enough on a daily basis, I also suffered from bullies at school. Those bullies caused me to lash out at everyone at school, mostly the teachers. Feeling not being helped, or listened to, I resorted to using a lot of foul language towards them. I would often go to them for assistance, trying to tell them how the bully would be persistent in their teasing, and how it was affecting me. I would tell any adult in my life about it, but I was left to deal with it on my own because it seemed they didn't want to be bothered by it. Resorting to foul language at first, became a way to deal with the pain I was left feeling. I didn't know how to properly deal with it, and my actions caused a lot of turmoil within the classroom.

When I think back to my stay at the Lakeview foster home that came to a messy end in the summer of 2002, I almost need to think of the worst things first. There were some great memories I had, but in order to think about them, I had to come to terms with the bad. I had to remember some of the pain I inflicted and created. I needed to be able to accept that I had some problems, some serious concerns that needed to be addressed so they wouldn't keep occurring.

The violence with the two female bullies became the first thing I had to think about over and over. I couldn't forget what had happened, because it was a reminder of what I didn't want to become. My greatest fear was to become like my biological father, as he would beat my mother, and us, and the violence he brought to others in their lives was something becoming too real to me. I was acting so much like him, and it terrified me. If I wanted to totally change and not become him, I needed to always remember what I had done, so I wouldn't make the same mistakes.

Thankfully, I was able to hold onto those memories to fuel my desire to become a better person. The end pain I brought to those girls is something I can never take back, but it is something that I would always try to make up for. Never again had I reacted in such a way to another girl. The only thing I had been left with was the hope that they would one day be able to find forgiveness in me.

By the time the end of grade six came around in June 2002, my fighting at school had become serious. I was getting in fights with some boys who would bully me, and my teacher once again wasn't listening when I would ask for help. She would ignore everything I would say, and with not being heard or helped, I would take matters in my own hands. The fighting was never to the extent of unleashing the rage monster but was still bad enough. I was refused the end of the year trip because I was told had I wanted to go, I would need additional adults in attendance to be there in case of my fighting.

I felt as though going back to that school in September was only going to make things worse for me. I knew that I needed to get away from troubling situations because I wanted to do better in my life. I requested to changed schools for the new year. The request was being considered at first. By the time September came around, I would be in a new foster home so I ended up getting my wish for a new school.

While bullying and fighting became a growing concern for my worker and foster parents, there always seemed to be something else that brought worry to the adults. Since moving to the Lakeview home, I began smoking. I was the youngest of the three initial children living within the home when I first moved. The other two were fifteen and seventeen. The two of them smoked, and it seemed as though smoking was something that everyone on my road did.

My foster parents did not approve of smoking and did not allow us to. We were too young to smoke, and therefore it had to be kept hidden. If cigarettes were found, they would be confiscated. My foster parents and worker were aware that I was still smoking although not allowed to. They couldn't stop me, as they couldn't be with me every moment of every day, but they could take preventative steps to try to help me not.

When the cigarettes would be confiscated, they would be placed in my foster parents' room. At times when wanting to get them back, I would wait until they would be out of the house, so I could try and get them back. I would sneak inside the house and would try to sneak in their room to look for them. When I would find them, I would get into trouble. For one, I was sneaking in the house when I shouldn't be. Second, I was found "stealing," because I shouldn't be having them. The house, in the end, had to be locked up to prevent me from sneaking in when I shouldn't be there.

Sneaking into the house was something I wasn't supposed to be doing when my foster parents weren't home. Sneaking out of the house at night was also something I wasn't supposed to be doing. I did though. At times I would sneak out to see my friends. I was caught quite a few times sneaking out. At first, I learned how to sneak out from watching other foster siblings sneak out, which gave me the idea. About 90% of the time, everyone was caught. My foster mom actually had amazing hearing, and always seemed to know when something was going on. While often being caught, still we would all try.

Some of the worst things I have done in my life, leaving me feeling guilt and shame well into adulthood, occurred during my second round of the Lakeview home. My rage monster reactions were the incidents that have always made me feel the most guilt and shame. When thinking of the remaining incidents involving the most shame and guilt, they were non-violent.

Before my move in mid-2002, I think I had experienced every worst trait a teenager could face. I tried smoking marijuana for the first time in an abandoned house across the street from where I lived. The older kids in the area would use that house as their party place. They would drink and smoke weed in there all of the time. I tried it for the first time, and I actually kind of liked it. At the time, I was in a really bad place involving my adoptive family and was growing tired of my feelings. The weed made me feel numb, and it became something I enjoyed feeling. It became something that allowed me to forget the pain and heartache.

No one was allowed to be in that house, so every time we would be in it, we were technically breaking and entering. That was something I found myself doing a lot during my Lakeview stay. The first time was with a different foster sister who was living with me and a few other older kids on my road. There were about four of us in total. We had heard about a known pedophile living on our road, and that kept a lot of money in his house. One day we all decided to break in and look to see what we could find. He had a small safe, and so we stole it.

After breaking into the small safe, there was practically nothing in it. A bit of jewelry, and coins. My foster sister took a ring that was in it. I wanted it for my girlfriend, but she took it. When she was removed from my foster home, I was in her room with my foster mom "helping" her pack it up, when I spotted the ring. I took it back, along with some of the cigarettes she had. I was caught stealing the ring, but not until after I had given it away. It wasn't known what we had done, so I had to pay to replace it.

The next time I found myself breaking and entering, was with a vehicle at the end of my road towards the end of my stay. I was with friends, just finished swimming and hanging out, when we saw a parked truck with windows opened. We searched it to see if we could find smokes but got caught. Having recognized me, I was the only one who had been caught. She found compassion, as she had known some of my history. She knew me to not be completely terrible and wanted to give me a chance to make up for going into her truck. It was a kindness that I hadn't expected but was definitely something I needed. I needed to be shown that people make mistakes, some worse than others, but they can be redeemed if you are willing to work on it. I did some outside work for her at her house, and by the end of it, was able to feel thankful I was given a second chance.

The last occurrence of breaking and entering occurred just before moving. I found myself sneaking into a house with a foster sibling who was only with me temporarily, and we were accompanied by a couple of friends. One being my first love. The whole incident had been instigated by the foster sibling as no one else actually wanted to. We didn't take anything or do damage, but still, it was known what we had done. My foster parents were notified, but by that time I had just moved.

Over the course of my life, I found myself to be a victim of some pretty horrifying situations. I found myself to be stuck in the middle of situations that I had no control over. When I moved in 2001 at the Lakeview home, that changed. I had become the reason for so many things going wrong in my life. When the issues and problems I had no control over became too much to handle, I found other means to deal with them. Acting out, doing things which

I thought would make me *cool* in the eyes of others became important. There had been some things that happened, and it left me feeling lost and damaged. I didn't respond to how I should have, but I was not capable of realizing how I truly felt.

At times my worker could sense how I didn't know how to react or feel about certain situations, and so she suggested I start writing things down. She wanted me to be able to understand my actions and to have written proof of it to look back on. This small writing suggestion at the time seemed "dumb" to me, but over time, became something to appreciate. I didn't realize it then, but it allowed me to look back at the things going on in my life, to understand how certain things made me feel. It allowed me a chance to see how not to react, and how to use the pain to strengthen my inner self. At times my writings had become somewhat difficult to read because, I would be able to feel the anger, frustrations, and sadness I had felt again. It was now a matter of being able to understand and accept those passages.

Often I found myself thinking that there had been more mistakes made then good choices the second time around at my foster home. Looking back to my time there, I believe that to be true. As much as I had hoped for a better time, I had just allowed the worst part of myself and of the situations to get to me. One of the best decisions I had made, however, came from the beginning of my stay.

Still feeling incredibly bad for how I left things with my previous foster home, my worker suggested I return to do a face to face apology. When I first heard her speak of this, I was instantly reminded of how my mom and dad would bring me to those I hurt, to apologize. The face to face actually seemed to help the problems I had during that time. The thought of doing this face to face though seemed impossible.

I couldn't help but feel scared and ashamed of what I had done. I didn't think there could be any way she could forgive me. I wasn't even so sure I deserved her forgiveness. At first, I was hesitant about going back to a home I once loved, but thankfully changed my mind in the end.

Sometimes we need that little extra nudge in the right direction to help put us on the right path. Listening to my worker and making my way back to apologize, was one of the best things I had done. I had felt so bad since the moment I left, so was given a chance to make things right. To no surprise, I was forgiven. The foster mom had always been known to me, to be a generous, gracious, and loving woman. She had such a big heart, and she definitely helped me with the desire for making amends. To make things even better for me, she had mentioned how pleased she was for me to return to correct the issue regarding me leaving. It even opened up the door for me to return for a relief stay.

Until my departure in July 2002, I found myself going away for relief quite a lot. When I lived with the Great Dane foster family, I never went away for relief. We had other children stay with us, but it was only once I moved that I found myself going away.

Aside from returning to my previous foster home, there had been another home to which I would spend a lot of time. I found myself enjoying the new home. They had two additional foster children who were also my age. The foster mom and dad seemed so full of energy and appeared to always be smiling.

When staying with new foster families, it becomes a matter of having to get accustomed to the new rules, and ways of living. When I first started staying with my new relief home, things seemed quite simple. As time went on, they remained simple, for me. Since I had been only staying at the home for a weekend at a time, I wasn't used to the ways they lived day in and day out. The other two kids at times, found themselves getting into trouble. Trying to stay clear of their situations the best I could, my goal was to just simply relax and enjoy my weekend away.

On weekends, the foster parents would get each child living there one bag of chips. This one bag could be eaten in one night, but the hope was for them to make it last all weekend. Every day, each child was given one hour of PlayStation playing. They had a specific game, that I came to quite love. Spyro! Playing that game became my favorite thing to do when I would visit! It also started my obsession with dragons!

While finding myself enjoying my relief visits, I would have to return to my usual routines at home. I became fond of the differences between the homes, although my friends were the reasons to prefer my Lakeview home.

Friendships come and go as we go through life. We develop feelings of the heart through different stages in our lives. There is much uncertainty we face with knowing which bonds and relationships will last. Being someone who had been bullied so much, it became difficult to make friends. The fear of possibly being teased was unavoidable, which made connecting with others difficult. With how much I moved within my life, having to say goodbye to the relationships I made, only worsened as time went on. Knowing that there was always a high probability of me leaving at some point, also affected the desire to make new friends.

While having a second go-around at the Lakeview home, I was gifted an opportunity to continue building on the friendships I already had the previous time. This opportunity rarely ever happened, and it became such a blessing. I was able to reunite with old friends from school and on my road. I had a best friend from school when I was in grade two, and seeing him again made me quite happy. To this day, we are not as close as we once were, but that's okay because we are both in different places in our lives. We had a second chance at our friendships, and that chance is something to appreciate.

The first time I shared a kiss with a girl, was another person I would be chanced with reuniting with. Seeing her brought back so many happy memories we had, and once again, were able to create new ones. To this day, we continue to remain in each other's lives, thanks to social media.

Of all of the friendships I had over the course of my life, the most important came from my first love. Friends since my first stay back in grade two, seeing each other after years made both of us extremely happy. The entire time I spent living at the Lakeview, we became quite close. Although we had our moments where we were being kids and didn't speak. That never lasted, and we always made up. Of everyone I had been friends with, she was the one person I wanted to spend the most time with. Before she became my first love, she was my best friend.

The thing I look back on with much appreciation for wasn't just what I had with her, but her family. She has a sister who was always close to her, and that allowed me to be able to create a friendship with her as well. I even quite loved her parents. In my past, I had issues with other kids' parents, because they weren't understanding of my foster life situation. I had always been viewed as too much trouble. They never understood that I wasn't responsible for being brought into the system. I've had a few friendships end because of this misguided view from parents. It was always something that was upsetting and unfortunate. I had always wanted someone to understand that just because I was a foster child, that doesn't mean I don't deserve friendships.

My first love's parents understood my unfortunate situation. Never had I been judged by them, and they always made me feel welcomed when I would be around. They knew how close I had become with their daughter, and they found no desire to get in the way of our building friendship. The way they made me feel was something I had longed for from friends' parents. I had seen some of that from my one bully's mom, but that was it. The compassion and understanding was something that traveled with me everywhere I went after my departure, for it became something to forever admire.

At first, we started to reunite as friends. We spent a lot of time together, and at times found ourselves getting into mischief. During the course of my time there, we dated on and off. We were kids. We were having fun and enjoying each other's company. I don't think I quite realized it at the time, but by the time I had to leave, she had become my first real love. I may have ended up gay in my adult life, but that love I felt was real. She was the only girl in my life to make me feel like that, and it is something I'll forever admire, and look back on with smiles.

She and I continued our friendship in the years to come. When I had to say my goodbyes, saying it to her was hardest of all. I remember barely being able to look at her without crying. Thankfully I was able to get her address, and for the next year, I would on occasion write to her. The letters I would receive in return would be kept locked away even to this current year of 2019. Opening them up during times of needed nostalgia, always makes me think back to the happiness we shared within our friendship.

When I'm left to think back to my leaving in July 2002, it's hard not to think of the possible influences. The definitive reasons were that I made such a mess of my life. Things had become so bad, and while actually enjoying my home, I had become too afraid and worried I couldn't pick up the pieces. I made such a mess, and I was beyond worried that whatever I try to do, I wouldn't be able to make things better. A part of me was too scared to try and see, and so I decided to run away instead. I decided to allow the bad overpower what could be good regained.

The summer of 2001 meant a lot of things for me. For one, it meant I had an opportunity to visit with my adoptive parents once again. My visit this summer allowed me to spend a bit more time in comparison to the previous year. Another great thing was that I wouldn't have to get together with my brother. Since the previous year, I wasn't able to sign up for the theatre camp, this time around I was fortunate enough to do so.

Every time I was given a chance to visit with my mom and dad, I was always left in good spirits. Every aspect of my life seemed to go well. Any aggression, sadness, or insecurities I had been feeling seemed to go away. My summer break seemed to come at a perfect time because my contact with my sister had been minimal, and I was feeling quite lonely. A break-away always felt nice, because all of the issues going on, seemed to become obsolete. My worker had also been asking again if I had any more thoughts on future adoption thoughts, so my time would hopefully give me a chance to think about it.

The first year I attended the theatre camp, I was a little underwhelmed with the outcome of my role within the performance. I was still quite pleased with the overall experience but was hoping for more. 2001 didn't give me the leading role, but I definitely found myself having more fun. I had more friends than the previous time, and I even built some friendships with the councilors there. One of which I became pen pals for almost a year.

I didn't have an active role within the performance, but I did have a few scene-stealer moments. My mom and dad had videotaped the theatre performance, which allowed me to have my first and only copy of any performance I had been a part of. Of course, years later I lent the tape to one of my aunts, who never returned it.

One day after rehearsal and my daily activities, instead of my mom or dad picking me up, my adoptive sister did. She had just gotten her driver's license, and out of excitement came to pick me up. I remember seeing how happy she was, and it was such a great sight. Deciding to go with the flow of happiness, we decided to spend some time together. There was a batting cage near where we were and thought we would spend a bit of time before meeting up with our mom.

My adoptive sister went first and began swinging the bat. We would talk to each other, while she would hit the balls. Seeing how well she was doing, and how much fun she seemed to be having, I became very excited for my turn. When her turn was up, and mine was about to start, out of excitement I opened the caged door. Still wanting to hit more balls, and I wasn't aware when I walked in, she swung the bat back. It made direct contact with my nose, and I honestly thought I was doing to die.

My nose began gushing blood, and I'm still surprised it didn't break. My whole face began to hurt, and my adoptive sister had started to panic. Not realizing I was standing behind her, she felt so bad because she had no idea how bad the injury was. Thankfully nothing bad came of it, although our bonding time came to an end.

The thing I loved most about my summer visit was how great it felt. We all actually felt like a family. It felt like it used to when I was living there. It was something I missed, and with each visit, it became more difficult to leave and say goodbye. I was told to figure out what I wanted and to make a decision, and after that summer break, all I wanted was to move back with them.

There were always things that caused conflict within my mind. I became quite certain all I wanted was to be readopted by my mom and dad again. When I was able to have visits with my sister, we started talking about how great it would be to become a family once again. Hearing her say that made me realize just how lonely she must have been feeling. I had my adoptive family, but she only had me, and even that wasn't often.

When thinking of our biological family, it was never something that came easy to us. We had always talked about whether or not they ever had any other children after giving us up. We had wondered what they looked like. We didn't know where they were even living. Well, I at least knew where our father was.

When I started going to the dentist while living at the Lakeview home, I ran into him once.

After years of being told to smile, but not always feeling a desire to smile, I was also embarrassed by my teeth. For so long I and others had feared that I would one day require braces from how messed up they appeared. I had gaps, missing teeth, and had even been teased from them. Smiling was not something I wanted to do. Picture day at school had always been my favorite day of the year because it allowed me a chance to show I was happier than I felt at home, but my smile always made me feel down.

Once I was adopted, thankfully my teeth began to correct themselves. The only thing that seemed to not correct itself were the white spots. My teeth filled in quite nicely where there were no more gaps, and they were even growing straight. The fear of needing braces was that of the past, but I was still left with my Bambie Spots. I went to the dentist to have them drilled and polished. When going to my dentist, I ran into my father for the second time since the goodbye visit, and so I knew he was still in the city of North Bay.

Spotting my biological father at the dentist, was after I had already seen him working at Walmart as a greeter. To me, he didn't appear as someone you would want greeting you into a store. He came off as an emotionless prick. He didn't even recognize me when I went up to him. I knew exactly who he was, and was curious if he would know who I was. When I asked him if his name was what it is, he replied yes, while staring at me confused. I waited a few seconds and then took off.

I remember telling my sister the story and we both had a good laugh from it. My sister and I would laugh so much about the old times we had together. With every story we would share, the more we laughed, and then the more she seemed hoping to become a family once again. Even talking about maybe one day finding a family where the two of us could be adopted into. She had even started throwing around the idea of perhaps looking into getting back in contact with our biological mother.

She knew I was still in contact with my adoptive family but had never understood what that meant. She would ask me if that means I would be leaving to live with them again. Every time the discussion came up, she always looked sad because I knew she worried if that meant I would leave her.

The sadness that she felt came mostly to my mind during Christmas 2001. I had plans to go see my adoptive family for the holidays. Once my plans were made, and was about to leave, I was told she would be staying at my foster home, without me. It devastated me that she had to be alone during the holidays, and it left a sour note that I couldn't shake. I was left worrying about whether she would be okay or not, and it became one of the reasons to draw panic for my visit.

Just before traveling to go visit with my family, I was told that my brother and his adoptive parents would be joining us on another skiing vacation. I was already having so much stress going on and was dealing with so much in my mind. The fact that I once again had to spend another holiday with him made me wonder how I was going to get through it.

The thought of excitement that I would be able to see my adoptive family again became overshadowed by the conflicting thoughts I was already having. Trying to piece everything together became too much to handle. I didn't know who to talk to, and regarding what subject. On one hand my I needed my sister in my life, but she seemed to not want me to have my adoptive family. I didn't want my brother at all but didn't know how to bring that up. The workers seemed to think that the decision regarding my future and adoption needed to be made right away. The workers informed me when talking about my sister that I needed to stop worrying and thinking about her, and to think about myself and what I wanted. They felt as though if I wanted to be happy, that I needed to consider the fact that might not include her. They indicated to me that should I go through with trying to be readopted, that would mean I wouldn't be able to have the contact with her that I now have.

Trying to juggle all of the information, and all of the situations seemed too much for my eleven-year-old mind. The entire visit did not seem to go over well. My brother had been avoiding me, to which I couldn't understand why. All I wanted to do was scream because my head was filled with so much noise but I couldn't. I ended up once again making my adoptive sister feel like crap from rude comments. I needed a way to let out some of the aggression, and it was becoming easy to do that with her.

Once returning to my foster home after the holidays, the only distraction I had was the play I was involved with. To date, it was one of my favorite experiences involving community theatre. I had one of the leads, two parts, and although a musical, to my surprise, was cast as one of the male leads. The play was *Briar Rose and The Prince*. It was such a beautiful play, and every day I spent rehearsing was just as rewarding as the final performance. I was able to invite my worker, supervisor, my foster mom, and even the Great Dane foster mom.

Knowing how many people in my life came to watch me perform felt so great. It was a feeling that filled my heart because it gave me the confidence to be a part of something. I had been causing a lot of problems around me, but this performance was a reminder that I was better than that. In a time where I had no idea what I was going to do with my life, and the decisions ahead, I was given a moment to create some good, while feeling like I mattered.

Once my favorite play had come to an end, the people involved with putting it on, invited me back for their next production, but during that time I found life to be difficult and so I declined. I thought I needed a break because there were too many things going on, and I didn't feel as though I could focus. Looking back, I regret not participating because I feel as though it could have been incredibly beneficial to distract myself.

March break of 2002 was difficult for me. By that point, the bullying all around me began to overwhelm me completely. I wasn't at the point of my blow-up, but I felt close. Between the many bullies, the thing that always got me was how they would comment on my home life. They would insist that my biological mother left because she couldn't love me. That she didn't care about me, nor wanted me in her life. I even remembered being told that she probably killed herself because of me. It wasn't the first time I had heard something similar to that. Remember one time being asked if I even know if she's alive.

When you're a child that is Crownward without access, there's a lot you don't know. There is a lot of information you aren't made aware of. You are left with only what you can remember, and from what others tell you. My sister and I had spoken a lot about what to do with our future selves. Seeing all of her pain was becoming too much to witness and to not try to do something about it. As much as I wanted a better life for myself, I was conflicted because I couldn't go on to my better life, knowing she couldn't have that. After hearing all of the hurting remarks from bullies, it really dug a hole in my mind and heart. What if my mother truly was dead? She did cause a lot of pain to my siblings and I, but did that mean she had to die for it?

When attending my adoptive family's home for March break, I was left thinking about everything for the last time. I was trying to internalize everything I had been feeling. *What to do about my sister? What do I do about my future happiness? What do I do about the comments involving my biological mother?* So many things to think about. Too many things to think about.

Being stuck in thought, caused some conflict with my mom. She and I got into a heated conversation because while thinking so much of my biological mother, she seemed distasteful hearing about her. She had only been told things from the caseworkers, which was different than what I was told. She had read things I didn't, as I had a specific view of her. My mom's view differed from mine, and it left me feeling upset. I overreacted in the moment, but it was only because of all the other things on my mind. I couldn't separate everything as I needed to, in order to see what she was saying, and where she was coming from.

What had been said wasn't to bash her in any way, but rather to make me realize that she had faults, a lot of them, which lead to my home being unsafe. That was the whole reason for me being put up for adoption. It was fine to think about her, or even wonder about her life now, but I needed to not live in the past and to embrace the present, and live for the future.

Unable to see the truth in what my mom was trying to tell me, I saw it as a sign and allowed it to fuel my rage in making a decision that seemed to be in constant ask from the workers. I went a bit of time after March Break not speaking with my adoptive family, in order to process the decision that I was still unsure of. One day I thought I had made up my mind, while the next day it became something different. It ended up coming down to whether or not I wanted my happiness with my adoptive family, or be a part of my sister's life.

In the end, I went with the decision I felt wasn't logically, emotionally, or mentally right with me. The love and admiration I had with my adoptive family was something I would never be able to experience again. I did know that considering how amazing and strong they were, they would be able to handle the bad news better than my sister. I couldn't help but think about what would happen to her if I would leave her again. She seemed to be only getting worse, and I just couldn't leave her in the world alone. It wasn't right, and it wasn't fair. I needed her in my life, and I know she needed and wanted me in hers.

Goodbyes are probably one of the hardest things to experience. There's always the fear of not knowing what will happen. You're left with so many worries and questions. When goodbye is in play, the longer amount of time spent up until it reflects on the feelings involved. The only thing you are left with, is what you're left with. The things to remember, mementos to hold. There becomes day to day small things that make you remember. A song, or a smell, perhaps an activity.

When I think about my final goodbye to my adoptive family, I'm left remembering so many different things. All of the firsts I had experienced with them, and because of them. I went to see The Lion King live with them, as well as a few other theatre performances. I sadly had to taste sour milk at school when I didn't know to read the expiry date. The first time I had ever gone to a movie theatre was with them. All of the artistic, academic, and sports-related lessons they involved me in. Getting me a tutor. Bringing me on my first zoo and safari trip. I attended a YTV achievement award, in the hope of meeting the cast of my favorite TV show. Although I was disappointed when they weren't there. I never knew how to tie my own shoes before I lived with them, and they taught me how to tie with bunny ears. To this day I still tie my shoes like that because it allows me to remember them.

There could be no amount of writing that could hold all of the things I was gifted with because of my adoptive family. The goodbye I had with them was not what I wanted. It did not go as I had hoped. It hurt more than I ever knew it could. I was not prepared for how it would make me feel.

Regardless of how much pain and sadness I was filled with from realizing I would not be speaking or seeing my mom and dad again, I had to try and somewhat pick myself up. I had made a decision to remain in foster care. The decision was made so that I could have my sister remain in my life, and for the two of us to become a family again. Knowing how difficult the decision was, I became determined to not allow it to be made in vain. It became an even bigger need to keep my sister in my life.

I had been feeling incredibly worried that my mother might actually be dead. The voices of my bullies kept making their way inside my thoughts, and so I needed answers. I needed to clear my conscience. I needed to begin looking for and going after the kind of life my sister and I had been discussing. I knew it was going to be long and tough, but after asking my worker to look into reconnecting with my biological mother, things would be able to start.

By the end of my stay at the Lakeview home, as much as I thought I was trying to work on my problems, things got worse. Time would pass, and while trying to look forward, and to the possibilities of the unknown, I was left wondering if I had made a mistake in my decision. Even thinking about whether it was a mistake, was beginning to hurt me. I again became conflicted, because I felt as though the mere thought was something I shouldn't have because of my sister. I felt as though it was an attack against her. It wasn't, but it felt wrong no matter how much I wondered whether it was the right decision.

I somehow won an award in June 2002 from the Children's Aid Society. It was called *The Betty Ralph Award* and was presented to a child, who shows incredible desire to try and do better with their life. I had heard about the award sometime earlier, and with how much I had been trying to improve myself, felt as though I did deserve it. I didn't see *try* the same as succeeding. I knew as much as I was trying, things were somehow getting worse. As happy as I was for the award, and is something I can always look at while remembering the moments I did try, it still feels undeserving.

So much about my life made me start thinking whether or not I was capable of anything good. Anytime I was placed somewhere great, and where I actually enjoyed, I ruined it. Friendships didn't always last. The relationship with my sister no matter how much I fought for it, seemed to be unreachable. I gave up the purest of happiness because I had too many conflicting thoughts flutter around my head. Too many instances in my life were beginning to fall apart, and it was becoming too much to handle. It got to the point where I just had to go with it. The only thing I could do was try to hold onto some hope.

Once realizing that adoption was not something in my future, I was left fearing what would happen. I was then beginning proceedings to start communication with my biological mother with my sister, but what if that wouldn't happen. Living within my Lakeview home, there were two incidents that I had witnessed involving what happens to a child at the end of their time in foster care.

There are a number of different cases and definitions of the type of foster child living in foster care. You can be someone who is short term, long term, Crownwardship with or without access. There are different circumstances involving the type of care and length of care received based on your title. When I first moved back to the Lakeview home, there were two other foster children in the home. The first one was a fifteen-year-old girl, and because of her status, she would only be in care until her sixteenth birthday. Literally UNTIL. On her birthday, she had to leave our home and would have to be on her own. The other foster child was seventeen, and the same went for him once he turned eighteen. On the days of their birthdays, their time within the system was at a close and therefore had to leave.

Once my decision had been made to remain in the foster system, all I could think about and fear was how this would now be my possible fate. If something were to happen, and I don't get back into contact with my mother, I would have to be forced out of my "home" on my eighteenth birthday. That would mean while still being in high school, I would have to have found an apartment, a job, all while trying to finish my final year of school. It scared me because that seemed incredibly scary, and I was unsure if I would be able to handle it. I just had to make sure that this process was successful so that I wouldn't be placed in that predicament.

Just before moving, I was given a letter from my biological mother. The Children's Aid had reached out, and she responded favorably. She seemed to have an interest in reconnecting, and so it had been decided to begin the process to allow access.

While things were seeming utterly hopeless, I now needed to have faith that this letter was what I needed in my life. I needed something to help turn things around for me. When I think back to the final days at my foster home, I had the letter. I had the knowledge that things were being looked into to reconnect us. And yet, I found myself breaking into a home down the street. Treating my foster mom like garbage. It made me wonder if the reconnecting was really the thing that would help turn things around. The truth in it all was that all I have ever wanted in my life was for a family. To be a part of a family, and feel as though I belong. I just didn't know yet if that was this.

Chapter Twelve
The Falls of Thought

I was always lead to believe that the number seven represented good luck and fortune. Having heard this, I think that's the reason why the number seven has always remained my favorite number. The thing is, in my life, the number seven represented the complete opposite. When I was seven years old, I had my goodbye visit. I smashed my head against the mirror in an attempt to shield myself from the pain I was afflicted with. I was always lead to believe that when you break a mirror, you are cursed with seven years of bad luck. All I was left to believe were the facts. From when I broke that mirror with my head, I still have a year or so left on my sentence.

Things in my life got to an all-time low these past few months, and I didn't think things could get worse for me. I was wrong in every way. Since determining that I would no longer have the desire to be adopted, it had seemed as though I had just simply given up. In so many ways I felt as though nothing I did matter because I was always going to find a way to get myself in trouble. I felt as though nothing I did seemed to have an effect on how others viewed me. Every time I thought I was trying to pick myself up, it felt as though those around me were conspiring against me. Every time I thought I was trying to do what was asked, it turned out it wasn't. I was beginning to wonder if things were ever going to get better. I didn't think that I was ever going to find some happiness, as everything had been taking forever.

In a hast made decision, I opted out of being adopted again. I began to feel as though my life had already been written that I was never going to become a part of a family again. I had been told on numerous occasions that I could manage independence on my own once I turn 18 since I had been found capable of doing so. I never wanted to be on my own. I had always insisted that I wanted to have a family. I had always stated that having a family to call my own was extremely important to me. I never understood why it kept being said that I could move out of foster care at the age of eighteen, to live on my own. That went against everything I had wanted for myself.

By the end of the sixth grade, I had become taken over with rage and aggression. I was at my wit's end with trying to ask for help with bullies. No one seemed to want to help, and actually pay attention to the pain and suffering I had been dealing with on a daily basis, on my own. It got to the extent of suspensions, kicked off the bus, extremely hurting two different girls, that people finally had seen what happened. Even then, the only ones who were made aware of the situation and how bad it had got, were the girls, their parents, my friends, and their parents. None of the people I had ever gone to had been woken up because all they could do was think about punishing me for my behavior, and worry if it could get even worse.

Things had gotten so bad in the end at my foster home on the lake. This was a foster home that I actually loved being a part of, and yet, I had been going through so much, unable to ascertain how to handle the situations. I felt as though I needed to deal with it all on my own because that's how I was left feeling. Things became so bad, that I knew they could get even worse, which would be something I wouldn't want. I was already living with the knowledge that I ruined another amazing relationship with people I cared a lot for, and so I needed to run. I couldn't face them anymore, because I was too afraid.

Before being able to sort through any of the problems I had caused, I once again requested to be moved from my foster home. My worker having heard most of the problems had become incredibly disappointed in me. Knowing how bad things were though, she agreed and picked me up.

I had just been caught with the breaking and entering with the house down the street just before my move. Once I made my way to my new foster home, I had a few conversations over the phone with the woman. She, bless her heart, found forgiveness in what I, my friend, and foster sibling had done. As disturbed as the situation was, she didn't want to cause even more trouble for any of us. After speaking with her, apologizing, she said she would not press charges so long as I would agree to doing some community service, and one selfless good deed.

I couldn't believe the level of compassion and forgiveness of this woman. I had already seen such kindness from the other time I broke into that woman's truck. I thought I had honestly run out of good luck, but as it would seem, this was in fact the last time.

As time went on, it would seem as though I would make my way further and further outside of North Bay. It might have actually been a good thing since the town had brought me nothing but misery and pain. My worker brought me to my new foster home in Bonfield. A really small town, that was basically made up of a single road.

With nothing in my life seeming to go well, creating chaos and trouble seemed to be an easy task. The less fortunate I felt, the more I acted out. The more lonely I felt, the more I pushed myself away from people. The more I felt as though I wasn't being heard, the more I refused to share. It became a vicious cycle, and in the end, I began to stop caring about everything.

Within the next eleven months, I would find myself living in two different foster homes. My stay in Bonfield lasted between July 2002 and February 2003. Looking back at my entire stay within the foster system, there were times where I swore I showed signs of depression. If the constant and ever-growing acting out wasn't a sign, then the fact that my mood changes should have been. If none of those two were indications something wasn't right, then dealing with all of the losses over the course of my life definitely should have been. Even the mere thought that since I seemed to keep distancing myself away from people, should have been an indication.

There were so many instances that should have made someone wonder what was going on. Still, no one questioned it. Still, no one thought to seek possible treatment, or even get me tested just to make sure. The fact that it seemed no matter how much I felt I was crying out in trouble, no one was listening. It hurt so much and caused me to lash out even more. I didn't know how to ask for help, especially since it didn't seem anyone cared enough.

Since adoption was no longer a thought in anyone's mind, looking into contact with my biological mother had begun. Before I moved to Bonfield, I received my first initial letter from her. It had been the first time I had read a letter from her since my Lifebook sessions. Feeling as though I was very much alone, that letter was read almost on a daily basis. I was still in pain from deciding against my adoptive family, and my sister was practically non-existent in my life. That one letter was all I had.

My worker and others at the CAS office had begun to wonder if contact with my mother was even in my best interest. They were fully aware of all the recent issues and troubles I was finding myself in. They were unsure if reconnecting would be a solution, or even deserving. Reading my files, on quite a few occasions, they wrote how unsure they were about the decision to look into possible contact. One way or another, the final decision had been planned for September 2002 to overturn the Crownwardship to *With Access*.

Before starting the seventh grade, at a new school in North Bay, I found myself spending the rest of the summer alone. I had been requesting to visit with my sister since I knew she had been moved to a foster home not too far from where I was. I was told I couldn't because she had to settle in her new home. On a few occasions, I made my way on my bike to the foster home anyways, because I knew exactly where it was. I didn't end up getting to see her, which only made me even more sad.

I didn't have much to do and hadn't made new friends yet, so found myself aimlessly making my way around the small town. One day, I stumbled across this little path, that leads out to a small stream, falls, rapids. I don't know exactly what it was, but the water was running down a hill, with many large rocks. Kinda like a small fall, with rapids. That's the best way I can describe it. There were trees on either side of the stream, and once standing beside it, you couldn't see any houses or any part of the town. Standing in that area, brought some peace to me. I had always enjoyed being out in nature because it allowed me to escape my life. It reminded me of when I lived in the Hell House, and I would cross the street to sit on my log.

I spent most of my days beside that stream, just staring at the water flowing by, hitting the rocks as it would at times splash back at me. When my mind would be screaming at me with all of the things being said to me from people in my life, the sound of the water took over. Slowly my mind was becoming blank with thought, and all I could hear was the water. It felt so freeing, so relaxing. Sadly, I would always have to make my way back to my foster home.

I had always known wherever I would be living, there would be chores to do. I'm not an idiot. Not now, and not back in my foster years. Some placements had more than others, but that was just how things were. In my Bonfield home though, it became more than just chores. There were two other foster children living with me, and the foster parents had two sons of their own in the home.

When I moved into the home, I noticed that one of the other foster children was actually about fifteen or sixteen. The difference with her, however, was that she had a mental disability. She had down syndrome. Never in my life had I met someone with DS, and never in my life had anyone explained to me what it even was. When I moved into my foster home, all I was told was that *she was slow, and had the mind of a two-year-old*. That gave me no information. Her speech was impaired as well, so that was another thing I didn't understand, or know why it was like that.

The other foster child in the home was about four or five years old. Actually reminded me of a younger version of myself. The two children of my foster parents were older, high school students. Although living in the home, the two of them seemed to rarely be there. They always spent their time in the backyard in **their** shed, or in the living room when they wanted to watch TV.

While knowing I would have to do certain chores around the home, I didn't realize I would be the only person to do them. The house I was living in was oddly small but was on a massive piece of property, covered in grass. My chores began with having to cut the entire property of grass, which always took two full days to do, with a push mower. I understood the teenage girl had some disadvantages due to hearing she had the mind of a two-year-old.

While I would be out cutting the grass, which never seemed to end, she would stand around, staring at me. All of the time, and it freaked me out. I would ask her to stop, but she would continue. After several times each day asking her to stop staring at me, I got in trouble. No one explained anything to me regarding her Down-Syndrome, and now I was the foster kid who *yelled at a disabled foster sibling*.

When I wasn't cutting the grass, I was sweeping the floors, cleaning the bathrooms, doing the dishes. I honestly felt like I was the male version of Cinderella. While I had to do all of these things, not one other person had to do anything. It seemed as though my new foster parents got exactly what they wanted, a child to do the chores, so they didn't have to. I was never asked if I wanted help, and I sure as hell complained. I didn't think it was fair that I was the only child or person in the house having to do any type of chores.

I complained to my worker on a few occasions, but of course, my claims didn't seem to hold any weight. My foster parents and worker, as per my files, just made the conclusion that I was expecting to be treated like the baby in the family not having to do chores. I never once stated that I didn't want to do any chores. I just didn't want to be made feel as though my only purpose for living in this home, was to become Cinderella. It was bad enough that my room was smaller than a jail cell. There was just enough room for my single bed, on a folding metal bottom frame, and one small dresser. The shower in the basement looked bigger than my room. Not even joking. That small.

If I already wasn't feeling used, and alone at the beginning of my new foster home, not being believed surely added to it. My foster parents noticed a purchase of an adult film on the paper-view bill. Before asking anyone else in the home, they accused me of purchasing it. The thing was, I barely had an opportunity to watch TV. Any time I would try, and once the fall came around where I could watch my favorite Vampire show, their sons would change the channel. I would have ten or so minutes left, but once they were inside and wanted the TV, I had no say in the matter.

My worker was notified, and of course, I got into trouble. I tried to explain that I didn't purchase the movie. I tried to tell everyone, but no one wanted to believe me. Even after reading my files, it stated that the issue was brought up to my foster parents' sons, and then the issue had been resolved. No indication of finding out that they were wrong in accusing me. Nothing is written about how I was telling the truth. They put a lock on the purchasing option so that in the future it wouldn't happen again.

On days where I was found to be getting into trouble, depending on my reactions to the situations, I had found myself leaving the dinner table to my room without my meal. This happened quite a few times. Not to mention that even my lunches barely had anything in them. I often found myself hungry. I was twelve years old, growing, and at times not being allowed to finish my meals. During the night, I became even more hungry. I would sneak into the freezer and would eat whatever I could find. Of course, I had been discovered and then called a thief for stealing the food. I once again tried to explain that it was because of how hungry I would become, but no one was listening.

With the growing concerns of aggression, finally, the Children's Aid had the thought that perhaps therapy was something to be considered. With how things ended at my last foster home, anger management therapy began in September 2002. It was with a male therapist, and he was not someone I liked. I didn't have many sessions with him, as it was not very easy for me to trust and open up to a man. I had also been annoyed that of all the things to send me for therapy, they finally chose now, and for my anger issues. There were issues caused by multiple, more severe issues in my life. It just made no sense, and I started refusing to go. And then they just stopped when my worker realized I didn't want to go.

To my surprise, once I began attending school, on my second day, I saw my sister waiting for the bus after school. I had been asking to see her, been refused, and there she was, at my school, and no one even bothered to tell me. Since we were both going to school, there wasn't a lot of time that we had to spend with one another. I continued to ask if I would be able to have visits with her, after school hours. I was told no since we were both going to the same school, it was found to be enough. Plus, her foster mother having heard of my troubles didn't want me around her home.

I started spending my lunch hours with my sister and her friends. At first, everything was great, and I was even meeting new friends. We would cross the street to a path, and everyone would smoke during the lunch breaks. What was just initially cigarettes, turned into smoking weed. I remembered smoking weed from my last foster home and remembered how funny I felt, and yet numbed. I found it to be a perfect solution to resting the stress in my foster home, and so began to smoke it, almost daily.

With being in a group of people every lunch hour smoking cigarettes and marijuana, it was brought to my attention that I would have to pitch in once in a while. I didn't exactly know where to get it, or even money for it. At first.

Every week I would have to cut the grass, which always took two days to do. One day while cutting the grass, everyone in the house was out. I was left alone and became curious when I was cutting the grass in the backyard. I went to look into the shed that the sons and foster father would always be in. From the small door window, I could see inside, and to my surprise, saw marijuana paraphernalia.

Knowing that the sons and foster father clearly smoked weed, I had wondered if there was any around the house. A couple of times the shed door had been unlocked, so I would go in to see if there was any I could take for school, to share. Other times prior to leaving for my bus, I would quickly sneak into one of the sons' bedrooms, and of course, I would find their stash. I could only take a little bit at a time, so they wouldn't notice. On days that I wouldn't take their weed, I would see if they had loose change so that I could at least offer money to pitch in.

One day, while looking for weed to bring to school, I went in one of the drawers of one of the sons. To my disgust, when I opened one of the drawers to his dresser, I saw that the entire thing was filled with used Kleenex. As soon as the drawer was opened, a foul smell hit me in the face. My eyes began to water, and for a second didn't know what it was, or why he would keep a drawer full of bunched up Kleenex. Turns out, for some reason he decided to keep and store all of the used Kleenex from masturbating. When I realized what the Kleenex was, I nearly vomited. I mean, there are garbage pales for a reason. Sure, when I would have to empty the garbage, I might have wondered why it was full of so much smelly Kleenex, but it would be better than storing it in your dresser. One would think.

After a little while of sneaking into the sons' rooms for their weed, and the odd change, I was seen one day. My foster parents notified my worker, and the situation was partly explained. My worker was informed that I was sneaking into the rooms stealing money, and so they began to lock their doors. Of course, they never bothered to tell my worker I was really mostly stealing the family's supply of marijuana. That would have got them in trouble, so just mentioning the change was all they wanted to talk about.

Since I had now stolen food, and the odd change, any time something had been misplaced or appeared stolen, I was the only suspect in the eyes of my foster parents. My foster mother had misplaced a ring of hers, and anytime she had mentioned something about it, would stare at me. She knew she couldn't just come out and accuse me but always insinuated that I had taken it. She had even spoken with my worker about it, saying how she thinks I did.

While the ring was still missing, the foster parents said in front of me that *if the ring just shows back up, as long as it's returned, no trouble will come to who took it*. I rolled my eyes because the entire time they were looking at me as if to tell me to go get it. I didn't have the ring, and I tried to tell everyone I didn't, but no one seemed to believe me. Without mentioning it to my worker, my foster mother found it one day when cleaning up her room. No apology for accusing me, and I don't even know where it was found. All I know is that the issue of the ring went away, but I had just hoped they realized how wrong they were.

When Halloween was approaching, I was becoming very excited to be able to go out trick or treating, while getting lots of candy. It gave me something to look forward to, and I had been wondering what I would even be. When I mentioned to my foster parents about my excitement, they squashed it almost instantly. Apparently, 12 years old was too old to be going out trick or treating. Since moving to this foster home, I had nothing to look forward to.

Although approved for the start of contact with my biological mother, the phone calls and letters were very few. I wasn't allowed to see my sister, and she seemed to be going back and forth between the detention center and her foster home. I needed something positive in my life. I needed at least one small thing that would make me smile. I found that in going out for Halloween, and yet, even that I couldn't seem to have.

I had been told that I was too old and that no one would give me candy, so I shouldn't be going. The thing was, they couldn't stop me, because how would you explain that to my worker. Denying a child the pleasure of going out on Halloween? I did feel so down about it though, that I mentioned to my worker how I might not go because of my age. Thankfully, my worker picked up my spirits and insisted that I should go out, have a blast, get lots of candy, and not stress about feeling like being too old.

Initially being so excited for an opportunity to have contact with my biological mother after so many years, soon after became questionable. I had to take my phone calls upstairs because my foster parents wanted to be in earshot of them, to make sure I wasn't saying anything bad. A few times, when I would complain about something happening in my home, I would get a warning to stop talking about it, or they would just hang up on me. I became quite upset about this and spoke to my worker about feeling as though my rights had been violated. I was feeling upset and had the right to complain to someone who would listen. No one seemed to be hearing my concerns, and so I wanted to share it with my mother. Apparently, my right to complain wasn't even a right, and I was told I wasn't allowed to mention issues within my foster home.

Since my adoption not continuing, the only good thing that came from it, was the fact that I no longer had the worry of having any contact with my brother. It was becoming a more difficult issue to have him in my life, and without being asked any questions about my decision, I opted out from further contact. Not being with my adoptive family helped with that as well.

Since my brother had still been living in his adoptive home, the crown wardship that was granted for with access, only meant for my sister and I. Knowing this, and shortly into the beginning of our communication, it seemed important for my mother to ask about him. At first, she was just asking a few simple questions; what he looked like, was he happy, do I have any pictures. What started out harmless questions about my brother, seemed to be the only thing she ever wanted to talk about. Not knowing anything that had happened, it was becoming annoying to me how she seemed to almost only want to discuss him. Here I was, living in my foster home, going through some stuff, and she didn't seem to care what I was going through.

She kept asking if I had any photos of him and if I would be able to send them to her. All I could hear from my mother was how she remembered him, and then went on to tell me stories. It was becoming clear to me, that I didn't seem to matter to her. Feeling this way, only added to the already growing frustrations in my foster home. The more frustrated I became about everything, the more I looked forward to going to school, so I could smoke pot and forget about the pain I had.

My grades began to slip, as I was usually stoned, but no one knew. Every time I was high, I felt as though I was drifting on a cloud, and all the frustrations and pain I had just went away. It numbed everything I was feeling and became something I looked forward to. A couple of times during lunch when everyone would be smoking pot, some older high school kids began hanging out with us all. Not often, but sometimes, not only would they smoke pot, but at times would snort cocaine.

At the point of being in grade seven, I had never done any other drug, other than marijuana. All of these kids were friends of my sisters, and on the days when she wasn't around, I still hung out with them. When she would return, I felt as though I needed to remain friends with hers, so we could hang out. When the kids with cocaine started hanging around, I had been asked if I wanted any. I had never done it before, and so they told me that it was fun, and I should try it. I figured why not. I was already stoned from the weed, so what harm could a little cocaine do. First and last time I snorted cocaine until I was much older.

No matter how much I thought I was helping my mind settle while feeling alone, unappreciative, not listened to, judged, and undesirable, the thoughts would never leave. I thought the numbing from the weed would help, and it didn't. Nothing seemed to be settling at home. My mother didn't even seem to want to talk to me, because I wasn't her precious oldest child. No matter what I tried to do to make myself feel better, nothing was working.

I often found myself making my way to the falls or rapids. I would go there and usually cry because I didn't know what else to do. I tried holding my cross while laying in bed praying for answers. I prayed for a sign to show me what to do. I would have conversations with myself while listening to the water in the background. I would pace back and forth, letting out the frustrations that I wasn't allowed to share with anyone. No one seemed to be listening to me anyway, so why couldn't I say what I want. I was beginning to consider how I made the worst decision by looking into contact with my biological mother. I found myself thinking of my mom and dad more and more as time went on. I was becoming desperate, and I was running out of options.

Before the snow covered the ground, I became completely lost. It was at the point, where I was so numb, I barely felt anything. I didn't care anymore. If I was getting into trouble, so what. There became no filter, and when being told something from my foster parents, I would say what I always wanted to. When asked to do yet another chore, I would suggest he get off his fat ass and do it himself. He was extremely overweight, and I felt had maybe he done some of the things I had to do, he wouldn't be so big. I was becoming belligerent in tone, and I didn't care.

One day, things felt like they couldn't get any worse for me. I once again made my way to my reflection spot by the rapids. At this point, it was freezing outside, and yet the water was still not frozen. The ground I was pacing on was hard and had been covered in fallen leaves. I was at my breaking point. All I wanted to do was scream at the top of my lungs. I just wanted anyone to hear me. I was crying. I was pacing. I was stuck in my head on what to do. I didn't know anymore, and I didn't know how to make the pain go away. I stopped, and I stared at the water. It was flowing past me, hitting the rocks as it fell to the calmness at the end of the stream.

I had been looking for an answer to making the pain go away. For so long I had been wondering what I could do, and it was always there. In the moment of looking at the water, an idea popped into my mind. Still crying, I thought if I were to jump into the rapids, there could be no way I would come out of that. The heavy stream would take me, and all the pain and frustrations I had would get washed away. Finally, it would all just go away. In the moment I didn't even think I would be missed. I felt as though at least all the troubles I seemed to be causing would go away, making everyone happy. After feeling like such a failure and disappointment, I decided to jump.

Had I landed into the water, the falls, or rapids, whatever they were, easily would have ended my suffering. To my stupidity, and thanks to my clumsiness, my foot got caught on a tree root, which held my one foot, and leg from jumping into the water. I ended up falling directly in front of it, and only a part of my head ended up seeing water. Looking up while laying smacked on the ground, I could see the water running past me. I looked at my feet as I didn't know what happened, and I saw the root. I remember shaking my head, and I blurted out *Are you fucking kidding me*. And then I started to laugh.

I limped back to my foster parents after tripping. In the moment of realizing what I had tried to do, I knew it wasn't quite my time. In that moment I knew regardless of the struggles and problems I was facing, I had to keep going. There had to be a reason for being stopped, other than the fact that I am just clumsy. I knew that I was going to have difficult days and that all of my worries weren't just going to go away, but I needed to find the joys in my life.

Before the Christmas holidays of 2002, shortly after my falls incident, my foster mother got herself into a bit of an accident. I had been searching for signs to remind me to keep going. Finally, I was given the best kind of reminders making me realize things could get better for me.

When needing to find a temporary relief home for me while my foster mother recovered, I was sent to one of my favorite relief homes. This family had three children, two boys, and one girl. The girl was the oldest, and the middle son was my age. Everything about this home made me feel welcomed, and had shown me everything I was looking for. I got along with everyone for the most part, and it ignited the flame inside me that I thought had gone out.

I had been searching for something to smile about, and it was my time at this home that I started to think back to some of the few things I already did have going for me. I had been so stuck in my head that the small things that did bring me simple joys, were forgotten. Since moving from my Lakeview foster home, I remained in contact through letters with my first love. Having a longtime friend meant a great deal to me because it had shown me that there were people out there who thought of me, and who listened to me.

Regardless of the fact that I felt ignored by my biological mother, after so many years of wanting a family, I was given another chance at it. I needed to give it a chance, time, and hope that it will work out. A visit was being planned for January 2003 with my sister as well, so I needed to wait out for it before allowing my mind to be made of how I felt about her. So many years had gone by without her, I needed to allow this adjustment period to pass.

I felt like a slave to my current foster parents because it seemed all they wanted me around for, was to do all of the household chores, while they didn't. I needed to suck it up and just go with the flow. I had already made noise about how it made me feel, and I just had to have hope that maybe one day someone will finally see the truth, and believe me.

I felt as though I wasn't allowed to be the child I was, because there was no one in my life who I could play with, and spend time with. Unless I was on relief somewhere that had other children, I was left by myself. Typically I was left in my room, drawing or writing down my feelings. Thinking no one would listen, writing down how I felt gave me a sense of freedom, and as though I was sharing my thoughts and feelings.

This family during the Christmas relief made me smile, which was something I didn't think would happen. It felt like it had been such a long time since I truly smiled and had been happy about something. I was able to play, be free, be a child. I wasn't treated like a slave, forced to do every household chore. Everyone ate together, and always left everyone full. Everything about my stay filled me with what was missing and needed in my life.

Although incredibly happy within my relief, I did have my days where I was in thought. I couldn't help it, because there were so many unresolved issues. It almost felt as though no issues had actually been resolved. During times where I was stuck thinking about everything, I liked to be on my own. Turning the TV on allowed me to do this.

One day towards the end of my relief stay, I was in thought, watching TV when everyone else was outside or playing. The foster dad turned the TV off and suggested that I go outside or play with the others. He said that I shouldn't just keep myself in front of the television. While deep in my thoughts, I was already emotional thinking about my life and what to do, and so I didn't know how to interpret what had been said.

His comment was harmless, and he just didn't want to see me stuck in front of the TV while I could be having fun with everyone else. Sadly, I took it as attacking me. It made me feel bad about the decisions I was making, which made me slightly retreat. I had thought he and his family liked me, but hearing what he said, made me feel like he didn't. That wasn't the case at all, but my fragile mind heard the worst in usually everything.

I requested to return to my foster home oddly enough. Unsure why the sudden change of wanting to leave their home, the foster parents had asked my worker what happened. They didn't understand why I would all of a sudden decide to go back to a place they knew I didn't even like. I was too afraid to share what I was feeling with the relief family, and a little bit embarrassed.

Hoping that the couple week break might help my living situation, it would soon return to how it was prior. Since I was unable to cut the grass, since the ground was covered in snow, it was my responsibility to shovel the laneway. No one else, just me.

In the beginning of the year, after so long waiting for another theatre opportunity, finally I found one. There was a musical production of Charlie Brown being put on. Auditions were being held in February, and so all I had to do was wait.

When returning to my foster home, I had so hoped things would get better. Sadly, they didn't. School wasn't going well for me, and my sister was absent in my life. My mother still seemed to only want to talk about my brother, and once again asked for pictures of him. I said to myself, fine. I'll send the couple of photos I had, and then she could hopefully be silent on the matter.

I had to wait to send out the letter and photos until I got a stamp. In the fall when I asked for a stamp to mail a letter, I wasn't given any, and so I tried to reuse one. Little did I know, that was apparently against the law, and I got into a lot of trouble. I was told that the post office was considering pressing charges against me, but I had no idea reusing a stamp, was that big a deal. I didn't want to get into any more trouble, so I figured I would wait until I could get a stamp to mail the stuff out to my mother.

By the middle of February 2003, while things at school didn't seem to be getting any better for me, I found myself getting suspended. Usually, when I would get in trouble, it was for skipping classes, smoking on property, or using foul language towards teachers. Being incredibly upset that I was suspended, and now having to stay at home, my foster parents told me I would have to remain outside during my suspended days.

I didn't so much mind having to stay outside, but I found having to do that all day long to be a bit much. Especially considering the fact that it was the middle of winter, and it was freezing. It had just snowed, and I was told that I had to remove all of the snow and ice in the driveway. I needed something to do, and so away I went.

I shoveled the snow, but apparently, that wasn't enough. I was told that I also needed to get rid of the ice in the driveway so no one would trip. The driveway took me hours, and I was already freezing. The ice was thick, and I had a plastic shovel. I was beginning to get really cold and asked to go inside. I was told that I couldn't go in until the ice was gone.

I tried and I tried to break that ice, but I couldn't. Again, I asked to go inside as I was cold, but was told no. I was told that this was my punishment, and I needed to learn my lesson. I said the hell to this. I dropped the shovel and ran off.

At first, I didn't know what to do, or where to go. I just knew I wasn't sticking around my foster home. My falls were frozen, so thought maybe I'd hitchhike to North Bay, which was about twenty or so minutes.

I got picked up almost instantly and asked to go to my school because I had missed my bus, and couldn't get a ride. Yes I lied, but I needed to hurry up and get away. I met up with a friend from school, and I decided that I wanted to try and run away to go see my mother in Ottawa.

I was at the point where I felt like I had no other option but to leave. My friend offered to join me, which was great because at least I wouldn't have to be alone during my running away. Once school ended, we stayed at her house for a bit, had something to eat, and then took off. At first, we aimlessly walked around North Bay, trying to stay out of sight, since it had been suspected people were looking for me. When night came around, we began making our way to the highway.

Right away we were picked up from a trucker, and driven all the way to Ottawa. I knew where my mother lived from getting her address off of the letters she wrote to me, so I knew she wasn't directly in the city. She was on the outskirts of the city, in a tiny town where she rented a house. The trucker dropped us off on the side of the highway and pointed in what direction we needed to go in, to get to my mothers. He wasn't going in that direction, and so he couldn't drive us any further.

Not long after beginning our walk on the highway, we were stopped by the police. It kind of came as a relief because of how cold we were. It kind of was a disappointment because of how close we had become. The Ottawa police had been on the lookout in case I were to have made my way there, since running away. We were asked our names, and for some reason, I told my actual name, and so he knew right away I was the "missing" foster child.

He asked where I was headed, and I told him I wanted to go see my mother. He appeared to be somewhat impressed that I had made my way all the way from North Bay, at twelve years old. He could tell that I was in a bad situation, and since making the trip, I should at least get to see her. He brought us to her house so I could at least say hello and then brought us to the station where everyone had been called indicating we were found. Later he spoke with me and talked about all of the dangers involved with running away and hitchhiking.

After spending a night in an Ottawa group home until I was able to be driven back to North Bay, I returned to my foster home. When I got to my room, it was completely turned upside down. Pages from my art book, torn out. Pages from my notebooks, torn out. Considering how small the room was, it was a disaster.

I became incredibly pissed off. When uncertain where I was, the police had gone through everything. Living in my previous home, I made myself a wooden stake out of white wood that I found in the woods. I even carved designs on it, as it became an art project to pay tribute to my favorite show. I guess the police found it to be unsafe and took it away. The unsent letter to my mother with my brother's photos, gone. Every single one of the photos I had of him was gone. I didn't so much mind, but still couldn't believe that they would just take them all. Most of my letters with my mother were also taken. Rage filled me so much that day. I had felt so violated, and as though any bit of privacy I was supposed to have, had been completely gone.

I never received my photos back. I never received my letters back. I wasn't expecting to receive my stake back, though I did miss it. It took a long time to make and had become symbolic for me. I ended up getting in more trouble once I returned than I had ever thought possible. I was told that from now on, I would only be allowed to send letters after they had been reviewed. My phone calls would have to be monitored, and I would have to continue my suspension outside. This time, I refused to do any more shoveling.

After requesting to be moved instantly from returning, it was found to be a good idea. Things were only getting worse for everyone in the home, and so the thought was that I needed a new placement. It was the hope that a fresh start, at a home I was already familiar with would be the change I needed.

Chapter Thirteen

A Dragon of Hope

If there is one thing I've learned in life, it's that the low points can really suck. When things become so dire that you begin to lose all hope, what do you do? Having the slightest idea of what I should do had been something I never knew. A lot of the time, I thought I knew what to do, but that usually resorted to finding myself in trouble.

Often the small things in my life were the ones that made the biggest difference. I never felt as though I had much in the world. I had spent years trying to hold onto things that at some point brought value and meaning to my life. During the times where I was left feeling down on myself, down from those around me, it was the small momentum that I held onto to spark something within me.

I can remember feeling down and absolutely crumby more often than feeling good. Feeling as I had, it became extremely important and a necessity to look for joys, reasons to smile, and positivity in my life. Whiling losing the hope I had worked so hard to keep, regaining it became a detriment to my survival within the foster system.

With each move I made in my life, there were things I always had to do. Reflection on my time in the foster home was typically the most important. Whether I wanted to or not, I had to come to terms that once moved, there was no going back. I had learned that early on, and as much as I may have wanted to at times, I couldn't. There was only moving forwards, although with reflection, allowed me to look back.

I have always found reflection, memory, and remembering to be completely different, even though sounding the same. If you are a person of knowledge, you may assume that should be obvious. To a twelve-year-old, who struggled with literacy issues all of his life, this quite often had not been made obvious.

Once moved to a new foster home, I would first reflect on all of the decisions made throughout my stay. What leads me to my leaving. What alternatives were in place that I either ignored or were unaware of. Had I been given the opportunity, if and how would I do things differently? I would have to take each incident and situation, breaking it down completely. I would have to analyze all of the options in order to move forward.

Once it was time to move, the second most important thing I found I had to do was to remember. While always finding how much I could remember to be both a gift and a curse, it became important to never forget. Forgiveness with wrongdoing seemed to be something I always hoped to achieve, but that doesn't mean people forget. At times, people will remember, and not want to forgive to move on. At times people will remember what they want, for instance, to allow them to think they do no wrong.

I had been accused of this many times in my life because no one wanted to listen to me. People found me guilty of always doing this because, in their minds, adults could do no wrong. Remembering what you choose to, and deciding what to repeat are different things. Admittedly I had negated certain aspects of the truth regarding certain situations. The difference with me in those situations was that in the end, I had always told the full truth. The negating certain things weren't all the time, as I only did it when feeling attacked, or that I needed to get my point across.

I made a crap ton of mistakes in my life. In some ways, I'm still paying for them. I allowed things at times to get so bad. I chose not to speak up, or out. I became violent and allowed my aggression to take control. I became belligerent to anyone who either got in my way, felt deserved it, or when I needed to lash out. I felt the need to numb my pain with drugs for a period of time, and even tried to kill myself. I lied, I stole, I even broke into homes and vehicles that didn't belong to me. I ignored those who brought great meaning to my life. I was an incredibly emotional person, which made it difficult to attach myself to things and people. I allowed my emotions to control most aspects of my life.

Remembering all of my flaws was never something I didn't do. Remembering all of the bad things I had done, was something I always had to do. If I wasn't constantly being reminded of them, I needed to pinpoint the times they occurred in my life, so I would always remember how I felt about them. I needed to remember how I was made to feel about them from those in my life. Had I not been believed, or felt like anyone was on my side, I needed the memory of it so I could retell my side.

Memory was typically the least important aspect of moving somewhere new for me. Being so similar to the other two, and yet was so different. When I think of my memory, I think of everything communicatively within a certain time frame. It became something of an overall mindset of things and people. While having full knowledge of all of the events that took place, the memory is how my mind chooses to remember something.

For instance, my social worker. I complained a lot about feeling as though she had never listened to me and my needs. For a long time, I felt as though she was oblivious to my depression and signs of needing help. A lot of times I was left feeling undesired and uncared for. The thing was, these were simply just how I was left to feel. Whether the feelings weren't intentional or not by her, it was how I went by my days. The feelings were valid regardless of how anyone else felt about them, because they were mine, in the moment. Although I may not have only the best forms of feelings when I remember my foster care days, I chose to keep her in my memory in a positive way.

In my memory, I know she did care, although I may not have always thought so. She usually always made me smile when we would speak. She never teased me and had always found things to compliment me on while knowing I would be down. She encouraged me to have my interests regardless if others disapproved. When things became dim within certain situations, she always tried to find something positive knowing that I would feel attacked. Although not as much as I had hoped, in the end, I know she tried. In my memory moving forward, I choose to allow the good things about her to be what I remember most.

We are all human, and mistakes are made on both parts. There's nothing wrong with making mistakes. It just becomes a matter of finding the strength to admit when we do make a mistake. In order to grow, change, do better, seeing the truth within the mistake, we need to come to terms with it and accept it for what it is.

On February 18th, 2003, I entered the last official foster home I would be living in. I would remain there until June 2003, and once moved, would still remain within the Children's Aid Society.

There had only been one instance where I actually had a choice in where I lived. The last few times of being placed somewhere new, I was the one to initiate the desire for a change. With each of the moves that I made, there was a specific, and different reason.

When I moved from home right after my adoption, I had grown quite attached to the family. With each bad behavior, I had grown worried that I was becoming too close. I didn't want to be disappointed when they would decide they no longer wanted me in their home and life. It wasn't because it was going to happen, it was because it had been a fear of mine. It became a crippling insecurity since I had grown quite fond of them, and wanted them to remain in my life. I had just become so detached with some problems, and I was filled with much shame.

Moving from the Lakeview home was not intentional. In my files, it had been repeated that once I am no longer able to manipulate my environment, I request a move. That wasn't the case at all. The home was a place I had also quite enjoyed living at, however, I was beginning to feel at my all-time low. Having my adoptive family officially, and finalizing the fact that I would not try a life with them again, hurt me more than I could ever imagine. I didn't know how to process everything going on in my life, and so I kept acting out. Knowing how much damage I was causing in my home, it felt as though there was no chance in regaining the view they once had of me. That frightened me, and I felt the need to run, instead of staying and try to come back to reality with them.

The move from the Bonfield residence was in my opinion obvious. It had got to the point of a mutual beneficial need for me to leave. There was no possible way things were going to work out, and I was honestly fine with that.

I have had quite a few relief stays, at multiple different foster homes over the years. There had been a few that were good, but prior to my move from Bonfield, only two stood out. Only two relief foster homes made me always hope to return because the time I had spent there had been nothing but enjoyable.

I needed something good to happen in my life. I had to find something that I was able to make those around me see the good in me. I had been on a downward spiral, and I needed to find something to ground me. The move in February was something I was hoping would do such a thing.

What was once good, then made to feel bad, can it once again become good? The million-dollar question that often struck my mind when moving somewhere. I had been told that I would be moved to Mattawa, at the foster home I started going to for relief while at the Lakeview foster home. It was a place I remembered to make me feel good, left me in smiles, and the people actually seemed to enjoy having me around. When hearing about how I would be moving there, I had hope again. I had thought I had a real chance. I thought things could actually start going better for me.

The thing about hope is as nice as it is to have, it can become disappointing to one's mind. Living somewhere on relief is not the same as living there for a long-term period. I remembered how much fun I had with everyone, especially when I was able to play that dragon video game. They always seemed so nice to me, and I was in good open thoughts when I first moved. I found whenever I moved somewhere, there had always been a short period of time, that seemed like a *honeymoon phase*. Things would always start out well, and then, shit hits the fan.

Prior to my move, I was already experiencing quite a lot of issues and problems within my life. While hoping my move would go well, and help me turn things around, the issues and problems that were around before, were still there. It had been something that slipped my mind because I wasn't thinking about it. I was pissed off at my mother as I felt she was the reason for getting me into trouble with the caseworkers regarding my brother. I was upset at my teachers because I needed someone to lash out at. I was upset with my worker because I kept being denied visitation, or at least to the extent I wanted with my sister. Not to mention the ever-growing list of conflicting emotions and feelings I had inside of me. Things I had been trying to keep buried, and things that I didn't care to share.

All of the situations hadn't just gone away from moving. They were very much still there, and it was only a matter of time until they would surface. The biggest problem with my foster parents that I hadn't realized at first, were how certain characteristics of them reminded me of other previous homes. It seemed as though the worst and least favorable aspects of some of my earlier foster homes, were evident within their home.

When I found myself getting suspended from school, or even getting into trouble, I had to remain outside all day long. Regardless of the weather, I wouldn't be allowed to step foot inside all day long. When there were issues or problems in my foster home that related to only me, those were discussed with the other foster children. Not to simply inform them on what was going on, but in a manner to discuss my own personal problems, where everyone would be allowed to comment on. When I found myself also getting in trouble regarding certain issues, as part of a punishment, all I would be allowed to eat was peanut butter and jam sandwich for dinner. I had to eat it at the table, with everyone present, where I had to watch as everyone else would eat a normal dinner meal. It was to show me what I was missing due to my acting out.

The thing I think I hated the most, was how no matter what I did, no matter how much I had tried to do better within the home, my past mistakes were the only way I was viewed. Regardless if and when I would try to make up for my mistakes and problems, I was shown *too little too late*. How I would be perceived and related to was based on what I had already done, and not what I was trying to do.

The first couple of months seemed to go fairly well, for the most part. When April 2003 made its way around, that's when things started to escalate once again. The little things within my foster home I had issues on, started to surface, which caused me the need to speak out. I found certain things to be unfair, but I wasn't allowed an opinion. They once in a while would bring in a foster child for relief, and since the other two foster kids shared a room, that meant I always had to share a room with the relief child.

This one time everyone was outside walking to the river a little way behind our property. In all honesty, this guy was a prick. He seemed to feel the need to tease me for once again my girlish demeanor. On our walk, I was walking behind everyone slightly because he kind of scared me. All of a sudden, he speaks up, looked back at me, and mentioned how he and the other two should take me in the woods and rape me. I stopped in my track, as I had no idea how to process that. He began to laugh, while the other two also seemed unsure how to process what he had said. It was completely out of nowhere, and as jokes go, not that funny.

I made my way to my foster parents, as I felt attacked, frightened, and didn't know what to do. I was already working really hard to somewhat forget and move on from the incidents involving my brother, so this did not help with that. I knew since this incident had been completely separate, saw it as an opportunity to get ahead of the situation. The sad thing was that they seemed unbothered by the comment. They only saw it as a joke, and that I had nothing to worry about. They did say if anything more would be said, or done, to let them know. And **then** they would look into doing something.

With issues coming up at my foster home, barely speaking to my mother because I felt a disconnect, and my attitude only progressing towards my teachers, I found myself getting into a lot of trouble. My sister was out of detention and was also finding herself in trouble. After being suspended, we decided to run away together. I had some experience previously, and so thought it would be a way to get far away from all of my problems.

We were caught after a day, and when I was returned to my foster family, a bleached blond, everyone seemed to be aware of what had happened. Everyone seemed to know completely of my suspension, running away with my sister, the issues at school, all of it. And to make matters worse, started teasing me for my hair. It felt like a violation that they all knew, when it had nothing to do with them, was none of their business, and yet there was no privacy.

I wasn't allowed to dye my hair back once I was returned, because it was thought I had to live with some consequences for my actions. The biggest consequence that I was faced with was that the Charlie Brown play I was a part of since the beginning of the year, had decided to kick me out. I missed auditions and ended up becoming a part of the main chorus, but then with my getting into trouble, kept missing rehearsals. I was given a ticket to the final performance but was told I couldn't be in it. It hurt a lot. For so long I went without being in a theatre performance, and so was really looking forward to this.

Any time I found myself getting into trouble, and suspended, I found solace in running away. It felt as though the only way to escape it all, was to actually escape and run away. I always knew I would be caught, but I needed the feeling of being in control when wanting to get away from my problems. I ran away seven times that month. The last time I did it, I found myself being sent to the juvenile detention center as a flight risk. I wasn't being charged with anything, but with how much I ran away, I needed some time to realize the risk in what I was doing.

I spent a couple of weeks in the detention center. Once it was time for me to leave, I actually cried because of how upset I was to return to my foster home. I had a couple of encounters in there that made a bit of trouble for me, but aside from that, quite enjoyed myself. There was this one older kid who kept calling me a queer and faggot. There was this one older female teenager, who kept asking me to masturbate in toilet paper and then give it to her. Honestly, these two situations had felt insane, and actually made me question where I was. Either way, the two individual's antics didn't last long, which gave me the chance to enjoy the rest of my stay.

Once I was released and made my way back to my foster home, it had been decided that I should no longer attend my school in North Bay. I had found myself getting into troubling situations over and over, and it was the thought that removing me from temptation might help matters. One thing that came from switching schools for the remaining six weeks of living at my foster home, was the fact that I had an opportunity to make some form of amends with my teacher. I was given an opportunity to go and say goodbye and apologize for my behavior in his classroom. The brief moment I had with him, actually felt good. He seemed to welcome my apology and wished me all the best in my future. He gave me some encouraging words, telling me how he felt I could be quite capable of excelling should I stay focused. It became a moment to which I didn't realize I even needed, but was something to look back on with a smile.

There were a few good things that came from switching schools for the last little bit of the year. For one, most of everything I would be taught in my classes were lessons I had already been over at my previous school. Having already been through it, it helped me find confidence in my classes because I felt as though I was at an advantage already knowing. The other aspect I found to enjoy was that I knew some people.

The two other foster children I lived with, now attended the same school as me. Having them at the same school as me helped when needing to meet new people. As well, the son to my favorite relief home also attended my school, and classes. He and I were friends, and having another familiar face became welcoming. For the duration of my stay, he and I would hang out together a lot during school hours. He wasn't a troubled preteen, which I found to really help me stay away from getting into trouble.

Once I moved schools, I stopped smoking cigarettes, smoking marijuana, and found myself picking up the lost pieces of my goodwill. I found myself getting involved with track and field again. That was something I hadn't done in years and actually felt really good. To everyone's surprise, I was quite a fast short-distance runner. The ribbons I ended up winning have been something I kept to look back and remind me of how capable I can be when I put my mind to it.

When there are many problems going on in one's life, it can be difficult to pay attention to everything going on. There are slight encounters, situations, and even words that are said that you may become oblivious to. For so long I had specific ideologies regarding certain people and places. In certain heat of the moment situations, things get said, and without realizing it at the time, they can have a much larger effect than expected.

During my month of running away, and even during my time at my previous foster home, there had been certain small moments I hadn't paid attention to. Words I had said I never found harm in, until moving schools. For so long, I looked back at my favorite relief home as being my favorite because of how amazing the people were, and how they always made me feel. I felt true kindness with them, and it was something that carried with me for years to come. Something I didn't realize was a conversation I had with my foster parents, that would in result try to squash those feelings.

My relief foster family were only temporary foster parents. During my stay with them, I so badly wished I could stay there long term because of how much I enjoyed myself with them. I so badly wished in times of needing a safe feeling in my home life, that I could find that with the family in their home. I had been told by the family that they enjoyed having me stay with them. The only issue was that they don't foster children long term. They are only short-term relief foster parents. This information was something I had always known. Of course, I wish things could have been different, but still, I knew the difference. I was told that had the relief home been capable or willing to foster long term, they would have liked me to stay with them. HAD been the word used. IF they were able to foster long term. Never had I been told by someone that they would foster long term, because they didn't nor would give false information, or false hope.

When discussing with my foster parents about feeling as though I felt my needs and rights weren't being met, I said I wished I had somewhere else to live. I was told there was nowhere else for me to go because I keep ruining my relationships with my behavior. I specifically remember explaining that that wasn't true. I said that if my relief home was allowed to foster long term they said they would have been happy to look into taking me. They seemed to enjoy having me around, so I know I hadn't ruined all of my relationships.

I am uncertain if they felt attacked from what I said to them, or the fact that they realized some of the things in their home weren't going right, so they decided to share with my caseworkers. The thing is, they decided to say that I was told, my relief home mentioned they <u>would</u> take me regardless of the fact they actually couldn't. Certain details that I remember being clear on, were left out. Telling a foster child certain things that are false, especially giving them false hope about moving placements, isn't something they look on kindly. It's like playing telephone, except in this case my foster parents knew full well of the corrections they made with their story.

When this got back to the workers, I was told they ended up getting my relief home in trouble for what they thought was said. To my surprise, one day at my new school, we were all practicing for track, when I ran into the relief foster dad. He was very upset. Very angry towards me. The whole situation had caused trouble for him, and I had no idea what was going on. He obviously didn't know that I didn't actually say anything against his family, because I wouldn't. I didn't even have a chance to explain to him because he was yelling at me. This relationship with my favorite relief foster home had become tarnished because my current and previous foster parents decided to switch around my words. Both sets of foster parents felt the desire to ruin the one great remaining relationship I had.

I felt betrayed, upset, and once again left feeling as though no matter how much I try to make my life better, something happens to set me back.

After years of feeling as though I had no voice or say in my own life, making sure my rights were being met became important. I had found people to not listen to me almost daily, and my worker had suggested while living at the lake, to start writing things down. I was told to write down my feelings, and when certain things happen, to keep notes about them so they can be discussed. At times I still felt as though this didn't help, but still, I did it. Sometimes I would even make sure my worker or supervisor would get my notes or letters.

Once released from the detention center, I had only one last big blow up. It lasted a few days and had been led up to by my foster parents and their decision to ignore, instigate, and encourage bad behavior at my expense.

On May 18th, 2003 my last blow up started with me feeling as though I wasn't being properly fed. With the issues surrounding my last suspension, I was still being punished even sometime later. Any bit of attitude towards them felt unwarranted, and although I shouldn't have, I felt as though I was being treated unfairly within their home. When speaking up about my feelings, they took away my dinner. They made me sit and watch as everyone got to eat pizza and cake, while I could only have one PB&J sandwich. It felt cruel just because I wanted to speak up about being treated unfairly, in my eyes.

I was also upset that night because when feeling incredibly hungry, I tried to eat licorice that I paid for with any own money. They took it away, threw it out, and I was sent to my room. I could hear everyone talking about me because of how small the house was. I was getting quite upset, and my first instinct was to run. I was getting fed up of feeling mistreated. I started to make my way to the front door to grab my shoes.

While trying to put on my shoes, I was asked to take them off. I replied no, and that I wasn't going to remove them. I continued to put on my shoes, but my foster father continued to ask me to take them off. While still trying to tie up my second shoe, he forcefully grabbed my foot to take off the one shoe. It was slightly difficult since I had just tied it tight, so there was a lot of tugging. With having difficulty taking the shoe off, he told me to take it off again. Trying to free myself from his grasp, I replied no. He told me if I don't take it off, that he would push me down the stairs so I wouldn't be able to leave. He then grabbed me by the arm, which was something I didn't care for. I tried to push him off of me, but it didn't work.

The next day, I was still upset about the incident in the evening. We had a relief foster kid staying with us, which only added to the sharing of my problems. All-day in the blistering heat that we were struck with, I had to remain outside. From first thing in the morning, until the evening. There was a certain area to which I had to stay in, which had no shade, and direct sun in all directions. The others were all working in the scrapyard, which I had actually wanted to do. I wanted something to do for a distraction but was told no.

After realizing how hot it was outside, later in the afternoon everyone went to go swimming. I was told I couldn't go because swimming was a privilege for those who helped work during the day. Hearing that pissed me off because they knew full well that I offered to help, but they refused it and made me sit in the sun. Still, I couldn't go swimming and continued to work on my sunburn.

On May 20th, 2003 things within my home became quite disturbing to me. Still being treated unfairly, everyone wasn't even trying to hide talking about me. I would be in the same room and they still found the need to discuss my troubles over the last couple of days. There was this one incident, I don't even quite remember because I wasn't involved. I had spent so much time on my own, that I wasn't allowed to be around others. I was blamed for the incident, and then once again got yelled at by the foster parents. The other three kids laughing, blamed me, and when I was sent to my room after trying to say it wasn't my fault, I became upset.

I locked the door behind me because I knew I needed space. Things over the last couple of days had not been kind to me, and I needed to be alone so I could calm down. I felt like one of those chemistry beakers when you mix two chemicals together, and they explode out the top. It was getting to the point of the explosion, and so I knew I needed to distance myself before things got worse.

I was told to unlock the door right away but refused. I knew unlocking it wasn't going to help my situation, even though keeping it locked wasn't either. It was becoming clear there wasn't a win here, so I did what I felt I needed to. I told them I wasn't going to unlock the door. I was then told from the foster father that if I don't unlock it, he will kick the door down, and make me pay for replacing it. Still, I kept the door locked.

When I wouldn't unlock and open the door, the foster father used a key to open the door. When it opened he was standing there, smiling, almost laughing, and then hit me over the head. The hitting over the head wasn't a forceful hit, it was when you say to someone, *what's wrong with you* while hitting over the head. Regardless of the intent of it, I didn't want to be touched. The situation wasn't pleasant, and I just wanted him away from me. I told him not to touch me. He found it funny, looked back at his wife, who also began to smile, and somewhat laugh, and then he continued to hit me on the side of the head. I tried to push his hands away, while I kept telling him to not touch me. At this point, I was becoming very upset and included profanity because he didn't seem to listen when asked without.

Finding the situation humorous, his wife then began to hit me on the side of the head when I had been trying to push the foster fathers away. At that point, I had enough and when she hit me, I got a hold of her arm. When trying to pull her arm back I asked how she likes being handled. She didn't like that and then grabbed me by the ear. I released her arm, but still, she kept hold of my ear, and with her ring, ended up cutting my ear.

The two of them while still having my ear in the foster mother's hand, proceeded to walk me towards my bed. She let go of my ear, and then each of them grabbed one of my arms with the tightest grip anyone has ever had on me. During this incident, because of the severity of everything, it was the first time I hadn't been reminded of what my brother had done when grabbing my arm. I was too in the moment and was dealing with a new trauma.

While holding and squeezing both of my arms while walking me back to my bed, my arms became twisted, like a rug burn. I was feeling a lot of pain and tried to push them off of me. I yelled at them. I called them names and used profanity. I was more angry at this moment than ever before, but the difference was how powerless I felt. The foster father was at least three times my size, and trying to push them off of me to release their grip was something I couldn't do.

While being held down from the foster mother, her gum fell out of her mouth and got tangled in my hair. While I was held down on my bed, the foster father began going through my things on my dresser, throwing everything on the floor, making a mess of my stuff. Once again, I yelled with profanity to tell him to stop. I tried to free myself from my foster mother. I tried to push her off of me, and then she tried to grab my hand to stop me. She ended up only grabbing my pinky finger and held it tight. It got twisted, and almost felt as though it became broken. It wasn't, but hurt like hell.

Finally, I was released, and they left my room. Before they left me in my room alone fuming with rage, and in pain, everything thrown on the floor, I was told my light had to remain off. Having a light was thought to be a privilege, one I wasn't allowed. I was told to stay in my room, which was something I tried to do from the beginning.

In the past, there had been times where I exaggerated certain things in order to move from my placement. It was never that I exaggerated things that didn't happen, but rather to make my workers realize certain pains I was feeling. When it came to this incident, there was no need. Never had I dealt with something like this in a foster home. I knew full well that I wasn't to be blamed, because from the beginning I had tried to remove myself from the situation, taking time to be by myself. I didn't even try to run, on the final night. Within my 11-page letter to my worker, I made sure to include every detail. I even told her about my choice words, and how I tried to defend myself by blocking their limbs with mine.

The thing that also made me realize there was no need for exaggerating anything about what had been done to me, were the marks on my body. I can remember everything about the night to the full extent, and I have never doubted myself when thinking if I was in the wrong. I wasn't. For the first moment, they took things way too far. I had cuts on my ear, marks on both of my arms from where they grabbed and twisted. I had gum stuck in my hair. My pinky was swollen and red. And I even had a few small red marks on the side of my head.

The thing that really upset me about that night, was that by the end of it, I really needed to pee. I wasn't allowed to leave my room, and that meant I wasn't allowed to use the bathroom. I wasn't allowed to turn my light on, so I was stuck in the dark, with a giant mess everywhere. I could hear everyone talking and laughing about what had happened. When my sister phoned to speak with me, my foster father went into detail to explain I couldn't talk because of what happened.

I disagreed with being blamed for something I hadn't done, and when that was found to be unacceptable, I tried to remove myself from the situation. With the growing issues, I was never allowed to be truthful to their ears. They never gave me a chance to speak or explain, or just talk. It was like the hell house where no matter what I tried to do or say, they had their minds made up that I was only troubled, and to always be the cause for trouble.

At my foster home, there were certain days we were allowed to have showers. We weren't allowed to have one daily, and they had to be no longer than five minutes. If anyone went over five minutes, which they were timed, they would shut the hot water off. The day after the final incident was my day for a shower. Having to go the night without using the washroom, I remained sitting on my bed feeling disturbed about what had happened. To top it off, the gum was still stuck in my hair, and so I definitely needed my shower.

When it was time for the other foster child sharing my room, to go to sleep, I was told that if I don't go to sleep, then I can take a hike, because he no longer cared if I ran away. I was told not to play with anything in my room, and not to make a sound. There was a light on the radio beside my bed, which I was using to try and remove the gum from my hair, and to look at my pinky finger. The foster child found my light annoying, so told my foster father, who then came in and began grabbing all of my stuff, including the dirty laundry, and took it out of my room.

Once again, I was becoming frustrated with this night, having all of my belongings removed from my room. Before falling asleep, I was told to *run now, because it would be better than running tomorrow*. I was frustrated, tired, in pain, needing to pee, needing a shower, hungry, so I was not going to run.

The next day, it seemed as though my foster father had alternative thoughts to wanting me to run. All I was fed that day were a couple of pieces of toast because he didn't want to give me any energy for taking off. All of my belongings were thrown on the kitchen floor, so I had to spend my time having to put everything back inside my room.

To this day, I still don't know what happened in result of my letter to my worker. The whole situation was messy and became something I felt to be unnecessary. I never understood how they could do what they did. Yes, I had my errors within the situation, but I know what they had done, was something no foster parent should have. In this particular incident, they were the ones at fault. For the first time, I actually felt like I was the better-behaved individual.

Before the end of the school year, about four or so weeks after the blow-up, I got a visit at my school. Leading up to the school visit, there hadn't been any other incident, and I barely had spoken words with my foster parents. They barely wanted to even look at me. It is the thought that they had known the things they had done were too far in nature and that for this one and only incident, they were at fault. Not me. Unsure how to come back from what had happened, I just assumed they were trying to keep at a distance until I would leave.

My worker came to my school and informed me that I would be moving. I would not be finishing the last week or so at my school. It was nearly the end of the school day, and it was then that I had to make my goodbyes to some of my friends. I was told that I would be moving to a group home, where my sister is living. I was told that with everything that had happened the past year, and even leading up to it, things only seem to be escalating. I needed to be in a place with more structure, and it is the hope that the group home would offer this. The bonus was that my sister would be living with me, and with our stay, we would be able to work on sibling group therapy.

While being completely thrown from this news, mostly because since the May 18-21 blow-up, I had thought I worked really hard to move forward. I was at a new school, improving and not getting into trouble. I was doing everything I could to not lash out, or act out at my foster parents. Things were actually going really well, so this news confused me. I didn't understand why if they wanted to move me, that they waited so long. Another unfortunate thing about this move, was that I would be getting a new social worker.

I once, and at first admired, and really liked my foster parents. When it was time to leave, I couldn't help but remember the good times I once had with them. There were times spent with them that brought excitement to my life. The problem was that the bad, overpowered the good. The issues and incidents became too difficult to deal with and be around. This was something that happened on both sides. Things went too far in the moment of hostility. It was a shame that things had to end so poorly, but the only thing I could do was use that experience to hopefully make better choices in the time to come.

The letter that had been written, became a mystery to my life because I had no idea what came of it. Being dropped off by my once liked foster parents, hurt me. After the incident, I really tried to make amends, and make things better between us. I didn't use foul language, didn't get into trouble, and I even apologized for my part. I didn't even get a goodbye. They wouldn't look at me, and not a single word said. As much as I had hoped for at least a goodbye, I was able to feel somewhat proud of the situation. I was able to move on knowing I tried. For one of the first times in my life, I was able to leave knowing I tried. It may not have been enough, but I knew in that moment I didn't need to feel shame or wonder what else I could have done to better the situation.

Chapter Fourteen

Falling Apart

Who I Admire The Most and Why
June 10th, 2004

The person that I admire the most would have to be my sister. The reasoning for that would be because my sister and I are really close. I mean, we are close in age so we can relate to each other. We have grown up together. No matter where we are, we always talk to each other somehow. Growing up with her, I always relied on her showing me the routes to go. She always had helped me out with things. We never had gotten into fights. When we do, we resolve it the next day or so, never lasts long. She had always been an awesome sister to me. I have always looked up to her. I guess you can also say that she is a role model to me. She is a role model to me because I always depend on her to help me out when I need it. No matter where she is, she always finds a way to help. Also she supports me when I'm doing a play, or a sport. Plus I know that she will encourage me to do things. Whenever she promises something to me, she always keeps her promises. When I need help, I know that if I ask my sister, she would help me. She has never really let me down. I love her, and always will. I admire her for who she is. She is my friend. She is my sister, and that is special. She is the person I admire the most.

As time goes on, people change in one way or another. Looking back to when I wrote this admiration description in grade eight, I can see how my writing style has changed. Not changing a single thing except for the removal of her name, I did so to show you how I used to write in comparison to now. I even left the punctuation the same, and I can spot so many things that nowadays I would have written differently. If there was one thing that I wouldn't need to change about what I wrote, it would be how I felt.

The relationship between siblings can be a powerful bond that can last a lifetime. That's not to say that every sibling will be close, because I even know that to not be true. I am not at all close with my half-brother, but I am with my sister. People have said that twins have a special telepathic connection, and with all of the twins I have known over the course of my life, they have even said the same thing to me. The bond that they share is something that most people can never come close to understanding or even experience. My sister and I may not be twins, but with everything, the two have been through together, and on our own, I feel as though we developed our very own version.

During the brief stays at our biological family's home, the two of us were inseparable. We could always be found playing together or even getting into trouble. Okay, quite often the two of us were getting up to know good causing trouble. What can I say, for the most part, we were bored and needed something to keep ourselves busy. You make the most with what you have, and the two of us didn't have much, and so we would make our own fun. That usually entailed running around causing mischief.

As the two of us got older, we became separated from one another which affected us more than most of the adults could have known, or in the very least cared to know. We had spent the beginning of our lives depending on the other for support when we would witness our parents fight. One of us would give comfort to the other so they knew that there was someone in this world who would never bring that much pain and sorrow to them. We relied on each other. We were there for the other. In that time we didn't have anyone else in our lives who could offer security in day to day living. We needed each other to feel safe.

Being separated from each other created a bit of chaos for my sister and I. We no longer had that safe feeling that we relied on for so long. Since our first separation when I was only six years old, for the rest of our time in the foster system, our number one fight was for the other. There were so many events and situations in each of our lives that made us need the other. We struggled so much, and in the end, we always knew that the one thing we needed was to just have the smallest bit of family. For each of us, that meant the other. We spent years begging to be reunited but were most times denied because our visitation became not only a *privilege* but a *reward for good behavior*. We were the only family each of us had for so long, and yet it was never considered a right to be in each other's lives. We were constrained to other people's opinions on whether or not we were allowed to be siblings.

The life-long fight to be reunited with one another created this unusual, and at times terrifying connection. When I have spoken about it in the past, I tend to resemble it to that of a twin bond. To myself, it feels as though because of how strongly we ought to be in each other's lives, and being a part so long, our minds created a way to know how the other one is. This bond we developed all the way into adulthood, and as strange as it sounds, I believe it to be true.

To this day I would often know when there is something wrong in my sister's life. She often wonders how I could know, and every time I would explain. For instance, out of nowhere, I would get a sharp pain in my chest, or shortness of breath, and would have no idea why. Within seconds, the thought of my sister would cross my mind, and the next time I would speak with her, before saying anything, she would go on to tell me how she had a panic attack or something. At times, I have even been woken up in the middle of the night with a really uneasy feeling and would have vivid dreams of my sister. The next morning I would be told from her of specific things in my dreams being a reality. Like if she would have a fight with her boyfriend or something. It would actually weird me out a little but just goes to show the unusual and probably coincidence connection the two of us have.

I have always cared about my sister more than anyone else. At times it may have felt like a curse because I should have focused less on her, and more about myself. Regardless of what was said on either side, how much we speak or see each other, and how much we may fight. Being only eleven months apart, it should have come to no surprise that we would be so close. If I was somewhere getting into trouble, you would know that my sister wasn't too far away leaving me to take the blame. Up until I was three, I had blond hair, which made everyone think we were twins because of how much we looked alike. We may have looked like two little angels, but together we were demonic little shit disturbers.

At a certain age, all kids would get themselves into some sort of trouble, but we would always take it one step further. I remember this one time when I was around five, maybe four, we were in our biological parents' basement playing, when we came across some matches. We were having a good time but wanted to light up the matches just like the grown-ups did. They all caught fire, got too hot to hold causing them to drop. Of course, dropping the lit matches on a cement floor would have been fine for it wouldn't have done anything, but no. We had to drop them on the couch. The entire couch caught ablaze, had to be thrown out, and we pretended as though we had no idea what just happened.

Our brother wasn't as close with the two of us, and my sister would at times torment him so he wouldn't want to be with us as often. We never really brought him into our endeavors. He had his own misfortunes, and we just left him out of our curious behaviors. At the time it wasn't so much that we didn't care for him at all, but it was more to the fact that we wanted to pick on our older brother. I think that it was more that my sister would enjoy tormenting him, but what she did or what she said, I had to follow.

When our family moved to North Bay to live *permanently* in 1996, we had this neighbor on the one side of our house, who had a huge tree separating our house and theirs. My sister and I, at times our brother too, would always be climbing it to get onto our neighbor's roof. Obviously, we weren't supposed to be up in the tree, or even on the roof, but nonetheless, we didn't care. Our mother would be expecting us to be in the small backyard playing, yet when she would check on us, we wouldn't be anywhere in sight. I can still hear the constant yelling of our names with worry that something had happened to us. After letting her panic for a few yells, we would respond with a laughing "hello" letting her know where-about we were. The first couple of times of going up on the roof, we wouldn't let her know where we were, we would just say "hello" while watching her try to figure out where we were hiding. That got quite a few giggles out of us, until she would call us by our first and middle names to tell us to get down at once. When you heard your middle name while being called, you knew she meant business! She never understood why we would always be going up there, but being so high up, away from everyone, everything, just gave us the freedom and thrill we wanted. My sister and I have always been carefree, her more than myself though.

Back then I was more of a sheep, and would just follow her every move, having her be the leader. I relied on my big sister to guide me through the scary world around us. Funny story. While we lived in Ottawa before moving to North Bay (spring of 1995), I had just learned how to ride a two-wheel bicycle thanks a lot to her, and once I mastered that, I was always on the go. The two of us would always be biking around, and at the end of the day when it was time to go inside, our parents would have the hardest time trying to get us both to come in. One would go one way, while the other would go another. One evening when our mother was trying to get us inside, we were doing our usual opposite biking away to stay out longer. Normally we would just go around the blocks by our house, and this time was no different. When we were biking back towards the front yard, we weren't paying attention to where we were going and slammed our bikes right into each other. Nothing happened to me, however, my sister flew off over the handlebars and bashed her face into the ground. Keep in mind this all happened so fast, something no one saw coming, and when I lifted my head, I looked over and saw blood spewing from her mouth.

Our parents we not pleased with what had happened. Both of our parents screamed because no one knew the full extent of the damage caused by us not listening to when being called. I got screamed at so much from my mother as it became my fault because nothing had happened to me. I got smacked from both of them because I could have "killed" my sister from not paying attention to where I was biking. My sister knew it was an accident and assured me that she wasn't mad at me. We actually ended up laughing about the situation. It was just another time that one of us got in trouble for causing our parents grief because one of us got hurt.

While still living in Ottawa, when we would be playing, our brother would usually be off with his own friends, which was the reason he wasn't with us as often. My sister and I had friends, but we would just prefer hanging out with each other. I quite enjoyed playing with my sister, because it allowed me the opportunity to play with dolls, which was something I began to like doing, even though our father would disapprove. Boys weren't allowed to play with girly things according to him and his family. My sister never felt that way and seemed actually happy that I would play them with her. Our brother wouldn't, so that was something the two of us could do together.

When I was five years old, my mother's best friend got married to my biological father's brother. The two of them were the only ones from my father's family who I actually came to like, so their wedding made a great memory to hold on to. My sister and I were even part of the wedding party. I was the ring bearer, while my sister was the flower girl. What should have been such a happy day filled with only fond memories, brought one of the scariest memories I have ever been faced with.

While everyone was beginning to get ready for the special day, my sister and I were playing in the basement to my aunt's house. Like always, we were getting into things we shouldn't have. All of the adults were busy, and our brother was somewhere else doing, well, we had no idea. My sister and I spotted a gumball machine, and from that instant, all we wanted was the gum inside. The machine was tucked away in front of a large shelving unit that was storing empty beer and liquor bottles. There was a lot of other junk in front of the shelves as well. Carefully the two of us tried to make our way to the gumball machine.

Not paying close attention to what we were doing, we bumped into the shelves, and all of the empties began to fall on us. Being slightly quicker than my sister, and also pushing myself ahead of her, I rushed out of the way. Once I cleared the area, I had thought she too made it out, but when I looked back, I had seen her on the ground with broken glass all around her. I helped her up as she was screaming, and blood seemed to be everywhere. Her tiny arm was gashed open from the broken glass shards.

At first, my sister was crying from the pain, but seeing all of that blood fearing that she was going to die because I pushed her out of my way so I wouldn't be trapped under the glass, I think I was more freaked than she was. Also, I think she was beginning to be in shock, that she wasn't crying as much. We rushed upstairs where all of the adults were, and that's when everyone started freaking out. After my sister was rushed to the hospital, I spent the entire time she was gone crying, pacing back and forth in wait for her return. I had no idea what was going to happen, and I just wanted to make sure she was okay.

So many terrible things I had witnessed and been a part of in my life and the fear of not knowing what was happening to my sister was the most scared I had ever been. For a bit, I had actually thought I killed my sister. There was so much blood, and I didn't even care if I was going to get into trouble, because I just wanted to make sure she was going to be okay. Thankfully she returned from the hospital with a stitched-up arm, and all I could do was be grateful she was going to be okay and I gave her the biggest hug.

While growing up, it's the little memories that hold great power to a person. As time went on, the little memories with my sister became all I would have of her. I would do everything I could to hold on to them in the fear of somehow forgetting about her. At least, forgetting the best times I've had with her. Even the memories where we might have had disagreements became important. Holding onto those memories allowed me to know that no matter what we may have gone through, at the end of the day, we were still there for each other.

Once living in North Bay before we moved back to our first foster home for the second time, my sister and I had an unforgettable misunderstanding while playing in our driveway. There was this lady that we remembered seeing on occasion but was someone our mother did not like. Our mother didn't like her at all, and we would always hear her call the lady a "bitch." One day while writing on our driveway in chalk, we heard arguing coming from inside our house, but we weren't distracted from it because it was an occurrence that seemed to happen often. The lady our mother didn't like was across the street, and as soon as I had seen her, I automatically just blurted out "bitch." It became a habit to refer to her in that way because of our mother, and so it just came out of my mouth.

Having heard what I had said, my sister was oblivious to whom I was referring to because she was busy sitting on the driveway drawing in chalk. She assumed I had called her that. She quickly stood up, and not paying attention to her as I was still glaring at the lady across the street, she threw me to the ground. I scrapped my knee on the pavement, started crying, and asking my sister why she had done that. I told her I was talking about the lady across the street. Our parents heard me crying and came rushing outside to see what had happened. I told them that my sister threw me to the ground, and it was now her time to be punished. Our mother gave her a spanking as she was told not to hurt her brother.

Looking back at that incident, the two of us laugh because of how silly the whole thing was. We wouldn't laugh at the part where our mother would yell and hit my sister, but the misunderstanding was just something that brought a laugh to each of us. We were able to turn that memory, into something that brought some joy to our minds. Turning hurtful memories into joyful ones, became something needed because true joyful memories weren't ones that came around often.

When it came to the fear of losing my sister from some freak accident, there are only two memories I have. The first being our aunt's wedding, and the second came before being turned to the foster system. Not realizing it at the time, someone we thought was just a friend of both our parents, was actually a "mister" to our mother. One of the affairs she was having, was with a man that she and my sister would often go and visit with. With trusting this man a lot, at times my sister by herself would stay with him. Something none of us knew until years later, was that this was the man who was the father to my mother's second miscarriage. Bullet dodged.

On one of the times my sister was visiting this "mister" in his apartment, the unit directly below him caught fire. The teenage girl was cooking and spilled oil onto the stovetop. From what we all knew, the oil spill caused a huge flame that lit up her face first and then spread throughout the apartment. My sister was on the top floor of what was believed to be a two or three-story apartment building. I was at my house when we all heard about the fire. Since it was only a couple of blocks away, we all ran quickly over to make sure my sister was okay.

Once we arrived to check on my sister, the fire department was there, and I had seen them bringing out the girl from below out on a stretcher. All I could see was her covered in blood as the fire burned most of her skin off, and we could hear the loud piercing screams ignited from her pain. At first, we were worried that was my sister, but then we noticed she was in the top window. The fire department wasn't able to reach the mister's unit, and so the two of them had to jump onto a held-up sheet.

I had so much panic and worries running through my mind and body. Hearing about the fire and that my sister was stuck inside made me cry so much because I didn't want anything to happen to her. Seeing the bloody neighbor girl being brought out of the house-made me worry even more because at first, I didn't know if that was my sister, not paying attention to the size of her. And then I had to worry that she was going to be able to jump from the window and not get hurt. I could only imagine how she would have felt that day, but knowing how worried and sad I was as an outside viewer, was enough cause for panic. I was just glad she made it through without injury.

Once we were sent back to our first foster home for the second time, my sister and I found ourselves getting into mischief and trouble more than ever before. There was this one time I remember, we were bored in the back yard, so we snuck off in the trees to go onto our neighbors' property. Once we reached the tree line of our neighbors, we noticed they had a pool close to where we were. I can't recall ever jumping in it, but I do know I had wanted to! We ended up splashing each other, throwing rocks and frogs in it, laughing at the frogs while watching them swimming around the pool. We threw a lot of stuff in that pool until the owners saw and heard us and yelled for us to leave. As soon as we heard them, we ducked down, frightened in our tiny shoes, and took off running. Of course, our foster parents were told what we had done, and then we would get into trouble.

For so long my sister and I went to the same school. This at times may not have been the best for either of us, as we tended to get ourselves in a lot of trouble. When we still lived with our parents, we would barely have lunch and would get hungry. During recess, we would sneak inside and steal parts of other kids' lunches so that we would be able to get something to eat. We spent so much time sneaking inside, and when not stealing food would just aimlessly run around the halls. The teachers would catch on eventually and would call our parents to complain. Once returning to foster care, it was determined that we needed to attend different schools so that we were no longer getting into mischief.

It was fortunate how the three of us lived together in the same foster home, for it's not often that siblings, especially three, would get to live together. There I go burning the oil because it wasn't long living there that the three of us would be split up. While grieving over the fact that we weren't living at home, and not being close to our other family, the three of us all acted out differently.

My brother and I were never as close as my sister and I were, which came as no surprise to anyone. Not being able to see her as often, or even living with or near her, left me feeling very much alone. I was used to spending so much time with her, which allowed me to keep my mind off what was going on in our lives, and every day with my sister became a new adventure. I hated the fact that she wasn't living with me, and I would always want to see her.

All the way until we were separated in the foster system, my sister and I relied on the other for comfort after witnessing the abuses in our home. So many times I can remember when we were so scared of watching our parents fight, hitting each other while screaming, we would be off somewhere hugging each other until it was finished. We would tell the other that everything was going to be okay, holding each other just waiting for it to be done. At times we would close our eyes so we couldn't see the fighting, even though we could still hear it. The only thing that managed to get us through it was knowing that the other was never going to let go which offered a type of security. It was a way that the two of us could make it through intact. We weren't often shown affection from anyone, and so being able to hug each other made us know that there was someone out there who cared.

Once being returned into foster care, we were told that we needed to not hug so much as that wasn't something siblings were supposed to do. It was described by our social worker that we hugged too long, and that stemmed from the sexual abuse allegations brought on from our father and others in our home life. From witnessing and being exposed to sexual behaviors, they felt as though my sister and I needed separation, and to have our hugs come to a stop. The thing is, they never asked either of us about it, and just assumed when we saw each other, or when we would get into trouble, we would hug because it gave a form of calmness and safe feeling. Our hugging was never sexual in any nature and was the only thing either of us had that offered safe feeling from the violence in our life. I mean, we were six and seven years old for crying out loud.

Obviously, I didn't understand much about anything at this point because I was only six, and with not understanding the circumstances for why things kept happening, made it worse. I wanted to understand, I wanted to be able to listen to my worker and really know what the hell he was saying, but my mind just wasn't developed yet for me to comprehend it all. Occasionally, our social worker would get us together to spend some time with one another, and we would just go to the park or something simple like that. I didn't really know then, but now it makes sense, that back then I had an idea that I was less frequently visiting my parents because things weren't looking so good. I was beginning to be under the impression that my sister and I would be the family we would have left. Slowly we were being driven away from our biological parents, and eventually even each other. With the less frequent visits with our parents, rarely seeing our brother, now living in our own foster homes, I wanted to do everything I could to try and fight for visitation with my sister. They had already separated us so much, and I didn't want them to continue. That was a choice that neither of us was allowed to make though.

In June 1997 it was determined that in the best interest of the three of us, an adoption into different homes would be the best course of action. Our parents had come to the realization that we were not going to be able to return to a safe home environment, and things were only progressing. The three of us were never asked if we wanted to be adopted together or separately. The decision was made without us, and it was not a decision my sister and I especially had cared for.

We had a "goodbye visit" with our biological parents that in so many ways was something we couldn't have understood. I had hoped so much that my sister and I could have been adopted together, but being the ages that we were, the CAS indicated that it was going to be hard enough to find an adoptive family for one, let alone for two. After the goodbye visit, none of us were allowed to have any further contact with any family members other than each other. We then became Crown Ward children without access. That meant according to the laws we were to have no further contact with any family members, something that our worker seemed to think we could just understand from being told, without a proper and full explanation.

During the two years I was in the adoption process, I had seen my sister a couple of times, had spoken over the phone several times, and had passed letters back and forth. Adopted families were found for all three of us, however, my sister's never lasted at all. I was later in a life informed during a stint at a group home, during what felt like a "bonding" conversation to the owner, that she apparently tried to adopt my sister.

Everyone perceives and handles situations differently, for not everyone has the same mental capacity, and with my sister, it had seemed her past caught up with her sooner than later. Hearing how her adoption didn't work out, frustrated me because I knew what would happen to her. She would return to foster care, adoption having failed, no siblings close by, left completely alone. If letting go of my biological parents was hard enough, the thought of my sister being all alone without either of her brothers was causing me much sorrow for her, which played a part in making me unable to be happy where I was.

Here I was with two new adopted sisters, and even though I tried to get close with them, trying to get them to like me, they weren't my own sister. It took a really long time to accept the fact that I was a part of a new family, and had new sisters. At first, everything was new, fresh, and allowed me to experience a childhood that wasn't filled with anger, disappointment, and fear. It wasn't long after that it sunk in that this was to be my life from then on. Realizing that living a life from the sister I knew, without having her always close to me, tore me up inside. I tried to move on with my life, from my biological family, but I wasn't ready to move on without her. Having lost everything at an age where things weren't clear to me, where I wasn't able to understand, towards the end of my adoption, I was finally old enough to start. Not a single day passed where I wouldn't worry about her. Every day I had hoped she was doing okay. Not a single day passed where I stopped caring and loving her.

Once my adoption failed and I was returned to foster care in 2000, as sad, upset, and scared that I was, I knew things were going to get better because I would be able to once again have my sister back in my life. Being back in foster care allowed me to have more contact with my her because I was no longer a part of an adoptive family.

My foster family was very family-oriented and understood the importance of a ten-year-old in need of a familiar bond. Having known how my failed adoption played on my emotions, they were very sympathetic and supportive. I would speak with my sister often over the phone, and when it was convenient, and allowed from our caseworkers, I would have arranged visits to where she was staying.

At first, our contact didn't occur often, with my sister's two failed adoption attempts, and mine also failing, we both needed time to work on our own individual problems. Once I learned of my adoption wasn't going to work out, I was sort of relieved that I would be allowed a chance to be reunited with my sister to become a family. Well, if two people could count as a family. Sure I would have wished that both of us could have had the opportunity at life with a permanent family, but having moved around so much, seeing hatred, tension, and violence being built in our home, we were at the age where it would be really difficult to just move on and forget.

Those memories haunted me, not giving me the chance to get close to anyone, and I knew it was the same with my sister. She was the only bit of light that had shown through the darkness that I had been building up inside of me. If ever I felt alone, sad, and not sure what my purpose was, just thinking of her or reading one of her letters would cheer me up.

AUGUST.1998
DEAR CASEY;
   I HOPE YOU ARE DOING WELL BECAUSE I LIKE KNOWING YOU ARE HAPPY. YOU DO NOT HAVE TO WORRY ABOUT ME BECAUSE I AM DOING JUST FINE.I HAVE MADE YOU NECKLACES AND I MADE ONE FOR ME, MINE HAS AN ELEPHANT ON IT WITH TWO GREEN BEADS. WHEN YOU HAVE TIME PLEASE WRITE TO ME, I LIKE TO KNOW THAT YOU ARE OKAY.I AM BUSY FINDING THINGS TO DO AND

HAVE MADE SOME NEW FRIENDS. ONCE A DAY I GET TO GO TO THE PLAY-GROUND, TODAY WE WENT FOR A NATURE WALK, THAT WAS FUN.THIS LETTER WAS DONE ON MY FOSTERMOM'S COMPUTER. I GET TO PLAY GAMES ON THE COMPUTER AND IT'S LOTS OF FUN.I HOPE TO HEAR FROM YOU SOON.

LOVE,

If there was one trait people who know me, know of, it's that I tend to keep everything. For so long I used the yellow cigar box I got when I was six, to hold all of my most prized possessions. The box became too small, and so I had to find other means to hold memorable things to me. I received many letters from my sister, especially during my adoption, and whether I always wrote back or not, I would keep them close to me. I often found myself reading them over and over, crying every time. The above letter was sent to me, which was one of the first I received during my adoption, and it brought so much meaning to me, and I found myself always going back to read it when I would think about her.

Throughout the year 2000, there were several times where I was too upset to converse with anyone. Not just my sister, but in general. She had always been the only person who I would want to talk with, but still, I neglected to. While going through some old letters that she had written to me, and just from reading them, I could tell how she felt, even if it wasn't written. I could sense that she was feeling left out, and the ability to connect with me was starting to fade.

She had always written me letters even if it was to just say hello and that she loved me. The thing that affected me the most at this time, was when I was first brought back into foster care, I was too upset to talk with anyone, which included her. In her letters, she would tell me that she missed me, that she loved me, and she even asked if I did? The mere fact that she had to ask me a question like that when she was only eleven hurt me. Having to question something like that at such an early age, saddened me because I had always thought I did my best to show her I would always be in her life. I thought she knew that I would always be there for her. Clearly, it was becoming evident that I wasn't doing so. I was just so distracted from my own problems, which mostly involved around my failed adoption.

The realization that she couldn't talk to me when she needed me; that perhaps she was really hurting, but I wasn't there for her, made me feel low because she always made time for me. I don't know why exactly, because I had so many thoughts going through my head, but that year was the hardest for me to get close to anyone, even my sister. I guess since feeling abandoned once we had our goodbye visit with our biological parents before my adoption, and after my adoption failed, all those feelings came rushing back.

Towards the end of my adoption, as troubled as I had become, I honestly thought I was starting to accept being part of a new family. Being back in foster care made me constantly think about how no one wanted me, how I didn't belong anywhere. That is why it was hard to connect with anyone, especially my sister. Since I'm sure that's how she felt as well, I should have been able to talk with her and share our common depression, but I just couldn't.

Towards the end of the year 2000, one of my foster parents' sons, and his wife took up fostering. Of the six children they had, who were the ones I knew the most, and at the time were closest with. Before the Christmas holidays, I was hoping that I would be able to see my sister since this was the first year that I was alone. In the end, it worked out because my sister would be able to stay with my foster family's son's home.

Even while I was excited to be able to spend Christmas with my sister after hoping and praying, I couldn't help but feel down. Before I was adopted I had spent Christmas with my biological parents and siblings, and then with my adoptive family. This was my very first Christmas spent without a family, without being part of a family. I was very grateful for what my foster parents had done for me, and even though they always made me and others feel like part of their family, it wasn't the same. I still wanted to distance myself. Seeing their big family coming together, sharing such a joyous occasion, made me jealous because I couldn't have that of my own.

While dealing with so many ongoing issues in my life, aside from being the reason for my adoption failing, Christmas was creating many worries for me that I didn't feel as though I could share with anyone, especially my sister. After hearing that I would have my sister with me on Christmas morning, I was also told about a visit to my old adoptive family. I had been keeping in contact with them, which was making things very confusing because I was under the impression that the adoption was over as it had failed. I felt such sadness and guilt for allowing it to end, and so in many ways regardless of how confused I was, was happy to still have them in my life.

When I was told about my visit with them, it created panic inside my mind because not only would that mean I would be leaving my sister, but it made me remember the events that happened the previous Christmas with my brother while visiting with his adoptive family. At this time, still, no one had known about what happened, as I still didn't know how to process it. I tried so hard to move forward while putting what happened behind me, but not having contact with him helped with doing so.

My sister had always been the one person I felt as though I could share anything with, but knowing what she had to deal with regarding our father, a subject like this was not going to help anyone, and the last thing I wanted to do was bring up any old and horrific memories for her. The entire day on Christmas, I kept quiet, tried to have a smile on, while completely ignoring my sister. Having her there made it worse for a couple of different reasons. One reason was because she reminded me of our past family that was no longer with us, which was making me remember so many horrible things. The other was because all I wanted to do was confide in her about my own dilemma, but didn't feel comfortable enough to do so.

One of the gifts I got that morning was the new (at the time) Pokémon Silver game for game-boy, and so to shut out my thoughts and how I felt, I played it all day. I got pretty far at least! My sister was clueless about what was going on and was left upset because I wouldn't want to talk with her, wouldn't want to be near her. All I did was play that "damn game." Since my foster family had got my sister to stay with them so I wouldn't be alone and could spend Christmas with her after so long not being able to, they couldn't understand why I was ignoring her and instead, playing that game. Knowing how upset that day made her, how I made her feel ignored, still hurts me today.

I hate feeling upset and hurt by those that I love, and how I made her feel is something I can't take back nor something I would ever want her to feel from me. My sister was the last person I would want to hurt, but at times I couldn't control how over-whelming things made me feel. That was probably one of the biggest problems of mine growing up. When something troubled me, instead of talking with someone about it, I wouldn't say anything and kept it bottled up. I felt as though if I wouldn't say anything, not talking about something on my mind, would mean that it wasn't real, that the problems in my life weren't really happening. I always neglected things, people, even my sister at times when she was the only person who understood everything that I was going through.

After having my sister stay with them for the holidays, my foster family's son and daughter-in-law decided to start fostering her here and there more often. This was to give us an opportunity to have more contact with each other, in the hope that it would give us the thing we longed for so much, a family. When my sister would stay with them, usually we would always go for a walk to the store, for it would take about half an hour, so we were able to really talk about things. One weekend, we were on our walk, and the topic for discussion was our father. It had been a while since he had come up in a conversation between us. We got into an argument, because in her own way, my sister really missed him, where I did not. Ever since learning what he had done, the pain that he caused my sister, I could never forgive him. During our walk on the side of the road, I made a comment against him, which rubbed my sister the wrong way. She had a reaction to it, and ended up pushing me. Had I not tripped on the rocks on the side of the road, I could have very well fallen into the busy road where cars where speeding by. I didn't get hit, but it definitely woke both of us up. We quickly made up, and the whole incident was left in the past.

In 2001 I found myself moving once again, although it was due to issues created by myself in my foster home. I returned to the foster home that I previously lived at just before the start of my adoption. I had so many fond memories while living there as a child, I had hoped that in a dark time, I would be able to create new and meaningful ones. These foster parents had known me from a traumatic time in my past and were aware of the importance my sister had on my life since she was the only family I had left.

Although I had still found myself being in contact with my adopted family, especially with the visitation, still I was left unsure what it all meant. I still had my sister in my life, and that part I understood. Like my previous foster family whom I had wronged, my Lakeview foster family wanted to help in keeping my sister and I in close contact. On occasion when it persisted, my sister was given access to my foster family on weekends for a relief visit.

The weekends we had spent together meant a great deal to me because I was beginning to feel us starting to grow back together. Our contact was starting to become more frequent, and I had felt as though we were actually siblings once again. When I would be told of my sister's weekend visit, I would do everything I could to think of things we could do. I tried to save a few dollars from my allowance so that we could walk down the road for snacks and a movie rental. One time towards the end of the year, I wanted to never forget our weekend visits, and so I wanted to find a way to capture the amazing feeling it left me in. I didn't have enough money at the time, and so when I was at the grocery store during my school lunch break, I stole a disposable camera.

During my time at the Lakeview foster home, my sister was still residing at the group home and had quite a few personal issues she was still trying to work out. A way one of the staff members thought would help her to feel connected to something, to feel appreciated, was to make a bet with her. The two of them shaved their heads, and the first one to cut it had to owe the other a professional hair day at the salon. At the time when I had seen my sister in incredibly short hair, I didn't understand it, but it was later that it made sense. The simple and yet strange bet gave my sister something to look forward to. It allowed her to feel close to someone. Once I came to realize it's importance, it made me incredibly happy to know that she had someone in her life who could show that much kindness.

In one of my sister's weekend visits, her hair was still quite short, and when people had seen her, they wouldn't understand why her hair was so short. Mostly, it was none of their business, but kids will be kids. There was a dance down the road at the firehall, and I was hesitant about going because I knew a few of my bullies would be there, and I was fearful of being teased. After seeing my sister tie her bandana around her head as she liked to do, the last thing I wanted was for my bullies to also bully her. This was supposed to be a weekend to bring us both happiness, and I didn't want anything to mess that up.

Regardless of any potential teasing, the two of us made our way to the dance. My friends were there, and none of them had met my sister yet, and so I was actually excited for them to meet her. As I had been worried about earlier, the fact that her hair was so short, seemed to create much conflict in my main bully's mind. She found the need to verbally attack her, which was a mistake. My sister was not myself, where I would take it for so long before snapping. If someone was to say or do something to her, she will instantly act upon it. I could tell my friends were slightly curious about her bandana and super short hair, but because they were actually my friend didn't say anything.

We left the dance quite early that night because we knew nothing good was going to come from staying. I just wanted my friends to be able to meet the most important person in my life and have a night of laughs, free from wrongdoings. Thankfully we were able to recover our night by watching TV and eating junk food together.

So many times the topic of adoption came up between us in our many conversations together. She had given up on the idea of trying once again, but was aware that I was still in contact with the family that tried to adopt me. In so many ways, the two of us shared the same notion that having each other back in our lives was something very much needed. Being so young taken away from our parents, we needed a familiar bond, and being so close early on, felt necessary to once again being back together as brother and sister. The two of us had found real happiness while being in the foster system because we were finally able to reconnect. It was becoming the idea that we didn't even need any other family. The problem with that though was that I was still in talks with my adoptive family.

As happy as I was to have my sister back in my life, I wasn't ready to let go, and lose hope for the possibility of a second chance with my adoptive family. The time I had spent with them were the best times of my life, and they made me feel everything I only hoped I could feel. They became the light at the end of my very dark and lonely tunnel, but it was as if there was always still something missing.

The dilemma I was in constant turmoil with, was how I felt about my sister separate from my adoptive family. The thought and memories of my sister were just too strong to forget, and the love I had for her was something I couldn't just put aside. No matter the fact that my adoptive family resembled everything I could have hoped for, it just meant I couldn't have her in my life. That was something I don't think I could have ever let go for good. Had I been given a choice to pick one over the other, I couldn't. At least, I didn't think I could.

The holidays didn't seem to go over well for me. There seemed to be something in the universe that wouldn't allow one to pass without any issues. Before any plans had been made for my 2001 Christmas, I had been persistent in asking to have my sister stay with me. At first, I was told that it is possible to happen, but considering her ongoing troubles in her own placement, that might not be something that could work out. I was left with the impression that she was not going to be able to spend the holidays with me, and so I made other plans.

I had still not made any decision regarding my failed adoption situation, and so plans were made for me to go and visit them over the Christmas break. The only unfortunate thing about it was that we would be making this Christmas a joint holiday with my brother's adoptive family. That was the only drawback that I was faced with. I was no way ready to have to deal with seeing him, or the possibility of having to discuss the events from a couple of years ago. It just seemed too soon, and too overwhelming.

Just before I was about to leave for my visit, my foster mom informed me that there was a surprise for me; My sister was given permission to spend the holidays with me at my foster home. I was incredibly confused because now I wouldn't even be there, so why would they send her for Christmas. Everyone knew that I was leaving for the Christmas break, and prior to making arrangements, I had asked several times for her to stay with me. I was told it wouldn't be possible because of problems in her own placement. Why bother sending her to a home, where she will be left alone. It was confusing and very frustrating.

My plans were already set in motion, and my foster mom who only found out just before myself felt my frustration. I knew regardless of the fact that I wouldn't be there, my foster mom would ensure my sister would be taken care of and would do everything she could to make sure it would be a great Christmas for her. For a bit, I had actually considered canceling my trip, because I felt so much guilt that my sister had to be left without me during the holidays. Knowing that I would have to see and be near my brother only added to me wanting to stay, but I was told I couldn't cancel the night before I was supposed to leave.

I wasn't even able to see my sister before I left. She was set to arrive after I had already left. There were so many things that bothered me that Christmas, and yet knowing of this situation was at the top of the list. The thing that pissed me off, even more, was the fact that her visit was scheduled to end just before I would get back to my foster home. So, the workers had planned a visit for my sister to join myself at my foster home, while knowing I wouldn't even be there. Then they planned for her to arrive after I leave, and would have her leave before I arrive. What the hell! The only good thing was that I was able to speak with her over the phone on Christmas. I became so filled with rage because I couldn't believe the incompetence, and this felt like such a tease for our need for needing family in our lives.

When I returned from my Christmas break, my sister had left me a letter. She was aware of the situation, however, she wasn't informed by her own worker that the visit was planned after plans were already made for me to leave. My foster mom spoke with her and explained how I didn't know she was supposed to stay, which was why I left. In her letter, she wrote how sad she was that she couldn't see me, but that she hoped I would have a great Christmas. She even went on to write how she was able to buy a disposable camera to take pictures of what was thought to be another Christmas together. After things didn't go well last year, it was hoped that this one was to be better for both of us. I couldn't help but come to tears from reading the letter.

A part of me felt as though this was a way to show me from the Children's Aid that I couldn't have both. There was going to come a time where I would be forced to choose between access and contact with my sister, and being reunited with my adoptive family. There was much discussion with my adoptive family, as well as my worker on the subject. Since 2000 when I was returned to foster care, my adoptive family and I had worked really hard to try and get back on track to be a family once again. There was interest on both sides to give it a second chance, but it came with restrictions. We had all been through so much, and if things were going to be tried again, we needed to make sure that it would last this time.

Within numerous conversations I had with my caseworker, as well as others in the Children's Aid, I had been asked about if I wanted to try re-adoption. There were too many things to consider, and I wasn't sure if I was ready to make a decision. Still, I had been asked again and again. I was also asked that if I wouldn't be adopted again from the same family if I would want to try with another family. I was asked if I wanted to remain in foster care. These were questions I didn't want to make, especially hasty. These questions were speaking to what would happen to me for the rest of my life. The only thing I knew for certain was that I didn't want to be adopted from a different family.

The family that I was adopted in really were the perfect family. When I thought of the things that made a perfect family, every single trait described them; Unconditional love. Patience. They always took the time to work out the struggles I had. Never hit me. Never screamed at me. Included me in everything. From day one treated me as their family, and not some orphan they took in. The list to describe what they represented to me goes on and on. I had it all with them, and yet I in my self-destructive ways ruined it. For a while, I was left with the fear of it not working out again, and I didn't know if I would be able to handle that a second time.

In mid-2002, before the end of grade six, I was told for the last time that I needed to make a decision. If I was to choose to try being adopted again, the thing that would have to happen this time would be leaving my sister in my past. In order for me to move forward, I had to say goodbye to her to give myself a chance. I was told to think about myself and what I wanted. I wanted both, and yet I couldn't have both. If I choose my sister, it would mean that I had to say goodbye to my adoptive family. Either way, I would have to write a letter to someone saying my goodbyes.

I sat alone in my classroom with my caseworker while we discussed this. It was a decision that I had to make right there. I had felt as though I had been berated so many times on a subject I didn't want to speak about. No matter how much I wanted to try my adoption again because of the love I had for them, I couldn't leave my sister alone in the world, with no one to be there for her. I asked for her to tell them for me, but was told it had to be something that came from me. I thought and already had the fear of the adoption failing again, and so I used that for my letter.

At twelve years old, writing my goodbye to a family who meant everything to me, who would be the only people to truly deserve the title of "Mom" and "Dad" in a way needed to hate me. I used anything I could think of which meant a small conversation we once had about how my biological parents were capable of parenting three children considering all of their continuous and growing problems. The only way I thought I was going to get through saying goodbye, would be to write a letter hoping to receive some form of hate from them. If I sounded cold and distant, perhaps it would make the situation easier. That's at least what I thought, and how I felt.

Dear, Adoptive Parents. *May 1ˢᵗ, 2002*
How are you two doing?
I'm fine!
If your wondering, school's fine.
I have some bad news for you.
I don't want to be addopted by
you guys. You both have been very nice
and kind to me, but I don't think we
make a family.

The reason why I don't want to
be addopted is because of the way
you talk about my parents. And also
because It did not work once so
who says its going to work this
time? And I don't want to always
fight with your daughter. *And I think I*
belong in North Bay in Childrens Aid
Society. But I will never forget
you because you guys have been a
great deal of my life.

I wish not to come over
there this summer. And I think it
would be best if we would not
talk, visit, and write. No affense. Well
I'm sorry. If you have any questions
call my worker *and she will help you,*
bye.

From
Casey

The hardest letter I have ever had to write in my life. Writing this made me feel more sadness than I ever felt before. At times I wasn't sure if I was going to be able to move on with myself because all I could think about was if I had made the right decision.

My sister almost meant more to me at this point if that's possible. It was after choosing to not be adopted that I made a point to not let the decision go to waste. It was now my number one goal to continue our sibling relationship and didn't want to accept the fact that I would often be told "no" when asking for visitation because of her own behavioral issues. My sister and I had spoken about one day reuniting with our biological mother, and since the decision was done for no more adoptions, it seemed like the logical next step.

The process to grant crown wardship to my mother for my sister and I was a lengthy one, and although I knew it would take some time, I didn't want to wait. Once our workers started on getting things in order so that we could have contact with our mother, every time my sister and I would speak, that's all we could talk about! This having been such a big deal to us because the last time we spoke or even saw her was at our goodbye visit back in 1997.

We would constantly ask each other the same questions over and over. What does she look like? Where does she live? Would she recognize us? Did she have any more kids? Has she missed us? As silly as it may have been, we were just overjoyed that sometime in the near future we could actually start talking with our mother again. It wouldn't be for about a year that we would have that first conversation with her.

The summer of 2002 was when I moved to Bonfield, and my sister was living not far away in Asterville. It was about a 20-minute drive from each other. I wasn't aware right away that she was living there, but shortly before having to go back to school, I was told. Being the outdoors kind of guy I was and am, so many times even though I was told not to, would bike towards my sister's new foster home desperately wanting to see her. It took me about an hour and a half to bike to where she was living. The people who owned the diner I had gone to so many times while living with the Great Dane foster family, had become foster parents themselves.

That summer, I didn't get to see her, but I did however get to speak with her over the phone a lot. Normally when I move to a new foster home there is so much to dread. Whether or not I can have contact with my sister, and what my new school will be like. This time I was fortunate enough that I didn't have to. My sister lived not far away, and the school I would be going to was the same one that all my friends from grades four and five would be attending. Not going to lie, I was disappointed that I didn't get a chance to see her before school, but it all worked out in the end because who did I see waiting for a school bus at the end of the second day, but my sister.

Surprised and curious as to what she was doing there, and not being told by anyone that we would be going to the same school, I ran up to her in shock, gave her a hug and asked what she was doing there. Obviously, I could see her school bag and could put the pieces together, but I felt I needed to ask to make sure this was real. The last time I was at the same school as my sister was in grade one, her being in grade two, so this was a huge deal. I would finally be able to see her every day. Her bus had come shortly after I saw her, so we weren't able to get into any deep conversation.

It had been a while since I had seen my sister that second day of grade seven. Her hair had finally grown back, and she almost looked like a completely different person. The two of us had started with our own workers the process to be reunited with our biological mother, but there was still so much to do. So many things had to occur before we would be given access, including court hearings on the matter. For the most part, my sister and I just had to sit back, and wait to be told anything from our workers.

The school year of September 2002 – June 2003 was one of the toughest years for me and was especially tough on my relationship with my sister. While beyond excited for a chance to become a family once again with our biological mother, we would be faced with some of our worst issues to date. I had already been exposed to drinking, delinquency, as well as *the pot*. My sister was in the same boat, but probably slightly more since most of her friends would be described as bad influences.

I was just so happy to finally being able to see my sister every day instead of waiting and hoping for a monthly visit. During lunch periods, we would cross the road to smoke cigarettes and most days pot. Her friends at the time weren't my friends, so it was a new crowd, but I was just there for her. After a while, I become part of the group, while everyone would be getting stoned during our lunch break. The first time I ever tried coke was in my seventh school grade after some of my sisters' friends were doing it and had asked me. I wanted my sister's friends to like me, and so I did it. I wanted to fit into her world, and at this time, that world involved these other kids who on occasion would drink, smoke, and snort coke.

After my move from my Bonfield foster home, I found myself living in Mattawa. With my sister being the number one reason to continue at the same school, although it was a longer commute, I was given permission to remain there. I was so worried that once again I would be denied contact with my sister because of problems in my life. While I was being faced with some struggles in my new foster home, as well as at school, I found myself making plans with my sister to run away.

She herself was having issues in her foster home, and so we thought it to be the perfect way to escape. I had already previously run away once, although that was under different circumstances. The two of us took off, and since I had been suspended from school, I found it to be the perfect timing.

For the majority of the day, we aimlessly walked around, meeting up with different friends of hers until the nighttime came around. She had a much older friend, who I believe was eighteen, while we were only thirteen and fourteen. I was just surprised that she even knew and was friends with someone who was that age. Nonetheless, we were continuing our journey to elude from being caught by the police. We knew that our descriptions would be given to them so we had to do everything we could to stay hidden. While at the grocery store, I had stolen bleach blonde hair dye. My sister's eighteen-year-old friend said that we could hang with him for the night so we could get some sleep.

After walking around all day, my sister and I were definitely tired, and considering how slow my sister walks with her short legs, it made things that much more painful. When it came time for us to get some sleep, I found myself on one of the couches, while my sister and her friend were snuggled on another with his arm reached around her. After I closed my eyes, I must have fallen asleep right away, because I don't remember anything.

The next morning when we all woke up, her friend had to take off, while my sister and I stayed to clean up before taking off again. I bleached my hair for the first time that morning, in hopes that having blonde hair would throw off the cops. That was a decision I would quickly regret, as it became a punching bag for many to tease me about.

When I looked at my sister, since we had woken up, she just seemed quiet, and out of place. Her mind looked to be elsewhere, and just from looking at her, I knew something was up. I had seen that look before, so I feared that her friend got a little too handsy with her. I had asked her if she was okay, and what happened. She insisted that she was fine and that he was only kissing her and rubbing on her top half. For what she was saying, it insinuated that it was okay because he allowed us to stay at his house while we were running away. As if letting him kiss her and grab her boobs was a payment of some sort.

I grew beyond angry once I heard that. I was even angry at myself for passing out right away before I had a chance to try to stop him. I would have had my butt kicked for sure since he was at least twice my size, but I didn't care. My sister had been hurt before, and it hurts me to know that she would once again be hurt. She begged me to just let it go. I told her I would, except in the back of my mind I knew I wouldn't. I couldn't. We took off on our run right after that conversation and were quickly caught. We tried to keep to not so busy roads, but because of how slow we walked, we were easily caught.

After the police picked us up, the first thing I did was report her "friend." I told not only the police officer but also my foster parents, caseworker, who ended up speaking with my sister and her foster parents and worker. I'm uncertain exactly what came of that situation on my sister's end, but I know the next time I saw her, for a second was upset for saying something, and then became grateful. She knew I was only trying to look out for her, and that what happened shouldn't have happened for so many reasons. Considering all of the sexual abuse the both of us had to deal with in our short lives, it was something I needed to try and fight against.

One day in the early spring of 2003, my sister found herself in some particular trouble, as she had been prior since starting at our shared school. She was arrested and was being held in the back of a police cruiser. Some albino at our school, who was in my grade, and had given me grief on occasion teasing me, let her out. She made her way to wherever I was that day, which was in the back of the school at the back entrance, having a smoke.

I saw her running towards me with her hands tied behind her back in handcuffs. I didn't know what to expect or what had happened. I tried to join her in her run from the cops, but it didn't last long. After they chased us, they tackled her down and took her away. I was already late to class that afternoon, so figured I would just skip. Being that I would be skipping, I knew I would be getting into a heap of trouble from my foster parents, and so I figured I might as well just run away. That's when I ran away for the third time since February and resulted in my desire for continuous AWOLing.

Once my sister was removed by the police from my school, she found herself in juvenile detention, once again. She had found herself going back and forth between the detention center and her foster home. It was while she was at the detention facility that we would be told we would be allowed to have our first face to face visit with our biological mother. We had spent the past few months having phone calls, and mailed letters back and forth, and finally, it was felt as though we were ready to have our first visit in person. The first visit occurred in January 2003.

Prior to our first visit with our mother after almost six years of not seeing her, my worker brought me to the detention facility to speak with my sister about what to expect. Details about everything had been gone over, and we discussed things that had happened in our past which lead to being sent to foster care. The things that were talked about wasn't what I had learned from reading my case files, but what we already knew. At that point, we didn't care about what was being told to us, just as long as we could see her.

That visit at the detention center brought up so many feelings I didn't know how to handle. It had been so long since I had seen my mother, and under the circumstances, felt weird to even see my sister there. As nice as the visit was as a whole, so much about it just felt strange. I think because there were such high expectations for having us all together again in the same room. Since everything had to go slowly involving our reintegration into each other's lives, the next time I would be allowed to visit with my mother would be at the end of summer, before I begin the eighth grade.

Since that visit with our mother, I had developed some feelings I didn't want to have. I had thoughts I didn't think I would ever feel. I was already having doubts leading up to the visit that I was trying to figure out. It was that day having seen her again after so long, that I realized this wasn't what I truly wanted. I felt as though I had made a grave mistake by turning away from my adoptive family, even though that included my sister. I knew the choice had already been made, and so there was no turning back. I knew I wouldn't have been able to say anything, because it wasn't going to make anything better for anyone, especially myself. My sister seemed happier than ever having our mother back in her life, and so I figured I should stand by her, and hope things seem better.

My sister was released from the detention center and then sent to the same group home she used to live at before. With all of the issues going on in her life, and with wanting to be integrated back into home life with our mother, CAS felt as though the group home was going to be her best option. After issues growing intensely larger in my foster home, and after running away seven times in one month, I was told that I too may benefit from being sent to a group home. It had become evident that I required stricter care than what could be offered from my foster family, and so I would have to move.

The only good thing that came from being told I would be moved from my foster home to a group home, was that it was at the same place my sister resided at. The last couple of months put quite a strain on my relationship with not only my sister, as our communication practically came to a halt due to our caseworkers wanting separation, but also with my mother. I didn't know how to deal with the thought of making a possible mistake having her back in my life, and with not being able to talk with my sister, things in my life just became difficult. We had spent so long, so many years coming together as a family, trying to be there for each other, and now, it felt as though we were just falling apart. The only thing I was left with, was the hope that living together for the first time since we were six and seven, would give us the chance to find our place once again.

Our minds are like a book for endless possibilities. They're filled with so much knowledge, but the access can be limited. Do we stand on the sidelines and choose when and how to acquire it? And the question is why? With every memory that passes, that we make, it never goes away. We simply just store it, and either lock it away deep at the back, or we face it and surround ourselves with that. To define the person we are today, it's because of those memories and it's because of what we choose to keep close. What we do with the knowledge we have, the memories we keep close is what is on the surface.

There are those that we try to forget, that we try to run away from, but what is it really doing to us. It's the unbreakable gate that blocks us from fully being ourselves. We deny, we "forget," but really that's a lie. We never actually forget, we choose to hide it beneath what we want, what we yearn for.

Circumstances and situations take heart-ache on our body and soul, it brings us down. They can belittle us, turning us against what we believe in, what we think is right. The cloud that blinds how we really feel becomes solid, and we don't know how to break free.

To find a balance, THE balance we need. withers with time. Like a tree, time murders the beauty, it kills the memory. All we can do now is unlock what we had, what we were, and try to grasp a piece of what we used to be. One by one recalling those not lost, but misplaced memories. To remember, and to not deceive who we're meant to be. Because the thought of losing the "us," is more painful with all we had to endure.

Chapter Fifteen

Locked Away

Considering how much traveling I've done in the past, you would think that a two or so hour car ride would be nothing. Well, turns out it's not so much the length of the ride itself, but rather the thoughts that fill one's head to make the ride seem ever so longing. Typically when traveling, I think it's safe to assume that one way usually goes by faster than the other. I don't know why considering if you take the exact same route, it's the EXACT same. I believe that it's all in your head and the thoughts that fill it determine how fast or slow the journey takes.

One thing that is for certain, is that from start to finish of that short car ride, I was living in my head. It was like I was living all the best and worst moments of my life. The bulk of my thoughts were of course about my sister as I couldn't be more excited to be finally getting a chance to live with her again. Just saying that, hearing it out loud sounds odd. I mean, you would think that it's normal to live with your sister no? The fact that it's been seven years since we've lived under the same roof, the same home, is just crazy. I was filled with so many emotions I don't even think someone with multiple personalities would know what to do in that situation.

I have always been a highly emotional person. I guess that's a good thing, being able to feel things. I think it would be something to worry about if I had no feelings. I did however had no control over them though. I think that was my weakness. I was often told that I needed to learn to control them because if gone unchecked, it could destroy me and make things difficult for me. Of course, I tried, but in the end, I didn't really listen. Nothing like a car ride that seemed to never end to make you think back to all of those unchecked emotional times. I had a tendency to bottle things up and not share, so I didn't feel the need or want to share with both my current and soon to be new worker who was driving me.

Every time a troubling memory crossed my mind, I would find I moved my head to look out the side window so in case I would begin to tear, my workers wouldn't be able to see. I would then try to replace that with the thought that soon I would be able to see my sister. Immediately I would begin to smile and I could feel my whole body fill with so much excitement. I found that my excitement level was higher in that brief moment knowing I had another chance to actually live somewhat like a family. In the case of happiness in my life, however, it was usually short-lived.

Close to the end of the drive, probably within the last ten to fifteen minutes, one of my workers were told to be prepared as there was an incident at the group home. Not given too much detail, I was then told the same. At that very moment, I could feel every ounce of happiness and excitement just completely freeze inside of me. I had no idea what was happening, or what this meant for me and my sister.

I had so many questions, and of course, I wanted answers. I knew my workers didn't know what was happening as we were all in the car together, but still somehow expected them to know. We were told that the incident involved my sister, but not too much more detail. Not knowing felt like it was killing me. Of all the fond and happy memories that I had been reminiscing about on this drive, had all of a sudden changed, and then couldn't help but think of the disappointment in other memories.

I just wanted to burst out and scream, and then cry. We were finally on the road that the group home was on, and I didn't even want to go there now. I didn't have a choice regardless, although I wish I had. I mean, was there any point now? I had thought the point of the two of us being there was to hopefully help both of us get back on track. Help us both find meaning in life while slowly working our way to moving away from foster care and into the home of our biological mother. I was told with all of the issues and troubles of late, that if we wanted to move back home, there was work to be done before that could happen. Living at this group home was the logical step since nothing else had seemed to be doing anything. And things needed to change. And believe me, while looking back, things really did need to change.

It's funny how quickly people's emotions can change. I think in the last ten minutes I've felt close to every emotion out there. By the time we pulled up to the driveway, and then up to the house, I was just tired of feeling anything. I didn't know what was happening and didn't know what to expect. I looked at the giant house, and massive property it was on, and all I could think of was how beautiful the place looked, and yet for some reason still hated it. I didn't actually hate it but was trying to make a point to myself.

The owner of the group home came outside, and I gave one of those fake smiles, just so I didn't give off the impression I was going to be a handful. She had what some might refer to as a resting bitch face. Moving to a new place is never easy. You don't know anything about the people, and being that this was my first group home, I had no idea what to expect. How many other kids were there, and did I know any of them. I think my greatest fear was that I would have to share a room with someone. I liked my privacy and didn't want some stranger in my personal space. I had so many questions, and I hadn't even walked through the front door.

I grabbed my luggage and started walking up the elevated front porch. After getting inside we walked past a staircase leading upstairs, down a tiny hallway that led to an open area that had a kitchen, dining room, and what looked like a closed-off living room. There were railings all around the living area, and at the back, you could see two other rooms. Everything looked so strange, and at this point, I hadn't made up my mind if I was going to like it or not. All I had seen so far were adults, and not a single kid so that at least was a plus. What I didn't know, is that in the basement, they had a school where most of the kids would go.

Like every place I've lived at, the initial visit would consist of meeting the foster parents to discuss me; who I am, what troubles I've been up to, what things are good about me, you know, the usual meet and greet. Although technically there are no foster parents, just group home staff, this was no different. The only difference this time is that all I could think about was what was going on with my sister. I gave it everything I had to not get too emotional, as I could feel myself about to burst out crying. I had waited seven years for an opportunity to live with her again. Had a failed adoption that consisted of me realizing how much I missed her and made me wonder if I was ever going to see her again.

After a long conversation about what was expected of me at the home, and after discussing my latest "fails" in my foster home, we finally talked about my sister. Turned out that there was an altercation between her, the other couple girls, and a couple of the boys. An altercation so bad that it resulted in a fight, and then the girls fled the property. The group home called the police after their AWOL, which apparently happened shortly before I arrived. It was until after arriving that they arrested them after breaking into some cottage while trying to steal a boat. Oh, and how could I forget that they also stole booze and started drinking. Sounds like one hell of a party they had.

My initial thought made me want to burst out laughing because of how ridiculous that sounded. Thankfully I didn't actually laugh out loud. I then turned to wondering how all of this happened in such a short time, and why while knowing I was on my way that she would do that. I tried to make sense of everything, but at that point, I just wanted my workers to leave, and to go to my room where I could be alone and have a good cry. The one good thing was that after talking with the owner of the Group Home, she actually seemed pretty nice. That somewhat lifted my spirits, as I could relax a little knowing at least this lady seemed decent. I did want to wait until my workers left though to make my final decision about her personality. I've seen it before where someone will put on a good show, and then behind closed doors turn into the spawn of the devil.

After my workers left, I was briefly shown around the home, and after seeing the one really large hallway that had about 10 small rooms, I asked where my room was. The next form of relief came when I was told it was upstairs. Apparently, the boys stayed downstairs, while the girls were upstairs. They wanted to make an exception for me since they knew this was a big deal for my sister and I, and wanted us to be close to one another. Also because I think they knew I wasn't as troubled as much as some of the other kids. That's at least the impression I got.

I brought my things upstairs, and I was so glad my room was up there. The rooms were larger, and I basically had my own bathroom. Since no one else was allowed up there, it was now my domain. The bedroom they had for me was sort of right across from where my sister's room was. Right across from her room, was a small hallway that had one room on either side of it. My room, and later I found out was the room that one of the weekend staff would stay in.

I was given a bit of time to settle in, and that was something I definitely needed. Once I was alone, the first thing I did was grab my pillow while sitting on the edge of my bed and yelled into it, and then started to cry. I was trying to be quiet because I didn't want anyone to hear me. I think they would understand why I would want to, but I didn't want to show that kind of weakness. Instead, it seemed like I had about an hour of self-reflection talk about my plans. Of course, it was probably about ten minutes.

In that moment, I told myself that although I no longer had the opportunity to live with my sister and become somewhat of a family, it was my time to make some changes. Changes that I would need to make in order better myself. For so long I had struggled with the thought of being alone, and not knowing if I would ever be part of a family again. I acted out, misbehaved, and ruined many great relationships. I had it stuck in my head that if I couldn't get the things I had always wanted, then what mattered if I was good. Well, in that moment, I finally listened to some of the things that people over the years had told me. They told me how I needed to focus on myself and to start putting my sister in the back of my head. I needed to not focus on her, and rather to focus on what I needed. For some reason, this felt like the last straw, and what resonated in me was finally being able to hear what had always been told to me.

As much as I loved her, it was time that I focused solely on myself if I ever wanted to leave that group home and start over. The hope was to one day live with my biological mother, so that's what I had to go by. The bond I had with my sister was strong, and it wasn't that I was forgetting about her, but that I needed to let her deal with her own issues and mistakes on her own. I needed to not let myself get down because of something she did. I needed to not let her mistakes, poor judgment, and misbehaviors determine how I acted in my homes. It had always been difficult for me to put her on a time out because she had always been the only family I had, that I knew. Finally, that day came, and it actually surprised me how that sudden and instant decision change felt. It may sound foolish or strange to some, but making that choice in that instant, regardless if I had just made it, made me feel different and more focused.

While knowing that I was now living at this group home to work on the issues that had sent me there, although not knowing how long that would take, I was ready to head downstairs and get started. At this point, the school had let out, and the kids from downstairs had come inside. Being the new kid, of course, everyone couldn't help but stare and ask questions. I thought that I handled myself pretty well though. Interacted while not being "too much" and trying to separate the mixed feelings I had about everything. It was after meeting the boys, because the only girls there had run away, that I realized I could easily get through this experience alive, and the best way to do so.

As petty as this may sound, I thought the best way for me to succeed there and help myself get back on track, would be to look at myself differently. I felt that it was time I finally focused on who I am, who I was, and who I wanted myself to be. In order for me to do that, I had to figure out who Casey Hardman was. Everything that I had been doing needed to change and changes were needed so that this experience could be different and better. The way I decided to look at myself, was that I was better than them.

Petty I know. Selfish, probably. Nothing else in the past seemed to work, so I figured it was time to have a different outlook on things. After meeting these boys, I noticed certain things about each. Issues and personal flaws about each after an initial meet. It actually made me feel better about myself because I thought I was somehow better behaved, or at least presented myself in a better fashion. Knowing that yes, I did have anger issues, and many other problems, but me being there probably wouldn't have happened if I wasn't going to live with my sister.

With all of the recent problems my last foster home had with me, things were starting to work out, but was a little too late. There was an opportunity not only for me to grow and work on issues in a new environment, but also a chance at a family. So, the decision to move me happened, and suddenly too. Somehow I felt in control because I could see and hear that the kids at this group home, were actually worse off than me. I didn't actually know that.

Perhaps I was the one who was worse, but I had an interesting opportunity to take advantage of it.

These kids had lived at the group home for a while now, with each of their issues brought to light, and yet no one has seen mine. No one had dealt with my misfortunes of acting out, and so in a way, I felt as though I had the advantage of being better. Why not use that. If I truly wanted to better myself and work on my anger issues, and other struggles, why wouldn't I want to start thinking that I was better than how I saw myself. If I wanted others to see myself differently and to have them respect me, I needed to find a way for myself to see that first. I needed a way to feel better in order to actually be better, and as terrible as this sounds, it actually somewhat worked.

When you live a life unsure of how things are supposed to work, how you're supposed to act, and the high expectations of others, it can be difficult to create your own version of yourself. Moving around as much as I had, being a part of so many different homes with different ideologies, made things extremely difficult because I had always been changing to conform to different people. It was hard to keep track of how I was supposed to act and be because there were always different variations of myself that others had wanted. Finally, being at this group home was an opportunity to create the kind of person I wanted to be. No one else. So, I needed to elevate myself a little so that I could actually see myself better.

Being the new kid, while having my room upstairs separated from the others gave me my first advantage. Knowing that my anger issues and other issues weren't as evident and voiced as the others, was my next advantage. I remember sitting in the living room, or common room for the residents, looking around at everyone thinking of the differences between myself and them. At this point, just hours after being there, some of the kids started acting out, screaming at each other, nearly fist fighting. It was at that moment I realized that was not the kind of person I wanted to be. For once in my life, I wanted to be viewed as "the good kid" and have others think highly of me. I knew I was capable of doing well, I just needed to work on it. Why create chaos when there isn't a need for it? It's strange, but I actually felt a smile on the inside, because I felt like this was the move I needed to reevaluate myself.

A couple of weeks went by, and after trying my new outlook on things, things had seemed to be going pretty well. The only issue I think I had was how I felt about my sister. I was still upset, angry, and disappointed in her for what she did. I was starting to understand that things actually do happen for a reason, and her leaving was the only way for me to actually make good changes for myself. It sucked that she couldn't be there, but at the same time, I was finally happy to be working on just me. Holding onto some resentment still, I felt that it was time I write to her to explain how I felt. If I wanted to move on and past the disappointment, she needed to know. As hard as it would be to say that to her, not knowing how she would feel, I too had feelings that deserved to be heard.

To this current day, over ten years later, writing that letter to my sister expressing how I felt about her running away, was one of the hardest things I ever had to do. That was the first time I chose to think of myself first instead of her because at that time, I needed to. I remember sitting on my bed in my room, and each line I wrote, made me feel every emotion I felt that day. I probably spent most of the time writing that letter crying. As exhilarating as I may have felt for finally telling her how she made me feel, I couldn't help but feel bad. And let me tell you, I let her have it. I didn't hold back.

By the end of writing that letter, I felt rage. I was able to push past the sadness I had felt, and was over it. At that point, all I could feel was anger. Instead of going downstairs and making a scene, because I was still on good behavior and wanted to remain like that, I stayed until I was calm. What do I do when I'm angry though? I break things. After years of breaking my personal possessions because of the temper tantrums, I was running out. And of course, I still didn't know how to filter my rage towards the right people or about the current situations. Being enraged from writing that letter, it brought up other feelings I still had about the fight I had a while back with my mother, and because of that, I directed my feelings towards that.

Once again, I did what I didn't want to do. What I wanted to start working on. Directing my feelings where they belong. Instead of keeping my feelings pointed at my sister, they were all focused on my mother. I ended up ripping up photos I had kept over the years, and even the goodbye letter, and the first letter I got from her before we started contact again. Once I finished taking my little fit, I felt better. I killed two birds with one stone, so to speak. I was able to confront my sister in a way about how she made me feel, and also in a way got back at my mother for our fight, even though we had made up. Of course, it was an overreaction on my part but was proud that I was able to let out my feelings in a sort of healthy way. I let out away from others, and not having other people having to deal with my issues, and backlash from it. I didn't leave my room until I was calm and relaxed, so that's growth in my opinion.

Before returning downstairs, I remember a split second of realization of what I had done, and it almost made me start crying again because I didn't want to tear those things up, but what was done was done, and there was no way to fix it. I needed to accept what I had done and to move on from that. I grabbed the letter I had written to my sister, and while walking downstairs, I felt proud of how I handled that situation. Dealing with inner struggles can at times seem crazy, and I definitely had wondered at times if I was. That day reliving what I had done, if others had seen that, they probably would have thought so too. In retrospect though, it was because I chose to deal with situations like that, on my own, so I wouldn't end up crazy. I needed to listen to what others had told me in the past, and finally start using that to help in situations on my own, so that when faced with other situations involving other people, I would have a better handle on things. Little self-reflections and situation building was what I needed, so that little freakout was definitely what I needed to start growing.

After my sister had received her letter, I was informed of something that I didn't know. Something that was a game-changer because I learned that there was something that she herself wasn't aware of. Apparently, the decision was made to not inform her that I was moving to the group home to live with her. It was decided that me moving there was to be a surprise for her. Yeah, how well did that turn out? Hearing that made me feel even worse for what I had said to her, especially because who knows what would have happened if she had known. Although knowing that truth changed certain things about how I felt, I had to accept what I had done. In one way or another, she needed to hear how I felt. The letter wasn't just about her running away moments before I moved to the group home. I included other instances where I felt betrayed or disappointed, so it was needed. The letter in the end I believe had helped. She understood where I was coming from and was very apologetic. It was a moment of realization for her that I believe she needed in order for us to get back to some normalcy. It was just difficult to know how upset it made her, to hear what I wrote because she had never heard that side from me before.

The two of us had so many issues that needed to be worked out, and those issues had to be done separately. As emotionally unstable as both of us were, things would only get worse if we continued to go down the path we were currently on. As hard as it was to realize I needed time away from her so that I could improve on myself, it was also difficult to come to terms with the knowledge that she too needed time apart from me. She had a very different past than I did. I had always known she needed extra help because she felt as though I had it easier than her. I never wanted to believe that, but in some instances, I know that to be true. I also know that being so different and yet the same, her difference was how she accepted certain situations, which resulted in different end results.

Every person will act and react differently. That's what makes us different and unique. We are supposed to be different. Being torn from family, friends, more than one failed adoption, my sister felt more betrayed than anything, which led to low patience and self-esteem levels. We viewed our relationships differently. We had different ways of handling situations. With all of the disappointments she faced and inner demons she kept within, there was very little room for trust. She was left thinking about why to get close to people because they're just going to leave. Although we sound very similar on paper, the two of us faced many different situations in our lives. She had things to deal with that I didn't and vice versa.

I don't think I necessarily had it "better" than her, but rather, I handled things differently which may have made things better in the end. I think I was just prone to handle things easier, which made people more wanting to try to help me. My sister was left with very little trust as I had stated. I found this made people so frustrated, that in some ways ended with them practically giving up on her. Although she had been given very similar chances for growth as me, some of the people she was given, were different from mine and gave up when things got bad. It was that feeling of abandonment that I hadn't faced before. That was our biggest difference and was something she couldn't move on from.

In the end, the two of us just needed time to work on ourselves. As much as I wanted to be there for her and help her, I couldn't. It was time for me to step back and hope that she could help herself. I just didn't want her to think that I was just like the other people who gave up on her, because I would never do that. Anytime she would fall, I would do what I could to reach out and help her get back up. This time as hard as it was, I needed to walk away as she fell. We needed to part ways, for now.

Being part of a group home made certain things easier. When you get stuck in your mind about feeling a certain way, even though you shouldn't, you can always count on a distraction. Distractions definitely came often.

After a month or so, my plan of improving on myself wasn't so much a plan anymore. It became a way of living. I was actually thriving and happy. I started building great relationships with people there. Other kids and staff alike. I wasn't so much thinking myself better than others but was using their acting out to help me to not want to. Seeing how silly it was, or how unneeded certain reactions can be, I was actually able to self-medicate my feelings. I found I was starting to channel my emotions better. I had no distractions at this point, which made it much easier. I had begun to see a therapist, or shrink. Well, to be honest, I'm not exactly sure what they were. Throughout the time I had spent in that group home, there were two people I spoke with about all kinds of things. A woman and a man. All I know is that even though I was hesitant at first, I felt as though I was able to open up a bit, and it felt good.

Starting to feel much better about things, mid-summer I once again began to have more frequent communication with my mother. I felt as though I was in a better place, and would be able to handle it. Even though we were talking on the phone occasionally since moving to the group home, it took some time for things to pick up again. She had even mentioned that perhaps at the end of the summer, she would be able to come visit me. Of course, something like that would have to be approved by my worker, who would have to check with the group home to see how I was doing. The idea gave me hope though, and brought some excitement, and who wouldn't want that.

The days spent at the group home were okay. The more time that passed there, the more I realized I definitely didn't belong there. Yes, I had issues, but seeing the other kids made me think that I wasn't *that* bad. I at least was not as bad or had fits as often as they did. Apparently, the group home had also thought I was doing well. So well in fact that they thought I could benefit from occasionally spending some days at their more "privileged" home.

The thing I didn't know about the group home initially was that the owners technically had three establishments. Their Group Home consisted of three different levels, based on different needs for the kids. The one I was currently in, was the main house, and where from Monday to Friday the owners would stay. The types of kids that would go there were made up of a wide variety of behavioral or otherwise issues. Perhaps the type of kids that needed slightly more attention.

The second home that was part of the Group Home establishment, was a place that housed a group of boys that would maybe prosper better in the wilderness. To explain its purpose is difficult being that not many of the kids where I was knew much about it. All we knew was that the owners would travel and stay there on weekends. It was in the middle of nowhere and took a couple of hours to drive there. That's how it felt, in any case, the one time I went to visit it. The boys that stayed there were disciplined in outdoor activities, and I guess you could say were made up of older youth. Your "manly" types. Aside from being stuck in the middle of nowhere in the wilderness, I didn't think there was anything worthwhile about that place.

The third home was my favorite of the three. It's what I referred to as the more privileged home. It was actually right next door, which made things quite convenient. On the side of the main property, there was a mini forest with beautiful tall trees. There was a pathway that allowed you to walk from home to home. The main house housed quite a number of boys, where the next-door home only had up to four. At the time I first got there, there were only three that lived there. Each residence would typically do their own thing, their own activities. On occasion, both homes would get together and spend time integrating. When that happened, I was definitely happy. The kids were closer to my age and were for the most part better behaved. Not to mention the four staff members that would change week to week, because only two would be on at a time.

The staff members next door to me were my favorite. Not only had I found them to be more charismatic and fun, but I believe having to deal with less stress than the main house staff, they seemed happier to be there. Throughout my entire time at the Group Home, the next-door staff changed quite a bit. It was sad because losing any of them was difficult as they were so beloved by everyone. The kids anyways. It was additionally sad because their replacements were also great. Of course, I feel as though for the most part everyone preferred the original staff.

With my behavior being so well, it was agreed that I would join the next-door home on some of their group activities. They wanted to slowly integrate me into their home to see how I would fit in. I couldn't have been happier. There were screaming matches and fights daily at the main house, and I wanted no part of that. I was finally feeling better about things, and actually making such a strong effort to better myself. It was a surprise because one of the staff members next door was a man that I had seen working at the detention center during my very brief stay.

His weekly partner was actually my favorite of all the workers at any of the branches of the Group Home. Her husband also worked at the privileged home, although on the opposite week. It made sense that his wife was so great, because so was he. And his weekly partner. After I met the four staff members, I quickly realized that all those workers were equally incredible to be around. It didn't take long for me to want to get things started with moving next door. I'm not saying that the workers were all bad at the main house, I just didn't find that they were as sincere or enjoyable to be around.

One thing that I don't think anyone realized at the main house, was that I was a night owl. I've always been that way, and even to this current day, I still am. It's always been difficult for me to fall asleep, and am always trying to find ways to keep busy if I can't sleep. In the past, I would sneak to watch TV, write, play with toys, and even eavesdrop. The Group Home didn't seem to know that, and with my bedroom being right above where their smoking deck was, it was a no brainer what I would do. Ever since I moved there, I would slightly open my window so I could hear all kinds of things. And they talked. A LOT!

Wanting to change so much, and being actually genially proud of how things had been going for me, I heard something one night, and I didn't know what to do about it. The staff often talked about the kids, and would either get each other to chuckle about certain things that happened, or they would just complain about each other. When it came to me, they felt it was funny to start a bet as to how long it would take for me to mess up. Yeah, I said that right.

Instead of wanting and hoping I would continue to do well and maybe be an example, they chose the ladder. How long it would take for me to act out and ruin my good behavior. Quite a number thought I wouldn't make it past the summer. One of my favorite workers at the main house, who didn't say anything to the bet, actually told me about it in private. I acted as though I didn't already know, and her telling me actually made me like her even more. She was such a sweet French lady who was actually from Sturgeon. So, we always had things to talk about.

As upset as I was about the bet, I couldn't and wouldn't let it distract me from my goal. I needed to continue to do well so that I could move next door. Thankfully I got the distraction I needed.

On one of the outings, we were at this location that we would often go to for swimming. A quiet little beach that had a floating dock and slide. In the background, there was a cliff surrounded by forest. The spot reminded me of a small paradise. While swimming on and off the dock, I had decided to stand at the end of the slide to jump and dive off. The water was quite deep, and there were only a few of us around the dock, so didn't have to worry about hitting anyone. The slide was positioned at the corner of the dock. What I didn't realize, was that being soaking wet myself, as well as the slide, when I began to crouch to get momentum to jump, I slipped.

You would probably assume that it would be obvious to not jump off a slide, and you would be right. No one should obviously stand at the edge of a wet slide and try to jump off of it. Regardless of the fact that I was not thinking, and in the moment of having fun, I still did it. The moment I slipped and fell off into the water, my side smacked against the edge of the dock before I plunged into the water. The wind had been knocked out of me, and there was a loud smacking sound from hitting the dock. I was unable to take a breath and began to fall deeper into the water.

I remember sinking while feeling a little out of it. I didn't have a chance to take a deep breath before going under, and so I began to struggle. I tried to swim to the surface, but my side was in so much pain I couldn't move. My arm felt numb and I didn't know what to do. I knew at that moment I had to suffer through whatever pain I was in because I was going to drown if I didn't. I used my other arm and legs to get me a little closer to shore so I could stand. Once I was able to stand up, I lifted my head out of the water, and while taking a massive breath of air, I let out a big scream. A couple of the other kids tried to help me as no one really knew what had happened, but I was in too much pain and wanted everyone to leave me alone.

Walking, breathing, just moving in any way seemed to hurt like hell. There was a gash on my ribs, a big bruise was forming, and I just wanted to fall down hoping it would stop. I was helped into the car, and we all drove to the group home. The staff member dropped everyone off, and the two of us rushed to the hospital so I could get checked out. I was actually really glad it was him because I actually liked him, so it made having to be in pain, stuck at a hospital that much better.

We waited at the hospital for a while, but then finally someone brought me for X-rays and checked me out. I had a couple fractured ribs with bruising but was told it would heal and I would be fine. With ribs, there isn't much you can do. It's not as though you can get a cast, and so pain is going to be your new best friend. I was told to take Advil for the pain, and that's it. Away I went.

For the next couple of weeks while I was recovering, I was told to take it easy, but to take small walks to help. I remember coughing to be the worst part of my injury. Well, getting out of bed as well. Quite a few times I needed help because to sit up, and then stand up, moved my ribs more than anything, and so it hurt. A lot! I did everything I could to not sneeze because I knew it was going to vibrate all over me, and that's not what I wanted. Coughing though seemed to hurt the most. Especially if I was having a coughing fit, and couldn't stop. At least I had Advil for the pain.

My whole life, I had been blessed with not needing to be on mediation. Aside from the occasional flu or something, I didn't need a daily dose of pharmaceuticals. At times I'm surprised no one tried to put me on some sort of mood stabilizer, but in the end, I wasn't. From my rib injury though, I would need to take Advil every several hours to help levitate the pain. At times, it felt as though I was on some heavy-duty pain medication though.

Some of the other children were on some form of medication, and when given their doses, they would have to be monitored. I understood that because the staff couldn't allow the kids to pretend to take it, and then hell breaks loose. That, or they collect, and then overdose. There are a lot of different scenarios that could happen, but that's why the staff watch. When given medication, you first put it in your mouth. Usually, it's on the tongue, and then you show the staff that it's in fact in your mouth. They will then hand you some water, and watch you drink and swallow. You must then reopen your mouth so that they look inside to make sure the pill(s) are gone. Usually, the staff will also get you to lift your tongue. It's what you would see when watching a show or movie that involves a mental institution. The same pill delivery system.

Apparently, Advil is no different than any other medication, because I too had to do this pill-taking ritual. It actually seemed pretty strange to me, because I wasn't used to this, and I didn't know what harm Advil of all things could do to me. Plus, considering the kind of pain I was in, there was no chance I was skipping a dose.

It took a couple of weeks, but thankfully my ribs were healing quite nicely. I was even given a scar that to this day will forever be a reminder of my stupidity. Never again will I stand on the corner of a wet slide. The lesson had been learned.

It was getting really close to the end of summer, which meant a couple of things. The first thing was that at the end of August 2003 I was going to have a visit with my biological mother and her boyfriend. I had very slowly begun to start communication with her, and after having phone calls, I decided a fresh start was in order. I was trying to give myself a fresh start, and so I felt it was best to give the same treatment to all in my life.

While trying to give a fresh perspective to certain aspects of my life, one place I didn't want to, was to the kids in the group home. Being around so much younger, and very problematic children really gave me an enlightening perspective. Seeing all of them, especially with their short fuses, made it easier for me to not act out. My good behavior at this point was continuing, and my outings with the house next door was becoming more frequent. I couldn't have been happier. I was told that at the end of the summer depending how I was doing, I would be able to move there.

The thing I didn't realize at the time was that being in the main house might have actually been better for me. The three kids that were next door, were older than the ones at the main house, closer to my age, while also being better behaved. In a way, it was a very different atmosphere, but a better one. The thing I didn't know was that while trying to make myself better, being around others who were more wild in nature than myself is what was actually helping me to keep myself from acting out. For so many years, I had been viewed as the problem child. The child with a never-ending list of problems.

Being around other children with more behavioral issues than myself was keeping me from acting out, making me want to be better. It made me want to appear better in nature which in a way was healing my mind. It showed me what I looked like when I acted out, and it was something I didn't want for myself. As selfish as it may have been, it still helped while I was there. Being the child who wasn't acting out, getting the glory if you will, made me feel so good. It was a feeling that was new to me. Like all things in my life though, it's ending would soon make an appearance.

In the last week of August, I had my visit with my mother, my move to the next door, and then getting ready to begin grade eight. I had left word with the staff to get in touch with my worker so I could get back to school clothing, and the proper work gear. There were so many good things happening to me, I couldn't decide which of the three I was most excited for. Back to school shopping was beginning to be my favorite thing to do, as I found it to set up my school year, which for the most part I actually liked. So, I think the back to school shopping was my number one choice for excitement.

One night before my mother and her boyfriend were going to make their way to the group home for our visit, I was laying in my room unable to sleep. It was still summer, and so the temperature was still quite warm. I needed my window open so I could get some fresh air. I was laying in bed, thinking about how great it would be to see my mother again, and my living at the group home was a stepping stone to moving back to her permanently. While laying there I could overhear the chatty staff members out on the patio while having their smokes.

One of the staff members was talking about how my mother called to ask about hotel information since she had never been to Huntsville before. Just had a couple of standard questions like what kind of hotels are there in the area, and restaurants. The staff member talked as if my mother had asked for her kidney because her tone was so annoyed and displeasing. I overheard her telling one of the other staff members that my mother should have just picked up a phone book and looked through it for that kind of information, because what was she, an information teller?

As silly as it may have been, hearing what I did, put a sour note in my mouth. It was a staff member that I actually really liked. Hearing once again such crude things just ticked me off. I decided to just let it go, and just think about my visit, and allow that to continue making me happy.

My visit seemed to go really well with my mother. It was about a week until school starts up, and still hadn't heard anything from my worker about new clothing, and school books and whatnot. When I spent the night at my mother's hotel, she took me shopping for some clothing. She knew how important it was for me to have some new clothes for the beginning of school. I had told her about how important it was for me to make a great first impression. First impressions at school was everything. It was going to be the thing that everyone will always remember. Whether you show up with fire red hair in a sweater vest, or in your pajamas. No matter what kind of school, or what grade you are in, it's that first day that really matters.

My mother barely had any money, and so she was only able to afford a couple of outfits for me. Then again, she technically didn't have to get me anything because the crown wardship still hadn't been turned over to her, and it was the Children's Aid Society that was responsible for my school clothing. She just knew that there was nothing from my worker, and so she wanted to help me out.

The moment I returned from my night out with my mother, all of my belongings had been searched to make sure I wasn't bringing anything I shouldn't have back. With my new clothing, another thing I wanted was the soundtrack CD for the musical episode of Buffy. I got it, and over the next several months, I would listen to it daily. I never even got tired of it because every time I would play it, it would shoot a sort of peace throughout my body and just reminded me of all the good things in my life.

When one of the staff members was going through my new stuff, they seemed to be like, Oh, why do you get to get all of this new stuff. It just rubbed me the wrong way. They had even said something that seemed hostile, and so of course I sarcastically responded. I did it in a way that couldn't allow me to get in trouble, but enough to make them aware I knew of their attitude towards me. Once everything was given the okay for me to have, I also had to have a therapy session with the group home's therapist. I had only seen this woman a couple of times prior, and in all honesty, I did not like her.

It seemed strange that after a day of happiness with my mother that I would have to go sit down and speak to this woman because they wanted to make sure I was okay since my visit. Yes, of course, I am okay, but having to go through all of this isn't making me okay. Nonetheless, I did it and that was that. Maybe I was a little pissed off about the window comments, and was holding onto a bit of a grudge?

The move next door came, and that was one of the few moves that was for good reasons. My behavior seemed great, and I was showing that I belonged in a better, more intimate environment with fewer children.

Before I knew it, it was time to go back to school. So many times I had asked various staff members about getting back to school clothing and belongings from my worker, but nothing ever came of it. Thankfully I had a couple of outfits from my mother, but that was it. No paper, no pencils, no gym clothing. The second I had to take the bus for my first day, not only was I filled with nerves because I was going to another new school, with new kids who were probably going to start bullying me at some point, but I didn't even have a new pencil for my classes.

All-day all I could think about was how crappy this was. My old worker knew how much I loved back to school shopping, and she never would have allowed me to go to school for the first day without a single thing. I had brought the subject up to the group home's owner, who told me that on my visit with my mother, she should have purchased back to school things. I explained that it wasn't her responsibility for doing that since technically it was the Children's Aid who were in fact responsible. They were the ones who were my legal guardians and were to make sure that I was prepared for my new school year. It's funny because when I explained the best way I knew to her, she didn't have much else to say. It was almost as if she knew I was right. I didn't explain with hostility or anything, but I was a bit pissed since it was something I had talked about for a while, and yet school had officially started but nothing had been done.

My first week at the new school was a bit of a headache for me. It's never easy being integrated into a new setting, no matter how many times you may do so. Everything was different, and yet it seemed like I was the only new person, which was exhausting. Everyone had their clicks, and I only knew one person, the granddaughter to the group home's owner. We weren't really close, so it didn't really help too much. Even the courses seemed strange because so much of what was being discussed seemed so different from everything I knew from my previous schools.

Our first big assignment was asking us in math class to design a room, with furniture, giving dimensions for everyone. Looking back, it didn't even seem like a big deal, but I got so stuck into my head about it, and I didn't even have a ruler to use. The assignment was due at the end of the first week, which seemed to have come very quickly. I woke up the morning of the first Friday, and my assignment was not finished. I was so stuck in my head about what exactly I had to do and was annoyed about not having anything to actually use for the class.

I decided instead of not handing in my first assignment, I would just skip the day which would give me the weekend to find a way to finish it. When I was supposed to go catch my bus, I waited out in the woods between the two houses. Once I had seen the bus drive away, I made my way into the huge open field across the road. I spent the whole day walking around there. The day seemed to go by incredibly slow. I knew once the bus would return, I would have to make my way back to the house, since that's where we have to go meet after school, before making our way to our house with our staff members who would begin their shift.

I spent the whole day trying to figure out what I was going to say because I knew the group home would have been notified about my absence. In my mind, I was also going over possible scenarios as to what would be spoken to me. I didn't know what to expect, but I knew it couldn't have been good.

I was right. The conversation I had when the school day had ended did not go well. More than anything everyone seemed very disappointed in me because I had been doing so well, and had shown I wanted to continue to do great. I did explain my situation, but it didn't seem to make a difference. I was told that they gave me a chance to attend school in a normal school setting, and what I did only showed how ungrateful I was. During the little meeting I had, I was becoming overwhelmed with everything, but I knew I couldn't freak out and make a big scene. I just wanted to end it as best as possible. As much as I tried to hold in my anger and speech, I just wasn't strong enough to do so yet. I wasn't at the point in my life where I could.

I was annoyed and frustrated about the whole school situation, and so then I said that maybe I just wasn't ready for it and that I should just join everyone in the downstairs school setting. I was asked if I was sure about that decision, and I should have taken that second chance, but I didn't. In the moment, it seemed like a safe bet because I had much less to worry about being at that school. The curriculum for starters wasn't what you would find at a traditional school. It just appeared like the easy way out, and safe bet, and so I took it. Little did I know, had I not, and taken the second chance, so many things could have gone different for me, and better.

It's insane how some very tiny things and situations can be a catalyst for so many, much larger things. At times we never know the outcome to something, but it all stems back to that initial instance. My decision to attend the group home's basement school setting was the small decision I made that shaped the rest of my time there. It was something that no one else including myself could have thought to have brought so much pain and problems.

Over the next month or so after school had started, tensions in my home started to cause issues between me and another boy. He wasn't sent to the group home from Children's Aid, but his parents to deal with his own issues. He and I at first got along great and became friends. While living in the same home with three other guys, tensions began to take shape. It was gradual but was becoming quite an issue. Our staff members knew of the tension and did what they could, but there's only so much you can do with four teenage boys who are full of testosterone and hormones. Things just get away from you at times, and you try to be a peacekeeper, but it doesn't always work out.

Mid-September was our first blowout as I had been enraged from comments by the group home's owner regarding my school situation, and I had also noticed my wallet was misplaced. I looked everywhere but couldn't find it. Admittedly I was in my head and didn't care about anyone else, and just wanted to speak with the staff member. She was speaking with the guy I was butting heads with while interrupting them, I tried to steal her away for my own problems. He had made some comments while I was trying to speak with the staff, and in my rage, I was not going to stand for it. Words were shared between us, and then I started to make my way to my room. He then made some nasty comments about my sister, which was the number one way to piss me off. I turned around and jumped on him, beginning to punch him. Our fight didn't last long and only ended when the staff member said that if we didn't stop, she would call the police. That was the one thing I didn't want because I did not want to go down that road.

The next day at the group home I got in a lot of trouble. I tried to explain the situation and that I just wanted to speak with the staff, and then the other guy had instigated me. Regardless of what happened, the owner deemed the situation all of my fault. When I received my files, I read the incident reports written by the staff and owner, and I was surprisingly not surprised at the owner's comments. She went on about how my attitude and behavior was obviously escalating because I attempt to gain power and control over every situation. She even went on about how interesting enough I waited until the end of the staff members shift before getting into a fight.

Ummm, I'm sorry. I didn't realize that about 9:30 pm, is the same as 11 pm. I also didn't know that I asked the other kid to start calling my sister names so I may start punching him when he did. Nothing about it was obvious, and it certainly wasn't about gaining power and control. It was merely about an enraged thirteen year old who didn't want to hear mean comments about his sister.

The aggression that I tried to keep bottled up inside myself was starting to be too much for me. Without properly talking about the issues, because I was beginning to feel unheard from the adults at the group home, it was only a matter of time until I blew. The bickering between myself and the other kid was now more frequent. At the end of September 2003, we once again had another fight. While now knowing since the last time about what drives me crazy and full of rage, he continued to call my sister names. He had also spoken to the fact that I was a foster child, and that I didn't have parents, because no one loves or cares about me. The same crap I heard so many times from others in my life. No matter how many times I hear it, it's as if I'm hearing it for the first time, and it triggers whatever rage and anger bottled up inside of me.

Like other times in my past, the threat of taking away phone calls and letters to my biological mother was what the owner and other staff members found to be the perfect consequence for my outbursts. Since the mid-September fight, I was told that speaking on the phone was a privilege and if I continue to act out, I would not be allowed my supervised phone calls. My letters to my mother were already being screened, as well the phone calls "had" to be listened to by a member of the staff. Reconnecting with my mother meant a great deal to me, and everyone at the group home knew this because of the years I had spent without family. Knowing how much contact with her meant to me, they used it as a way to show their dominance and power over me. Separating a child from their family isn't a punishment. It's a cruel abuse of power.

For years I had tried to make it clear to so many people that all I wanted was a family. All I had wanted was to be a part of a family. When I was adopted, there was so much I hadn't dealt with, as well as so many things I didn't understand. This made it too difficult for me to accept the fact that everything I needed and wanted was right in front of me. The adoption failed because I didn't know then exactly what I wanted and needed, and was searching for what I all along had. Since then, I was able to come to terms with what I needed to find a sort of peace of mind, but no one was listening. The threat of taking away access to the fraction of a family I had was the number one go to for everyone.

With Thanksgiving around the corner, there was a possibility of me being able to go to my biological mothers, however, I was told that it probably wasn't in my best interest because of my growing anger and bad behavior. Before the end of September's fight, I had been teased from another boy quite a few times, and while trying to get the group home's attention on the matter, because of my previous problems, I was the one who was blamed and told to just simply ignore. The funny thing was though, the few staff members at my home were more inclined to try to do something, where the staff at the main house were less inclined. The main house staff seemed to hold more power, and in their minds, I was the only problem.

When the staff were able to separate the two of us from our fight, we were each to remain in our rooms. I was beyond pissed about everything. There had seemed to be so much chaos going on around me, and it made me feel as though I was left with no options. I was being teased, my phone calls were being taken away, my school situation wasn't going well, and was feeling much hostility from all of the staff. Prior to the fight, I and the other kids were outside and used our fingers to write on one of the staff members' car doors, but it apparently scratched it. Of course, I was the one who got into trouble, and then the main house turned it around by saying I purposely scratched the car door. Once again, I wasn't being heard, believed, or listened to, although the staff member who owned the car did, but of course not the main house.

Everything overwhelmed me, and so when I was left in my room after the fight, I destroyed it in frustration. I had hand cream and shampoo bottles in my room, and not really knowing how else to let loose the feelings inside, I emptied the bottles on the walls. A punching bag probably would have helped, but I didn't have one and needed to let out the pain that I was feeling. I couldn't think of any other way to calm down as no one would talk to me, even though I had asked.

After the fight with the same boy because of the ongoing teasing which nothing was being done, the following morning left me in frustration. We all made our way next door as we always do before school. I was walking in the back of the others, as I could still feel the anger from what had happened. When I reached the front of the house, before making my way to the side where the door was to go inside, I was stopped from one of the main houses staff members. She was the one who I had overheard on numerous occasions speaking ill about myself and others from my bedroom window.

No child at the group home was allowed to walk on the front porch or use the front door. The porch and door was to be used by the staff only, but the steps leading up to the porch was often deemed acceptable. It always felt as though because of how the porch was raised, it allowed the staff to be taller, and higher than us. This almost gave them a sort of power over all of us for when they had to speak with us. When the staff member stopped me that morning of September 30th, 2003, she appeared on the porch as if she was all mighty while looking down on me.

The staff member had heard about the previous night, and what I had done to my room. She told me that because of everything I had done, I was to remain outside to calm down. Sure, I was frustrated because of the incident, but I just wanted to get on with my day, and in a way forget about what had happened. Her tone didn't seem to have any concern for me, but more of a *I'm going to tell you what you need to do, and you have no choice in the matter.* A little annoyed about her demand to stay outside when I wasn't properly dressed to sit outside in the chilly fall weather, I responded admittedly hostile towards her. I told her I was fine and that I didn't need to calm down. She insisted that it wasn't a question and that I had to stay outside and couldn't join the rest inside. I then got angry at her, and told her she was a bitch, and that it was "fucking bullshit."

I shouldn't have used the language I did, especially using the foul name at her, but it just came out. I was left sitting at the picnic table, chilled, arms crossed, with my anger only growing because I felt what was happening was unfair. The other kids and staff members walked around the house to go into the other side door that leads to the basement school. As everyone walked by I was stared at, pointed at, and laughed at. The staff said nothing about that and completely ignored me. I had already been out there for an hour, and before they completely made their way in, I yelled for one of the staff members' attention. I tried to say that I was ready to join everyone inside and that I was sorry. I didn't go into detail, but I thought it was a start to show that I wanted to put what happened behind me. The same staff member as before said that she didn't feel as though I was ready and needed to stay outside longer. I mentioned that I was cold and that I did feel as though I was ready to go inside, but still nothing.

They all went inside and closed the door behind them. I was really starting to get pissed again. I began pacing back and forth by the picnic table talking to myself, calling them bitches to myself. I could barely feel my fingers, but the rage I was feeling almost seemed to warm me up a little. Every so often someone would walk by one of the windows to just stare at me, and then would proceed to walk away. A couple of times a kid would, and they would smile and start to laugh, and so I would respond by giving them the finger.

I was outside for a few hours, and no one would talk to me. From the beginning of the morning, I wasn't spoken with which really upset me. They knew about what had happened, and instead of trying to get to the bottom of it, and try to resolve it, they just put me aside and chose not to deal with me right away. They allowed the feelings I had to grow. I was the one who allowed my anger to get the better of me, but I didn't know how else to get their attention since asking didn't work. I tried to go inside to go on with the day but was refused it. Seeing the kids and staff constantly walk by the window just to take a look at me, I just couldn't take it anymore. I continued to make faces and gave them the finger. One of the staff didn't like that, and so she covered up the windows while giving me a smirk beforehand. As if to almost laugh at me because I couldn't see them any longer while giving them the finger again. I was freezing, hungry and full of anger. I then picked up a rock and threw it through the window.

I waited a bit, and being able to see the shadows, I knew no one was in throwing view of the window and that I wouldn't hit them. I didn't want to hurt anyone, but I did want to get their attention. A few small glass fragments fell on one of the staff members' shirt but no one was hurt. Not a scratch. They immediately called the police, and then told me they had done so. While they were telling me they called the police, they insinuated that I was going to get what I deserved, which rubbed me the wrong way. I picked up another rock and threw it through a larger window, where no one was near so I definitely wasn't going to hit anyone. They pissed me off, and I needed them to know it.

There were many things I had said and done that I shouldn't have that day. Vulgar language, the destruction of property, and giving in to the growing anger inside of myself. While looking back on the events of that day, there were other ways of dealing with the situation. The problem was that in the heat of the moment, I hadn't thought of other ways to get through it. The one thing I didn't want to have happened, was for the police to be called because of the possibility of being incarcerated. That was one path I did not want to venture down. Perhaps at the time, I deserved it, because whether I didn't hurt anyone or not, it had to have been a cause for alarm having a couple of rocks being thrown through the windows. I knew I wasn't wanting or going to hurt anyone, but in the moment, no one could have known that. Especially since no one had any desire to speak with me at all that day.

When the police showed up at the group home to take me to the station, I feared the worst. I thought this was too much, and I was going to be making my way to juvenile detention. Thankfully I didn't, but I was charged with destruction of property to which I would have to appear in court come November. I was incredibly lucky, and since that moment, I made a vow to myself that I would not allow anything like that to happen again. That was too lose a call, and I didn't think I would have any more luck to keep me out of baby jail.

Since none of the staff seemed to have listened to the events leading up to the rock-throwing, I took advantage of having the police around me and explained everything to them. They had asked me what had happened anyway, so I figured it was now my chance to finally talk to someone who actually seemed to want to listen. Nothing seemed to come out of it, but perhaps hearing what had happened, being told, and forced to stay outside in the cold when I didn't want to, could have had some way with keeping me out of jail. As much as I didn't want to go to jail, a small part of me kind of wanted it, because I didn't want to go back to the group home.

Once I returned to the group home that evening, I didn't know what to expect. Everyone seemed pissed off at me, which I understood. I explained everything to the police, tried to the staff that morning, but they didn't care to listen, and then I had a chance to speak with the on-site therapy councilor. I even spoke with the group home's owner, trying to make sure everyone knew about exactly what had happened. My CAS worker also seemed to want to speak with me, and so once again I relayed the same details to him. With all of the people I had to speak with, my side of what had happened never changed, because it was the truth. The unfair injustice that I had felt starting with no one listening to me about the teasing which lead to the fighting, followed by my room being destroyed by me, and then without question or reasoning, or listening, forced to remain outside in the cold.

I had strongly felt that so much could have been avoided had anyone cared enough to listen to me. The staff at my house were the only ones who actually cared enough to ask what was happening, but in my moment's rage didn't want to speak properly. While reading my case files, and all of the incident reports and notes made by staff members from both houses, only my staff members were the ones who never tried to lesson any situation to make themselves look better in the eyes of the reader. Their accounts for this incident and others were written accordingly, but while reading the main house's staff's notes, it just made me laugh.

In their notes, the staff member who forced me outside made it so that I was the one who wanted to remain outside. I was the one who somehow made others walk by the window so that I could instigate them. She wrote it in a way that showed she calmly asked me a few times to join everyone. Just like previous foster homes when things occur, certain details change to what the adult feels is right and what others need to read in order to make them out to seem like the victim. I most definitely didn't want to stay outside. I tried to speak with the staff, but every chance I was declined for their own personal reasons and power grab. Before these notes were written, I had spoken with numerous people that I felt should be made aware. The funny thing is, my side of the story was never written down. My side of what went down was never recorded. The only thing that was ever written down was a version that allowed the group home to stay in the right. They needed to cover their asses because they knew their avoidance of what lead up to that day was their fault.

I knew the severity of what I had done, and I knew it could never happen again. I knew no matter how many times I would tell someone what had happened, for the rest of my time at the group home, I was never going to get the proper attention or listening because of what I had done. I was right because, for the most part, that was true. I gave in to the anger that I tried to put behind me, and I needed to find other ways of dealing with it so this wouldn't happen again. I knew that I had to swallow whatever bullshit the group home, and my worker was going to say, and whatever consequences given to me so I could get through this intact. I needed to show that I wasn't just a problem child with so many issues, and that I am a strong-willed young man who just wanted to be listened to. I just wanted to be believed, heard, appreciated, but there was work that had to be done first before anyone could see this.

Even though the school was in the basement of the group home, at times they acted like a real school. I was suspended for a few days for the windows, along with losing half of my seven or nine dollars weekly allowance. During my suspension, I had to remain outside for the whole day, for each of my suspended days. I was to remain on the property while trying to find things to do on my own. I spent those days aimlessly walking around while in deep thought. My possible Thanksgiving trip to my mother's was confirmed to be canceled due to what had happened. As much as I wanted to freak out about that, I knew I couldn't.

For the next couple of months, there was much hostility from all of the staff. At first, I understood it because of what I had done, but I really did try to make things right. I just knew that if I ever wanted to leave this place, I needed to show that I was better than my fits of rage. Even when they would be rude towards me, I wouldn't say anything because it wasn't going to do me any good. No matter what I tried to do, no matter how much I tried to show the happy and positive version of myself to the school's teacher, she never seemed to want to accept it. Until the time she left which was until the new year, she never seemed to care that I was trying to make up for my mistakes. It stung because I truly was doing better, but that was just another thing I couldn't let get me down.

Aside from my house's staff members, the only person from the main house who actually somewhat shown they understood and appreciated me trying to do better was the owner. I was actually surprised, but a part of me figured it was because of the fact that she knew some of her staff were at fault for ignoring certain truths. I guess she wasn't the only person there, because the French lady, as well as the overnight lady from the main house, had always shown they were on my side. They were both always so kind towards me, and always shown that they understood kids with issues are going to mess up, but it's about correcting the problems. They both knew I was trying to fix my mistakes and had shown they weren't going to hold that against me. It was definitely kindness that I needed.

Fighting between myself and the other kid in my home seemed to settle down quite a lot for a while. It was never completely gone, but definitely not as bad has it had gotten. It was until a new older guy had moved next door. Just before the Christmas holidays. I had messed my chances of going home for Thanksgiving, and I was not going to let my outbursts ruin my chances of leaving for Christmas. I had learned that after leaving juvenile detention, my sister was allowed to move back home. This actually upset me, because I felt as though she had so many internal issues that needed to be worked out, that I personally didn't feel as though she could have. I knew she had a lot more other problems involving law-breaking, that I didn't have, and yet, she was allowed to move back home.

I was jealous. I was incredibly jealous of my sister because she was able to move back to our biological mother's house. I knew everything we had to deal with as young children, especially the issues involving our father, were things that the CAS hadn't tried to work out with her. It just made no sense to me that they would move her *home* before making sure she was properly taken care of regarding her mental state. If they wanted her to have everything work out for her benefit, they needed to make sure she was being properly counseled. They needed to make sure that all of the issues, even the buried deep ones, were being talked about. She needed to be able to live her life not in fear while being able to trust others. My sister needed the proper guidance so that these burried issues wouldn't surface making it impossible for her to mess up again. Instead of giving her the help that she needed to promise success, she was just sent to live at our mother's. It was as if they were like, *there you go. She's your problem now, as we are not going to bother with it.* As happy as I'm sure it was for my sister, it wasn't fair to her, because they chose not to give her a chance for recovery.

I had been warned so many times to be careful of my behavior because they would take away my Christmas visit had I shown the anger as I had previously. I went day to day fearful and watchful because I needed that break away. I felt so suffocated at the group home, having everyone judge me, not giving me a chance to change. At times I knew people were in the wrong, and yet I had to allow for it because I just needed the time to go by so I could be allowed to leave. The problem was that it was causing a lot of internal grief. It actually hurt that even at times when I knew I was wrongfully handled or judged, I couldn't say or do anything because I would once again have my phone calls taken away, or even my visit. I was already told by my worker that he felt as though I would need at least another year or two living at the group home to work on all of the problems I had. Hearing that I would have to stay there that long nearly made me want to die. I didn't think I would be able to handle that long living there.

When I first arrived at the group home, I was beginning weekly therapy sessions with an onsite lady, and I did not enjoy them. I had found her to be cold, unresponsive, and that she never really listened to me. Once November came around, I began seeing and speaking with another one. At first, it was difficult for me to open up, as I have always been like that with new people. Over time, I actually came to quite enjoy my sessions. The new therapist or councilor, however you wish to describe him, was someone who really showed how much he cared for his patients. It was strange because I usually don't open up to or get close to males because of my biological father, but this man seemed different. He had shown me that I could trust him, which made me want to speak with him.

Leading up to my Christmas visit, when I found as though the staff weren't listening to me, I would speak with the therapist. It seemed to help quite a lot, as my temper wasn't as bad as it had been. The only problem I was faced with was that I still didn't feel as though I was being heard, and when having meetings with my worker, I was uncooperative because of it. I tried to explain how I felt, but I was described as someone who only wanted to blame, and not takes responsibility. That wasn't the case. I knew of the mistakes I had made, but I also wanted something done about the treatment I was being faced with. Still, I wasn't being heard, again!

When the fighting with the one kid in my home was on a hiatus, it seemed as though the universe was trying to correct that. He became close friends with the new kid at the main home which only made things worse for me. This new kid seemed to hate me and had the desire to pick on me quite a lot. He was much larger than me, so I definitely didn't want to get into a fight with him. I just wanted to try and avoid him as much as I could. I tried to tell the staff about the issues, but they seemed to still be pissed at me for my window incident. Even the owner at times didn't really want to do anything to correct the teasing I was being faced with. I was just told to stay away and ignore it. The things I was always told when an adult didn't want or cared to help. Thankfully, there would come a time where they would have no choice but to help.

While making my way from the main house to mine through the woods, I was jumped by this kid. I had done exactly what was asked of me by ignoring him the best I could. When someone jumps out of nowhere, especially on a path in the woods, doesn't exactly make ignoring or walking away easy. Even though I did try to find a way around him, I couldn't and he started punching me. He punched me in the face, and thankfully the situation made its way to the main house. This time they had no choice but to listen. In many instances, I had tried to explain how he was bullying me, but they chose not to. Now here I am, bleeding, bruised because this kid was able to jump me, and beat me. It was on them, but they didn't want to take responsibility. This was something I tried to bring up in the plan of care meetings because these conversations were never recorded because it was something that had shown how the group home was at fault. When that happens, nothing is recorded. Looking through my files, this incident was never recorded, and no incident report was created.

Christmas couldn't have come at a better time. For so long, I knew that all I needed in order to find happiness and peace of mind, was to be reunited with my biological family. This was something all of my workers and even the supervisor knew, and yet none of them felt as though this was the solution for me. My visit that was unsupervised, at *home*, brought me so much joy. It was the first time in a very long time that I felt somewhat normal. It was a time where I could speak with anyone, where they would truly listen. I was actually being heard and had people on my side. For the first time in so long, I felt a sort of release of so much negativity. I was able to breathe again.

As amazing as it was to feel like a family again, I knew it was for only a week. That one week was going to be something that I would hold dear, and I would use it to help me keep in mind what I was fighting for. Not only was I reunited with my mother and sister, but I also had the opportunity to see my aunt and her children. I hadn't seen them since I was about five or six, and so it was another thing that made me feel incredible. Every day while I was at my mother's, I lived in the moment, and it was something that I desperately needed. It was a teaser for my end prize. After a lifelong struggle bouncing around foster homes, being faced with so many troubling situations, being at my mother's felt right. All of the problems and all of the bad things I had done and said prior, seemed to be a distant memory and was almost as if they had been done by a different person.

Since this was the first Christmas we were all celebrating together after many years not being allowed to be together, my mother actually went all out. Our house was decorated with tons of Christmas decorations. It wasn't a big house, but it was enough considering we didn't exactly have a lot of money. I had even heard my mother say that she and her boyfriend went completely broke and even took out a loan in order for us to have an exceptional Christmas. I felt bad because just being together was going to be enough for my sister and I. We didn't need all of the presents, decorations, or even food. We hadn't spent a Christmas together since I was six years old, so this was definitely the only present either of us needed.

Since my sister had already moved into our mother's house before my visit, it was assumed that she had her moment where she was able to visit with everyone. Having it been years since seeing any of our family or old friends, it would have been such an amazing feeling to be able to see either of us again. She seemed to be close to one of our cousins, and I had just hoped she received the same praise and surprise when everyone had seen her for the first time as they had with me. While it was slightly overwhelming because everyone seemed so happy, with a million questions for me, it was still a really great feeling.

I spent my week at my mother's taking it all in. It was a feeling I had longed to feel, and it truly was a well worth the wait feeling. When I wasn't visiting with my family, I found myself in my room that had a TV in it. It seemed like such an awesome thing. I mean, I had my own television in my own room. As strange as it may sound, for me at that time, having my own television was a huge deal. The best part of it though was that during that Christmas holiday, there was a rerun marathon of my fav show! I had missed the series finale, and so I was able to get myself caught up. There wasn't a single other thing I wanted to watch. I sat in my room, soaking in the feeling of belonging somewhere, while the best show ever was on my TV. It seriously couldn't get any better than that!

My return to the group home felt necessary. As much as I didn't want to go back, I knew I had to. The end felt so close, and I knew exactly what I was fighting for. I became determined and wasn't going to allow anyone to stop me from doing better, showing that I deserve a chance at normalcy and family. It wasn't easy, and I had my moments. I especially had moments where I didn't always agree with things being said, but I was slowly learning that the group home, and my worker, were the type that needed justification to their own ideas. I was learning that I had to give them what they wanted regardless of how I personally felt. So I did exactly that. Regardless if I would agree or not, I would let them know I agreed with them with a smile. It's what they wanted, and it was actually working.

My schooling was improving up until the end of the year. My interactions with others in the group home, staff, and other kids had also improved. In January 2004, I started a drama work program in the community. It had been a while since I was a part of a theatre endeavor, and so it was important for me to be able to get back into that. Performing was my escape from reality, and allowed me to forget about all of the troubles in my life, and made me feel as though I had a purpose. I knew that if I were to continue on the path I was heading down, my time at the group home would be coming to an end. I wanted the remainder of that time to go by fast so I could get the hell out of there. I figured if I were to be able to get involved in another theatre performance, it would help.

During a couple of months that I was involved with the drama program, I was reminded of what I missed so very much. The last time I was a part of a play, because of my actions, I was removed from it and couldn't perform. That weighed on me so much, so I didn't want that to happen again. Although there were brief moments where I would argue with others in the group home, and even some of my staff, I would do all that I could to try and keep composure because I knew it couldn't get too bad. Thankfully I had a great bond with the on-site therapist, who actually helped a lot. He even came to watch my performance when the drama program came to an end. Having someone there in the audience was always something that meant a great deal to me. The group home's owner was also there, but her granddaughter was in the program as well, so she was there for her. The owner did tell me how great of a job I had done, and so that actually meant a lot to me. It especially meant a lot because of all of the hostility I had felt from her during my time there, but I think she was starting to see just how much I was trying to do better.

Up until the end of my stay at the group home, I never felt as though the main house's staff liked me or had any respect for me. It all went back to that window incident. Ever since then there had always been a cold shoulder from the main house. I realize what had happened was terrible, but I was trying my hardest to make up for my mistakes. I felt as though I deserved it. Everyone makes mistakes. Some people make larger ones than others, but as long as they know what they have done, and are truly trying to make peace with others and themselves about it so it doesn't happen again, it would make sense that they should deserve some sort of forgiveness. I was a troubled child, and I knew it. It was coming to a point where I did all that I could to try and get their forgiveness, but if they were unresponsive, what more could I have done.

My house's staff seemed to offer me forgiveness, and at times I was truly terrible towards them when they didn't deserve it. Like most times, I tend to spread my frustrations and anger towards others who aren't the center of it, but because they are there, I lash out. Still, it seemed as though my staff were understanding for what was happening, and it was something that meant a lot to me, knowing things I had said and done, and yet, they could forgive me. The memory of them and the kindness they had always shown me, would be something I could appreciate for years to follow. Even the CD made for me from one of them during our house's Christmas exchange is something that I've kept with me all of these years because it represents how much respect I had for them whether I had shown it or not.

If there is one thing I have learned from all of my years, it's that there is only so much a person can do to help someone else. Regardless of the fact that I deeply appreciated my staff at the group home, there was only so much they could do. They can't control every person, things done and said. They can't make a person like others. They were limited to what was in their control. When it came to others teasing me, there was only so much they could do. I had shown a lot of aggression in the past, and it was not pleasant to them. The best thing they could have done was to try and clear the room so no one would get hurt. The best thing for me was to be kept in my room where no one else was.

Around Easter time 2004, I would have my second home visit to my mother's. My sister at the time was still there, although was apparently having problems. My visit came at a great time because I felt as though I needed an escape once again. I was doing well with trying to improve myself but felt as though I needed a break. My visit went really well, aside from the fact that my sister and I went to some friends of hers and got really stoned.

I hadn't smoked the pot since my troubling seventh grade, so it hit me hard! I ended up getting pretty sick, and we tried to conceal it from our mother. We told her I ate bad yogurt. She didn't believe us, and we both got a stern talking to. Although, my sister got into a lot more trouble. The incident wasn't reported to my worker, because of the fear of having my return be jeopardized. We figured since nothing really bad came of it, that we would keep it as an *in house incident*. At least it gave my sister and me something to look back on and laugh. Being around my sister was always my favorite thing to do because I always knew so long as I was with her, I would never be teased. She would always stick up for me, and it was something I definitely needed at the group home.

Although I had done so much better in the last few months of my time at the group home, things weren't perfect. I was still being teased by others. Anytime I would argue with other kids or staff, especially at the main house, I had privileges taken away. The thing that was the number one choice to take away from me, were my phone calls to my mother. I was also being continuously told that every time I would mess up, more time would be added to my stay there. My worker almost seemed joyful whenever we spoke, and he would talk about my wrongdoings. He seemed to find joy in telling me that he felt I needed to stay longer and that moving home to my mother's wasn't the solution I needed. I found it ridiculous that trying to stick up for myself after being teased would result in having to stay longer. Why am I the one to always be found responsible for other people teasing and picking on me? There is only so much I can take.

I was becoming incredibly exhausted from the constant threat of having to remain at the group home. I was emotionally drained from all of the teasing, unable to do anything about it, especially since no one wanted to help correct it. Every time I felt as though I was making progress to my release, it seemed I was blocked. Whenever I thought I was one step closer to being able to live with my biological mother, my worker or the group home would kick me back two steps. I was just beginning to feel as though nothing would ever change, and I would be locked away from life, forever.

One of the lowest points in my life came that spring. I had felt so defeated and didn't know what more I could do. One night I was arguing with the same kid as always, getting fed up with his teasing. I retaliated with screaming back at him. I was told to stay in my room, to which I slammed the door. One of my favorite staff members knocked on my door to see if I was okay, but I was so full of emotions. I yelled at her to leave me alone, although using foul language to say so. The thing that no one knew, or at least for the most part didn't know, was that any time I would say to leave me alone, I didn't actually want them to.

As silly or stupid as it may seem, saying for someone to leave me alone, was a test. I had gone my whole life feeling alone, and I hated that feeling more than anything. When I would say for someone to leave me alone, I would wait to see if they actually would. Although emotions would be high, I always knew things would be able to settle had they shown me they cared enough to not let me be alone. When I was adopted, and even the foster family with the Great Dane, knew this. I think that may be one of the reasons they mean so much to me. They would never just let me be alone. They may have at times given me some space, but they always made sure I knew I wasn't alone, and they wouldn't go away until they made sure I knew this.

I realize this stupid little test wasn't exactly fair, as they were just doing what I had asked, but in my mind, it was the only way I could find out how I meant to someone. After yelling at my staff to leave me alone, she did. That day I was in a really rough space. The teasing didn't seem to ever want to settle.

My future seemed uncertain which caused me to worry. Since returning from my Easter visit at my mother's, my sister found herself in trouble and was moved to a detention facility in Ottawa. Everything I was excited for seemed to be crumbling all around me. I just wanted all of the pain to end.

I had a small pocket knife that I had bought from the dollar store in my room. After being listened to, I was alone in my room. All I could think about was how I wished all of the pain I was feeling would go away. It was pain that I seemed to have my entire life, and I didn't think it was ever going to go away. I looked at my arms, wrists, with my eyes full of tears, and I became hesitant. So many things crossed my mind. In the end, all I could think about was how I was tired of it all. I began to cut my wrists, but the blade was incredibly dull. Thank you dollar store.

I made a few cuts, but nothing too deep. My staff I think got a little worried when I had become somewhat quite, and opened the door. Seeing what I was doing, the knife was taken away. The situation seemed too much and so help from the main house was asked for. The night time lady made her way over. I really liked her and had always found her to like me. If there was anyone who would be able to calm me down that night, I think it was her.

I yelled for her to leave me alone. I was crying, blood on my arms, and yelling for her to leave me alone. She didn't. She told me she wasn't going to leave me alone, because being alone was something I didn't need. Aside from the fact that there was a worry I would try to hurt myself again, she assured me that she wanted to be there to help me. She could see the pain in my eyes. We spoke for quite a while that night, and at that moment, it showed me what I wanted. In all of the current pain, sadness, and worry I was feeling, I needed to know I was appreciated and cared for. That night she had shown me that. She even told me that anytime I needed someone to talk with, to go to her before I even think about wanting to hurt myself.

Since the pocket knife night, everything changed. It opened my eyes to so many things. I let go of so many pent up feelings that night, and I didn't want to be held back because of what others were saying around me. For the remainder of my time at the group home, I didn't seem to have any more problems. Everything changed and for the better. My eyes were open, and I knew what I needed to do. In a healthy way, let go of all of the pain, grief, and trauma from my life.

Earlier in my time at the group home, I did something that in times to come, made me think back to when I wanted to try to let go. I knew I needed not only to move on from all of the issues in my life, but to accept them for being my past, and do not allow them to control my future. Everyone makes mistakes, but it's about being able to accept the mistakes, and doing everything we can

313

to make up for them. I had made so many mistakes in my life. I had hurt so many people where I knew were only trying to help me, for the most part. I focused so much on the mistakes I made, and I felt as though there was never anything I could do to correct it, and so I would just want to leave. To move. I couldn't though, because the problems wouldn't be fixed, and they would only resurface being that they were put on a time out.

Knowing that, in order to start being better, and coming to terms with everything I had done, I needed to apologize for my mistakes. The first step in showing remorse for all of my errors, to so many people. I wasn't expecting any responses, but I did at least want to try to make up for the wrong I had passed around. I wrote to my previous worker and supervisor, three foster homes I had done the wrongest at, and my failed adoptive family. Writing these letters gave me a chance to come to terms with the errors of my way, and I really did need to apologize for my time there. I didn't need them to respond, but at least I would know that I made an effort. That was enough for me.

I received three responses, thanking me for taking the step of reaching out. It was three responses more than what I expected. My previous worker and supervisor, the Great Dane foster family, and my old adoptive family all reached out. Their responses meant so much to me. The letters I received from the foster family and even the adoptive family are some of my most cherished items. To this day I still have them, and anytime I am feeling a need to be reminded that forgiveness is possible, I read them.

People change. Not always do people change, but I think it's dependent on whether or not they are given chances or reasons to change. A person's view on others may change, just as their attitude and behavior can. I had worked very hard to change. For so long I was trying to change for others, because of the fact I was constantly being asked to. It was only when I began changing for myself that I was truly able to.

Seeing just how much better I was doing in all aspects, it was determined that I was in a position to be moved back to my biological mother's care. I finished my eighth grade at the group home, and shortly afterward, I would be moving from there. I was living there for almost a year, and it was a roller coaster of a year. I had so many ups and downs, and it seemed like the longest year ever of my life. When I was to be returned to my mother, my sister wouldn't be there. As sad as I was, I knew I would be okay because I was going to do what I could to be there for her in her time of needing help. I spent so much time working on myself, and finally, I felt as though I made real progress.

Slowly towards the end of my time at the group home, I had worked really hard to make amends with those there, because I didn't want to leave on a sour note. It seemed like a long task but was definitely worth it. I had moved from so many homes on bad notes, I didn't want my last placement to be the same. I was able to pack my belongings and look to the future.

I had no idea what to expect once being released. My mind was just so excited to be given a chance at normalcy. This move to my mother's was a lifelong dream, and finally would be coming to fruition. The only thing left for me to do was to make my goodbyes, and wait for my social worker to pick me up. I would make my way inside his vehicle, and this time while looking back, I could do so while knowing I worked for this. I could smile with self-gratification for all that I had accomplished. I mean, I struggled, at times gave up, but picked myself back up and tried again, and again. If I could get myself through all these years in the foster system, I should be able to get through anything that life throws my way.

Chapter Sixteen

Transition to Reality

Is this seriously happening right now? I think the more important question to be asking is if I'm dreaming. Throughout my entire life, I had imagined the day I would be able to go and live with my biological mother and finally be rid of The Children's Aid Society. I knew and had hoped one day this would happen; I just didn't imagine I would finally get to that point. It seemed like this day was unreachable, and all I want to do is get through this drive before minds are changed, and I'm back at another foster home.

Often told better things to come. Often assured the grass is greener on the other side. Often illuminated with the brighter side to any impending darkness. I'm sorry, but what the hell? There is no great amount of metaphors that can truly fix a constant struggle that imposters our existence. As pure as someone's intention is for feeling the need to speak in such dribble, there comes a time and a place for them. When all you do is live by speaking these metaphors to someone who is in need of real help, just don't. It's not what they need, and although perhaps somewhere down the road they may think back on them, right now they need more than words.

Too often I have had people just speak to me in metaphors, somehow thinking just offering me that will help me in my life, and they were wrong. I'm not saying that you can't say them, it's just that they didn't read the room, and even had they just looked at me, smiled, told me I would be okay; As corny as that is, it would have at times felt so much better. In my current life, I am able to look back on all those sayings, and in some ways, they have made an impression on me. During my struggles, I wasn't in my right mind, and I surely didn't want to think about some metaphor that made no sense to me at the time. I needed to feel safe. I needed to feel appreciated, and most importantly, wanted. I needed to know that even during my tough and scary days I had someone in my corner hoping and rooting for me to succeed. I wanted unconditional love and not a fallback easy way out saying.

In order for a difference to be made, for the hope that lingers to surface, we need to truly want it to. Being someone who heard from countless amount of people all these sayings, they never made any difference to me. The words were in my head and I tried to think about them, analyzing what I could come from seeing them out. Truthfully though, in the end, it was what I wanted to do with myself that made the difference. A struggle is exactly that; a meek tug from what your conscience is telling you what you should do, say, etcetera.

No matter how many therapists I had seen growing up, nothing could change what my mind wanted to do except for what I truly wanted. I acted out, misbehaved as violence and destruction was all I knew. Being shown different methods of dealing with the pain, loss, and sadness, I didn't want to accept and see them, for my mind wanted only one solution. Deep down I knew some of the choices I made were wrong, and I did want to change. I always told myself that this wasn't how I wanted to view the world, nor how I wanted to act out, but with time, I was losing that choice. Being in one constant mindset for so long was actually dissolving the choice to change and be who and what I wanted. Thinking back to all the things my caseworkers, teachers, and foster parents had told me, the metaphors, they still didn't faze me.

The way I see how the *greener pasture* sayings work, is that they only come at the bad times because people don't want to have to deal with the situations, so they think of something to bring cheer. I can understand that, for having tension and chaos isn't something pleasant to deal with, but if a person really wants better, it all comes down to what they want by their actions. The thing that made me realize what I was doing, the person I was becoming was actually seeing what was becoming of my sister. We were in similar situations and yet handled them so very differently.

Every time I made a poor decision-m a k i n g response to something, I was left with a consequence. As I should have been. Yes, I had a shitty upbringing, but in the end, I knew it was time to start learning from it. It did take a very long time for me to understand this. Although I had believed I already knew this, it wasn't until the news of being able to move back with my biological mother that it fully sunk in.

With every bad choice I made, especially violent behavior, it scared me. The last thing I wanted was to become my father. I had hoped afterward that the next time I would be able to change the outcome, and not do as I had previously. While trying not to, I bottled up all of my emotions instead of dealing with them. With never actually dealing with the issues, it became too much to store, and I would lash out. The thing I was always missing was self-analyzing each situation. The remainder of what happens after lashing out was void in my mind. I would say I didn't want to become my father, and

I would say I didn't want to become violent but just saying it wasn't enough. At the time I thought just knowing was all I needed, but it wasn't actually being dealt with internally. Although it sounds like it should be super simple to deal with, it's not.

I had a lot of trust issues, and because of that, it was difficult to speak with therapists, caseworkers, and foster parents. Even though in therapy I would be given similar exercises to work on the internal issues, I needed to figure it out on my own. Anytime I would be spoken with, it would just go in one ear, and out the other. That's why things never clicked for me. Hearing that I would finally be home, made me start looking back on everything I had done, and one event at a time, I needed to start going over them. I needed to analyze and come to terms with what I had done, and actually put it all behind me creating a peace of mind. I needed a clean mental slate for when I move back, to give me the fresh start I desperately needed.

The car ride back to Ottawa was silent for me, not just because I didn't care for my worker, but because I needed the silence. I needed all that time to start processing everything over the years. One thing at a time I needed to understand the choices made in each situation. I couldn't think about the *what if's* regarding them because I needed to focus specifically on the *why's*. Why couldn't I have walked away? Why did I not speak up? Why did I hit them? Why did I steal? Why did I lie? Why was I afraid? Why was I scared?

Reliving all of your terrible moments in life is not an easy task. It especially isn't easy when you're trying to do it in such a short period of time. It made me think I must be some really horrible person for having done all that I have. But I couldn't think like that. I had a task to do, and a very limited amount of time to do it. As tough as it was to relive everything, the more I thought about each instance where I should have handled them better, it seemed to actually help. Focusing so much on everything was draining on my emotions, but it was the only time that I truly thought about what happened. It's difficult to put into words, but it almost felt like an epiphany.

A few times before, I believed I had some sort of self-realization, or epiphany, where I was sure that I learned my lessons. I was wrong. It wasn't so much that I had learned exactly what I had done, rather, it was that I just *wanted* to learn from my mistakes. I had hoped while knowing what I did was wrong, that I could change and be better. Everyone kept telling me that they wanted me to do better. That I am capable of doing better, and that I needed to start showing it. Every time I thought I was trying to do better, it was out of fear, and it was for others. I was getting tired of feeling like a disappointment to everyone around me and trying too hard to become something I thought everyone else wanted was actually what was holding me back.

I was surprised at how quiet the car ride was. As we were driving, as much as I had hoped my worker wouldn't talk to me, I couldn't believe he wouldn't. It's funny how those things happen. You hope for something, but when you get what you want, you start to want the opposite. I didn't want him to speak to me, but I did want him to want to speak to me. The thought that regardless of my feelings, having someone care enough to still want to talk while showing they care, that's all I wanted. It made me realize that this man wasn't in my life because he wanted to be, but because he had to be.

It felt as though throughout my entire life all I had were people telling me how *they* wanted me to be. They told me how they think I should act, what they wanted me to say. I was always told to smile more because I needed to show that I was happy, regardless if I was or not. I was told to walk away from situations that could lead to trouble, regardless of the fact that nothing was being done to prevent the situations from arising. I often felt as though the people around me weren't there to actually help me, but because they had to for their job and a paycheque. It's this feeling that not only me but others in similar situations should not have. We need to feel as though the people in our lives are there because they want to be. We children of foster care have enough struggles to deal with from our past, present, and family life, that the strangers who **chose** to be employed by the foster system need to be in it 100%.

One of the biggest lessons I have learned while being in foster care, living with, and meeting countless amounts of people, is that I can't rely on anyone else to help me. No matter how many times I had been told I had people who were on my side, the only person who was going to be there through it all, was in fact me. All I needed to do was not give up on myself, and to keep fighting. I did meet people who tried to help, who tried to be there for me, but in the end, they weren't there. There is only so much a person can do to help another individual, which is why the only person I could count on is me.

In some ways, there were a few people who had tried to convey this to me, but it never sunk in. It's probably due to the fact that it just wasn't the right time, and that I didn't want to hear it, or listen. We say things to one another that *we* feel is right, but it's not about what we feel, rather it needs to be about how the other feels. While growing up everyone told me what they felt was right, not thinking about what was right for me. That was something that was very clear to me. This was **my** life that we were discussing

319

and trying to figure out, and yet, they were talking as if it was about them. When I would speak out about it, I was considered to be bad talking them. It was a system that seemed to be going around and around. They would give me their thoughts on how I needed to be, and I would disagree because I'm not them. I'd then get into trouble, and once again, would be given advice as if I were them.

While reflecting over and over on everything, it became apparent that going forward, as happy as I was to be going back home, I couldn't rely on my mother. I need to listen to her and follow whatever rules she may have, but in the end, I need to believe in myself fully and put faith in knowing that I can succeed. I spent too much time trying to live a life in other people's eyes, and it was time I live my life for me and only me. I need to start doing what makes me happy, while of course knowing what is wrong, and by doing what I can to stay away from being stuck in situations that could jeopardize succeeding.

My sister had been the only constant person and thing in my life, and because she had been through so much, more than me, I wanted to be something she could count on. I did everything I could to never give up on her because everyone deserves someone like that. It was not always easy to stay by her side, but I felt as though I needed to. I knew she felt as though she didn't have anyone who truly cared for her, and I wanted to show her she was wrong because she had me. As much as it weighed on me, to watch her fall apart, I knew I had to take a few steps back to allow her to figure things out on her own. Similar to what others were trying to do to me, there was only so much I could do to help her if she wasn't willing to help herself. It was something that pained me from writing that letter to her, to seeing her during Christmas, and even hearing she was removed from our mother's house.

So many times I had seen things looking better for my sister, and yet, something would happen and she would fall apart. Things would turn really horrible for her, and every time it would hurt me. I just wanted to know she was happy, smiling, and in a good place. As much as I was now trying to distance myself in hopes she will figure things out, I just didn't feel as though she was ready to be alone. The seemingly long car ride made me feel as though she had too many internal issues going on, and no one was actually helping her to sort and deal with them. So many years of pent up feelings and memories, never being dealt with. I just knew that once I was back living at home, I needed to make an effort to show her she isn't alone, and that she does have someone on her side.

She had been released from juvenile detention to go back home without working on things. It was too soon for her, but that wasn't her fault. I'm certain to her it felt as though they gave up on her, and that they sent her home so that they didn't have to deal with her anymore. She never even stood a chance because she still had all of her issues with nothing being done about them. All of the buried abusive memories of what our father had done, was the root of everything, and they needed to be professionally looked after. My involvement was limited, and I knew this, but that didn't mean I wasn't going to try. I just knew that I had to keep some distance. Let her know I was there for her, and wait for her to come to me when she needed to while knowing she could. I didn't know how things would turn out for her, and I didn't know what was going to happen, but it was out of my control. It was now her time to be in control of what she chose to do, and I just had to be on the sidelines, hoping for the best.

One of the biggest motivations for wanting to be better was seeing what was becoming of my sister. I had witnessed all of her downfalls aside from my own, and in my quest for realization, I knew that wasn't the kind of life I wanted. Her downfalls weren't all of her own doing, but it was becoming difficult for her to do better because of them. I didn't want that for myself. I had enough of my own troubles and problems, that watching her and what resulted with her showed what could happen to me if I didn't truly change things. I felt bad because it was her fault that drove me to try and correct things moving forward. I had hoped that if I was able to do and be better than I would be in a better place to try and help her. Maybe even give her some motivation. All I knew at the time was that she had a really tough time ahead of her, and I wanted to do everything I could to be in a position to help.

Neither my sister nor I wanted to become our parents. One of the biggest struggles I had was the fear of following in my father's footsteps with how he treated women. Quite a few times I was left with worry as it seemed I was becoming him. The last time when I was twelve that I hit not only a girl but a girl who I had thought was a friend, was my wakeup call. It reminded me of the other two instances, and all three memories collided together creating one giant memory waking me up.

If there was any lesson to be grateful for the learning, it was that one for me. It was after that that I realized regardless of how much constant harassment brought on by a girl, I can't hit her. Even if she was to hit me, I needed to do everything I could to stay away from that thought and action. Not hitting back wasn't because I didn't think a girl couldn't defend herself. I couldn't hit a girl regardless of how much daily teasing or anything they were doing to me because hitting was what my father would do. I needed to show that I'm not him. I needed to show that I am better than him and that I can be my own person. A person that not only chooses not to resort to violence but one who wouldn't hit a girl.

Going forward, choosing not to respond with violence was going to be one of the biggest tasks I would have. For the record, I can honestly say that since the car ride to my mothers, that is one of the things I was fully successful with. Not since the group home had I been in a fight, and not since I was 12 had I hit a girl. As silly as it might seem to some, it is one of the things I am proud of because of how volatile I was becoming, and it was a huge improvement. Believe me, there were many times in my teenage years and onwards where I was faced with situations that the younger me would have responded with violence. I chose not to though, and I chose to take a better approach to dealing with things.

Looking back on my younger years, there were many times I had questioned what was the one thing that could have made everything go so much better for me. Was there ever really ONE solution to all of my problems? I often asked myself what was the one thing that if I had, could make all of my problems go away.

During the years in my foster homes, not having my biological family in my life was a key factor in reasons of feeling abnormal and abandoned. So many times all I wanted was to live somewhere that felt like home. When I was adopted, I did feel like I was finally "home," but I felt as though I was abandoning my sister. I also had a lot of other aggressive behaviors that were difficult to manage, and so I ruined that chance. I ruined the chance with people who cared more about me than any other people I came into contact with. As much as even to this day I wish I could take everything back, everything I had done to them, I can't. All I ever wanted was to be a part of a family and feel unconditional love, and that is exactly what I had with them. The thing about it though, is at that time I just wasn't ready to accept it, which was a true shame. They are my biggest regret to this current day, but they will forever be the fondest memory. Looking back on them and all that I have learned from having them in my life is what I use to bring shine and light to whatever darkness befalls me.

Growing up I often felt as though the thing I needed in order to find peace, was to have my sister in my life. I was denied such because no one thought it was a good idea. To this day I still feel as though it could have helped both of us out so much more being *brother and sister* as we should have been. We will never know, but it is known that all either of us wanted was to be a part of a family, and we were all we had. As much as either of us tried, again and again, we were always shut down from those requests.

I've always felt as though the one solution to all of my problems was to be back "home" with my family. I used to think that was just with my sister because I often viewed her as my only family. Looking back on my childhood, it seemed as though she was all the family I needed. After remembering everything my parents had done, she was definitely the only family I needed growing up, but what about the future? Right now, I have the chance at an opportunity to have that with my entire biological family. I would be foolish not to give that a shot right?

While sitting in this dead silent vehicle with my worker, the closer we were getting to my mother's house, the more he figured he should start speaking up. While assuming words of encouragement would be a topic he should stick with, it wasn't. Here I am reliving all the terrible things I had done, and instead of trying to pick up my spirits, he was almost preparing me to fail. I remember being told not to have high expectations because there is still so much I need to work on. He even told me that he didn't feel as though I was ready to go back home, but "You won't know until you try."

When someone doesn't believe in you or have faith that you can succeed in something, it shows. Whether a person doesn't mean for it to do that, it's almost inevitable it will. I didn't like my last worker, and I know he didn't like me. It's a shame because I really liked his wife, and I know in some ways my sister also did. He chose to be silent during our last drive, except for when he decided to remind me that there's a good chance my mother may not live up to my expectations. If history was to tell one thing, it's that she herself has many unresolved issues, and to not be surprised if living at home wasn't in my best interest. And then being returned into the foster system.

I chose to do my eighth grade in the group home's school. I had insecurities about being integrated into society and felt safer being at the group home. There wasn't risk being taken which in a way was the coward's way but was something I learned from. I chose that out of fear, not because I couldn't do it. To my worker, he brought up how I wasn't able to succeed in a regular school environment. He reminded me that the past year I wasn't able to acclimate in a regular school environment and had to be at the group home's school. Ummm, excuse me? Once I was at my mother's and we were discussing the steps needed for the integration back home to work, he repeated it.

In front of my mother, and her boyfriend, he went on about how I "failed" at school and that he didn't believe I would be able to make it in high school. He said that high school in a normal setting is difficult, but for me, it would be even more so. He went on about how my mother needed to watch out as he thought I might run from my troubles in the classroom and either refuse to go or drop out. She needed to be stern, make me go, and not let me. He clearly had so much faith me. Spoiler… I think I greatly proved him wrong because, in many instances, I had much success.

So many times it had felt as though I didn't have people on my side. Time often felt as though I was in this world alone, and all I was going to do was struggle. The car ride was exhilarating and needed in so many ways. It allowed me to relive and look back on all of my mistakes and really poor decisions. I was able to look over each of them, accept what had happened one last time, and then leave them on the highway behind me as I drove ahead. I wasn't forgetting all of my mistakes and struggles, but rather I was putting them to rest as I wake up the good memories. The memories that I could hold onto, and reflect on.

I needed to bring the good memories of people of my past and things that bring a real smile to my face to the surface because that is what I needed to start focusing on. I often felt left aside, but it wasn't always the case. As much as I wanted to forget this jerk of a caseworker, it made me remember and appreciate my worker before him.

She was someone who always tried everything with me, and I know she truly cared. Back then I didn't always want to know it, but I do. It's just like the big boss lady worker. The one who was there since the beginning. Someone even to this day I am grateful for. So many times I had thought she had given up on me, but she didn't. At times she had to take steps back to allow me to figure things out on my own. Although at times it was frustrating because she didn't always believe me, when she probably should have, she did care. And I am better because of it. I am able to look back and appreciate her for all that she had done. I can appreciate that she was nothing like this car ride guy.

Both of these women had a huge influence on my life. They will forever be memories of people to make me smile when I think of them. I had hoped regardless that I was troubled and a struggling child, that when bad things happened to me at school and at my foster parents' homes, they would take me more seriously. I know it wasn't always easy, mostly because I didn't always make things easy, but it was hard to take the word of a child over an adult. Nonetheless, they did do a lot for me, and it is something to look back on and be thankful for.

Although throughout my life there were more foster homes that left a sore note in my mouth than sweet, not all of my past foster parents were bad. I know I wasn't the easiest child to have in their home, but there were a few who tried to stick by me as much as I would allow them to. The two foster homes that will forever be cast as a memory of regret on my part because of how great they actually were, are the French family and the one after my failed adoption. Both had taught me so much, not just in life, but with myself. Those two homes as much as I didn't realize it back then, but do now, were beyond forgiving towards me, and gave me more happy memories than any other home. Even the relief foster home who thought poorly of me towards the end is a family I will never forget and will always appreciate for being there when I really needed them. They gave me a real reason to smile, and their three children gave me memories that a normal child should have while growing up. They allowed me to be a child, and to have fun while trying to put my past behind me.

As brief as some teachers may have been in my life, and although quite a few were dismissive with everything, there were a select few I couldn't forget. The eighth-grade teacher and the other from the same school are two of the brightest memories I have from people who showed they truly cared. More people to remember to help me creating and holding on memories of great things in my life. These are the memories that deserve to be highlighted in my mind, to hopefully take over and fuel the new me.

Moving back to my biological mother's is something I have always wanted. This move was the most important thing to have happened to me because it meant that my life had a chance at normalcy. I was finally given a chance to start over. With all of the struggles put behind me, I needed to hold onto the good things that had happened. I needed the people who have meant something to me to be my focus on bettering myself. For too long I have held onto bad memories, having the anger and frustrations that surrounded me dictating how my life would be. That needed to change, and I finally knew it. I finally know that although I always felt I didn't have people in my corner, I did. They just had to take a backseat so that I could learn on my own. I learned the hard way, but I think I did.

Just because I was finally getting a chance to move back home, that doesn't automatically mean everything is forgotten and all better. There was still work to be done, not just on my part, but my mothers. As great as I felt after the car ride from my sort of epiphany, feeling as though my mind had finally been cleared, was it? There were many reasons why I was placed in foster care in the first place, and many unanswered questions I still had. I had hoped this was an opportunity to not only learn the real truth but also work on things to make things better.

Although I did finally move back to my mother's, it was probationary. For the next year or so, we would have a strict schedule to keep with appointments, school, counseling, a few visits with my worker, and open communication with The Children's Aid Society. They needed to make sure this move wasn't rushed, and that it was in the best interest of all of us, especially me. My worker seemed convinced that this move wasn't going to work, as he felt it was too soon.

The end prize was inches from my grasp, and I was going to do everything I could to stretch out and grab it. The problem with the prize though, is if you can't see what it is, is it even worth fighting to get it? Let's say it's a box, decorated with jewels and shiny things. The appearance of it would make it seem perfect and a must-have. What if when you got it, open it up only to find out it was just a rock? Talk about a disappointment! That's the problem with a prize that you can't see. You just never know what's inside.

For so long I felt as though I didn't belong. I felt as though so much was missing from my life. I often didn't know what I was missing. I was left imagining things in my mind of how I wished things could have been. I was fourteen years old and finally given a chance to come back to reality. I spent too many years pretending I was with a perfect family, that I belonged, that I was loved. It was now time to transition myself back into reality as I had that chance. The thing of it though, is that there's still so much uncertainty. What if my mother resorts to her old ways. It's been nearly a decade since I lived with her full time. There are so many things I still don't know about what happened. What if what I have seen this past year is just a persona of the expected. That she is just showing not only the CAS but me what we want to see.

The sad truth of it is that at the time, signing the papers with my worker to allow me to live back home, I didn't know anything. I just had a dream. I was filled with hopes. I believed with every fiber of my being that this move was everything I needed, and wanted. I didn't want to think about the possibility that things could turn sideways. I didn't want to think that this move was a smokescreen. That my life wasn't as important to my mother as I had thought. I didn't want to relive the abuse and all of the yelling. I was living in the moment, and I didn't want to think about what could go wrong.

It's when you don't think or want things to go wrong, that they usually do. It's especially when you hope history doesn't repeat itself, that it does. All you're left with is what **you** can do differently this time around. You ask yourself while being older this time, what can you do that you couldn't before. You had hoped for better things. You worked hard to achieve better. You begin to question so many things and are left with so many choices. When things start out all smiles, but the bad is just lingering on the surface, what do you do? Do you yourself resort to old ways while others have, or do you continue to grow and find other means to deal? In the past things got worse with each situation, and now the worry is how much worse can things actually get?

I didn't want to think about the bad possible outcomes, because I didn't think I would be able to handle it if it came to be. I didn't think that after everything, only to be let down again that I would make it out alive. I just needed to stay positive. I needed to have faith that this could work. I just wanted a chance to regain what was lost. I wasn't able to have a childhood, and I didn't want the same for my teenage years. I needed this to work without struggle, and without worry. The path ahead of me was uncertain, and yet all I wanted was what I felt I deserved. I just wanted a life.